SIDREA Series in Accounting and Business Administration

This is the official book series of SIDREA - the Italian Society of Accounting and Business Administration. This book series is provided with a wide Scientific Committee composed of Academics by SIDREA. It publishes contributions (monographs, edited volumes and proceedings) as a result of the double blind review process by the SIDREA's thematic research groups, operating at the national and international levels. Particularly, the series aims to disseminate specialized findings on several topics – classical and cutting-edge alike – that are currently being discussed by the accounting and business administration communities. The series authors are respected researchers and professors in the fields of business valuation; governance and internal control; financial accounting; public accounting; management control; gender; turnaround predictive models; non-financial disclosure; intellectual capital, smart technologies, and digitalization; and university governance and performance measurement.

This book series is indexed in Scopus.

Alberto Incollingo • Andrea Lionzo
Editors

The European Harmonization of National Accounting Rules

The Application of Directive 2013/34/EU in Europe

Springer

Editors
Alberto Incollingo
Department of Political Science
University of Campania "Luigi Vanvitelli"
Caserta, Italy

Andrea Lionzo
Department of Economics and Business Management Sciences
Catholic University of the Sacred Heart
Milan, Milano, Italy

ISSN 2662-9879 ISSN 2662-9887 (electronic)
SIDREA Series in Accounting and Business Administration
ISBN 978-3-031-42930-9 ISBN 978-3-031-42931-6 (eBook)
https://doi.org/10.1007/978-3-031-42931-6

This Springer imprint is published by the registered company Springer Nature Switzerland AG
The registered company address is: Gewerbestrasse 11, 6330 Cham, Switzerland

Paper in this product is recyclable.

Foreword

As a fierce tenant of the idea that Europe needs a robust and simple set of accounting standards that serves the general interest and that supports European financial stability, it is with immense pleasure that I decided to answer positively to the editors' invitation to write a foreword for this book, dedicated to accounting standards in Europe.

Before I comment on the need for common accounting standards in Europe, about European Financial Reporting Advisory Group (EFRAG)'s work, and about the content of this book, it seems relevant to share my understanding of the fundamental role that accounting has historically played and still plays in constructing a desirable society. A premise to the emergence of accounting activities is the idea that societies are made of communities of individuals which seek to collectively face dangers originating from the unknown, and for that purpose, design conventions, rules, and habits that organize individuals' interrelations and the management of the resources available to the whole community. Early rules appeared 4000 years ago when human beings decided to settle down in areas where resources were abundant. They defined rights, obligations, and penalties. It is to materialize and organize the follow-up of those rights and obligations that accounting instruments were designed.

Because this book is co-authored by some members of the EFRAG academic panel, I convoke Mattessich and Ijiri, two eminent scholars who influenced the accounting thought, and borrow their definition of accounting both as a passive representation and as an active instrument likely to influence the behavior of economic actors. Indeed, by initially keeping records of receivables, early accounting offered, on the one hand, a description of a transaction, and on the other hand, the demonstration of the existence of an ordered relation between two individuals or entities. Moreover, it acts as a means of building trust by actualizing the commitments of involved parties. This is because the permanent registration of this transaction in various materials (clay bowls, clay tablets, papyrus, ledgers, books, etc.) perpetuates a memory and builds grounds for a durable relation. Concretely, an individual having historically fulfilled his commitments can be deemed trustworthy. This suggests that accounting be not originally concerned with the "measurement" of the profit obtained from a relation between two individuals or entities. The focus on transactions as results is recent and can even be seen as an epiphenomenon in the history of humankind. Before this shift, which likely occurred with the liberalization of the financial markets in the 1980s, transactions acted as a means of serving a higher-level goal.

As one of the oldest organized intellectual practices, if not the oldest, accounting played an essential role in the structuration of human society and in the development of revolutionary innovations. Writing was invented to support accounting records, alphabet was created to simplify bookkeeping, numbers were conceptualized for accounting issues, the zero first appeared in an accounting book, and algebra, financial mathematics, and probabilities also served accounting purposes. While no other instrument has played such a decisive role in the history of humankind, accounting has also created the circumstances for a Babelian mosaic. With the multiplication of human communities across the globe, accounting practices diffused but also differed, with a magnitude similar to that of languages. Nobes, another famous scholar, produced a seminal comparison of various accounting systems, observing that some national standards developed at the micro level are either inspired by business or professional practices, whereas other standards were developed at the macro level in order to follow tax or legal orientations. The European Union is a setting where those four types of accounting standard-setting orientations manifest themselves. As a result, preparers, auditors, and users of published financial statements meet complicated situations.

It is hence not a surprise that building a common and harmonized accounting environment has been a target of Europe since its early foundation. It is indeed mentioned in Article 54 Paragraph 3g of the Treaty of Rome (1957). Nevertheless, it remained a complex issue. Harmonization is undertaken through the publication of directives, among which are the famous fourth and seventh directives, respectively, adopted in 1978 and in 1983, now superseded by directive 2013/34/EU, which is the central topic of this book. A Directive is a regulatory instrument that is directly binding, when enforced, i.e., when Member States have transposed it in their national law, and specifically in their commercial codes. However, aimed to ease the movement toward a better comparability, the numerous remaining options present in the 4th and 7th accounting directives preserved the existing accounting traditions and weakened the reporting convergence process. They testified to a partial success (failure) in the European accounting harmonization process.

In search of an alternative path, and under the pressure of financial markets, by the middle of the 1990s, the European Commission (EC) started to support the efforts of the International Accounting Standards Committee (IASC) in their endeavor to develop the first principles-based international standards. Other world-level organizations also pledge for a greater harmonization and standardization of accounting systems and support the effort of the IASC and of its new form as the International Accounting Standards Board (IASB). These are the United Nations, the World Bank, the Organisation for Economic Co-operation and Development, the World Trade Organization, the European Union, and the International Organization of Securities Commission. It is in such context that the decision to adopt the set of International

Accounting Standards (IAS) in Europe was made in 2000 that became applicable in 2005, requiring that about 7000 listed companies prepared their financial statements in accordance with the IAS, now referred to as the International Financial Reporting Standards (IFRS), and issued by the IASB.

The Constitution of the IFRS Foundation, a not-for-profit corporation incorporated in the State of Delaware, USA, outlines the full criteria for the composition of the IASB. The members are appointed by the Trustees of the IFRS Foundation. Currently, they are six trustees representing North and Central America, six trustees representing Europe, seven trustees representing Asia, and three trustees originating from Commonwealth countries, namely, the United Kingdom and South Africa. The IASB being a private organization, located in the United Kingdom, a country no longer part of the European Union, those standards could not be adopted straightforward. The EU "*cannot delegate responsibility for setting financial reporting requirements for listed EU companies to a non-governmental third party*." A two-tier endorsement mechanism was designed that defines how to examine, challenge, and advise the European Commission on the adoption of those international standards. This is how EFRAG came to life.

EFRAG is a private association established in 2001 with the encouragement of the European Commission to serve the public interest. EFRAG extended its mission in 2022 following the new role assigned to EFRAG in the CSRD (Corporate Sustainability Reporting Disclosure), providing Technical Advice to the European Commission in the form of fully prepared draft EU Sustainability Reporting Standards and/or draft amendments to these standards. Its member organizations are European stakeholders, national organizations, and civil society organizations. EFRAG's activities are organized into two pillars. The first pillar addresses financial reporting and seeks to influence the development of IFRS Standards from a European perspective. The second pillar seeks the development of Sustainability Reporting Standards and their related amendments for the European Commission.

In its financial reporting activities, EFRAG ensures that the European views are properly incorporated into the IASB's standard-setting process and in related international debates. EFRAG ultimately provides advice to the European Commission on whether newly issued or revised IFRS Standards meet the criteria of the IAS Regulation for endorsement for use in the EU, including whether endorsement would be conducive to the European public good. In its sustainability reporting activities, EFRAG provides technical advice to the European Commission in the form of draft EU Sustainability Reporting Standards accompanied by bases of conclusions and cost benefit analysis. EFRAG also seeks input from all stakeholders and obtains evidence about specific European circumstances, throughout the standard-setting process. Its legitimacy is built on transparency, governance, due process (which may include field tests, impact analyses, and outreach), public accountability, and thought leadership. This enables EFRAG to speak convincingly, clearly, and consistently, and be recognized as the European voice in corporate reporting.

In 2016, the European Commission proposed my name for the role of President of the European Financial Reporting Advisory Group (EFRAG). To my credit, I had three decades of representation of the people, and an award of the deputy of the year

2009 for my activism toward a stronger stabilization of the financial system, after the occurrence of the subprime crisis. Following a hearing, members of the Association voted and the Committee on Economic and Monetary Affairs confirmed my nomination in May 2016. I remained in charge until 2022. I dedicated my mandate to the transformation of EFRAG.

This book provides the reader with a deeper understanding of the stakes at play in accounting standards. The focus is on Directive 2013/34/EU of the European Parliament and of the Council of June 26, 2013, on the annual financial statements, consolidated financial statements, and related reports of certain types of undertakings, amending Directive 2006/43/EC of the European Parliament and of the Council and repealing Council Directives 78/660/EEC and 83/349/EEC Text with EEA relevance.

In the first part of this book, authors from eight different countries relate the modalities of transposition of the directive in their country: Denmark, France, Germany, Italy, Spain, Sweden, the Netherlands, and the United Kingdom. This cross-country comparison is eased by the adoption of a common outline for all chapters. Authors first set the context by introducing the ecosystem of their country and by explaining the roles of the civil code, tax laws, and professional standards in the multiple approaches to the transposition of the directive. This interestingly sets the departure point of various European countries. I trust that readers will find insights that will inform them about the important initial diversity of accounting contexts. Next, the authors address the recent and current evolution of the standards, which generally testifies to a convergence of their national accounting systems toward that of IFRS. It is also the occasion to discuss the modalities of the national movement toward extra-financial reporting and to understand the different national paths and paces toward the Corporate Sustainability Reporting Directive. The current state and the key characteristics of national accounting rules are next exposed, as well as the recognition and measurement approaches that more or less converge toward IFRS. Nevertheless, differences still subsist; the notion of measurement in accounting is not straightforward across countries.

In a second part of the book, the spatial approach is discontinued to favor a focus on cross-cutting issues related to the following issues: the objectives, overriding principles and relevance of accounting standards, the components of financial statements and layouts, the write-down for impairment losses, the equity reserves and profit distribution, the income taxes in financial statements, and the sustainability reporting. The book finally ends as it has started in this foreword, with an overview of the evolution of private firm accounting in Europe.

I hope that this accounting journey within European countries will illuminate the reasons why some of us dedicate their time and effort to the issue of accounting in Europe, even finding some passion in playing that role.

Former EFRAG President and former
Member of the European Parliament,
Paris, France

J. P. Gauzès

Contents

The Evolution of Financial Statements Regulations in the Main European Countries

Paul André and Roberto Di Pietra

1 Introduction

In the context of corporate reporting within the member States of the European Union (EU), the European Commission (EC) establishes regulations and Directives. Once approved at the EU level, each member State must transpose Directives into their national legislation. In recent years, the EC has undertaken three significant projects: (1) adopted the International Accounting Standards/International Financial Report Standards (IAS/IFRS) framework of the International Accounting Standards Board (IASB) for financial reporting of certain undertakings, (2) developed Non-Financial reporting (NFR) requirements and (3) adopted the International Auditing Standards (IAudS) audit standards of the International Auditing and Assurance Standards Board (IAASB). This chapter focuses on the first two which deal with corporate reporting.

In the EU, all limited liability companies must prepare financial statements in order for stakeholders to assess the financial health of the business and provide a 'true and fair' view of their financial position. Over recent years, the EU's objective has been to 'promote the convergence of accounting standards at global level and ensure consistent and comparable financial reporting across the EU' (https://ec.

P. André
University of Lausanne, Lausanne, Switzerland
e-mail: paul.andre@unil.ch

R. Di Pietra (✉)
Department of Business and Law Studies, University of Siena, Siena, Italy
e-mail: dipietra@unisi.it

A. Incollingo, A. Lionzo (eds.), *The European Harmonization of National Accounting Rules*, SIDREA Series in Accounting and Business Administration,
https://doi.org/10.1007/978-3-031-42931-6_1

europa.eu/info/business-economy-euro/company-reporting-and-auditing/company-reporting/financial-reporting_en).

EU rules vary whether companies are listed on a regulated EU market or not. Listed companies on a regulated EU market must prepare their consolidated financial statements in accordance with IFRS as issued by the IASB and endorsed by the EC as detailed in Regulation EC 1606/2002 (IFRS financial statements). We describe the endorsement process in more detail in the following section.

Other EU requirements apply to nonconsolidated financial statements of listed companies and to non-listed companies and to small businesses (non-IFRS financial statements). The IASB also developed an IFRS for Small and Medium sized Entities (SMEs) standard, a simplified version of 'full' IFRS standards, issued in 2009.

1.1 Non-IFRS Financial Statements

The rules that companies must follow for non-IFRS financial statements are detailed in Directive 2013/34/EU of the European Parliament and of the Council of 26 June 2013 which is also known as the 'Accounting Directive'. Directive 2013/34/EU on the annual financial statements, consolidated financial statements and related reports of certain types of undertakings amended Directive 2006/43/EC of the European Parliament and of the Council and merged and improved Council Directives 78/660/EEC (known as the Fourth Directive which dealt with individual financial statements) and 83/349/EEC (known as the Seventh Directive which dealt with consolidated financial statements).

The directive attempts to harmonise national requirements about (1) presentation and content of annual or consolidated financial statements, (2) presentation and content of management reports, (3) the measurement basis companies use to prepare their financial statements, (4) audit of financial statements publication of financial statements and (5) the responsibility of management with regard to all the prior.

Directive 2013/34/EU was also developed following the 'think small first' approach wanting to eliminate unnecessary and disproportionate administrative costs on small companies. The directive allows a simplified reporting regime for SMEs and a very light approach for micro-companies (companies having less than ten employees). Present thresholds are as follows (Table 1):

Table 1 Thresholds defining micro-, small- and medium-sized companies

	Micro	Small	Medium-sized
Balance sheet total	≤350,000	≤6,000,000	≤20,000,000
Net turnover	≤700,000	≤12,000,000	≤40,000,000
Average no. of employees during the financial year	≤10	≤50	≤250

Source: https://ec.europa.eu/info/law/accounting-rules-directive-2013-34-eu/implementation/guidance-implementation-and-interpretation-law_en

Table 2 Use of IFRS in consolidated accounts of 'non-listed in a regulated market' nonfinancial undertakings trading for gain

Required by all	Required for some Permitted for all others	Required for some/ Permitted for some	Permitted for all	Permitted for some	Not permitted
Cyprus	Malta *(larger companies)* Spain *(groups which include at least one group company who is traded in regulated market)*	Croatia *(large entrepreneurs/ subs. of EU IFRS parent)* Greece *(significant subs of listed groups/if audit by CPA)*	Austria Belgium Czech Republic Denmark Estonia France Germany Ireland Netherlands Norway Portugal Romania Slovenia[a] Sweden Switzerland United Kingdom Turkey	Finland *(if independent audit)* Italy *(except small entities)* Poland *(filed for admission to public trading or subs. of EU IFRS parent)*	

Subs, subsidiaries
Source: André (2017), Table 1 IFRS profiles and articles in the *Accounting in Europe* 2017 special issue 14(1–2)
[a]Once IFRS adopted, must be used for at least 5 years

According to the EU Directive, micro-companies can prepare and present a very simplified financial statement with a minimum set of information included within the balance sheet and a short income statement. The level of information is higher in the case of the financial statement prepared by small companies including some simplified notes to the accounts.

As shown in André (2017), understanding the role and present status of IFRS in the completion of national accounting rules, at least for large non-listed industrials and even sometimes medium-sized firms, is not straightforward since only in-depth analysis by country can allow us to answer to what extent are IFRS required or permitted in their consolidated accounts or in separate accounts. Tables 2 and 3 are based on such an in-depth analysis of 25 European Countries as presented in the special issue of *Accounting in Europe* in 2017 (Issue 14, 1–2). André (2017) also shows that only the United Kingdom and Ireland have a significant group of large non-listed companies (about 9–10%) using IFRS.

Further, while the IASB developed IFRS for SMEs in 2009, the EU, following consultations, felt that these were still too complex to meet its objectives in particular

Table 3 Use of IFRS in annual/separate accounts of 'non-listed in a regulated market' nonfinancial undertakings trading for gain

Required by all	Required for some Permitted for all others	Required for some/ Permitted for some	Permitted for all	Permitted for some	Not permitted
Cyprus	Malta *(larger companies)*	Croatia *(large entrepreneurs/ subsidiaries of EU IFRS parent)* Greece *(significant subs. of listed groups/if audit by CPA)*	Denmark Estonia Ireland Italy *(except small entities)* Netherlands Norway Slovenia United Kingdom Turkey	Czech Rep. *(subs. of EU IFRS parent)* Finland *(if independent audit)* Poland *(filed for admission to public trading or subs. of EU IFRS parent)* Portugal *(subs. of EU IFRS parent)* Switzerland *(if no subs.)*	Austria Belgium France Germany Romania Spain Sweden

Subs., subsidiaries
Underlined Countries: Class A (strong equity, commercially driven) as per Nobes
Source: André (2017), Table 2, by author from data in ARC, IFRS profiles and articles in the *Accounting in Europe* 2017 special issue 14 (1–2)

referring to the above-mentioned simplification requested by the EU Accounting Directive 2013/34.[1] The only EU Country that has national standards based on IFRS for SMEs standard, but with significant modifications, is Ireland (similarly in the United Kingdom), and other Countries can be viewed as generally aligned with these standards such as Estonia, the Netherlands and Sweden (K3).[2]

Table 4 reflects André (2017)'s attempt to classify for some EU countries the level of convergence of IFRS and national GAAP for large non-listed nonfinancial undertakings countries based on five categories: (1) full IFRS, (2) generally aligned with IFRS and references/acknowledged, (3) generally aligned with IFRS for SMEs, (4) generally aligned with IFRS yet not referenced/not acknowledged and (5) some alignment but single accounts have other focus (tax, investor protection, etc.). While some of these classifications can be debated, the table shows the challenge in classifying accounting systems in Europe. See also André et al. (2021) for further analysis of book-tax and book-dividend conformity with IFRS within the EU which documents the complexity of determining clear categories.

[1] Summary report of the responses received to the Commission's Consultation on the International Financial Reporting Standard for Small- and Medium-Sized Entities, Directorate General for the Internal Market and Services, May 2010.

http://ec.europa.eu/internal_market/accounting/sme_accounting/review_directives_en.htm.

[2] The website https://www.ifrs.org/use-around-the-world/use-of-ifrs-standards-by-jurisdiction/ (searched on 6 June 2022) indicates that IFRS for SMEs is under consideration in Hungary.

Table 4 Convergence between IFRS and national GAAP of 'large' non-listed nonfinancial undertakings

Full IFRS	Generally aligned with IFRS and referenced/ acknowledged	Generally aligned with IFRS for SMEs	Generally aligned with IFRS yet not referenced/not acknowledged	Some alignment but single accounts have other focus (tax, investor protection, etc.)
Cyprus	Croatia Denmark Finland Greece Malta Poland Portugal Slovenia	Estonia Ireland (FRS102) Netherlands Norway Sweden (K3) United Kingdom (FRS102)	Romania Spain (PGC) Switzerland (FER)	Austria Belgium Czech Rep. France Germany Italy Switzerland (CO)

Underlined countries: Class A (strong equity, commercially driven) as per Nobes. Excludes Turkey where standards are undergoing revision
FER: Swiss GAAP; CO: Code des obligations
Source: André (2017), Table 4, by author from articles in the *Accounting in Europe* 2017 special issue 14(1–2)

1.2 IFRS Financial Statements

Regulation (EC) 1606/2002 requires all EU listed companies on a EU regulated market to prepare their consolidated financial statements in accordance with a single set of international standards, the IFRS (International Financial Reporting Standards), previously known as IAS (International Accounting Standards). Regulation (EC) no. 1606/2002 sets a mandatory rule that all EU listed companies must use IFRS as adopted by the EU for their consolidated financial statements and a discretionary provision that EU countries can opt to extend the use of IFRS to annual financial statements and non-listed companies as well.

Nevertheless, according to Pownall and Wieczynska (2018) a non-negligible number of EU listed do not use IFRS at different times between 2005 and 2012 either because of adoption deferral for certain categories of firms or firms on unregulated markets, because single entity reports are not required/permitted to use IFRS (see their Table 1), or some firms exploited definitions and exemptions or simply failed to comply with the regulation.

2 The Interaction Between EU and IFRS in Developing Present Project in the Accounting Field

Before presenting our analysis on the present projects about financial reporting within the EU, it could be useful to provide a description of the interrelations existing between the European Commission (EC) and the IFRS Foundation through the

European Financial Reporting Advisory Group (EFRAG) and the Accounting Regulatory Committee (ARC).

The involvement of the EC in the accounting area and, more specifically, on financial reporting has had a radical change with the issuing of Regulation no. 1606/2002/EC. Following this regulation, some other regulations have been approved by EC till Regulation no. 1126/2008. This regulation has been amended several times to include all the standards presented by the IASB since 2008, including certain amendments from 2012. A page on the EC website listing all the amendments to Commission Regulation (EC) no. 1126/2008 is published and updated regularly (https://eur-lex.europa.eu/legal-content/EN/ALL/?uri=CELEX%3A32008R1126).

In June 2015 (new governance implemented 31 October 2014), the EC adopted a report evaluating the regulation's operation (Maystadt 2013 report). It concludes overall that IFRSs have been successful in improving the efficiency of EU capital markets by enhancing the transparency and comparability of financial statements. Some areas for improvement were however identified, such as better collaboration between the parties involved in the endorsement process.

Regulation no. 1606/2002/EC (amended by Regulation EC no. 297/2008) empowers the EC to adopt certain implementing measures in accordance with the Regulatory Procedure with Scrutiny (RPS). This procedure must be applied every time the EC adopts newly issued International Accounting Standards (IAS/IFRS), amendments to existing accounting standards or interpretations of existing standards.

The most recent changes have been approved by EC through three specific Regulations 2017/1990, 2017/1989 and 2017/1988 in relation to some amendments changing the standards IAS 7 (Statement of Cash Flows), IAS 12 (Income Taxes) and IFRS 4 (Insurance Contracts), respectively.

As a consequence of Regulation no. 1606/2002/EC, a specific process for the endorsement of the International Accounting Standards (IAS/IFRS) in the EU was established. To ensure appropriate political oversight, the regulation introduces a mechanism to assess the IFRSs adopted by the IASB to give them enforceability within the EU. As above-mentioned two bodies play a role in this endorsement mechanism:

1. ARC, chaired by the European Commission and composed of EU countries' representatives, decides whether to endorse IFRSs based on Commission proposals. The ARC has a regulatory role in deciding whether the IFRSs are to be adopted.
2. EFRAG provides support and expertise to the Commission in the assessment of IFRS. It is composed of accounting experts from the private sector in several EU countries. EFRAG has a technical role in providing support and expertise as needed to assess IFRSs and to advise the EC on whether to adopt the IFRSs under consideration.

Through the endorsement mechanism, the EC could develop interaction with the IFRS Foundation in order to achieve the official endorsement of IFRS within the EU context.

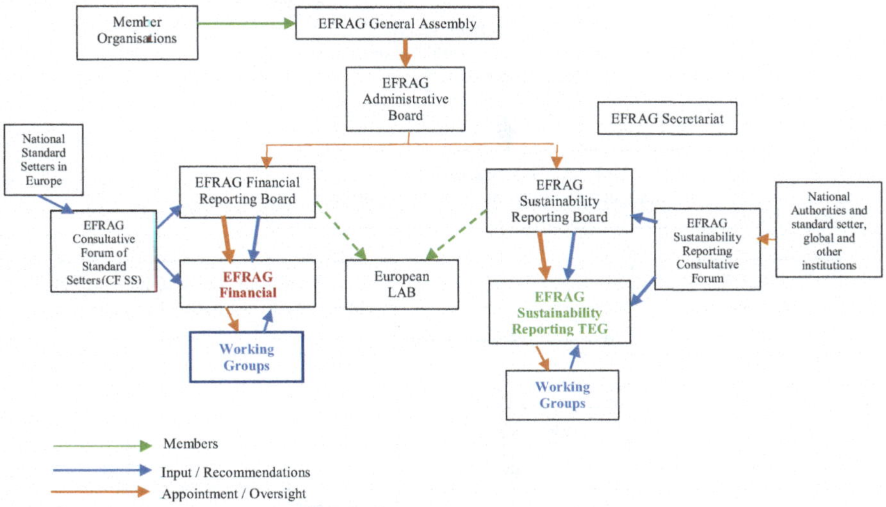

Fig. 1 EFRAG's organisation chart. Source: EFRAG Website (https://www.efrag.org/About/Facts)

As well, the IFRS Foundation plays a strategic role on the activity of the International Accounting Standards Board (IASB). The IASB is the independent body responsible for developing and publishing International Financial Reporting Standards. The EC monitors the operation of the IFRS Foundation, contributes to its consultations and reports on its activity. The IFRS Foundation receives financial contributions from the EU. In the financial year 2020, the EC funded the IFRS Foundation with an amount of 4,284,140 GBP (in Euro 5,125,000).

The consultative role played by the EFRAG within the EU context and considering the different relationships with the IFRS Foundation and the National standard setters have contributed to set its governance and the flows of its several activities (Fig. 1).

As to the endorsement system of the IFRS rules, the entire process could be schematised through the following scheme (Fig. 2).

To conclude this overview of the interaction between EU and IFRS, it is worth underlining the role played by the European Securities and Markets Authorities (ESMA). Within the described endorsement system, ESMA contributes as an official observer in the ARC and in the EFRAG and its working groups. ESMA plays a relevant role underlying the importance to support the development of corporate reporting and evaluation of the existing legislative framework. Through its comment letters try to improve the usefulness and transparency of the decisions regarding financial information and the enforceability of IFRS (https://www.esma.europa.eu/convergence/ias-regulation).

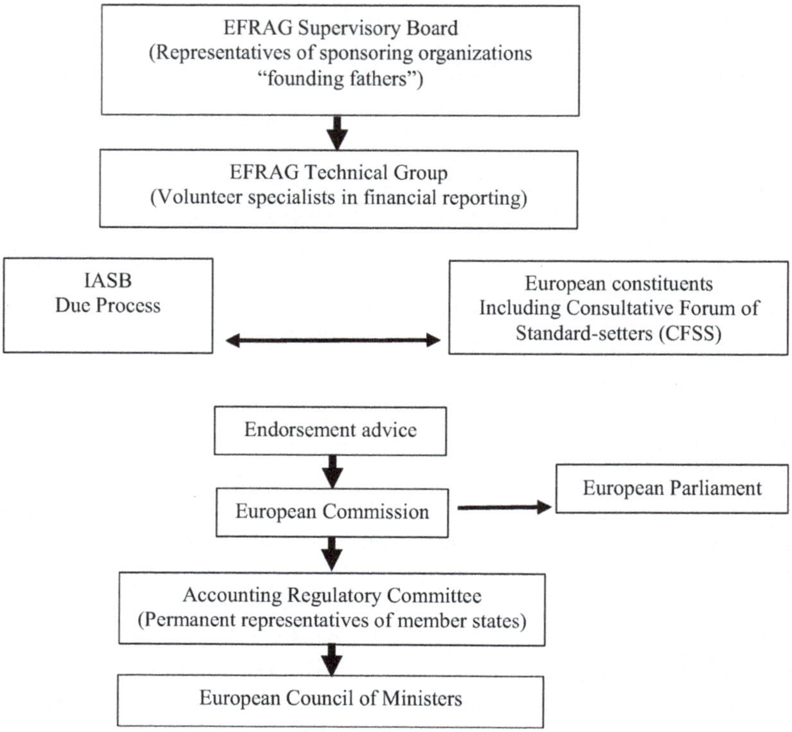

Fig. 2 The European IFRS endorsement system. Source: From van Mourik and Walton (2018)

3 Present Projects in Developing Financial Reporting Within the EU

As clarified in the previous section, the EU interacts with the IFRS Foundation and IASB through the EC and, more specifically, through the activities of EFRAG and ARC. These two bodies are involved in the issuing of new and revised standards or interpretations providing advice and verifying if they are consistent or not with the existing, accounting EU Directives. In other words, they play a consultative role.

3.1 EFRAG

EFRAG is an independent organisation that provides advice to the EC in the assessment of IFRS. EFRAG receives financial contributions from the EU (2,777,000 EUR) in order to support its activities. In 2014, the EU established a programme to support and fund in the medium term the activities of the IFRS Foundation and EFRAG for the period 2014–2020 (this programme was amended with an increase in the financial recourses provided in 2017 through Regulation 2017/827). The present initiatives involving EFRAG in projects related to the EC can be summarised by taking into consideration the different stages at which the advisory group is working or has completed its work. In this respect, EFRAG has identified the following phases: (a) communication, (b) research phase, (c) consultation, (d) re-consultation, (e) discussion paper (DP) consultation, (f) second DP consultation, (g) ED consultation, (h) re-ED consultation, (i) endorsement consultation, (j) phase 2 ED consultation, (k) phase 2 endorsement consultation, (l) monitoring, (m) completed and (n) publishing in the Official Journal (Source: EFRAG website, www.efrag.org, activities).

Examining Tables 5, 6, 7, 8 and 9 in the Appendix, we identify some relevant trends in its present projects with the EC and the IFRS Foundation but also internally.

As to the projects with the EC, this interaction has mainly focused on the 'sustainability reporting standards', the 'climate-related reporting' and the 'business model issue', confirming the growing relevance of this topic in the agenda of the regulators and standard setters (see Table 5).

As to the relationship with the IFRS Foundation, we distinguish the level of consultation and the level of standard setting and endorsement. In the most recent years, EFRAG has been consulted in order to share an opinion on the IASB agenda, the research agenda and the IASB due process in issuing standards (see Table 6). Another relevant activity has been with respect to the issuing of IFRS (new and revised) and their EC enforcement (see Table 7).

In this respect, the present projects mainly have been related to:

1. The research phase (disclosure initiative; equity method; IFRS 9 financial instruments; provisions).
2. The consultation (post-implementation review of IFRS 10, IFRS 11 and IFRS 12).
3. The DP consultation (business combinations).
4. The ED consultation (IAS 21; IFRIC 14; lease liability and sale and leaseback).
5. The endorsement consultation (IAS 1 amendments about the deferral of effective date, or the classification of liabilities; IFRS 17 Insurance Contracts).
6. The project monitoring (dynamic risk management; extractive activities).
7. The present projects completed (disclosure of accounting policies and IAS 8 amendments; financial instruments with characteristics of equity; IFRS Practice Statement 1 Management Commentary; IFRS 13: Fair Value Measurement).
8. The publication in the EU Official Journal (IAS 28 amendments; IFRS 16 and covid-19; IFRS 9 amendments).

Moreover, we can refer to some activities related to ad hoc projects stimulated by the EC (Table 8) in which we can emphasise the specific relevance of present projects devoted to the sustainability reporting standards, the link between risk opportunities and the characteristics of the business model and the growing importance of the climate-related reporting.

The EFRAG Board sometimes aims to stimulate attention on emerging issues by planning proactive research activities (Table 9) related to increasing role of crypto assets and currencies or the need to provide better information on intangibles and, in particular, to reflect on the impairment and amortisation processes related to Goodwill.

3.2 ARC

The Accounting Regulatory Committee (ARC) is a committee composed of representatives of the different EU countries. It provides opinions when the Commission proposes to endorse new accounting standards in the EU. Since 2008, ARC has scheduled an average of four meetings per year for a total of 60 meetings. Several amendments have affected many standards along the years. In Table 10, we propose the complete list of topics examined by the ARC (source: EC website, https://ec.europa.eu comitology register). As to the present projects, we refer to the last 3 years mentioning the opinion expressed on the amendments of the following standards:

1. IAS 1 Presentation of Financial Statement and IAS 8 Accounting Policies, Changes in Accounting Estimates and Errors.
2. IFRS 3 Business Combinations.
3. IFRS 7 Financial Instruments: Disclosures, IFRS 9 Financial Instruments, IAS 39 Financial Instruments: Recognition and Measurement.
4. IFRS 16 Leases.
5. IFRS 17 Insurance Contracts.
6. IAS 16 Property, Plant and Equipment; IAS 37 Provisions Contingent Liabilities and Contingent Assets; IAS 41 Agriculture; IFRS 1 First-Time Adoption of International Financial Reporting Standards.

From the analysis of the present project between the EU and IFRS Foundation, it emerges that in many cases they are representing some intervention of maintenance of existing IFRS. Due to the nature of the standards, they are subject to a continuous update. Present projects confirm how the EU, through the involvement of EC, is collaborating on IFRS development and is strongly supporting issuing activity. The EC is perfectly aware of this role having created an enforcement mechanism through EFRAG and ARC that is effective and efficient.

The interaction between EU and IFRS Foundation is particularly relevant if we consider the increase of new topics intro the agenda of these institutions. This is confirmed in the specific cases of the debate related to consideration of the business models and the discussion about nonfinancial reporting and sustainability issues.

4 Nonfinancial Reporting

The reporting activity of business entities traditionally and historically is based on the preparation and presentation of a financial statement. However, in the last 50 years, an increasing interest of the stakeholders and consequently of 'new' and 'traditional' regulators have contributed to the nonfinancial side of the business reporting. This trend is strongly connected with the awareness that an increasing number of stakeholders need a larger set of information to take their own specific economic decision, integrating the financial side with information related to different perspectives (social, labour, environmental, sustainability, gender, human rights, etc.).

On this basis, a double set of initiatives has started. From one side, it is possible to observe an enlargement of the financial statements' contents. From the other, it has emerged a phenomenon related to the introduction of new reports and the standardisation of their contents.

As to the first kind of initiative, many regulatory systems introduced modifications to enrich the nonfinancial side of the reporting activity, including within the Notes to the accounts and the Management Commentary several requirements related to information about the social, environmental and sustainable activities of the business entity. This is what happened within the European Union (EU) regulatory scenario where the Accounting Directives since 2003 have been modified introducing the requests to provide information about the risks and uncertainties related to the environment, the social context, the technology, etc. More specifically, Directive 2003/51/EC has required to include in Notes to the accounts and in the Management Commentary nonfinancial key performance indicators relevant to the specific business, including information relating to environmental and employee matters. Through the Directive 2006/46EC, the information related to the corporate governance area were increased.

As to the introduction of new reports and the need to standardise their contents, several initiatives started because of the activity of different international institutions and organisations such as the United Nations (UN), the Organisation for Economic Co-operation and Development (OECD), the International Labour Organization (ILO), the Eco-Management and Audit Scheme (EMAS), the International Organization for Standardization (ISO) and the Global Reporting Initiative (GRI).

Within the nonfinancial side of reporting, we can list the following seven experiences:

1. In 1976, the OECD Guidelines for Multinational Enterprises were issued for the first time. It is a set of voluntary principles and standards providing recommendations to multinational enterprises (MNE) for responsible business conduct. These guidelines provide non-binding standards aiming to ensure the coherence between economic, environmental and social objectives.
2. In 1977, the ILO's Tripartite Declaration of Principles was issued. The ILO is a United Nation agency issuing a set of labour standards and developing programs and policies promoting decent work. These principles concerned multinational

enterprises (MNE) and provided social policy guidelines to governments, employers and workers' organisations. These guidelines covered four different areas of interest: employment, training, conditions of work and life and industrial relations.

3. In 1993, the EMAS regulation was issued for the first time, and it was revised and modified in 2009 to achieve the European Commission's goals on sustainable development. The EMAS regulation aims to support all the organisations interested to assume economic and environmental responsibility, improving their environmental performance and communicating this performance to the stakeholders. To get the EMAS certification, the organisations must follow and comply with a detailed five steps procedure.
4. In 2000, the UN launched the Global Compact as a voluntary initiative for the development of socially responsible corporate practices. The main aim was to support the entities in doing their business in a responsible way. In this respect, the UN defined a framework composed of ten principles organised in four areas related to human rights, labour, environment and anticorruption.
5. In 2010, ISO issued standard 26000 with the aim to support a group of stakeholders (consumers, government, industry, labour, non-governmental organisations, academics and others) in several aspects of social responsibility. The ISO 26000 is structured in seven principles (accountability, transparency, ethical behaviour, respect for stakeholder interests, respect for the rule of law, respect for international norms of behaviour and respect for human rights) and covers seven core subjects of social responsibility (organisational governance, human rights, labour practices, the environment, fair operating practices, consumer issues and community involvement and development).
6. In 2011, the UN issued the Guiding Principles on Business and Human Rights. These principles constitute a set of guidelines for states and companies created to prevent, address and remedy human rights abuses committed in business operations. The UN Guiding Principles are based on three main pillars: the state duty to protect human rights, the corporate responsibility to respect human rights and the access to remedy. Within these three pillars, there are 31 foundational and operational principles aimed to prevent and address the risk of adverse impact on human rights related to business activity.
7. In 2016, GRI issued a set of 36 interrelated reporting standards to support on a voluntary basis companies in preparing their reports on their impacts on the economy, the environment and society. The first three standards (GRI 101, 102 and 103) are universal standards, useful as a guide for organisations preparing sustainability reports. The 200 series of the GRI Standards group together standards related to the material economic impact of an organisation. The 300 series of the GRI Standards include specific standards on the material environmental impact of an organisation. The 400 series of the GRI Standards contain standards focused on the material social impact of an organisation.

Observing the different topics covered by each of the seven initiatives, it emerges how some of them represent very most complete frameworks in the field of nonfinancial reporting (e.g. GRI Standards, ISO 26000, OECD Guidelines), while some other are proposing a specific list of topics (e.g. EMAS, UN Global Compact, UN Guiding Principles and ILO's Tripartite Declaration). Moreover, we must clarify that the previous list of initiatives is not exhaustive. Some other interventions in the field of nonfinancial reporting could be added (e.g. US Sustainability Accounting Standards Board, SASB; Carbon Disclosure Project, CDP; ISO 140001 on environmental management; ISO 13485 on medical device quality; RobecoSam Corporate Sustainability Assessment, CSA; Environmental, Social and Corporate Governance, ESG).

The growing importance of nonfinancial reporting is also confirmed considering how the idea to provide a large set of financial and nonfinancial information to the stakeholders has contributed to the affirmation of the integrated reporting (IR) initiative together with the gradual definition of its contents and the activity of a specific international regulator: the International Integrated Reporting Council (IIRC). The IIRC aims to define a framework on integrated reporting and to issue a set of integrated thinking principles. The IIRC pursues the idea to create an interrelation between integrated reporting and thinking of efficient and productive capital allocation, acting as a force for financial stability and sustainable development. This interrelation can contribute to: (a) improve the quality of information available to the providers of financial capital; (b) promote a more cohesive and efficient approach to corporate reporting; (c) enhance accountability and stewardship for the broad base of capitals (financial, intellectual, human, social, natural); and (d) support integrated thinking, decision-making and actions.

Summarising the previous developments, we can form a first conclusion. During the last 50 years, we have observed that together with the traditional financial reports, other reports have raised the growing importance of complementing the informative value of the first one. This was the case with the environmental reports, the social responsibility reports, the sustainability reports, the integrated reports and the economic, social and governance (ESG) reports.

To this first conclusion, we can add the recent initiative adopted by the EU and IFRS entering in the field of nonfinancial reporting.

In 2014, the EU issued Directive 2014/95/EC on nonfinancial reporting (NFR). Through this directive, the European Commission introduced within the member states the mandatory preparation of this kind of reporting on the public companies' performance and their impact on society and the environment. Public company under this mandatory requirement is large public-interest entities (or groups) exceeding on their balance sheet the criterion of the average number of 500 employees during the financial year (also turnover + asset criteria, etc.).

The mandatory preparation of the NFR reports has impacted the 27 EU member countries, among the few in the world (South Africa was the first country in the world to adopt a mandatory basis for this reporting). The requirement of the Directive 2014/95/EC became effective in 2017. The content of the Directive No. 2014/95 includes five nonfinancial areas to be disclosed and a list of required aspects: (1) environmental matters (present and foreseeable impact on the environment, use of renewable and/or nonrenewable energy, greenhouse gas emission, water use, air pollution, land use, use of materials), (2) social matters (dialogue with local communities, actions taken to ensure the protection and the development of those communities), (3) employee matters (actions taken to ensure gender equality, implementation of fundamental conventions of the International Labour Organisation, working conditions, social dialogue, rights of workers, rights of trade union, health and safety at work, diversity of competences, more diversified on boards), (4) human rights matters (prevention of human rights abuses) and (5) anticorruption and bribery matters (instruments to fight corruption and bribery).

The directive does not impose a specific framework to prepare the NFR. Formally, it is possible to refer to any of the nonfinancial reporting approaches mentioned before. However, most of the public companies obliged to prepare the NFR have chosen to follow the GRI framework.[3] In many cases, public companies have decided to refer to the Sustainable Development Goals (SDG) issued in 2015 by the UN as a fundamental part of the Agenda 2030.

As to the IFRS initiatives related to the nonfinancial reporting field, we can refer to the project related to the Management Commentary preparation and launching of the IASB International Sustainability reporting project.

The Management Commentary project has a long history within the activity of the IASB. A first attempt to issue a document about the Management Commentary dates back to 2010 (Practice statement 1).[4] In November 2017, after some years of pause, the Board has decided to launch again this topic in November 2017 taking into consideration the informational needs of investors and creditors for a narrative reporting related to specific industries and topics such as sustainability reporting. In other words, investors and creditors are affected by Environmental, Social and Governance (ESG) or sustainability matters, and they aim to find this issue within the narrative part of the annual reports. In this perspective, the Management Commentary is a report that complements a company's financial statement. In many jurisdictions, the Management Commentary is included within the annual report on a mandatory basis (this is the case in EU countries according to the Accounting Directives).

In May 2021, the Board published the Exposure Draft ED including the proposals for a comprehensive new framework for the Management Commentary preparation in order to provide investors and creditors the information they need to assess companies' prospects over all time horizons, including in the long term. The ED feedbacks are expected to be collected through comment letters and examined within the first quarter of 2022.

In September 2020, the Board published a consultation paper to collect the opinion on the relevance of sustainable reporting. The numerous feedbacks received have clearly highlighted how the international investors with global investment

[3] See Carungu et al. (2021); Stolowy and Paugam (2018). See also Borisova and André (2020), and Haller et al. (2017) for more on the impact of the Directive on the quality and impact of the Directive.

[4] On the first Practice Statement 1 issued in 2010, see Argento and Di Pietra (2014).

portfolios are increasingly calling for high quality, transparent, reliable and comparable reporting by companies on climate and other Environmental, Social and Governance (ESG) matters. On the basis of this reaction, in April 2021, an exposure draft was published in order to discuss the idea to involve the IFRS Foundation in the establishment of an international body in charge to issue sustainability standards for the preparation of these nonfinancial reports. Due to the feedbacks collected in November 2021, the IFRS Foundation decided to create the International Sustainability Standards Board (ISSB).

Through this decision of the Board of Trustees, a comprehensive framework on the activity of the IFRS Foundation was completed. In this complex layout of activities, the IASB is in charge to support through its standards the financial statement's preparation, while the ISSB will develop the standards to prepare sustainability reports. The Management Commentary will play an intermediate role between the financial statement, the sustainability report and the other information provided through the annual report.

The involvement of the EU and the IFRS Foundation in the nonfinancial reporting field is a relevant change after several years in which different initiatives were launched attempting to cover and legitimate the importance of this reporting area. The mandatory preparation of NFR within the EU and the forthcoming international standards on sustainability could contribute to determining two processes. The first process is on the one hand related to the NFR standardisation (searching for a growing level of comparability) while the second process is determining a gradual tension to integrate financial and nonfinancial reports.

In this respect, it is worth to note that in June 2020 EFRAG was involved by the European Commission in order to provide a technical support on the elaboration of possible EU nonfinancial reporting standards in a revised NFR Directive. The most recent status of this involvement (April 2021) is related with the EC proposal for a Corporate Sustainability Reporting Directive (CSRD) through the adoption of European sustainability reporting standards. The draft standards would be developed by EFRAG.

5 Concluding Remarks

In the previous sections, we have tried to provide an overview of the recent regulative evolution within the European Union interesting both the financial and nonfinancial reporting. During the last 20 years, we identify some general trends affecting the reporting of the business entities operating in the EU context.

As for financial reporting, it is evident that the EU through the EC and EFRAG is playing an institutionalised role with the IFRS Foundation. The mandatory adoption of the IFRS standards in the EU has greatly contributed to determining this role, and, at the same time, this has greatly changed the content of the EU Accounting Directives.

The issuing of the Directive 2013/34/EU represents a relevant result in this process. Its enactment in the national accounting rules of the EU member states has determined a radical change reducing the distance in many countries between the national accounting legislation and the IFRS rules. Nevertheless, identifying the level of convergence between IFRS and national GAAP remains challenging since some countries require full IFRS, are generally aligned with IFRS and reference or acknowledge so, are more aligned with IFRS for SMEs but with some or major modifications, are generally aligned with IFRS yet do not per se reference or acknowledge the fact or have some alignment but single accounts have other focus (tax, investor protection, dividend distribution, etc.).

Meanwhile, EFRAG and ARC continue to play their consultative role in the present projects of the IASB. In this interaction, it is evident how the EU and its advisory bodies contribute to the issuing activity of the international standard setter. In this respect, we have to emphasise a phenomenon related to the content of the financial statements. Over the years, we are observing how this is increasing and is enlarging with respect to not only financial information but also nonfinancial information. This is quite evident if we consider the project launched on the Management Commentary.

Moving from this trend, we refer to the growing importance assumed by nonfinancial reporting. As highlighted before, several experiences have contributed to this phenomenon. Different international initiatives were launched and developed over the years (EMAS, ISO, UN Global Compact, GRI, IIRC, etc.). Due to this, the EU has started to include this topic within the agenda of its regulatory activity (see the case of the mandatory adoption of the nonfinancial report and the consultative role played by the EFRAG). Moreover, the IFRS has decided to enter this regulative field creating the International Sustainability Standards Boards.

As a result of the above-mentioned trends, the present situation could be summarised in the following way: from one side, it is evident how the nonfinancial reporting area is an important area but also one that is crowded with many actors and their rules/standards/guidelines; from the other side, there is a clear attempt to bridge together financial and nonfinancial information within the unique regulatory activity of the international standards-setting body that is the IFRS Foundation. For the moment, it is difficult to say if the IFRS Foundation will succeed in maintaining its central role in the international reporting domain profiting from the EU collaboration in this strategic challenge.

Appendix

Table 5 EFRAG Board present projects classified by phases and topics in projects related to 'EC'

No.	Phase	Project title	Topic
1	Communication	*Ad personam* governance mandate	Specific activities, governance, politics, policies and priorities
2	Communication	European Lab facts	Specific activities
3	Communication	Risks, opportunities and business model	Specific activities
4	Communication	Sustainability reporting standards interim draft	Specific activities
5	Completed	Climate-related reporting	Specific activities
6	Completed	Sustainability reporting standards roadmap	Specific activities

Table 6 EFRAG Board present projects classified by phases and topics in projects related to 'IFRS Foundation consultation'

No.	Phase	Project title	Topic
1	Consultation	EFRAG consultation on IASB agenda and EFRAG research agenda	Specific activities
2	ED consultation	IASB's Due Process Handbook Review	Specific activities

Table 7 EFRAG Board present projects classified by phases and topics in projects related to 'IFRS Foundation standard setting and endorsement'

No.	Phase	Project title	Topic
1	Research phase	Disclosure Initiative: Comprehensive Project	Presentation of financial statements and disclosure unrelated to specific assets and liabilities
2	Research phase	Equity Method: IASB Research Project	Consolidation, interests in other entities and joint arrangements
3	Research phase	IFRS 9 Financial Instruments: Post-Implementation Review	Equity, financial instruments and hedging
4	Research phase	Provisions: Targeted Improvements (IASB Research Project)	Nonfinancial liabilities, provisions, contingent liabilities and contingent assets
5	Research phase	Variable and contingent consideration	Specific activities, nonfinancial assets
6	Consultation	Post-implementation Review of IFRS 10, IFRS 11 and IFRS 12	Consolidation, interests in other entities and joint arrangements
7	Consultation	Primary Financial Statements	Presentation of financial statements and disclosure unrelated to specific assets and liabilities
8	DP consultation	Business Combinations: Disclosures, Goodwill and Impairment	Consolidation, interests in other entities and joint arrangements, nonfinancial assets
9	ED consultation	Disclosure Requirements in IFRS Standards: A Pilot Approach	Presentation of financial statements and disclosure unrelated to specific assets and liabilities
10	ED consultation	IFRIC 14 Amendments: Availability of a refund from a defined benefit plan	Employee benefits
11	ED consultation	Lack of exchangeability: Amendments to IAS 21	
12	ED consultation	Lease Liability in a Sale and Leaseback (Proposed amendment to IFRS 16)	Specific activities
13	ED consultation	Subsidiaries without Public Accountability: Disclosures	Concepts and general guidance, SME accounting
14	ED consultation	Supplier Finance Arrangements	Equity, financial instruments and hedging, presentation of financial statements and disclosure unrelated to specific assets and liabilities
15	Re-ED consultation	Rate-regulated activities: IASB Comprehensive Project	Specific activities
16	Endorsement consultation	Costs Considered in Assessing Whether a Contract Is Onerous (Amendments to IAS 37)	Nonfinancial liabilities, provisions, contingent liabilities and contingent assets
17	Endorsement consultation	IAS 1: Deferral of Effective Date/ Classification of Liabilities	Presentation of financial statements and disclosure unrelated to specific assets and liabilities

(continued)

Table 7 (continued)

No.	Phase	Project title	Topic
18	Endorsement consultation	IAS 1 Amendments: Classification of Liabilities as Current or Non-current	Presentation of financial statements and disclosure unrelated to specific assets and liabilities
19	Endorsement consultation	IFRS 17: Insurance Contracts	Specific activities
20	Monitoring	Dynamic Risk Management	Equity, financial instruments and hedging
21	Monitoring	Extractive Activities	Specific activities
22	Monitoring	Primary Financial Statements: 2021 Standard Setting Activity	Presentation of financial statements and disclosure unrelated to specific assets and liabilities
23	Completed	Amendments to IAS 12 Deferred Tax Related to Assets and Liabilities Arising from a Single Transaction	Income taxes
24	Completed	Definition of Accounting Estimates (Amendments to IAS 8)	Concepts and general guidance
25	Completed	Disclosure of Accounting Policies	Presentation of financial statements and disclosure unrelated to specific assets and liabilities, concepts and general guidance
26	Completed	Financial Instruments with Characteristics of Equity (FICE): 2018 IASB Discussion Paper	Equity, financial instruments and hedging
27	Completed	IAS 8 Amendments: Accounting Policy Changes	Concepts and general guidance
28	Completed	IFRS 13: Fair Value Measurement—Post-implementation Review	Concepts and general guidance, consolidation, interests in other entities and joint arrangements
29	Completed	IFRS 8 Amendments Resulting from Post-implementation Review	Operating segments
30	Completed	IFRS Practice Statement 1 Management Commentary (2021 Revision)	Specific activities
31	Completed	Reference to the Conceptual Framework (Amendments to IFRS 3)	Concepts and general guidance, consolidation, interests in other entities and joint arrangements
32	Published in the Official Journal	Disclosure Initiative: Definition of Material	Concepts and general guidance
33	Published in the Official Journal	IAS 28 Amendments: Long-Term Interests in Associates and Joint Ventures	Consolidation, interests in other entities and joint arrangements, equity, financial instruments and hedging
34	Published in the Official Journal	IFRS 16 and covid-19	Specific activities

(continued)

Table 7 (continued)

No.	Phase	Project title	Topic
35	Published in the EU Official Journal	IFRS 9 Amendments: Prepayment Features with Negative Compensation	Equity, financial instruments and hedging

Table 8 EFRAG Board 'ad hoc projects for the EC' classified by phases and topics

No.	Phase	Project title	Topic
1	Communication	*Ad personam* governance mandate	Specific activities, governance, politics, policies and priorities
2	Communication	European Lab facts	Specific activities
3	Communication	Risk, opportunities and business model	Specific activities
4	Communication	Sustainability reporting standards—interim draft	Specific activities
5	Completed	Climate-related reporting	Specific activities
6	Completed	Sustainability reporting standards roadmap	Specific activities

Table 9 EFRAG Board 'proactive research activities' classified by phases and topics

No.	Phase	Project title	Topic
1	Research phase	EFRAG research project on crypto assets	
2	Research phase	Research on the theory and practice of discounting in financial reporting	Concepts and general guidance, employee benefits
3	DP consultation	Business combinations under common control	Consolidation, interests in other entities and joint arrangements
4	DP consultation	EFRAG research project on better information on intangibles	Nonfinancial assets
5	Completed	European research project Goodwill—impairment and amortisation	Nonfinancial assets

Table 10 ARC decisions on IAS/IFRS amendments classified by topics

No.	IAS/ IFRS	Title	Date
1	IFRS 1	First-Time Adoption of International Financial Reporting Standards	12 December 2009
2	IFRS 10 IFRS 13 IAS 27	Consolidated Financial Statements Fair Value Measurement Separate Financial Statements	17 June 2013
3	IAS 36	Impairment of Assets	5 September 2013
4	IAS 19	Employee Benefits	20 June 2014
5	IAS 16 IAS 38 IAS 41 IFRS 11	Property, Plant and Equipment Intangible Assets Agriculture Joint Arrangements	9 July 2015
6	IAS 27	Separate Financial Statements	28 August 2015
7	IAS 1	Presentation of Financial Statements	1 September 2015
8	IAS 28 IFRS 10 IFRS 12	Investments in Associates and Joint Ventures Consolidated Financial Statements Disclosure of Interests in Other Entities	18 April 2016
9	IFRS 4	Insurance Contracts	29 June 2017
10	IAS 12 IFRS 15	Income Taxes Revenue from Contracts with Customers	3 July 2017
11	IFRS 2	Share-Based Payment	6 October 2017
12	IAS 40	Agriculture	24 October 2017
13	IFRS 9	Financial Instruments	11 December 2017
14	IAS 19	Employee Benefits	9 October 2018
15	IAS 1 IAS 8	Presentation of Financial Statements Accounting Policies, Changes in Accounting Estimates and Errors	2 August 2019
16	IFRS 3	Business Combinations	19 August 2019
17	IFRS 7 IFRS 9 IAS 39	Financial Instruments: Disclosures Financial Instruments Financial Instruments: Recognition and Measurement	29 October 2019
18	IFRS 16	Leases	2 July 2020
19	IFRS 4	Insurance Contracts	28 August 2020
20	IAS 16 IAS 37 IAS 41 IFRS 1 IFRS 3 IFRS 9	Property, Plant and Equipment Provisions Contingent Liabilities and Contingent Assets Agriculture First-Time Adoption of International Financial Reporting Standards Business Combinations Financial Instruments	1 March 2021
21	IFRS 17	Insurance Contracts	16 July 2021

References

André, P. (2017). The role and current status of IFRS in the completion of national accounting rules—Evidence from European countries. *Accounting in Europe, 14*(1–2), 1–12.

André, P., Schaubschlaeger, M., & Schultze, W. (2021). The cash-relevance of IFRS—European Legislation regarding dividends and taxation in the context of IFRS reporting (May 19, 2021). Available at SSRN: https://ssrn.com/abstract=3849492

Argento, D., & Di Pietra, R. (2014). IASB ED management commentary versus European regulation: The impact on management's reports of companies listed on Italian Stock Exchange. In R. Di Pietra, S. McLeay, & J. Ronen (Eds.), *Accounting regulation. New insights on governance, markets and institutions* (pp. 291–310). Springer.

Borisova, A., & André, P. (2020). Measuring the impact of the transition to mandatory CSR reporting in Europe (December 10, 2020). Available at SSRN: https://ssrn.com/abstract=3746634 or https://doi.org/10.2139/ssrn.3746634

Carungu, J., Di Pietra, R., & Molinari, M. (2021). Mandatory vs. voluntary exercise on non-financial reporting: does a normative/coercive isomorphism facilitate an increase in quality? *Meditari Accountancy Research, 29*(3), 449–476.

Haller, A., Link, M., & Gross, T. (2017). The term 'non-financial information'—A semantic analysis of a key feature of current and future corporate reporting. *Accounting in Europe, 14*(1–2), 407–429.

Pownall, G., & Wieczynska, M. (2018). Deviations from mandatory adoption of IFRS in the European Union: Implementation, enforcement, incentives and compliance. *Contemporary Accounting Research, 35*(2), 1029–1066.

Stolowy, H., & Paugam, L. (2018). The explanation of non-financial reporting: an exploratory study. *Accounting and Business Research, 48*(5), 525–548.

van Mourik, C., & Walton, P. (2018). The European IFRS endorsement process—In search of a single voice. *Accounting in Europe, 15*(1), 1–32. https://doi.org/10.1080/17449480.2018.1438635

Part I
Country Analysis

Germany

Antonio De Vito, Martin Glaum, and Axel Haller

1 Introduction

Financial accounting in Germany has been traditionally characterized as strongly creditor-oriented and conservative, as well as linked to tax law, and consequently lacking in information value for investors (Haller, 2003; Leuz & Wüstemann, 2003). While this characterization may still be relevant, it does not fully describe the current German approach to financial reporting, which, in light of the legislative changes that have taken place over the last two decades, has moved the country somewhere on a spectrum between the traditional Continental European model of accounting and the Anglo-American model of accounting (Hellmann et al., 2013). Specifically, the changes have led to a complex situation, with at least two parallel financial accounting systems. On the one side, the German Generally Accepted Accounting Principles (German GAAP) are primarily codified in the German Commercial Code (*Handelsgesetzbuch* or HGB) and are used by all legal entities in their single financial statements. On the other side, the International Financial Reporting

A. De Vito (✉)
Department of Management, University of Bologna, Bologna, Italy
e-mail: a.devito@unibo.it

M. Glaum
WHU Otto Beisheim School of Management, Düsseldorf, Germany
e-mail: martin.glaum@whu.edu

A. Haller
Universität Regensburg, Regensburg, Germany
e-mail: axel.haller@wiwi.uni-regensburg.de

A. Incollingo, A. Lionzo (eds.), *The European Harmonization of National Accounting Rules*, SIDREA Series in Accounting and Business Administration,
https://doi.org/10.1007/978-3-031-42931-6_2

Standards (hereafter IFRS) must be used by publicly traded firms in their group financial statements (according to the EU/IAS Regulation of 2002).[1]

However, before delving into the evolution of the accounting changes that have occurred in the German financial system in recent years, we believe it is important to understand the economic and institutional infrastructures that characterize the country. As prior literature argues (Haller & Walton, 2003; Leuz & Wüstemann, 2003), the accounting system is an integral part of a country's financial architecture and, more generally, of a country's economic landscape. For this reason, a systematic analysis of the evolution of the German accounting system cannot disregard a preliminary evaluation of the key parties in the economy, which, depending on their financial claims and control rights, may have different informational and contracting needs.

1.1 The Economic System

While Germany has some large and well-known multinational companies, which are often stock-listed, small- and medium-sized firms (hereafter SMEs) are the backbone of the German economy and are often referred to as *Mittelstand* (Parella & Hernández, 2018). The SMEs are mostly family-owned and primarily rely on bank loans for their external financing.[2] Traditionally, most of these firms have developed long-standing and close relationships with one or few banks (*Hausbank*). In comparison, the stock market has always played a minor role in German firms' financing activities. Only relatively few firms are listed on a stock exchange, and those firms that are listed usually have concentrated ownership structures (Haller & Wehrfritz, 2011).

In line with this reasoning, in 2020, the Federal Statistical Office of Germany (*Statistisches Bundesamt*) reported that there were about 3.4 million registered firms in the country, of which only 454 were listed on the main stock exchange (*Deutsche Börse AG*). Table 1 reports the number of private sector firms registered in Germany as of December 2020 along with the workforce and the total sales by economic sector. Irrespective of the listing status, the majority of firms are nowadays concentrated in the service industry. Similar to other developed countries, the service industry now accounts for a large fraction of the country's gross domestic product. However, the manufacturing sector is still sizeable in the German economy, and it employs about seven million workers in total.

[1] Note that the IFRS may also be used for group financial statements of non-publicly traded entities (§ 315e (3) HGB).

[2] The Foundation for Family Businesses—a nonprofit foundation headquartered in Munich—estimates that about 91% of all registered firms in Germany are family-controlled and about 87% are family-led (Stiftung Familienunternehmen, 2019).

Table 1 Company distribution by economic sector, workforce, and total sales

Economic sectors	No. of firms	Workforce	Total sales (in 1000 of Euro)
Mining and construction	384,697	2,069,796	361,331,866
Manufacturing	219,449	7,336,297	2,025,383,227
Utilities	188,748	2,722,678	875,123,735
Wholesale and retail trade	577,161	5,374,101	2,208,078,458
Financial, insurance, and real estate	279,401	1,343,619	303,858,696
Services	1,725,127	16,085,669	1,106,075,207
Total	**3,374,583**	**34,932,160**	**6,879,851,189**

Source: Business register's statistics (2020)

1.2 *The Role of Civil Code and Financial Reporting Standards*

The German financing system has been characterized as a weak equity-outsider system in which banks play a dominant role in corporate finance, while stock markets are relatively less developed (Haller & Wehrfritz, 2011). The key insider financing parties, such as banks, typically have access to privileged private information and therefore have little demand for public information (Nobes, 1998, 2003). Hence, the historical role of German accounting has been not so much to disseminate information to the public. Rather, its role has been to smooth the path of relationship-based financing, for example, by computing income and by imposing restrictions on dividend payments to (minority) shareholders in the interest of creditors (Leuz & Wüstemann, 2003).

In the German accounting system, (1) the HGB, which is the German Commercial Code, enacted by the Parliament; (2) the German basic accounting rules (*Grundsätze ordnungsmäßiger Buchführung* or "GoB"), which have been developed over the last century by practice and academia; and (3) court decisions all play a fundamental role in financial reporting. These rules, standards, and court decisions apply to all legal forms of economic undertakings, such as sole proprietorships (*Einzelunternehmen*), partnerships (*Personengesellschaften*, such as *Offene Handelsgesellschaft* (*OHG*) or *Kommanditgesellschaft* (*KG*)), and entities with limited liability (*Kapitalgesellschaften*, such as *Gesellschaft mit beschränkter Haftung* (*GmbH*) or *Aktiengesellschaft* (*AG*)), albeit with stricter and more detailed regulation for the latter entities. Unlike in Anglo-American countries, the German accounting rules are codified laws (*Rechtsnormen*) and not professional standards (*Fachnormen*). Within this framework, German courts, including tax courts, also play a crucial role in interpreting legal rules and in applying the GoB to court cases. Closely related, another source of interpretation comes from the commentaries to the codified rules and uncodified principles written by accounting professionals and academics. Finally, the Accounting Standards Committee of Germany (*Deutsches Rechnungslegungs Standards Committee e.V.* or DRSC) is in charge of developing accounting standards for group accounts within the scope of the HGB (the role of the DRSC is discussed in more detail in Sect. 1.4).

1.3 The Role of the Tax Code

An important aspect of German accounting is the close relationship between financial accounting (*Handelsbilanz*) and tax accounting (*Steuerbilanz*) (Haller, 1992). This close relationship between the HGB and the German income tax code (i.e., *Einkommenssteuergesetz* or EStG) is due to the "authoritative principle" (*Maßgeblichkeitsprinzip*), which states that the financial statements prepared in compliance with the HGB are the basis for the determination of firms' taxable income (Haller, 2003; Pfaff & Schröer, 1996). The rationale for the book-tax alignment is twofold. The first rationale is conceptual, and it refers to the objective of financial accounting rules, which is to determine income that can be further distributed to equity providers without harming creditors' position. However, by being potentially distributable, the income can also be used as the basis for income taxes without harming the economic condition of the firm. The second rationale is practical, and it refers to the compliance costs, which can be minimized if only one set of books has to be prepared for financial and tax purposes. This is crucial for many small firms, which, by preparing only one set of accounts that complies with both the HGB and tax laws, can minimize compliance costs (Haller, 1992, 2003). However, as we shall see, while a certain degree of book-tax conformity still exists, the scope for the influence of tax accounting rules on unconsolidated financial statements, and even more so for the consolidated statements of listed companies, has significantly decreased over time (Gee et al., 2010).

1.4 The Role of the Professional Standards-Setting Body

An additional layer of complexity was introduced into the German accounting system in 1998 with the establishment of a private standards-setting body, namely, the DRSC. The German legislator allowed for the foundation of a private standards-setting body in line with § 342 HGB, which stipulates that the Federal Ministry of Justice and the Consumer Protection Authority may officially recognize such an institution and may delegate to it four functions: (1) developing recommendations for the application of codified and uncodified accounting rules (only) in the area of group financial reporting, (2) advising the Ministry of Justice and the Consumer Protection Authority on legislative initiatives regarding financial reporting, (3) representing Germany in international standards committees, and (4) developing interpretations on International Financial Reporting Standards. The introduction of a private standards-setting body into a system that traditionally has been characterized as a civil code-based system at times creates frictions. In particular, because § 342 HGB restricts the mandate of the private body explicitly to the area of group financial reporting, any mandate for the development of standards for the recognition and measurement of assets, liabilities, income, or expenses in single-entity statements is unclear and at times contentious (Haller, 2003).

1.5 *Summary*

Overall, our preliminary analysis has yielded four insights on the German financial and accounting systems. First, there are currently two financial accounting systems used in parallel in Germany. The German codified and uncodified accounting rules apply to single financial statements of all legal forms, whereas the IFRS apply to consolidated accounts of publicly traded companies and to non-publicly entities that adopt the IFRS for their consolidated accounts on a voluntary basis. Hence, from our analysis it has emerged a clear distinction between the single accounts and the consolidated accounts. This distinction becomes even more prominent when looking at the role of the private standards-setting body, the DRSC, whose accounting standards aim only at group financial accounts and do not have legal authority for single-entity financial statements. Second, the economic landscape is characterized by a significant presence of small- and medium-sized firms, which are often family-owned and account for the vast majority of all businesses in the country. These SMEs typically finance their activities via bank loans, while stock markets only play a minor role. Third, because of the bank-based financial system, there is less demand for public disclosure, since insiders have access to privileged private information. Fourth, unlike in Anglo-American countries, the HGB plays a crucial role in the system, since the most important accounting rules in Germany are subject to a legislative process and to a close scrutiny of courts, with implications also on a firm's taxable income.

Using these insights as guiding principles, the next section will then describe the key developments of the German financial accounting system over the last two decades.

2 The Evolution of the Accounting Regulation in Germany

In Germany, changes to accounting rules are the result of a legislative process that requires a legislative act and parliamentary approval.[3] The "starting point" for modern German accounting law was the reform in 1985, which transposed the Fourth (1978), the Seventh (1983), and the Eighth (1984) Directives of the European Economic Community into law. With this reform, the accounting rules for all legal forms of economic undertakings were summarized in the HGB by enacting the *Bilanzrichtliniengesetz* (BiRiLiG).[4] Prior to this reform, the German

[3]The legislative process also involves several stakeholder groups (see, e.g., Hellmann et al., 2010).

[4]It is worth pointing out that, in Germany, not only corporations but also sole proprietorships and private partnerships have to present single and consolidated financial statements, provided that certain size thresholds are met. The total sales (assets) must be higher than 130,000,000 (65,000,000) Euro, and the number of employees must be higher than 5000. A sole proprietorship or a private partnership (or a group with a parent company in the legal form of a sole proprietorship

accounting system had been very different, with detailed accounting rules codified only for stock corporations and written in many laws with different content.

In recent years, several elements of the HGB have been subject to change, of which the major reforms were the Accounting Law Reform Act in 2004 (i.e., *Bilanzrechtsreformgesetz*, BilReG), the Accounting Law Modernization Act in 2009 (i.e., *Bilanzrechtsmodernisierungsgesetz*, BilMoG), and the Accounting Directive Implementation Act (i.e., *Bilanzrichtlinie-Umsetzungsgesetz*, BilRUG) in 2015.

2.1 IFRS Adoption and Convergence

With the BilReG in 2004, the German legislator transposed the optional clauses of the EU Regulation No. 1606/2002 into German law as follows:

- All firms that were not listed but had applied for listing in the German stock exchange by the time of entry into force of the reform were required to adopt the IFRS on their consolidated financial statements.
- All firms that were not listed and had not applied for listing in the German stock exchange by the time of entry into force of the reform were allowed to choose whether to adopt the IFRS or the German rules codified in the HGB on their consolidated financial statements.
- All firms were required to follow the German rules codified in the HGB when preparing their unconsolidated, single-entity financial statements. Entities with limited liability may adopt the IFRS for disclosure purposes of their unconsolidated financial statements but only if a separate set of unconsolidated financial statements is further prepared according to the HGB.

The law also mandated other relevant changes to financial reporting, such as:

1. The disclosure of the audit fees and the financial instruments used by the disclosing entity
2. A considerable extension of the management's report with an analysis of the entity's competitive position, material risks, and disclosures of nonfinancial performance indicators related to Environmental, Social, and Governance (ESG) issues, which are deemed material to reveal the entity's financial position
3. The preparation of the cash flow statement and the statement of changes in owners' equity for consolidated financial statements

Finally, in line with the EU Directive 2003/38/EC, the BilReG also changed the size-based thresholds to classify small- and medium-sized enterprises.

---

or a private partnership) that meets at least two of the three thresholds in three consecutive fiscal years must publicly disclose a (consolidated group) balance sheet but is not required to disclose an income statement. This requirement, which is unique to Germany, goes beyond the demands of the EU Accounting Directives, and it dates back to 1969, when the Disclosure Act (*Publizitätsgesetz*, or PublG) was put into law.

	Single-entity financial statements	Consolidated financial statements
Publicly-traded entities	HGB rules mandatory[a]	IFRS mandatory
Non-publicly traded entities	HGB rules mandatory[a]	IFRS optional

[a]Large entities with limited liability may submit their single financial statements according to IFRS to the commercial register and the electronic Federal Gazette in addition to the financial statements according to codified German rules (§ 325 (2a and 2b) HGB).

Fig. 1 The transposition of the EU Regulation No. 1606/2002 into German law. [a]Large entities with limited liability may submit their single financial statements according to IFRS to the commercial register and the electronic Federal Gazette in addition to the financial statements according to codified German rules (§ 325 (2a and 2b) HGB)

In sum, after the enactment of the BilReG, the IFRS officially entered the HGB and thus the German accounting law. Before this reform, the IFRS were only allowed for consolidated financial statements of listed entities; after the reform, the IFRS became mandatory for the consolidated financial statements of publicly traded entities and are allowed for all other consolidated statements of non-publicly traded entities (see also Fig. 1). In this latter case, however, it is important to highlight that the empirical evidence finds that most non-publicly traded entities are still very reluctant to adopt IFRS on a voluntary basis. In particular, Bassemir (2018) and Bassemir and Novotny-Farkas (2018) find that only 12% of all German non-publicly traded entities that prepare consolidated financial statements have adopted IFRS in recent years.

2.2 *The Modernization of the German Commercial Code in 2009*

The push for reform of German accounting law did not stop with the BilReG. In 2009, the Federal Ministry of Justice signed into law the *Bilanzrichtlinienmodernisierungsgesetz* (BilMoG), which transposed two EU Directives (2006/43/EC; 2006/46/EC) into German law and introduced other significant changes to the HGB. Specifically, the reform softened the close alignment between financial accounting and tax accounting and introduced new valuation and recognition criteria, despite preserving the key principles of the German accounting system (Baetge et al., 2016). In particular, the BilMoG abolished the reverse authoritative principle (*Umgekehrte Maßgeblichkeit*), which was heavily criticized on the grounds that it would distort the information content of financial statements.[5] Hence, after the

[5]According to the reverse authoritative principle, tax regulations could determine the content disclosed in financial statements prepared under the HGB. An example of tax regulation driving

reform, the financial statements prepared under the HGB remain the basis for taxation, but the income tax laws codified in the EStG no longer drive the preparation of financial statements (Gee et al., 2010). Table 2 summarizes the most important regulatory changes with respect to valuation and recognition criteria that were put into law to *partly* align the German accounting rules to the IFRS. However, it is important to point out that, despite these changes, the legislator did not alter the fundamental function of the HGB financial statements, which is the prudent calculation of a distributable income that also serves as the basis for income tax purposes.

Taken together, the changes brought about by the BilMoG marked the most comprehensive revisions to German accounting law in recent years. The reform *partly* aligned German accounting rules to the international accounting standards by removing old recognition, valuation, and disclosure options and by introducing fair value measurement—albeit to a very limited extent—for pension plan assets for all entities, as well as for trading securities of financial institutions. Importantly, one of the objectives of the BilMoG was to make financial statements according to German rules more attractive relative to the IFRS for SMEs, which was published by the International Accounting Standards Board (IASB) in 2009 (Becker et al., 2021). Hence, the German legislator intended to provide German SMEs with a less complex and a less costly set of accounting rules that could be alternatively applied in lieu of the IFRS for SMEs (Bundesministerium der Justiz, 2009; Gross, 2016).

2.3 The Transposition of EU Directive 2013/34: The BilRUG and the Accounting for SMEs

The next reform to German accounting law took place in 2015. Specifically, on June 26, 2013, the Council of the European Union issued the Directive 2013/34/EU, which replaced the former Fourth and Seventh Directives on annual and consolidated financial statements. In Germany, the Directive 2013/34/EU was transposed into law with the *Bilanzrichtlinie-Umsetzungsgesetz* (BilRUG) on July 17, 2015, and it applies to all fiscal periods beginning on or after January 1, 2016. With this reform, the German legislator did not intend to further align the HGB with international accounting standards (Fülbier et al., 2017). Instead, the reform mainly aimed at lowering the regulatory burden of SMEs.

To achieve this, the legislator transposed only the mandatory provisions of the Directive 2013/34/EU into national legislation, since the last major reform, the BilMoG, and the transposition of the Micro-Directive (Directive 2012/6/EU)

---

financial reporting was the special entry in capital surplus (*Sonderposten mit Rücklageanteil*). This controversial entry consisted of both a nontaxable reserve and a tax depreciation allowance, which allowed delaying tax liabilities since a portion of it was considered future tax liability, while the remaining portion was treated as equity. As such, these entries in capital surplus were disclosed on the balance sheet between the liabilities and the equity.

Table 2 Major changes to German accounting law introduced by the BilMoG in 2009

Scope	Regulatory changes
Intangible assets	Providing the option to capitalize internally generated intangible assets (§ 248 (2) HGB) If such an option is exercised, then internally generated intangible assets have to be valued at their development cost (§ 255 (2a) HGB). The general approach, along with the distinction of research and development (R&D), was almost fully adapted from IAS 38—Intangible Assets
Provisions	Elimination of the option to recognize expense provisions (apart from two exceptions, § 249 HGB), similar to what is stated in IAS 37—Provisions, Contingent Liabilities and Contingent Assets. Importantly, noncurrent provisions must now be discounted with a market-based discount rate (§ 253 (2) HGB)
Pension liabilities	Option to measure pension liabilities with the projected unit credit method, similar to what is stated in IAS 19—Employee Benefits Introduction of a maturity period adjusted long-term average interest rate (of the last 10 years) that is currently published by the German Central Bank (§ 253 (2) HGB). Before the BilMoG, the measurement of pensions followed tax rules of the EStG, which mandated a uniform discount rate of 6%
Deferred taxes	Introduction of the temporary concept, similar to IAS 12—Income Taxes, while retaining the option to recognize deferred tax assets with the explicit inclusion of carryforward losses (§ 274 HGB)
Financial instruments	Implementation of the requirement for financial institutions only to measure financial instruments held for trading at their fair value minus a risk discount (§ 340e (3) HGB). Hence, the BilMoG introduces the concept of "fair value" for financial institutions by stating that the valuation of financial instruments, such as stocks, debt securities, and derivatives, should follow the fair market value if the financial instruments were acquired for trading purposes
Dividend restrictions	Introduction of dividend payout restrictions with respect to capitalized intangible assets, net deferred tax assets, and held-for-trading financial instruments of financial institutions (§ 268 (8) HGB)
Foreign currency payables and receivables	For short-term receivables and payables (settlement within 12 months), the closing rate method must be applied (§ 256a HGB). For mid- and long-term receivables and payables, this method is not allowed if it leads to higher net assets than the application of the temporal principle method

Source: Authors' adaptation from Fülbier and Klein (2015, p. 360)

through the *Kleinstkapitalgesellschaften-Bilanzrechtsänderungsgesetz* (MicroBilG) of 2012 had only occurred a few years earlier. In particular, the BilRUG removed the extraordinary line items from the profit and loss statement and broadly changed the content of the notes to financial statements (§§ 275 and 285 HGB). Moreover, intangible assets as well as goodwill must now be amortized over their useful economic life. However, in cases when the useful life of goodwill and capitalized development costs cannot be reliably estimated, such assets must then be amortized over 10 years (§253). Moreover, the law increased the size thresholds for the determination of the sizes under §267 of the HGB for the single financial statements and under §293 HGB for the consolidated financial statements and introduced the report on payments to governments for entities active in the extractive industry in §341 of the HGB in line with Art. 41 Directive 2013/34/EU.

2.4 The EU Directive 2014/95: Nonfinancial Disclosure in Germany

In recognition of the political and societal need to follow a sustainable development path within Europe and the growing interest in nonfinancial information disclosure among capital markets' participants, just a year after the publication of the Directive 2013/34/EU, the Council of the European Union issued the Directive 2014/95/EU on the disclosure of a nonfinancial statement by certain large undertakings and groups (public interest entities with over 500 employees). According to the newly introduced Art. 19a in the Directive 2013/34/EU, the nonfinancial statement must "contain information to the extent necessary for an understanding of the undertaking's development, performance, position and impact of its activity, relating to, as a minimum, environmental, social and employment matters, respect for human rights, anti-corruption and bribery matters." This requirement includes a brief description of the business model, the policies, the due diligence processes, and the risks on these matters. The entities should also inform about the outcomes of their policies and relevant nonfinancial key performance indicators. The nonfinancial statement can either be published as a separate report or within the management report (Art. 19a (4)). The auditor must assure the existence of such statement but not its content (Art. 19a (5)). Member states may also require the nonfinancial statement to be audited by an "independent assurance services provider," not necessarily an auditor (Art. 19a (6)). But the members of the administrative, management, and supervisory bodies of an undertaking always have collective responsibility for it (Art. 33). In Germany, the Directive was transposed with the *CSR-Richtlinie-Umsetzungsgesetz* (CSR-RUG) into the HGB on April 11, 2017, with the political intention to transpose only the minimum requirements of the Directive and to pass all the options included in the Directive to the German entities. Therefore, the CSR-RUG applies to all public interest entities (PIEs), that is, all large publicly traded entities[6] according to §267 (3) (for size criteria, see Table 4) and §264d HGB with more than 500 employees.

With regard to the materiality concept included in Art. 19a and 29a, the German legislator and the German financial reporting community have chosen a particular

[6]These are either capital market-oriented companies with limited liability (i.e., use of an organized market for their own equity or debt securities; § 264d HGB) (§ 289b HGB) or financial institutions (§ 340a (1a) HGB) and insurance companies (§ 341a (1a) HGB).

Table 4 Size classes in the HGB

Size class	Total assets (Euro)	Total sales (Euro)	Average employees
Micro (§267a HGB)	<350,000	<700,000	<10
Small (§267 (1) HGB)	<6,000,000	<12,000,000	<50
Medium (§267 (2) HGB)	<20,000,000	<40,000,000	<250
Large	>20,000,000	>40,000,000	>250

Source: authors' elaboration

interpretation. As stated in the Directive, the nonfinancial information needs only to be disclosed, "(. . .)to the extend necessary for an understanding of the undertaking's development, performance, position and impact of its activity (. . .)." Hence, it is perceived that the nonfinancial information must only be provided in cases where a sustainability matter has an impact on the entity (the so-called outside-in impact) and, at the same time, an impact on the environment or on the stakeholders of the entity (the so-called inside-out impact). This "cumulative" materiality perspective has led to a smaller volume of disclosed nonfinancial information in German nonfinancial statements compared to other EU member states, especially with regard to the "inside-out impacts" of the corporate activities.[7]

Within the scope of the corporate governance system of the disclosing entity, the management board (*Vorstand*) is responsible for preparing the nonfinancial statement, while the supervisory board (*Aufsichtsrat*) is required to examine it and to ensure that all requirements imposed by the law are fulfilled before the report is published. The legislator did not intend to further impose a mandatory external audit of the nonfinancial statement on the disclosing entity. The auditor of the financial statements of the disclosing entity is only required to confirm the existence of the nonfinancial statement without formulating an opinion on its content. This results in a greater responsibility of the supervisory board. However, the supervisory board may still mandate its auditor (or another assurance provider) to conduct an audit of the nonfinancial statement's content, in which case the auditor's opinion has to be disclosed along with the nonfinancial statement (§ 289b (4) HGB).

3 The Current State and the Key Characteristics of German Accounting Rules

3.1 General Provisions and Principles

In contrast to outsider financing systems (e.g., the United Kingdom, the United States), in which equity investors are the main users of accounting information, in

[7]This is why the EU has explicitly introduced the "double materiality" in the Corporate Sustainability Reporting Directive (CSRD) to make it clear that sustainability-related information must be provided if there is either an "outside-in" or an "inside-out" impact (Art 19a according to the CSRD).

insider financing systems, such as in Germany, the main addressees of financial statements are the management, the owners, and banks, and their relative importance differs with the number of owners and the firms' dependence on bank financing (Glaum, 2020). As previously argued, the central principles of German accounting aim at preserving capital with great emphasis on creditor protection. In particular, the HGB (§ 243 (1)) prescribes for enterprises of any legal form that the annual accounts must be prepared in accordance with the "GoB" (the basic accounting principles) that require the accounts to be clear, correct, complete, comparable, consistent, transparent, as well as prepared in a prudent and conservative way. Moreover, § 264 HGB further requires corporations in their annual accounts to give an accurate and complete state of the affairs of the financial (assets, liabilities, and equity) and performance situation of the company (Ordelheide, 1993).[8] The structure of the balance sheet and the income statement must be in compliance with legal requirements, that is, the name of account items and the order of account items must comply with the rules codified in the HGB (§ 267 and § 275 HGB). Finally, according to § 246 (1) HGB, the financial statements must include all assets and liabilities at the closing date. This means that transactions occurring after such date may not be recognized, but in the case of material transactions corporations must inform interested parties in the management report. In contrast, if new information about a transaction that has already occurred before the end of the fiscal year becomes available after the closing date, this information must be used in the preparation of the financial statements.

With respect to the other principles underlying the German accounting system, the principle of *prudence* is the most important, because it makes German accounting different from many other accounting systems. This principle stems from the idea of an honorable businessman who has to assess all risks and losses carefully (§ 252 (1) no. 4 HGB). The risk-averse approach to German accounting is in line with the aim of protecting creditors by making sure that the net assets reported are truly available to repay creditors in the event of bankruptcy. Closely related, the *realization* principle states any income and gain may be recognized only once they are realized. Hence, unrealized gains that may exist at the closing date cannot be recognized. Income or gains are realized when the underlying transaction is completed, i.e., the firm has fulfilled all its obligations by supplying the products or delivering the services, and it can reliably expect the counterparty to fulfill its contractual obligation. Finally, the information provided by financial statements should follow the *accrual basis of accounting* (§252 sect. 1 no. 5), and to be decision useful, it should further be *comparable* (§ 252 (1) no. 6) and satisfy the *going concern* test (§252 (1) no. 2).

[8] This is referred to as a *true and fair view* of the economic situation of the company. The true and fair view notion was introduced into German law when the EU Directives from 1978 and 1983 were transposed into law through the BiRiLiG in 1995. Due to the objective to calculate a distributable income, the prudence principle is very dominant and leads to a conservative interpretation of the true and fair view (Haller, 2002).

Table 3 Content and publication requirements of financial statements for partnerships and corporations

	Partnership	Corporation
Key financial statements		
Balance sheet	Aggregated structure (noncurrent assets, current assets, equity, liabilities, deferred items; §247 (1) HGB)	Detailed structure (§266 HGB)
Income statement	Aggregated structure (income and expense, §242 (2) HGB)	Detailed structure (§275 HGB)
Other reports		
Notes to financial statements	Not required	Detailed rules (§§284–285 HGB)
Management report	Not required	Detailed rules (§289 HGB)
Audit report	Not required	Detailed rules (§§ 316–324a HGB)
Publication	Not required	Detailed rules (§§ 325–329 HGB)

Source: authors' elaboration

3.2 *Accounting Rules Depending on Legal Form and Size of the Firm*

The HGB differentiates between partnerships and corporations. All entities have to follow §§238–263 HGB, whereas corporations have to additionally comply with §264–335b HGB. Table 3 summarizes the content and the publicity requirements of financial statements for partnerships and corporations, respectively.

3.3 *Simplifications for SMEs*

As Table 3 shows, the content and the publication requirements of financial statements for corporations are much more comprehensive than for partnerships. However, fulfilling these requirements can be particularly burdensome, especially for smaller firms whose compliance costs can significantly outweigh the benefits of providing stakeholders with more granular financial information. For this reason, the HGB further differentiates corporations among size classes. According to the Directive 2013/34/EU, the size classes use three accounting criteria: total assets, total sales, and the average number of employees over the fiscal year. To be classified in a size class, at least two of the three criteria must be fulfilled for two consecutive fiscal years. Importantly, if a corporation is capital market oriented, it is always treated as large regardless of its size class (§264d). Table 4 displays the current size classes in the HGB taking into account the changes brought about by the BilRUG.

Finally, Table 5 summarizes the accounting rules for partnerships and corporations by also differentiating for size classes. Note that, if a firm is capital market

Table 5 Content and publication requirements of financial statements for partnerships and corporations by size classes (all paragraphs refer to the HGB)

	Partnership	Corporation			
	Not large[a]	Micro	Small	Medium	Large
Balance sheet	Aggregated structure (§247 (1))	Reduced form (§266 (1))	Reduced form (§ 266 (1))	Detailed structure (§266)	Detailed structure (§266)
Income statement	Aggregated structure (§242 (2))	Reduced form (§275 (5))	Reduced form (§ 276)	Reduced form (§ 276)	Detailed structure (§ 275)
Notes	Not required	Not required	Reduced form (§288 (1))	Reduced form (§288 (2))	Detailed rules (§§284–285)
Management report	Not required	Not required	Not required	Detailed rules (§289)	Detailed rules (§289)
Audit report	Not required	Not required	Not required	Detailed rules (§§ 316–324a)	Detailed rules (§§ 316–324a)
Time to prepare financial statements after the closing date	Not specified	Within 6 months	Within 6 months	Within 3 months	Within 3 months
Publication	Not required	Not required (§326 (2))	Only balance sheet and notes to financial statement (§326 (1))	Reduced form of balance sheet and notes to financial statement (§ 327)	Detailed rules (§§ 325–329)
Time to publish financial statements	Not required	Within 12 months	Within 12 months	Within 12 months	Within12 months

Source: authors' elaboration

[a]Note that large partnerships that fall under the PublG (see footnote 4) must also comply with the rules of large corporations (§5 subseq. HGB)

oriented, but it does not prepare consolidated financial statements, it has to prepare a cash flow statement as part of its single-entity financial statements (§ 264 (1) HGB).[9]

[9]It is worth pointing out that, if a corporation controls at least another entity, the corporation must prepare consolidated financial statements (§290 HGB). According to §297 HGB, the consolidated financial statements consist of (1) a consolidated balance sheet, (2) a consolidated income statement, (3) a consolidated cash flow statement, (4) a consolidated statement of changes in equity, (5) consolidated notes, and (6) a consolidated management report that must be prepared as an additional information instrument next to the consolidated financial statements (§315 HGB).

4 Recognition and Measurement Approaches

Table 6 presents a summary of the recognition and measurement rules that entities preparing their financial statements according to the HGB must follow. In general, the historical cost model represents the baseline measurement approach of the HGB and the GoB (fair value model is only allowed for assets exclusively held for coverage of pension liabilities and for trading securities of financial institutions). This is because, unlike in Anglo-American countries, the accounting system in Germany is historically rooted in conservatism and strict realization principles with an emphasis on early loss recognition, which are in line with the contracting-based nature of German accounting rules mostly catering to the needs of both creditors and tax authorities.

5 Conclusion

The civil law legal origin, the key role of bank lending as the main source of finance for German firms, and the connection between financial and tax accounting have historically played a crucial role in shaping the financial accounting systems of the country (e.g., La Porta et al., 1997, 1998). As argued earlier, the vast majority of firms in Germany are SMEs, often family-owned, which rarely rely on stock markets to finance their operations. Hence, for these firms, there is typically less demand for public disclosure to reduce information asymmetries between outside capital providers and managers. On the contrary, the primary role of financial statements is to determine income and dividend distribution (Glaum, 2020). Because of this role, the German Commercial Code, the HGB, constitutes the backbone of the financial reporting system of the country, since the most important German basic accounting principles (i.e., the GoB) are codified in the HGB.

Hence, the central tenet of the German accounting tradition has been, and still arguably is, the prudence principle (*Vorsichtsprinzip*), which implies that the historical cost model continues to represent the baseline measurement approach. Indeed, despite several changes in the Germany accounting system in recent years, the legislator has not embraced the use of fair value as a measurement basis yet (apart from very few exceptions). For example, the most comprehensive reform over the last two decades in Germany, the BilMoG in 2009, *only partly* aligned the German accounting to the international accounting standards. In particular, with the BilMoG, the legislator's intent was rather to provide German firms with a set of rules codified in the HGB that could serve as a viable alternative to the IFRS. Similarly, the most recent reform incorporating the EU Directive 2013/34, the BilRUG in 2015, did not intend to further align the HGB with the IFRS. Hence, whether the German legislator will continue the harmonization process initiated by the European Union about two decades ago by further converging toward the IFRS and the use of fair value measurement remains to be seen. Nonetheless, the prudence principle will arguably

Table 6 Recognition and measurement rules

Balance sheet/income statement line item	Recognition and valuation rules
Property, plant, and equipment (PPE)	– The initial measurement of property, plant, and equipment that qualify for recognition as an asset is at cost (cost of acquisition or cost of production) – After recognition, PPE are carried at cost less any accumulated depreciation and any accumulated impairment loss – An entity has to depreciate the amount initially recognized of PPE on a systematic basis over their useful life – Depreciation and impairment losses are recognized in the income statement – The impairment test is performed at the individual asset level – Land and buildings are separable assets and accounted for separately – In general, land has an unlimited useful life and therefore is not depreciated
Intangible assets (other than goodwill)	– An intangible asset is initially recognized at cost if: (1) it is likely that the expected future economic benefits that are attributable to the asset will flow to the entity; (2) the cost of the asset can be measured reliably, and (3) it can be separated from the business – Internally generated intangible assets may be recognized (optional) under certain conditions, and the measurement base is the development costs, but the recognized amount is not available for distribution to shareholders – Similar to PPE, intangible assets require: (1) a regular amortization over the expected useful life (in exceptional cases in which the useful life of internally generated intangible assets cannot be determined, the useful life is deemed to be 10 years); (2) a write-down if the intangible asset's value is likely to be permanently impaired
Goodwill	– Goodwill from acquisitions is computed as the difference between the consideration transferred and the acquirer's share of the fair value of assets and liabilities acquired – Goodwill is considered an intangible asset but with a finite useful life and is amortized over its useful life. If the useful life of the goodwill cannot be determined, it is deemed to be 10 years. The reason for the choice of useful life has to be disclosed in the notes to financial statement – Negative goodwill is recognized in the equity section and dissolved over the coming years according to its character – In business combinations, identifiable assets are to be measured at the acquisition-date fair value – Liabilities are measured at their acquisition-date settlement value – Acquisition-related costs are part of the consideration transferred, and therefore they increase the goodwill
Inventory	– Inventories must be recognized and measured at acquisition or production cost – Subsequent measurements take the lowest between the cost and the market value (replacement or net realizable value) – First-in, first-out (FIFO), weighted average cost method, and last-in, first-out (LIFO) are generally permitted

(continued)

Table 6 (continued)

Balance sheet/income statement line item	Recognition and valuation rules
Lease contracts	– If the lessee is the beneficial owner of the lease asset, the lease contract is referred to as a finance lease. In this case, the lease asset and the lease liability are recognized in the balance sheet of the lessee (i.e., present value of the lease payments at the starting date). The beneficial owner is the party that bears risks and rewards (e.g., the right to use or sell the asset, the risks and opportunities from changes of the asset's value, or the risk of loss from accidental destruction of the asset) from the use of the asset during its useful life – A lease asset is depreciated over its useful life – If the lessee is not the beneficial owner of the asset (operating lease contract), the lease payments are recognized in the income statement as an expense
Financial instruments	– Financial assets are generally measured at cost, after deduction of any impairment loss in the income statement – Exceptions apply to short-term assets and liabilities (settlement within 1 year) in foreign currency, which are measured at the closing rate of the balance sheet date – Doubtful accounts receivable are impaired using a valuation allowance on an individual basis and in addition on a general basis – Liabilities (e.g., accounts payable) are recognized when the entity enters into a contractual agreement, and they are measured at the settlement amount – Specific rules apply to the accounting for financial assets and liabilities in financial institutions
Investments in associates (significant influence)	– Single accounts: the cost model must be applied – Group accounts: the equity method must be applied
Investments in joint ventures	– Single accounts: the cost model must be applied – Group accounts: an option exists to apply either the proportionate consolidation or the equity method
Provisions and contingent liabilities	– A provision is recognized for uncertain liabilities and for potential losses from pending transactions (onerous contracts) – Specifically, following the prudence principle, a provision is accounted for when: (1) a legal obligation as a result of a past event exists; (2) it is likely that an outflow of the entity's resources will be required to settle the obligation; and (3) a reliable estimate of the settlement of the obligation can be made. The recognition and the measurement of provision is impacted by the prudence principle
Pensions	– The HGB differentiates between direct and indirect pension obligations. The distinction depends on who provides the benefit to the pension beneficiary. Benefits are provided either directly by the employer or indirectly through an external pension fund – Indirect pension obligations can be both defined contribution plans or defined benefit plans

(continued)

Table 6 (continued)

Balance sheet/income statement line item	Recognition and valuation rules
	– Direct pension obligations are recognized as a provision. The current contribution to the pension plan of an indirect obligation is expensed. The amount of future contributions needs to be mentioned in the notes – For defined benefit plans, if the fair value of the assets exceeds that of the liabilities, the excess amount has to be reported under a separate item on the assets side of the balance sheet. Any recognized but unrealized gain is not available for distribution – Plan assets exclusively held to cover pension liabilities may not be accessed by other creditors and exclusively serve the purpose of fulfilling liabilities arising from pension obligations. They are measured at fair value
Revenues	– Revenues are the proceedings from the sale, rental, or leasing of products or from the provision of services net of sales deductions (e.g., discounts, bonuses, and rebates) and value-added tax – Following the realization principle, revenues are recognized when the product (service) has been transferred (performed) and the risk has passed to the buyer
Deferred taxes	– The recognition of deferred tax assets is optional. However, they may only be recognized for deductible temporary differences to the extent that it is likely that future taxable income will be available against which the deductible temporary difference can be utilized – Deferred tax liabilities must be recognized for taxable temporary differences – A deferred tax asset (liability) is measured at the tax rate that is expected to apply in the period when the asset (liability) is realized (settled), based on the tax rate enacted at the reporting date – The carrying amount of a previously recognized deferred tax asset is reduced to the extent that it is no longer likely that sufficient taxable income will be available to enable the asset to be recovered – All changes in the carrying amount of a deferred tax asset (liability) are recognized in the income statement within the income taxes line item
Related party transactions	– Related party transactions must be disclosed in the notes if they were carried out other than on an arm's length basis

Source: authors' elaboration

remain dominant and will likely hinder a wider application of the fair value model. On the contrary, a greater convergence will be reached with respect to the sustainability disclosures in the management report, in light of the transposition of the CSR Directive in 2023.

References

Baetge, J., Panzer, A., & Flügel, A. (2016). German accounting and IFRS: Limitations in the convergence potential of German national accounting standards towards International Accounting Standards. In D. Bensadon & N. Praquin (Eds.), *IFRS in a global world*. Springer.

Bassemir, M. (2018). Why do private firms adopt IFRS? *Accounting and Business Research, 48*(3), 237–263.

Bassemir, M., & Novotny-Farkas, Z. (2018). IFRS adoption, reporting incentives and financial reporting quality in private firms. *Journal of Business, Finance, and Accounting, 45*(7–8), 759–796.

Becker, K., Bischof, J., & Daske, H. (2021). IFRS: Markets, practice, and politics. *Foundations and Trends in Accounting, 15*(1–2), 1–262.

Bundesministerium der Justiz. (2009). Neues Bilanzrecht: Milliardenentlastung für den deutschen Mittelstand beschlossen.

Fülbier, R. U., & Klein, M. (2015). Balancing past and present: The impact of accounting internationalization on German accounting regulations. *Accounting History, 20*(3), 342–374.

Fülbier, R. U., Pelger, C., Kuntner, E., & Bravidor, M. (2017). The role and current status of IFRS in the completion of national accounting rules—Evidence from Austria and Germany. *Accounting in Europe, 14*(1–2), 13–28.

Gee, M., Haller, A., & Nobes, C. (2010). The influence of tax on IFRS consolidated statements: The convergence of Germany and the UK. *Accounting in Europe, 7*(1), 97–122.

Glaum, M. (2020). Financial reporting in non-listed family firms: Insights from interviews with CFOs. *Schmalenbach Business Review, 72*, 225–270.

Gross, C. (2016). The effect of the German accounting law modernization act on the comparability of private local GAAP and IFRS firms. *Schmalenbach Business Review, 17*, 423–460.

Haller, A. (1992). Der Grundsatz der maßgeblichkeit der handels- für die steuerbilanz—Ein wesentlicher grund für die mangelnde harmonisierung der jahresabschlußerstellung in Europa. *Recht der Internationalen Wirtschaft, 38*, 43–48.

Haller, A. (2002). Financial accounting developments in the European Union: past events and future prospects. *European Accounting Review, 11*, 153–190.

Haller, A. (2003). Accounting in Germany. In P. Walton, A. Haller, & B. Raffournier (Eds.), *International accounting* (2nd ed.). Thomson.

Haller, A., & Walton, P. (2003). Country differences and harmonization. In P. Walton, A. Haller, & B. Raffournier (Eds.), *International accounting* (2nd ed.). Thomson.

Haller, A., & Wehrfritz, M. (2011). Analysis of changing institutional environments, new accounting policies, and corporate governance practices in Germany. In V. Krivogorsky (Ed.), *In law, corporate governance, and accounting: European perspectives*. Routledge.

Hellmann, A., Perera, H., & Patel, C. (2010). Contextual issues of the convergence of International Financial Reporting Standards: The case of Germany. *Advances in Accounting, 26*(1), 108–116.

Hellmann, A., Perera, H., & Patel, C. (2013). Continental European accounting model and accounting modernization in Germany. *Advances in Accounting, 29*, 124–133.

La Porta, R., Lopez-de-Silanes, F., Shleifer, A., & Vishny, R. W. (1997). Legal determinants of external finance. *Journal of Finance, 52*, 1131–1150.

La Porta, R., Lopez-de-Silanes, F., Shleifer, A., & Vishny, R. W. (1998). Law and finance. *Journal of Political Economy, 106*, 1113–1155.

Leuz, C., & Wüstemann, J. (2003). The role of accounting in the German financial system. In J. P. Krahnen & R. H. Schmidt (Eds.), *The German financial system*. Oxford University Press.

Nobes, C. (1998). Towards a general model of the reasons for International differences in financial reporting. *Abacus, 34*(2), 162–187.

Nobes, C. (2003). On the myth of "Anglo-Saxon" financial accounting: a comment. *The International Journal of Accounting, 38*(1), 95–104.

Ordelheide, D. (1993). True and fair view. A European and a German perspective. *European Accounting Review, 1*, 81–90.

Parella, J. F., & Hernández, G. C. (2018). The German business model: The role of the Mittelstand. *Journal of Management Policies and Practices, 6*(1), 10–16.

Pfaff, D., & Schröer, T. (1996). The relationship between financial and tax accounting in Germany—The authoritativeness and reverse authoritativeness principle. *European Accounting Review, 5*(1), 963–979.

Stiftung Familienunternehmen. (2019). *Die volkswirtschaftliche Bedeutung der Familienunternehmen*. Stiftung Familienunternehmen.

United Kingdom

Stefano Cascino and Maria Correia

1 Introduction: The National Accounting Scenario

1.1 The Role of Company Law and Financial Reporting Standards

The financial reporting framework for private sector companies in the United Kingdom rests on two key pillars: (1) company law and (2) financial reporting standards. UK company law is set out in the *Companies Act 2006*, which essentially provides a general framework for the preparation and filing of financial statements. UK generally accepted accounting standards (GAAP), in contrast, offer detailed guidance on the specific set of reporting rules that UK domestic entities are required to comply with.

Unlike the rule-based accounting system in the United States, the UK financial reporting framework is generally regarded as principles-based, thus allowing preparers greater professional judgment and reporting discretion. In fact, the law allows company directors to override accounting rules if the financial statements do not present a true and fair view of the reporting entity's assets, liabilities, financial position, and profit or loss (the *true and fair view* principle).

The *Companies Act 2006* requires companies domiciled in the United Kingdom to publish their financial reports on public record at the Companies House, the official business register of the United Kingdom. The *Companies Act 2006* has

S. Cascino (✉) · M. Correia
London School of Economics and Political Science, London, UK
e-mail: s.cascino@lse.ac.uk; m.m.correia@lse.ac.uk

A. Incollingo, A. Lionzo (eds.), *The European Harmonization of National Accounting Rules*, SIDREA Series in Accounting and Business Administration,
https://doi.org/10.1007/978-3-031-42931-6_3

historically brought into force the laws, regulations, and administrative provisions of the relevant accounting directives issued by the European Parliament and Council. On January 31, 2020, however, the United Kingdom formally ceased to be a member state of the European Union (under the so-called *Withdrawal Agreement*) and, as such, entered a transition period in which it continued to follow EU regulation until December 31, 2020, when UK domestic law became applicable. As of the end of the transition period, public interest entities—that is, companies whose securities are traded on a UK regulated market—are required to prepare their consolidated financial statements following UK-endorsed International Financial Reporting Standards (IFRS) but are allowed the option between UK GAAP and IFRS for their individual (i.e., separate) financial statements (IFRS Foundation, 2022). Nonpublic interest entities (i.e., private companies), in contrast, have the option between UK GAAP and IFRS for both their individual and consolidated financial statements.

1.2 Professional Standard Setting, Endorsement, and Oversight Bodies

The Financial Reporting Council (FRC) is an independent private sector body responsible for setting the UK financial reporting standards, as well as for regulating and exercising oversight over the accounting, auditing, and actuarial professions.

The FRC board has the power to approve all standards and rules issued by the FRC and has responsibility over key governance and strategy issues. The members of the FRC board are appointed by the Secretary of State for Business, Energy, and Industrial Strategy. The FRC board conducts its operations through: (1) two governance committees (i.e., the People Committee and the Audit and Risk Committee) and (2) three business committees (i.e., the Conduct Committee, the Supervision Committee, and the Regulatory Standards and Codes Committee).

The recently established UK Endorsement Board (UKEB) endorses, adopts, and exercises influence over the development of new (or amended) IFRS as issued by the International Accounting Standards Board (IASB).[1] Before the establishment of the UKEB, the *2019 International Accounting Standards and European Public Limited-Liability Company (EU Exit)* regulations brought into force IFRS as endorsed by the European Union.

Following a restructuring in 2013, the enforcement of accounting standards in the United Kingdom currently falls under the remit of the FRC's Conduct Committee, which has responsibility for investigating cases that have the potential to negatively

[1]The UKEB has recently announced its first major accounting standard for use in the United Kingdom, that is, IFRS 17 *Insurance Contracts*.

affect the UK public interest and for initiating disciplinary proceedings against cases of misconduct.[2]

1.3 Tax Regulation

In line with the capital market-oriented Anglo-Saxon accounting tradition (Hopwood, 1994), the objective of the financial reporting under UK law is for companies to provide their shareholders with a true and fair view of their economic activities. As such, the degree of alignment between financial reporting regulation and tax regulation in the United Kingdom is relatively minimal compared with several continental European countries. A direct consequence of the limited level of tax-book conformity in the United Kingdom is that domestic companies are allowed to use IFRS for their individual financial statements. This is in contrast to countries such as Austria, Belgium, France, Germany, Romania, Spain, and Sweden where, because of a strong link between accounting and tax rules, companies are required to use local GAAP for their individual financial statements (e.g., Beuselinck et al., 2023).[3]

1.4 The Economic System

The United Kingdom is one of the most globalized market economies in the world. Unlike continental European countries, whose financial systems strongly rely on bank capital, the UK economy traditionally stands out for the relative importance of its well-developed capital markets (both equity and debt) characterized by high levels of investor protection (Djankov et al., 2008; La Porta et al., 1997, 1998). Because of the arm's length nature of the UK economic system, corporate ownership is typically widely dispersed. Most of the largest British firms have their shares traded on the equity market, and the extent of overlap between ownership and control is fairly limited (Christensen & Nikolaev, 2013).

Notwithstanding the importance of large publicly traded corporations, small- and medium-sized enterprises (SMEs) can be regarded as the backbone of the UK economy with 98% of private sector companies employing less than 20 employees (Table 1, Panel A). Like in other developed countries, the most prominent sectors of the UK economy are in the service industry (Table 1, Panel B), which accounts for a large fraction of the country's gross domestic product.

---

[2]Previously, the enforcement of accounting standards was delegated to the Financial Reporting Review Panel (FRRP), a former subsidiary of the FRC (Christensen et al., 2020; Florou et al., 2020).

[3]In other countries (e.g., Italy), individual financial statements may be prepared according to IFRS. In fact, tax regulations, which are based on individual financial statements, have evolved over time to accommodate the transition to IFRS.

Table 1 UK private sector companies

Panel A: Company distribution by employee size band		
Employee size band	Companies	%
0	4,174,920	74.7
1	134,340	2.4
2–4	764,955	13.7
5–9	262,860	4.7
10–19	136,880	2.4
20–49	73,670	1.3
50–99	23,515	0.4
100–199	10,090	0.2
200–249	2015	0.0
250–499	3890	0.1
>500	3765	0.1
Total	**5,590,900**	**100.0**

Panel B: Company distribution by industry		
Industry	Companies	%
Agriculture, forestry, and fishing	152,620	2.7
Mining, electricity, gas, and water supply	29,190	0.5
Manufacturing	270,000	4.8
Construction	913,820	16.3
Wholesale and retail trade	556,930	10.0
Transportation and storage	310,550	5.6
Accommodation and food service activities	200,645	3.6
Information and communication	352,865	6.3
Financial and insurance activities	98,260	1.8
Real estate activities	134,095	2.4
Professional, scientific, and technical activities	848,770	15.2
Administrative and support service activities	465,905	8.3
Education	298,250	5.3
Human health and social work activities	339,055	6.1
Arts, entertainment, and recreation	278,160	5.0
Other service activities	341,785	6.1
Total	**5,590,900**	**100.0**

This table reports the number of private sector companies domiciled in the United Kingdom as of January 2021 based on population estimates reported by the Department for Business, Energy, and Industrial Strategy published on October 7, 2021. Panel A presents the company distribution by employee size band. Panel B presents the company distribution by industry

Source: https://www.gov.uk/government/statistics/business-population-estimates-2021/business-population-estimates-for-the-uk-and-regions-2021-statistical-release-html

2 The Evolution of Accounting Regulation in the United Kingdom

2.1 The Extent of IFRS Adoption and Convergence

As a former EU member state, the United Kingdom has played a central role in the process of convergence of European countries' local accounting rules toward IFRS (Camfferman & Zeff, 2007). When in 1973 the United Kingdom joined the European Economic Community (EEC), which then developed into the European Union, the regulatory power shifted somewhat away from Germany in favor of the United Kingdom. As a result, for example, European regulation adopted the true and fair view principle (through the fourth EEC Directive 1978/660), which has always been a cornerstone of UK company law (Alexander, 1993).

Since January 1, 2005, public interest entities—that is, companies whose shares or other securities are listed on the London Stock Exchange—are required to prepare their consolidated financial statements in compliance with IFRS (Regulation (EC) No. 1606/2002). Listed companies are also allowed to apply IFRS for their individual financial statements as an alternative to UK GAAP. While mandatory adoption of IFRS became widespread in 2005, certain companies were initially exempt from the IFRS mandate. Specifically, companies listed on the Alternative Investment Market (AIM) were only required to file their consolidated accounts following IFRS on or after January 1, 2007.

As previously mentioned, after the withdrawal of the United Kingdom from the European Union, EU-endorsed IFRS were incorporated into UK law. As such, UK listed companies were required to apply EU-endorsed IFRS for fiscal years beginning on or before December 31, 2020. As of the end of the transition period, however, UK domestic law has acquired the formal power to adopt and endorse IFRS through the work of the UKEB. Therefore, since then, listed companies are required to apply UK-endorsed IFRS for fiscal years beginning after December 31, 2020.

UK-domiciled nonpublic interest entities (e.g., private companies) are permitted to file both their individual and consolidated financial statements following IFRS. Yet, even though allowed to use IFRS, most private companies—especially SMEs—usually choose to prepare their financial statements in accordance with UK GAAP.

Local accounting standards for private companies in the United Kingdom have undergone several iterations of reforms aimed at encouraging a continuing convergence toward IFRS. A simplified set of IFRS for SMEs (so-called IFRS light) was issued by the IASB in July 2009 to incentivize more companies to move closer to IFRS in their financial reporting (Becker et al., 2021). In the same year, the Accounting Standards Board (ASB) issued a consultation paper on *The future of UK GAAP* (ASB, 2009), which detailed a proposed strategy for convergence and analyzed potential costs and benefits of developing UK accounting rules based on IFRS principles. In essence, the ASB consultation paper was aimed at assessing whether IFRS for SMEs could represent a blueprint for the accounting rules followed by UK nonpublic interest entities. Ultimately, the UK regulators waited for the EU Directive 2013/34 (so-called Accounting Directive) to be finalized and opted for applying a set of modifications to the IFRS for SMEs when translating the directive into national law (Gassen, 2017; Kaya & Koch, 2015).

2.2 *The Transposition of EU Directive 2013/34: Accounting for SMEs*

The Accounting Directive (EU Directive 2013/34) became EU law in 2013. The process of transposition of the Accounting Directive into UK law started in 2011 when the government published a discussion paper seeking views from different stakeholders (Collis et al., 2017; Kaya & Koch, 2015).[4] Soon after, the UK government launched a public consultation, which was meant to stimulate preparers, auditors, regulators, and a vast array of other stakeholders to provide their views on the best way to reform UK GAAP.[5]

The key objective of UK policy makers was to develop a new set of financial reporting standards that were close enough to those followed by listed companies but that would also offer to private companies a simplified, more principles-based accounting regime (Gassen, 2017).

The Accounting Directive was ultimately transposed into UK law by the *Companies, Partnerships and Groups (Accounts and Reports) Regulations 2015 (SI 2015/980)*, which amended: (1) the *Companies Act 2006*, (2) the *Smallest Companies and Groups (Accounts and Directors' Report) Regulations 2008 (SI 2008/409)*, and (3) the *Large- and Medium-Sized Companies and Groups (Accounts and Reports) Regulations 2008 (SI 2008/410)*.

The *Companies, Partnerships and Groups (Accounts and Reports) Regulations 2015 (SI 2015/980)*, which entered into force in April 2015, became applicable to companies' financial statements with fiscal year starting on or after January 1, 2016 (Collis et al., 2017).

2.3 *The EU Directive 2014/95: Nonfinancial Disclosure*

In recognition of the importance of nonfinancial information disclosure for different types of users, the EU Directive 2014/95 (so-called Non-financial Reporting Directive) sought to harmonize the ways in which EU member states' companies disclose information about social, environmental, and diversity issues. In 2016, the UK

---

[4] *Simpler reporting for the smallest businesses* (BIS/FRC, 2011).

[5] *Simpler reporting for micro-entities: The UK's proposal to implement the "micros directive"* (BIS, 2013).

government initiated a public consultation to identify the most effective way to transpose the Non-financial Reporting Directive. An important goal of this public consultation was to assess the extent of differences between the existing UK and EU frameworks and to understand how to best use the discretion offered by the directive to accomplish a meaningful regulatory implementation. Following the consultation, the UK Department for Business, Energy, and Industrial Strategy enacted specific regulations to transpose the Non-financial Reporting Directive.[6] These new regulations, designed for large companies and business groups to include nonfinancial disclosures in their strategic reports beginning on or after January 1, 2017, essentially transposed the minimum requirements of the Non-financial Reporting Directive.

According to the Non-financial Reporting Directive, reporting entities must set out the objectives of their diversity policies (e.g., on age, gender, educational, and professional background), explain the ways in which these are implemented, and assess the results of their implementation efforts. Following a *comply-or-explain* approach, in the event in which a reporting entity does not have a diversity policy in place, it is required to explain why this is the case. In 2016, the Financial Conduct Authority (FCA) amended the *UK Disclosure and Transparency Rules* to implement this specific requirement of the Non-financial Reporting Directive. The new regulations effectively complemented the preexisting UK narrative reporting rules, which already required reporting entities to disclose specific information on corporate strategy, business model, gender diversity, and human rights in their strategic reports.

Following the transposition of the EU Non-financial Reporting Directive into UK law, large public interest entities—that is, listed companies with 500 employees or more—apply both the requirements of the Non-financial Reporting Directive and the UK requirements for the strategic report, which the directive does not cover. In contrast, public interest entities with fewer than 500 employees continue to apply the existing UK requirements for the strategic report.

3 The Implementation of the EU Directive 2013/34

3.1 The Multitier UK GAAP System

Although most of the changes made to UK laws in order to transpose the Accounting Directive were mainly amendments to filing and disclosure requirements (Collis et al., 2017), the FRC took the opportunity to reorganize the whole of UK accounting standards with a view of reducing the burden associated with the multitude of financial reporting requirements that companies hitherto had to comply with (Arafat

[6] *The Companies, Partnerships and Groups (Accounts and Non-financial Reporting) Regulations 2016 (SI 2016/1245).*

et al., 2020). As such, all previous accounting standards were withdrawn, and, as of January 2016, a new set of accounting standards based on a multitier financial reporting system were adopted. Under the new multitier system, the financial reporting requirements become progressively more demanding depending on the size and organizational complexity of the reporting entity (Deloitte, 2015). In all cases, however, reporting entities in lower tiers may elect to opt for a more demanding reporting regime if they wish so.

The new suite of UK GAAP comprises the following accounting standards:

- FRS 100 *Application of Financial Reporting Requirements* sets out the relevant financial reporting framework for all entities that prepare their financial statements in accordance with the laws, regulations, or accounting standards applicable in the United Kingdom and the Republic of Ireland. As previously stated, public interest entities are required to file their consolidated financial statements in compliance with UK-endorsed IFRS (previously EU-endorsed IFRS), whereas they can choose between UK GAAP and IFRS for their individual financial statements.
- FRS 101 *Reduced Disclosure Framework* allows for reduced disclosure requirements enabling most subsidiaries and parents to use the recognition and measurement rules of IFRS in their individual financial statements but with a lower disclosure burden.
- FRS 102 *The Financial Reporting Standard Applicable in the UK and the Republic of Ireland*, a single financial reporting standard based on IFRS for SMEs, effectively replaces the old UK GAAP. Any nonpublic interest entity can use FRS 102. However, Section 1A of FRS 102 is specifically designed for small entities. Moreover, FRS 102 allows for reduced disclosure requirements for individual financial statements of companies within a business group.
- FRS 103 *Insurance Contracts* provides specific financial reporting requirements for all entities with insurance contracts issued and/or reinsurance contracts held.
- FRS 104 *Interim Financial Reporting* is largely based on IAS 34 and provides the framework for the preparation of interim financial statements for all entities that apply FRS 101 and FRS 102.
- FRS 105 *The Financial Reporting Standard Applicable to the Micro-entities Regime* applies to micro-entities as defined by the *Companies Act 2006*. The financial reporting requirements for micro-entities are largely based on those of FRS 102 but are adapted to conform to the legal requirements applicable to micro-entities and to take into account the smaller size and simpler organizational structure of this type of companies.

Table 2 details the relevant accounting standards that reporting entities domiciled in the United Kingdom must follow depending on their size and whether they qualify or not as public interest entities.

The most important advantage of the UK multitier financial reporting system is that smaller companies are spared from the disclosure burden of the (more demanding) upper tiers. At the same time, the freedom to choose a more demanding tier

Table 2 Applicable financial reporting standards

Company type	Individual financial statements	Consolidated financial statements
Micro-nonpublic interest entities	FRS 105	FRS 105
Small nonpublic interest entities	FRS 102—Section 1A	FRS 102—Section 1A
Other nonpublic interest entities	FRS 102	FRS 102
Public interest entities	FRS 102	IFRS

This table presents the financial reporting standards applicable to UK entities based on their size and organizational structure

Table 3 Financial reporting standards by size thresholds

	Micro-entities FRS 105	Small entities FRS 102—Section 1A	Medium entities FRS 102
Turnover	GBP 0.632m	GBP 10. 2m	GBP 36.0m
Total assets	GBP 0.316m	GBP 5.1m	GBP 18.0m
Average number of employees	10	50	250

This table reports the financial reporting standards applicable to UK entities based on size thresholds defined by company law (Collis et al., 2017)

tames the potential loss of comparability inherent to a multitier financial reporting system.

The choice of accounting regime to apply to a specific entity depends on several important factors (FRC, 2015). First, an entity must be eligible to apply a certain regime. Eligibility criteria depend on: (1) the type of entity (i.e., public interest or nonpublic interest entity), (2) size thresholds, and (3) the type of financial statements (i.e., individual or consolidated financial statements).

The United Kingdom has adopted the maximum EU size thresholds as revised in the Accounting Directive (Collis et al., 2017). Since January 1, 2016, an entity has been qualified for a particular size threshold if, in its first year, it does not exceed two or more of the criteria presented in Table 3 (i.e., turnover, total assets, and average number of employees). For the following years, the entity must pass the size test of the current and previous years.

3.2 *General Provisions and Principles*

The common law legal origin and the relative importance of equity capital markets in the UK economy are thought to have shaped the nature of its financial reporting system and the development of accounting practice over time (Leuz, 2010; Nobes, 1998). Indeed, in contrast to insider financing systems (e.g., Germany, Italy), in which banks are the main users of accounting information, outsider financing systems like the United Kingdom are more geared toward the information needs of equity investors. In fact, company law specifically requires the directors of UK entities to prepare financial statements for their shareholders—that is, an implicit presumption that shareholders are the main users of financial accounting information. Consequently, as previously mentioned, a central tenet of UK GAAP and company law is the principle that financial statements are required to show a true and fair view of the company's economic activities to their shareholders. As such, UK company directors are required to use their professional judgment and can use the true and fair view principle to override accounting standards and/or company law, provided that a sensible justification can be given. For example, if the application of a specific accounting treatment prescribed by UK GAAP were to conflict with the objective to give a true and fair representation of the business under specific circumstances, a departure from such accounting treatment would be considered justified. Whereas under FRS 102 directors are *required* to prepare accounts that give a true and fair view of the entity, under FRS 105 the financial statements of micro-entities are *presumed* to give a true and fair view. In practical terms, this means that the directors of micro-entities need not to exercise their professional judgment beyond what is prescribed by FRS 105—that is, by preparing their financial statements in compliance with FRS 105, they are assumed to be providing a true and fair view of their companies' operations.

Similar to the principles underlying IFRS, the information provided by financial statements prepared according to FRS 102 should follow the accrual basis of accounting—that is, economic transactions should be recorded in the time period in which they occur, regardless of the actual timing of their associated cash flows. Moreover, to be decision useful, financial reporting information should possess the following qualitative characteristics: (1) understandability, (2) relevance, (3) materiality, (4) reliability, (5) substance over form, (6) prudence, (7) completeness, (8) timeliness, and (9) balance between benefit and cost.

3.3 Financial Statement Components and Formats

According to FRS 102, a complete set of financial statements should include (FRC, 2015):

- A statement of financial position (i.e., a balance sheet)
- Either:
  - A statement of comprehensive income detailing revenues, expenses, net income, and other comprehensive income, which essentially combines the presentation of profit and loss and other comprehensive income together (single-statement approach)
  - A separate income statement and a separate statement of comprehensive income (two-statement approach)

Table 4 Financial statement components by financial reporting standard

	FRS 105	FRS 102—Section 1A	FRS 102
Balance sheet	Condensed	Abridged	Yes
Income statement	Condensed (filing not required)	Abridged (filing not required)	Yes
Cash flow statement	No	No	Yes
Statement of changes in equity	No	No	Yes
Notes to the accounts	Yes (less details required)	Yes (less details required)	Yes
Management report	No	No	Yes

This table presents the components of financial statements required under UK law based on different financial reporting regimes (FRC, 2015)

- A statement of changes in equity
- A cash flow statement
- Notes to the accounts presenting detailed information on accounting policies and other explanatory information

Section 1A of FRS 102 and FRS 105 allow small and micro-entities, respectively, to prepare and file their financial statements in a simplified fashion.[7] Table 4 shows the required financial statement components for different reporting regimes.

3.4 *Simplifications for Small and Micro-entities*

As previously discussed, UK GAAP comprises two simplified financial reporting regimes for small and micro-entities (FRC, 2015).

Section 1A of FRS 102 sets out the reduced disclosure requirements of the small entities' financial reporting regime. An entity qualifies as small if at least two of the size criteria presented in Table 3 are satisfied. Listed companies, banks, insurance companies, and other types of financial services companies are by default excluded from the small entities' financial reporting regime. If an entity is a parent company, it qualifies as small only if the whole business group qualifies as small based on its consolidated financial statements. In contrast, if an entity is a parent company in a business group in which one or more affiliates are listed companies or companies that operate in the insurance and financial services business, then the parent company would not qualify as a small entity.

The directors of small entities that do not opt for higher-tier financial reporting regimes (i.e., full FRS 102 or IFRS) and, as such, take advantage of the significantly reduced reporting requirements of Section 1A of FRS 102 must still give a true and

[7] Section 3.4 discusses in detail the financial statement simplifications and exemptions for small and micro-entities.

fair view of the underlying financial performance and financial position of their companies. Therefore, the directors are required to take into account whether disclosure of additional information, which is not necessarily required by company law and accounting standards, is necessary to present a true and fair view.[8] The reporting framework for small entities gives directors the choice to prepare *abridged* financial statements if this option has been approved by shareholders (FRC, 2015).[9] In terms of publication and dissemination of financial statement information, small entities are allowed to file only their balance sheet and related notes to the Companies House—that is, they can omit the income statement from their filings (Deloitte, 2015).[10]

FRS 105 presents the reduced disclosure requirements of the micro-entities' financial reporting regime. An entity qualifies as micro if at least two of the size criteria presented in Table 3 are satisfied. However, the optional nature of the FRS 105 financial reporting regime is such that companies may opt for an upper-tier financial reporting framework even if they meet the eligibility criteria of micro-entities. Like in the case of small entities, listed companies, banks, insurance companies, and other types of financial services companies are by default excluded from the micro-entities' financial reporting regime. In contrast, unlike in the case of small entities, the financial statements of micro-entities are presumed to provide a true and fair view, which essentially reduces the burden of disclosure for these firms. The only financial statements that micro-entities are required to prepare for their shareholders are a balance sheet and an income statement. Hence, there is no requirement to prepare a comprehensive income statement, a cash flow statement, or a statement of changes in equity. Moreover, the information to be disclosed in the balance sheet and income statement is more condensed (e.g., no disaggregated

[8]For example, if the application of a specific accounting standard were to lead to misleading financial statements, then the directors of the company would have an obligation *not* to apply that accounting standard.

[9]The previous UK GAAP option to prepare *abbreviated* financial statements has been removed.

[10]Moreover, small entities are required to provide the following information in the notes to their accounts: (1) information regarding the accounting policies adopted; (2) a fixed assets revaluation table; (3) detailed information regarding financial commitments, guarantees, or contingencies not recognized on the balance sheet; (4) detailed information on advances and credit granted to administrative, managerial, and supervisory bodies; (5) exceptional items; (6) amounts due or payable after more than 5 years and debt covered by valuable security; (7) average number of employees during the fiscal year; (8) a fixed asset note; (9) detail information regarding the entities included in the consolidation perimeter; (10) detailed information regarding arrangements omitted from the balance sheet; (11) detailed information regarding events occurred after the fiscal year end; and (12) detailed information regarding related-party transactions.

information for tangible and intangible assets is required for fixed assets).[11] However, like in the case of small entities, micro-entities are also allowed to omit the income statement from their Companies House filings (Deloitte, 2015).

3.5 *Financial Reporting Regime for Entities That Are Part of a Business Group*

The new UK GAAP system encompasses two further optional reporting regimes for companies that are included in the consolidation perimeter of a business group parent firm (Deloitte, 2015; FRC, 2015). The first regime, which is provided by FRS 101 *Reduced Disclosure Framework*, allows for reduced disclosure requirements, essentially permitting most subsidiaries and parents to use the financial reporting rules of UK-endorsed IFRS (EU-endorsed IFRS before the end of the transition period) in their individual financial statements, but with a significantly reduced disclosure burden. The second regime, whose requirements for subsidiaries and ultimate parents are presented in FRS 102, is essentially based on the principles of FRS 102, but with a number of disclosure exemptions.

4 Valuation Approaches

Table 5 presents a summary of the initial recognition and subsequent measurement rules that companies preparing their financial statements following the requirements of FRS 102 must follow. Generally speaking, the *historical cost model* represents the baseline valuation approach informing the recognition criteria of FRS 102. That said, the United Kingdom has a long-standing tradition for certain financial statement items to have the option to be accounted for using the *fair value model*. This is because, unlike in several continental European countries, accounting practice in the United Kingdom has historically developed separately from tax regulation (Christensen & Nikolaev, 2013). Moreover, because ownership is dispersed even in medium-sized companies (Djankov et al., 2008; La Porta et al., 1997, 1998), financial reporting has the objective to reduce the information asymmetries between managers and shareholders. Therefore, the increasing reliance on fair value over time has served the purpose of conveying more timely and relevant information about companies' asset values.

[11] Furthermore, micro-entities are required to provide the following information in the notes to their accounts: (1) the total amount of financial commitments, guarantees, or contingencies not recognized on the balance sheet; (2) general information on any valuable security that the entity has provided; (3) the amounts of advances and credit granted to the entities' directors; (4) information on commitments entered into on behalf of the directors.

Table 5 Initial recognition and subsequent measurement rules (FRS 102)

Balance sheet/income statement line item	Initial recognition and subsequent measurement
Property, plant, and equipment	– Initial recognition at cost (borrowing costs may be capitalized) – Subsequent measurement at either (1) cost less accumulated depreciation and accumulated impairment losses (if any) or (2) fair value with changes in fair value recognized through other comprehensive income
Investment property	– Initial recognition at cost (directly attributable expenses may be capitalized) – Subsequent measurement at fair value through profit and loss unless fair value cannot be reliably estimated, in which case investment property is measured as property, plant, and equipment
Intangible assets (other than goodwill)	– Initial recognition at cost – Subsequent measurement at cost or at fair value less accumulated amortization and impairment losses (if certain conditions are met). Revaluation gains or losses are recognized through other comprehensive income if fair value is above cost and through profit and loss otherwise – Intangible assets are considered to have a definite useful life, which should not exceed 5 years unless reasonable estimates can be made – Research costs are expensed as incurred – Development costs may be capitalized (if certain conditions are met) – Costs for internally generated intangibles are expensed as incurred
Goodwill	– Initially recognized as the difference between acquisition cost and the fair value of the net assets acquired – Subsequently measured at cost less accumulated amortization and impairment losses – Goodwill is considered to have a definite useful life, which should not exceed 5 years unless reasonable estimates can be made
Inventory	– Initial recognition at the lower of cost and net realizable value. If inventory items are not interchangeable, they are measured based on individual costs. If inventory items are interchangeable, their cost is measured based on the first-in, first-out (FIFO) method or weighted average cost method. The last-in, first-out (LIFO) method is not allowed

(continued)

Table 5 (continued)

Balance sheet/income statement line item	Initial recognition and subsequent measurement
	– Inventory items are periodically tested for impairment
Leases	– Distinction between finance leases and operating leases. To qualify as a finance lease, all the risks and rewards of ownership need be transferred to the lessee – Finance leases: a depreciable asset and finance lease liability are recognized at the lower of fair value of the leased asset or the present value of the minimum lease payments on the balance sheet of the lessee – Operating leases: lease payments are expensed in the income statement of the lessee
Basic financial instruments (e.g., cash, receivables, payables, fixed-rate loans, variable-rate loans, etc.)	– Initial recognition at the transaction price, or at present value of the future payments in case of a financing transaction – Subsequent measurement of debt financial instruments at amortized cost less impairment losses. Fair value option allowed for specific debt financial instruments – Financial instruments such as nonconvertible preference shares, non-puttable ordinary shares, and non-puttable preference shares are subsequently recognized at fair value through profit and loss, or at cost less impairment losses if fair value cannot be reliably estimated
Other financial instruments	– Initial recognition at fair value – Subsequent measurement at fair value through profit and loss, or at cost less impairment losses if fair value cannot be reliably estimated
Controlling shareholdings	– The purchase accounting method is the required accounting treatment for most business combinations – Intangible assets acquired in a business combination are to be recognized separately from goodwill if all the following three conditions are met: (1) intangible assets recognition criteria are met; (2) intangible assets arise from contractual or legal rights; and (3) intangible assets are considered to be separable
Investments in associates	– In consolidated financial statements, investments in associates are generally accounted for using the equity method – In individual financial statements, investments in associates can be accounted for at (1) cost less impairment losses, or (2) fair value through other comprehensive income if fair

(continued)

Table 5 (continued)

Balance sheet/income statement line item	Initial recognition and subsequent measurement
	value remains above cost and fair value through profit and loss if fair value falls below cost, or (3) fair value through profit and loss
Investments in joint ventures	– In consolidated financial statements, investments in joint ventures that qualify as joint controlled entities (JCEs) are generally accounted for using the equity method – In individual financial statements, investments in joint ventures that qualify as joint controlled entities (JCEs) can be accounted for at (1) cost less impairment losses, or (2) fair value through other comprehensive income if fair value remains above cost and fair value through profit and loss if fair value falls below cost, or (3) fair value through profit and loss
Provisions and contingent liabilities	– Provisions are initially recognized based on the estimated amount required to settle the underlying obligation at the balance sheet date – Subsequent measurement of provisions involves an update to reflect the current value of the underlying obligation at the balance sheet date – Contingent liabilities are disclosed in the notes if the likelihood of an outflow of resources is not remote – Contingent liabilities are recognized as liabilities if acquired in the context of a business combination
Revenues	– Revenues are measured at the fair value of the consideration received (or receivable) and include trade discounts and rebates
Share-based payments	– Equity-settled share-based payment transactions are accounted for at fair value assuming this can be reliably estimated – Cash-settled share-based payment transactions are accounted for at the fair value of the liability incurred with changes in the value of the liability recognized in the income statement

This table presents initial recognition and subsequent measurement rules under FRS 102

In terms of measurement and recognition criteria, the key difference between FRS 102 and FRS 105 (the financial reporting regime for micro-entities) is that, under the micro-entity regime, companies cannot measure their assets at fair value or revalued amount. For example, land and buildings and investment properties are required to be accounted for using the historical cost model. In contrast, measurement and recognition criteria for small entities (FRS 102—Section 1A) encompass the use of the fair value model for derivatives, deferred taxes, and equity-settled share-based payments. Furthermore, under FRS 105, entities are not required to recognize deferred taxes and equity-settled share-based payments.

The major differences in terms of recognition criteria between FRS 102 and IFRS for SMEs (FRC, 2015) are instead:

- An option to revalue property, plant, and equipment and certain intangible assets
- An option to capitalize development costs conditional on these meeting specific recognition criteria
- An additional choice to use the recognition rules of IFRS 9 for certain financial instruments
- The replacement of hedge accounting requirements with the recognition rules of IFRS 9
- The allowed use of merger accounting (pooling of interest method) for business combinations under common control
- An option to capitalize borrowing costs on certain qualifying assets
- An accrual accounting option for government grants
- A required timing difference approach, as opposed to a temporary difference approach, for deferred income taxes
- An option to use the historical cost model for all types of biological assets

5 Conclusions

The common law legal origin and the key role of public equity as the main source of finance for UK corporations have historically shaped the nature of the financial reporting system in that the primary role financial statements play is to reduce information asymmetries between outside capital providers and managers (Christensen & Nikolaev, 2013; Leuz, 2010; Nobes, 1998). For this reason, like in other Anglo-Saxon countries, also in the United Kingdom the financial reporting system has naturally evolved to progressively embrace the use of fair value as a measurement basis, thus allowing managers to disclose more timely and more relevant information about their companies' asset values.

In the course of its history, the UK financial reporting system has experienced several reforms implying structural changes. Importantly, the United Kingdom has played a central role in the process of EU accounting harmonization (Camfferman & Zeff, 2007; Hopwood, 1994), always being at the forefront of the key initiative that led to the development of international accounting standards (IAS) first and IFRS later on.

In 2009, the IASB issued a simplified set of IFRS for SMEs with the objective to incentivize companies to prepare their financial statements following requirements that would be closer to those of the main IFRS (Becker et al., 2021). As a member of the EU at that time, the United Kingdom incorporated the EU Directive 2013/34 into company law. In doing so, it amended the previous reporting framework and accounting standards to essentially adopt a modified version of IFRS for SMEs.

The main modifications were meant to keep accounting rules for SMEs close enough to those followed by listed companies, but with simplified, less burdensome disclosure requirements (Gassen, 2017). Ultimately, the United Kingdom opted for a multitier system, with financial reporting requirements becoming progressively more demanding depending on the size and organizational complexity of the reporting entity.

The future of corporate reporting in the United Kingdom will certainly be shaped by the recent withdrawal from the European Union. Since the end of the transition period, UK domestic law has acquired the formal power to adopt and endorse IFRS. In fact, the recently established UKEB is now tasked with the adoption and endorsement of IFRS as issued by the IASB. As such, it is reasonable to assume that, in the future, UK-endorsed IFRS and EU-endorsed IFRS may start to exhibit differences, which could be viewed as a potential setback for the accounting harmonization process initiated by the European Union more than two decades ago.[12]

References

Alexander, D. (1993). A European true and fair view? *European Accounting Review, 2*(1), 17–46.

Arafat, I., Dunne, T., & Ahmed, A. H. (2020). Splitting accountability hairs: Anomalies in the adaptation of IFRS for SMEs in the UK and Ireland. *Accounting in Europe, 17*(2), 183–203.

ASB. (2009). *The future of UK GAAP*. Accounting Standards Board.

Becker, K., Bischof, J., & Daske, H. (2021). IFRS: Markets, practice, and politics. *Foundations and Trends in Accounting, 15*(1–2), 1–262.

Beuselinck, C., Elfers, F., Gassen, J., & Pierk, J. (2023). Private firm accounting: The European reporting environment, data and research perspectives. *Accounting and Business Research, 53*(1), 38–82.

BIS. (2013). Simpler financial reporting for micro-entities: The UK's proposal to implement the 'micros directive.' Consultation document.

BIS/FRC. (2011). *Simpler reporting for the smallest businesses*. Discussion paper.

Camfferman, K., & Zeff, S. (2007). *Financial reporting and global capital markets—A history of the International Accounting Standards Committee, 1973-2000*. Oxford University Press.

Christensen, H. B., Liu, L. Y., & Maffett, M. (2020). Proactive financial reporting enforcement and shareholder wealth. *Journal of Accounting and Economics, 69*(2–3), 1–23.

Christensen, H.B., & Nikolaev, V.V. (2013). Does fair value accounting for non-financial assets pass the market test? *Review of Accounting Studies, 18*, 734–775.

Collis, J., Jarvis, R., & Skerratt, L. (2017). The role and current status of IFRS in the completion of national accounting rules: Evidence from the UK. *Accounting in Europe, 14*(1–2), 235–247.

Deloitte. (2015). A closer look—UK implementation of the EU Accounting Directive.

Djankov, S., La Porta, R. L., Lopez-de-Silanes, F., & Shleifer, A. (2008). The law and economics of self-dealing. *Journal of Financial Economics, 88*(3), 430–465.

Florou, A., Morricone, S., & Pope, P. F. (2020). Proactive financial reporting enforcement: Audit fees and financial reporting quality effects. *The Accounting Review, 95*(2), 167–197.

FRC. (2015). *Overview of the financial reporting framework*. Financial Reporting Council.

Gassen, J. (2017). The effect of IFRS for SMEs on the financial reporting environment of private firms: An exploratory interview study. *Accounting and Business Research, 47*(5), 540–563.

[12]The process was initiated with the 4th EEC Directive 1978/660.

Hopwood, A. G. (1994). Some reflections on 'The harmonization of accounting within the EU'. *European Accounting Review, 3*(2), 241–253.

IFRS Foundation. (2022). IFRS application around the world. Jurisdictional profile: United Kingdom.

Kaya, D., & Koch, M. (2015). Countries' adoption of the international financial reporting standard for small and medium-sized entities (IFRS for SMEs)—Early empirical evidence. *Accounting and Business Research, 45*(1), 93–120.

La Porta, R. L., Lopez-de-Silanes, F., Shleifer, A., & Vishny, R. W. (1997). Legal determinants of external finance. *Journal of Finance, 52*(3), 1131–1150.

La Porta, R. L., Lopez-de-Silanes, F., Shleifer, A., & Vishny, R. W. (1998). Law and finance. *Journal of Political Economy, 106*(6), 1113–1155.

Leuz, C. (2010). Different approaches to corporate reporting regulation: How jurisdictions differ and why. *Accounting and Business Research, 40*(3), 229–256.

Nobes, C. (1998). Towards a general model of the reasons for international differences in financial reporting. *Abacus, 34*(2), 162–187.

France

Corinne Bessieux-Ollier, Véronique Blum, and Elisabeth Walliser

1 Introduction: The National Accounting Scenario

1.1 The Role of Civil Code

France is a 68 million inhabitant country, which undertook a unification of its customary laws when practices were too diversified. The resulting Civil Code includes contractual laws but does not relate to commerce laws. This is the scope of the Commercial Code (CC—*code de commerce*[1]) that was enforced in 1807 and inspired by the medieval *Lex Mercatoria* and very similar to the 1673 Savary Code.[2] The codes establish the social function of accounting as the protection of creditors, by demonstrating the absence of manipulation. It is also expected to resolve disputes between merchants (Monéger, 2004). Notably, all merchants had to keep trade books

[1] https://www.legifrance.gouv.fr/codes/id/LEGITEXT000005634379/.

[2] https://books.google.fr/books?id=MjmhDIQwD4kC&pg=RA1-PA1#v=onepage&q&f=false.

C. Bessieux-Ollier
Montpellier Business School, Montpellier, France
e-mail: c.bessieux@Montpellier-BS.com

V. Blum (✉)
Université Grenoble Alpes, Saint-Martin-d'Hères, France
e-mail: veronique.blum@univ-grenoble-alpes.fr

E. Walliser
Université Côte d'Azur, Nice, France
e-mail: elisabeth.walliser@univ-cotedazur.fr

A. Incollingo, A. Lionzo (eds.), *The European Harmonization of National Accounting Rules*, SIDREA Series in Accounting and Business Administration,
https://doi.org/10.1007/978-3-031-42931-6_4

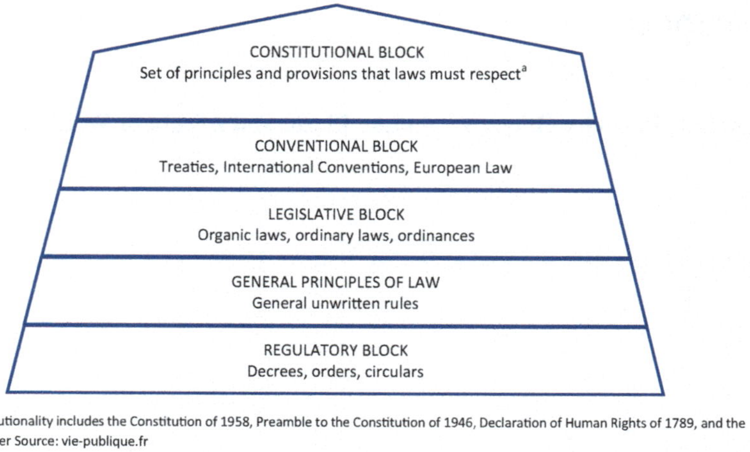

Fig. 1 The hierarchy of French laws. [a]The block of constitutionality includes the Constitution of 1958, Preamble to the Constitution of 1946, Declaration of Human Rights of 1789, and the environmental charter. Source: www.vie-publique.fr

and registers, but no accounting method was made compulsory. The establishment of a ledger was not required before 1984 (Coquery & Praquin, 2008).

Since 1969, all accounting regulations have been gathered under the concept of "accounting law," a branch of business law and part of private law, though independent of tax law. Accounting law sets on two pillars: the laws for accounting and the laws for accountants, as a regulated profession (Lamrani, 2013). First established at a national level, the international texts (treaties, European regulations, and directives) became the prominent sources of accounting law. A major transformation occurred with the publication of the fourth (78/660/EEC) and seventh (83/349/EEC) European directives as their transposition affected lower-level national laws (Fig. 1).

Indeed, the French accounting system is part of the continental tradition (Nobes, 1983) where the state plays a crucial role in standard-setting. The statutory rules governing the annual accounts of companies in France are set out in the CC and the compendium of accounting standards (*Recueil des normes comptables*). The CC, which structure has remained unchanged since 1807, presents the procedures for drawing up the annual accounts, in the form of laws and decrees. It contains both a legislative part and a regulatory part, with accounting obligations being mainly contained in articles L123-12 to L123-28. It is made up of articles, some relating specifically to merchants (*commerçants*) (Art. L. 123-12 to L. 123-28 and R. 123-172 to R. 123-208) and others to consolidated accounts (*comptes consolidés*) (L. 233-16 to L. 233-28 and R. 233-3 to R. 233-16). Laws are amended by the French Parliament or by ministerial decrees issued by the government. It is part of the legislative block in the French pyramidal hierarchy of laws (Fig. 1).

At a lower hierarchical level, the compendium of accounting standards brings together all the accounting texts issued by the institutions in charge of the accounting standard-setting process. It presents the rules for drawing up the annual accounts of industrial and commercial companies. The PCG (*Plan Comptable Général*) is the main document of the French accounting standards. It sets the accounting rules and principles. It is an integral part of the compendium and displays nearly the same structure, broken down in different books. The PCG was created in 1947 and has undergone many changes since, particularly in 2016 or 2019. It is currently undertaking a modernization process. The January 1, 2019, version[3] is in force but shall be replaced by the January 1, 2023, version, starting in 2025. Before it comes in force, it has to be approved by the Parliament. [4] The currently applicable PCG is detailed in Regulation ANC 2014-03, a document that develops in 221 pages and 948 articles and is freely available on the website of the standard-setter (www.anc.gouv.fr). It divides in four books. Book 1 covers the general arrangements applicable to the various items in the accounting statements (in particular assets, liabilities, expenses, and income). Book 2 deals with specific modalities (software, website, quarries, greenhouse gas emission allowances, financial instruments, merger operations, etc.). Book 3 provides 47 table templates and guidance for presenting annual statements and their notes (models of summary documents). It also contains a summary table of the applicable accounting methods (Art. 831-2). Finally, Book 4 deals with the maintenance, structure, and operation of the accounting statements.

The second document of importance is Regulation no. 2020-01, approved by decree, that superseded the CRC Regulation 99-02 and is dedicated to consolidated accounts of industrial and commercial companies. It develops in 100 pages and three books. [5] The version in force is that of October 9, 2020.

The third source of accounting law is made of jurisprudence and doctrines. It sets below the pyramid of laws and is sometimes described as its base. Notably, in France, jurisprudence is not a law per se. As decisions issued by the courts, jurisprudence serves as nonmandatory references for shedding light on possible solutions earlier adopted by judges in similar cases. A doctrine is an opinion related to an accounting law text. It takes the form of an interpretation, an advice, or a recommendation and is formulated by organizations such as the standard-setter or the Order of Chartered Accountants.

[3]https://www.anc.gouv.fr/files/live/sites/anc/files/contributed/ANC/1_Normes_françaises/Reglements/Recueils/PCG_Janvier2023/PCG_1er-janvier-2023.pdf.

[4]The proposed changes can be read in the regulation N° 2022-06 du 4 novembre 2022: https://www.anc.gouv.fr/files/live/sites/anc/files/contributed/ANC/1_Normes_françaises/Reglements/2022/R2022_06/R2022_06.pdf.

[5]Book 1 covers the general arrangements. Book 2 is dedicated to the consolidation statement and relates to perimeter, methods, control, and variations and contains templates. Book 3 addresses combined accounts and specific cases like insurance companies or agricultural cooperatives.

1.2 The Role of Professional Standard-Setting Body

The Accounting Standards Authority (*Autorité des Normes Comptables,* ANC) is the French standard-setting body. Created by Ordinance no. 2009-79 of January 22, 2009, it is the result of the merger of the former National Accounting Board (CNC) and the Accounting Regulatory Committee (CRC). Its missions are multiple: (1) It establishes, in the form of regulations, the general and sectoral accounting requirements that must be observed by natural or legal persons subject; (2) it gives an opinion on any legislative or regulatory provision containing measures of an accounting nature; (3) it issues opinions and positions and positions within the framework of the procedure for developing international accounting standards; and (4) it oversees the coordination and synthesis of the theoretical and methodological work carried out in accounting matters.

For listed companies, the French Securities and Markets Authority (*Autorité des Marchés Financiers*—AMF) also plays a key role. AMF is responsible for protecting savings invested in financial products, informing investors, and ensuring the smooth functioning of markets. While seeking better information for investors, AMF is involved in accounting standard-setting and has regulatory power for actors in its field of competence. It may be required to contribute to accounting doctrine in the form of instructions or recommendations and works tightly with the accounting profession.

Although the liberal accounting profession is not responsible for French standard-setting, it indirectly participates in the process through the recommendations and opinions published for its members. It also expresses its position in the development of international accounting standards. The profession is placed under the *Ordre des Experts Comptables* (OEC), the equivalent of an Institute of Chartered Accountants, placed under the supervision of the Ministry of Economy, Finance and Budget. The other prominent professional association is that of auditors, the *Compagnie Nationale des Commissaires aux Comptes* (CNCC), placed under the supervision of the Ministry of Justice. Both organizations have a code of ethics.

1.3 The Role of Tax Regulation

"Accounting and taxation have had a compelling relationship for several centuries" (Rossignol, 1999). As aforementioned, taxation was a major driver to establish accounting laws; thus, it has a strong influence on the structuration of individual accounts. Where there is an inconsistency between the tax rules and the accounting rules, the discrepancies result in deductions or restatements to determine the tax result.

The process is as follows. During the year, transactions are recorded using the accounting rules, without taking into account the tax rules. At the end of the year, when the accounting result is released, the taxable result is determined in three steps:

(1) the accounting net income is calculated, (2) nontaxable profits or revenues are deducted from (1), and (3) nondeductible expenses are added back.

This gives the following formula: tax earnings = accounting earnings + reintegrated items – deducted items. The tax payable over the tax period is calculated by multiplying the company's tax income by the tax rate.

In order to limit preparatory costs, financial statements have to adopt a standardized form called the "tax report" (*liasse fiscale*) which template is standardized [6] and available online.[7] The filing of the tax report is compulsory; it is transmitted to the registries of the Trade Tribunals that makes the report available online or on demand. Companies also need to complete a supplemental tax form.[8] Since January 1, 2021, the calculation of the tax due has applied the following scale: (1) a reduced rate of 15% is applied to the portion of profit that is inferior to 42,500 € (under certain conditions), and (2) a normal rate of 25% is applied to the part of the profit that is greater than 42,500 €.

1.4 *Economic System: Large-Sized Companies Versus SMEs*

1.4.1 Weight of SMEs/Listed Companies [9]

In 2019, 4.1 million French nonagricultural and nonfinancial companies—with 4.4M legal entities—generated 1240 B€ of added value, which represents 51% of the gross domestic product (GDP). They employed more than 13 million people, out of almost 30 million workers, and their tangible assets were worth 2.8 B€, whereas their recognized intangible assets almost reached 600 B€. French companies include 276 large undertakings ($6.7\times10^{-5\%}$ of the total number of companies), 5861 intermediary-sized enterprises (0.14%), 152,826 small- and medium-sized enterprises (3.7%), and almost 4 million micro-undertakings (96%). The organization into a group of companies is not reserved for large companies only: nearly one out of two SMEs excluding micro-enterprises has opted for this mode of organization. The tertiarization of the productive system is massive, including in industry or

[6] The tax report must contain at least: the earnings for the financial year subject to tax, the balance sheet and the profit and loss account, the table of fixed assets and depreciation, the table of provisions, as well as receivables and debts, the table of gains and losses on capital, the added value, the composition of the capital, and the identification of the main partners.

[7] https://www.impots.gouv.fr/sites/default/files/formulaires/2050-liasse/2022/2050-liasse_3731.pdf.

[8] https://www.impots.gouv.fr/sites/default/files/formulaires/2065-sd/2020/2065-sd_2851.pdf.

[9] Sources : https://www.economie.gouv.fr/cedef/chiffres-cles-des-pme
https://solutions.lesechos.fr/compta-gestion/c/barometre-des-tpe-pme-dans-leconomie-francaise-en-2019-19385/
https://www.insee.fr/en/statistiques/fichier/5759063/ENTFRA21.pdf.

construction, two sectors in which the large groups integrate more and more tertiary subsidiaries (Insee, 2021).

Until 2020, the classification of undertakings was defined by the decree implementing Article 51 of the law on the modernization of the economy (no. 2008-776) and the in decree 2008-1354, Art. 3, but the criteria have been modified in order to converge with the categories of the Directive 2013/34. Article D123-200 of the CC, modified by decree 2020-101 (Art.2), is currently the text of reference (Table 1). Article 7 of law 2019-486 related to PACTE law had earlier started the convergence process and created a new category of companies: the medium company, which characteristics are detailed in law 2019-539. However, because the breakdown in companies' categories was formerly different, data collection has until 2020 complied with the old system. Thus, because we do not yet have access to demographical data using the novel breakdown, Table 1 recalls the old and new thresholds but remains incomplete.

The economic fabric is made up of 4 million medium, small, and micro-companies, with nearly three-quarters of them having no employees and about 2 M being sole proprietorships. Very-small- and small- and medium-sized undertakings produce more than a third of the revenue of French companies, i.e., about 1400 B€. Their role is vital as they contribute to 9% of the GDP and hired 49% of the 14 million employees in France. In comparison, intermediary-sized enterprises hire 3 million employees and generate a 1184 B€ revenue. Family ownership characterizes half of the midcaps.

On the other hand, multinational corporations alone generate more than half of the value added and are responsible for nearly 90% of exports although the average exportation rate of French companies is merely 19%. Four of them currently belong to the top 100 market capitalization in the world (LVMH, L'Oréal, BNP Paribas, and TotalEnergies). As a consequence, the French productive apparatus remains very concentrated. Moreover, the capital of these very large French companies remains in the hands of local investors. Foreign investors held only 39.9% of the capital of the CAC 40 at the end of 2020, for companies having their registered office in France.[10]

1.4.2 Weight of Bank Financing, Weight of Financial Markets

The financing of the French economy has long been significantly based on bank credit.[11] At the end of the 1990s, this accounted for almost 75% of the debt financing of nonfinancial corporations. Since 2008, the dominant share of bank financing has declined significantly in favor of market financing with a market debt share multiplied by 2. Thus, debt financing has now stabilized around 36% (against 20% on average in the euro area). This development is mainly due to large enterprises and

[10] https://www.lesechos.fr/finance-marches/marches-financiers/le-cac-40-un-indice-a-lactionnariat-de-plus-en-plus-francais-1357243.

[11] https://www.banque-france.fr/en/node/359093.

Table 1 Panorama of the categories of French companies in 2019

	French acronym	Nb. of employees[a]	Maximum turnover		Maximum total balance sheet	Reference laws	Nb. of enterprises and (%)	Revenues in billion € & (exportation rate)
Micro-undertakings (after 2020)	MIC	Av. 10	700,000 €	And *[or]*	350,000 €	Art. D123-200	n.a.	n.a.
Very small enterprises (before 2020)	TPE or MIC	Max. 10	2 million €	Or	2 million €	2008-776 2008-1354	3,946,131 (96.1%)	514 (3.8%)
Small undertakings (and groups) (after 2020)	TPE	Av. 50	12 million € *[8 million €]*[b]	And *[or]*	6 million € *[4 million €]*	Art. D123-200	n.a.	n.a.
Small- and medium-sized enterprises (before 2020)	PME	Max. 249	50 million €	Or	43 million €	2008-776 2008-1354	12,826 (3.7%)	892 (9.8%)
Medium-sized undertakings (and groups) (after 2020)	ME	Av. 250	40 million €	And *[or]*	20 million €	2019-486 2019-539 and Art. D123-200	n.a.	n.a.
Intermediary-sized enterprises (before 2020)	ETI	Max. 4999	1.5 billion €	Or	2 billion €	2008-776 2008-1354	5861 (0.14%)	1124 (20.9%)
Large undertakings (and groups) (after 2020)	GE	Av. above 250	Above 40 million €	And *[or]*	Above 20 million €	Art. D123-200	n.a.	n.a.
Large enterprises (before 2020)	GE	5000 and above	Above 1.5 billion €	Or	2 billion €	2008-776 2008-1354	276	1397 (29%)

Example: A company with fewer than 250 employees but a turnover greater than 50 million € and a balance sheet exceeding 43 million € used to be considered as an intermediary-sized undertaking. It is now a large undertaking

Sources: https://www.insee.fr/fr/statistiques/5758732?sommaire=5759063 and https://www.economie.gouv.fr/cedef/definition-petites-et-moyennes-entreprises

[a]Av., average; max, maximum

[b]When criteria in the Directive 2013/34 and in French law differ, figures in italic and between brackets refer to the Directive 2013/34, whereas regular font figures refer to Art D213-200. It is the case for small undertakings

midcaps. On the other hand, SMEs remain structurally dependent on bank financing. The share of bank credit in their debt was still 85% in 2019 and 95% when leasing is included. It was about 85% for the intermediary-sized enterprises. Notably, in the same time lap, from the late 1990s to the early 2020s, the share of equity financing has increased from 30–35% to 36–42% of the total funds.

2 The Evolution of Accounting Regulations

2.1 EU Directive 2013/34 Transposition

The European Directive 2013/34 was transposed in France through Ordinance 2015-900 in July 2015 and by its implementing decree 2015-903. [12] As noted in Le Manh (2017), contrary to what has happened in other European countries, it has not been discussed nationally and was issued without consulting the French Parliament. This is because law 2014-1662 allowed the French government to transpose this directive by circumventing Parliament. The CC has been amended accordingly, and the Accounting Standards Authority (*ANC*) issued new regulations whose versions used today are ANC regulations 2014-03 and 2020-01.

2.2 The Level of IFRS Adoption

At the time of the National Accounting Council (CNC) in 2001, it was decided to bring the French regulations applicable to company accounts in line with IFRS. The rationale was that it would be difficult to support two different long-term regulations, since the mandatory application of IFRS to the consolidated accounts of listed French companies had already been programmed (Le Manh, 2017). Nevertheless, this convergence slowed down with the financial crisis of 2008. In France in particular, voices have been raised that criticized the IASB and its standards (Burlaud & Colasse, 2011; Marteau & Morand, 2009). They found an echo with the creation of the ANC that was led by a senior official at the Finance Ministry (i.e., a political leader), whereas the previous CNC was led by a member of the accounting profession. Subsequently, convergence with the individual accounts regulations was no longer on the agenda, and ANC outlawed IFRS-PME standards. Hence, there is in France a plurality of regulations, applying to different types of companies (Table 2) with different rules (Table 3).

[12] Other transposition texts are : LOI n° 2014-1 du 2 janvier 2014, v. init. ; Ordonnance n° 2014-86 du 30 janvier 2014, v. init. ; LOI n° 2014-1662 du 30 décembre 2014, v. init. ; DÉCRET n°2015-903 du 23 juillet 2015, v. init. ; Arrêté du 4 décembre 2015, v. init.

Table 2 Preparing financial statements in France, three levels of regulations

Regulation	Type of accounts	Companies concerned
PCG ANC regulation 2014-03	Individual accounts	French companies
ANC regulation 2020-01	Consolidated accounts	French companies that are not listed on a regulated market
IFRS standards	Consolidated accounts	French companies listed on a regulated market or **in option** for French companies with consolidated accounts that are not listed on a regulated market

2.3 Nonfinancial Disclosure Evolution

France has a long history of extra-accounting reporting. The demand for social information started at the beginning of the twentieth century but became imperative with the students' revolution of May 1968 (Chatriot, 2012). In response, Pierre Sudreau's report (1975) addressed a reform of the enterprise focused on social dialog and the place of the employee. As a consequence, law no. 77-769 was passed in 1977 and incorporated in the Labour Code[13] (art. L. 2323-68 to, L. 2323-72, and R. 2323-71). Still in force, it requires the publication of a social report for all companies employing more than 300 employees. The report covers issues such as employment, wages, work conditions, health, security, permanent education, professional relations, and many figures.

Testifying of the rise of corporate social responsibility (CSR) concepts, the New Economic Regulations Act (NRE) was promulgated by the Jospin government on May 15, 2001 (law 2001-420), concerning companies listed on stock exchanges. It was the first report addressing the environmental and social consequences of the enterprise's activity, including GHG emissions. It was followed by the "Grenelle 1 and 2" laws (laws 2009-967 and 2010-788, Art. 225, respectively), which formalized the commitments of the *Grenelle de l'environnement*. They extended the application of CSR rules to all companies with more than 500 employees.

In a third stage, Ordinance no. 2017-1180 of July 19, 2017, on the publication of nonfinancial information by certain large companies and groups of companies and its implementing decree (2017-1265) enables the transposition of the European Directive 2014/95/EU of October 22, 2014, on the publication of social and environmental information. It is incorporated in Art. L 225-102-1 of the French CC. This nonfinancial reporting directive (NFRD) has resulted in the obligation for large companies to publish an extra-financial performance statement (Ordinance 2017-1180, art. 1; L. 225-102-1 amended).

[13] https://www.legifrance.gouv.fr/codes/id/LEGITEXT000006072050/, the Code being sufficient, the law was repealed in February 2022 to obtain a better readability of French laws.

Table 3 Main differences between three levels of regulations

	French regulations for individual accounts	French regulations for consolidated accounts	IFRS
Objectives	Specified in Art. 111-1 to 112-4	Specified in Art. 111-1 to 111-3	Specified in conceptual framework
Statement of income	Net income only General requirements: Art. 112-3 & 511-1 to 515-2 Templates: 821-3 (table) and 821-4 (list)	Net income Templates: Art. 281-2 (by nature) and 281-3 (by destination)	Net income and other comprehensive income Open format
Balance sheet	Format template: before (Art. 821-1) or after (Art. 821-2) distribution of income Current and noncurrent financial liabilities are distinct in footnote, in the compulsory related notes, or in the extended balance sheet. Items are listed with raising chargeability when going down the balance sheet	Format template: Art. 281-1/281-2 Current and noncurrent financial liabilities are distinct in footnote, in the compulsory related notes, or in the extended balance sheet Items are listed with raising chargeability when going down the balance sheet	Open format, two sections are compulsory: current and noncurrent items
Statement of cash flow	Voluntary but three models exist: PCG, OEC, and Banque de France	Mandatory, part of the notes. Art. 282-41 to 282-44, with templates	Mandatory
Measurement of tangible and intangible assets	Cost model. Revaluation is possible under conditions. Investment properties are tangible assets	Cost model. Revaluation is possible under conditions Investment properties are tangible assets	Cost model or revaluation model. Investment properties can be recognized at fair value
Accounting for leases	Unrecognized until the purchase option is exercised. Usually retreated in the statement of cash flow	Art. 272-2. Leases are capitalized and considered as asset and liability	Leases are capitalized and considered as asset and liability
Measurement of financial assets	Recognition at cost model. Impairment when evaluation at usage value or fair value according to the intention (participation in the management or profitability seeking) is inferior to cost value. Art. 221-1 to 223-3	According to ANC 2014-03 Identical to French regulations for individual accounts	Cost model or fair value model
Goodwill	Goodwill does not exist in the individual accounts	Art. 231-11 Goodwill must be amortized over its useful life if predictable, or 10 years. If useful life is undefined, it is not amortized	At the time of the writing, goodwill is not amortized but subject to impairment test only
Development costs	Can be capitalized under condition or can be expensed (Art. 212-3)	Must be capitalized according to the requirement of ANC 2014-03	Must be capitalized
Postretirement benefits	Are preferably accounted for or in the notes (Art. 324-1, 831-2)	The existing benefits in an acquired companies must be recorded in the purchasing entity's account (Art. 232-1)	Must be accounted for

Adapted from Le Manh (2017)

More recently, with the PACTE law of May 22, 2019, new provisions have come into force to strengthen the dissemination of nonfinancial information through the consideration of social and environmental issues in French companies. This law proposes a "label" of mission-oriented undertaking that any company can choose to adopt and which confirms a voluntary commitment through an inscription in its constitution. Civil Code has been amended in two sections:

(i) Article 1833 now stipulates "The company is managed in its social interest, taking into account the social and environmental issues of its activity"—therefore, the PACTE law has changed the definition of the company in the Civil Code and the CC by breaking with the sole interest of the partners and imposing a management that considers the company's social and environmental issues.
(ii) Article 1835 adds: "The articles of association may specify a *raison d'être* (purpose), consisting of the principles which the company has established and for the respect of which it intends to allocate means in the performance of its activity."

The aim of this law is to bring entrepreneurs and businesses closer to their long-term environment. It thus encourages companies to no longer be guided by a single *raison d'avoir* (*owning goal*) but also by a *raison d'être*, a form of fruitful existential doubt that makes it possible to direct it toward a long-term path. Finally, in 2019, with a mission given by the French state, Patrick de Cambourg, president of the ANC, published a report advocating an extra-financial reporting framework initiated by the European Union (de Cambourg, 2019). Extra-financial reporting is now referred to as sustainability reporting to reflect the idea that it does not complement financial reporting but that it constitutes a second leg of corporate reporting. Arguments in favor of the standardization and development of extra-financial information are found in the context of an academic research demonstrating the utility of CSR information and the emergence of socially responsible investment, while NGOs and advocacy groups bring their contribution and voice in favor of more transparency and comparability. However, the available information is deemed lacking reliability, as it adopts privately constructed and non-converging frameworks and is not audited.

3 Which Implementation of EU Directive 2013/34 in France?

The directive shall apply to the laws, regulations, and administrative provisions of the member states relating to the types of undertakings listed (Chapter 1, article 1). In France, it shall apply to the *société anonyme*, the *société en commandite par actions*, the *société à responsabilité limitée*, the *société par actions simplifiée*, the *société en nom collectif*, and the *société en commandite simple*.

*3.1 General Provisions and Principles (*Dispositions et principes*)*

In Directive 2013/34/EU, Chapter 2, article 4, presents the general provisions, and Chapter 2, article 6, exposes the general financial reporting principles. They are transposed in CC L123-12 to L123-20, PCG 2023 Art. 121-1 to 121-5. Notably, the regulation 2014-03 makes explicit the general principles applied in the PCG. To clarify those, ANC has issued a note (ANC, 2022) detailing those.

3.1.1 True and Fair View, Conservatism, Accrual, and Realization Principles

The scope of the directive is principles-based (para. 6). In Chapter 2, article 6 (1), the directive cites the principles and precises that "Items presented in the annual and consolidated financial statements shall be *recognised and measured* in accordance with principles." Most of them are similar in the French regulation. The PCG considers the following principles for preparing the annual accounts: true and fair view, comparability and going concern, regularity and sincerity, prudence, and permanence of methods. They also appear in the French CC.

The annual accounts must give a **true and fair view** (*Image fidèle*) of the assets, the financial situation, and the results of the company (CC Art. L123-14). PCG 2023 Art.121-1 defines accounting statements as a system for organizing financial information that makes it possible to enter, classify, and record basic data in figures and present statements reflecting a *true and fair view* of the entity's assets, financial situation, and results at the end of year.

Accounting statements make it possible to carry out periodic comparisons and to assess the evolution of the entity with a view to business continuity (**comparability**, *comparabilité*; **going concern,** *continuité d'activité*, PCG 2023 Art.121-2). For their establishment, the merchant, natural or legal person, is presumed to continue his activities (*Continuité d'activité*, CC Art. L123-20).

The annual accounts must comply with the principle of **prudence** (CC Art. L123-20). Accounting statements are established on the basis of prudent assessments, to avoid the risk of transfer, to future periods, of present uncertainties likely to burden the entity's assets and results (PCG 2019 Art. 121-4).

The accounting methods used and the structure of the balance sheet and profit and loss account cannot be modified from 1 year to another (CC Art. L123-17). The consistency and comparability of accounting information over successive periods is based on the consistency of accounting methods and the structure of the balance sheet and profit and loss account (**consistently from one financial year to the next**—*cohérence et permanence des méthodes*, PCG 2023 Art. 121-5). In French, two words are necessary to capture both the consistency across methods (*cohérence*) and their internal consistency across time (*permanence*). A literal translation would only address the first meaning.

Some principles existing in France *(sincérité et régularité)* are not present in the European directive. The annual accounts are deemed **truthful and conform** (CC Art. L123-14) when they comply with the rules and procedures in force, which are applied with sincerity in order to reflect the knowledge that those responsible for preparing the accounts have of the reality and assuming a relative importance of the events recorded (PCG 2023 Art. 121-3). These principles, linked to the true and fair view concept, were already present in the decree law of August 31, 1937, modifying the law of July 24, 1867 (Obert, 2016 [14]), and in the PCG 1957.[15]

Some items appearing in the European directive are also present in the PCG (and/or the CC), but they are not the subject of a specific subtitle:

- The entity must prepare annual accounts at the end of the year in view of the accounting records and the inventory (**accruals bases**—*spécialisation, indépendance des exercices*, CC Art. L123-12).
- No compensation can be made between assets and liabilities (PCG 2023 Art. 112-2) or between expense and income items (PCG 2023 Art. 112-3, **set-offs**—*non compensation)*, except in exceptional cases provided for by a regulation of the ANC (CC Art. L123-19).
- Accounting statements comply with the rules and procedures in force, which are applied with sincerity in order to reflect the knowledge that those responsible for drawing up the accounts have of the reality and relative importance of the events recorded (**economic reality or substance commercial of the transaction**—*réalité économique ou substance commerciale de la transaction*/**materiality**—*importance relative*, PCG 2023 Art. 121-3). The predominance of the substance over form has however been deleted from the regulation 2020-01.

[14]Obert (2016) p. 133 "Ainsi, le décret-loi du 31 août 1937 modifiant la loi du 24 juillet 1867, a introduit les notions de régularité et de sincérité que l'on retrouve dans notre droit actuel en demandant au commissaire aux comptes 'de contrôler la régularité et la sincérité des inventaires et des bilans ainsi que l'exactitude des informations données sur les comptes de la société dans le rapport du conseil d'administration.'

[15]*PCG 1957 : Pour qu'une comptabilité ait une valeur certaine, il faut qu'elle respecte les PRINCIPES COMPTABLES FONDAMENTAUX : régularité et sincérité des comptes.*

- la régularité est la conformité à la règlementation ou en son absence aux principes généralement admis, - la sincérité ("true and fair view" anglo-saxon) : présentation des comptes donnant, en fonction des limites de la pratique comptable courante, une image aussi objective que possible, ne comportant pas de déformation intentionnelle, de manipulation, ni d'omission volontaire de faits significatifs.

L'appréciation de l'auditeur doit se faire essentiellement à partir de ces deux derniers éléments : la régularité des comptes, leur sincérité.

- The opening balance sheet of a year must correspond to the closing balance sheet of the previous year (CC Art. L123-19), stated before distribution of earnings (**opening/closing balance sheet**—*intangibilité du bilan d'ouverture*, PCG 2023 Art. 112-2).
- Assets and liabilities must be **valued separately** (*evaluation séparée*, CC Art. L123-19 and PCG 2023 Art. 112-2). Finally, goods acquired for consideration are recorded at their **acquisition cost** (*coût d'acquisition*), whereas goods acquired free of charge are accounted at their market value and goods produced are recognized at their **production cost** (*coût de production—coûts historiques*, CC Art. L123-18).

3.1.2 Disapplication in Exceptional Cases

Chapter 2, article 4 (4) and (9), of Directive 2013/34 considers that the disapplication of an accounting requirement shall be disclosed in the notes to the financial statements together with an explanation of the reasons for it. It should also relate its effect on the undertaking's assets, liabilities, financial position, and profit or loss. Exceptional cases should be understood as unusual transaction and unusual situations.

French regulations are identical on this subject. Indeed, "When the application of an accounting requirement is not sufficient to give the true and fair view, additional information must be provided in the notes. If, in an exceptional case, the application of an accounting prescription proves to be unsuitable for giving a true and fair view of the assets, the financial situation or the result, it must be waived. This derogation is mentioned in the notes and duly substantiated, with an indication of its influence on the assets, the financial situation and the results of the company" (Code commerce Art. L123-14). "In the exceptional case where the application of an accounting rule proves to be unsuitable for giving the true and fair view, it is waived. The justification and the consequences of the derogation are mentioned in the notes" (PCG 2023 Art. 121-3). This might be the case when one needs to justify a change in accounting policy. One example is that of stock valuations, where the true and fair view objective prevails over the principle of consistency in accounting methods.

3.2 *Balance Sheet and Profit and Loss Account (***Bilan et compte de résultat***)*

In France, following the CC Art. L123-12 and the PCG 2023 Art. 111-1 and 112-1, the annual accounts include the balance sheet, the profit and loss account, and the notes which form an inseparable whole. Financial statements are presented in accordance with one of the following systems (PCG 2023 Art. 810-7, Book 3 Models of annual accounts, Chapter 2): a basic system, a simplified or abridged system, and

Table 4 Financial statements requirements

	Large non-listed undertakings	Medium undertakings	Small undertakings	Micro-undertakings
Max. total balance sheet		20,000,000 €	6,000,000 €	350,000 €
Max. revenues		40,000,000 €	12,000,000 €	700,000 €
Av. nb of employees		250	50	10
Condition of classification the category		If less than two of the above thresholds are reached	If less than two of the above thresholds are reached	If less than two of the above thresholds are reached
System to apply	**Basic system–developed system in option**	**Simplified system**	**Simplified system (financial statements and simplified notes)**	**Simplified system (notes are not required)**

a developed system. The method of presentation of accounts depends on the size of the companies and their tax profile[16] (Table 4):

- The simplified or abridged system is applicable to micro- and small undertakings (cerfa 2033[17]).
- The basic system is applicable to the undertakings that exceed the thresholds set for presentation with an abridged system (cerfa 2050).
- The developed system is applicable to larger undertakings. This system is optional and little used. The entity has the option of drawing up more detailed documents than those corresponding to the minimum obligation to which it is subject. Thus, it can adopt the developed system which provides for documents highlighting the analysis of basic data in order to better inform its management.[18]

Standard balance sheet templates are provided (PCG 2023 Art. 821-1 to 823-1). The presentation is carried out either in the form of a table or in the form of a list (PCG 2023 Art. 810-2). In the basic system, there is a choice between a table (PCG 2023 Art. 821-1) or a list presentation, before distribution (PCG 2023 Art. 821-2). In the abridged system, there is a choice between a balance sheet in table before distribution (PCG 2023 Art. 822-1) or balance sheet in table after dividend distribution (PCG 2023 Art. 822-2). In the developed system, a balance sheet in table before and after dividend distribution is presented (PCG 2023 Art. 823-1). A presentation in the form of a table is a horizontal layout, and a presentation in the form of a list is a vertical layout.

---

[16] https://www.plancomptable.com/comptes_annuels/comptes_annuels.htm.

[17] https://entreprendre.service-public.fr/vosdroits/R52884.

[18] https://www.pcg.fr/recueil-3123200-plan-comptable-ss-sec-2-modele-de-compte-de-resultat.php.

Some distinctions remain with respect to Directive 2013/34: the possibility of distinguishing current and noncurrent assets is not emphasized in the French statement, as the presentation has favoured the traditional process of reading down a balance with increasing liquidity on the assets side and increasing chargeability on the equity and liabilities side. Nevertheless, the short-term financial debt is included in the financial debt. However, the PCG requires the publication of the short-term share of financial debt in a footnote to the balance sheet and in the notes. It is worth to note that debts are classified according to their term at the time of debt contraction but not according to their remaining term. The definitions of assets and stocks (PCG 2023 Art. 211-6 and 211-7, respectively) specify the long-term characteristics of an asset and the alignment of the stocks on the operating cycle.

Standard profit and loss account templates are also provided (PCG 2023 Art. 821-3 to 823-2). Income and expenses, classified by category, must be presented either in the form of tables or in the form of a list (CC L123-13, PCG 2023 Art. 810-2). This applies both to the basic system, (PCG Art. 821-3, 821-4) and to the abridged system (PCG 2023 Art. 822-3, 822-4). In the developed system, the profit and loss account takes the form of a table (PCG 2023 Art. 823-2).

The presentation of the profit and loss account breaks down the expenses by nature. Indeed, the presentation with a breakdown of expenses by function is not proposed in the PCG. A statement of performance exists in the developed system (in notes) in addition to but not instead of the profit and loss account: it is the profit and loss account performance indicators (*Tableau des Soldes Intermédiaires de Gestion*).

The structure of the accounting statements is also concerned by a high level of standardization, and any varying layout is forbidden: "The balance sheet, the profit and loss account and the notes must include as many headings and items as necessary to give a true image of the assets, the financial situation and the result of the entity" (CC L123-15), and "The balance sheet, the profit and loss account and the notes are detailed in headings and items. They present at least the headings and items set out in the models appearing in Articles 821-1 to 832-13" (PCG 2023 Art. 810-3).

Temporal comparison must be made easy as "Each of the balance sheet and profit and loss account items includes an indication of the figure relating to the corresponding item for the previous year" (CC L123-15 and PCG 2023 Art. 810-3).

3.3 Other (Only) Relevant Issues

3.3.1 Notes to the Financial Statements (Annexe)

Notes are standardized as well, and "The information is presented in the notes to the financial statements in the order in which the items to which they relate are presented in the balance sheet and the profit and loss account" (PCG 2023 Art. 832-1).

The required content of the notes depends on the category of the legal entity (see Table 3). This is required in many places in the PCG (PCG 2023 Art. 810-8, Chapter

III, and L.123-25 of the CC, PCG 2023 Art. 831-1, Art. L123-16 of the CC, PCG 2023 Art. 831-2 to 832-20, and PCG 2023 Art. 833-1). Those develop in 18 pages listing the headers of the required notes.

A list of significant information is required for companies subject to the simplified tax system: an abridged version (PCG 2023 Art. 831-2 to 831-1). Principles and accounting methods must be disclosed by entities (PCG 2023 Art. 832-2 to 832-14). "The accounting methods used and the structure of the balance sheet and profit and loss account cannot be changed from one financial year to another. If changes occur, they are described and justified in the notes and reported, where applicable, in the auditors' report" (CC Art. L123-17).

PCG 2023 Chapter 4 of Title 8 of Book 3 presents the information to be mentioned in the notes in the form of tables. This is in Articles 841-1 to 841-7 for the basic system and in Articles 842-1 to 842-4 for the developed system; the latter includes:

- Profit and loss account performance indicators—*tableau des soldes intermédiaires de gestion*, which include an item close to the EBITDA, and the value added
- A cash flow estimation—*détermination de la capacité d'autofinancement*
- A cash flow statement and a financing table—*modèle de tableau des emplois et des ressources*, which can be drawn with a horizontal or vertical layout (PCG 2023 Art. 810-7).

When the entities come under the abridged system or when they use the developed system, the content of the notes is modified accordingly, without this resulting in a reduction of the information necessary for the financial statements to a true and fair view (PCG 2023 Art. 810-7). [19]

3.3.2 Management Report (Rapport de gestion)

Information relating to the management report can be found in the French CC Book 2 Title 2, Chapter 5, Section 3, and Book 2 Title 3, Chapter 2, Section 1 (Art. L225-100-1 to L225-102-1 and L232-1[20] modified by law no.2018-727 of August 10, 2018—Art. 55 (V)). Its content is specified in Article L225-100-1-I; it includes:

(i) An objective and exhaustive analysis of the development of the company's business, results, and financial situation, in particular its debt situation, with regard to the volume and complexity of the business.
(ii) To the extent that the information is necessary in order to understand the development of the business, the results or the situation of the company, the key performance indicators of a financial nature, and, where applicable, the key

[19] An introduction with some versions of the templates is available in English at: https://www.plancomptable.com/en/french-notes-to-financial-statements.htm.

[20] https://www.legifrance.gouv.fr/codes/article_lc/LEGIARTI000042339777/

performance indicators of a nonfinancial nature relating to the specific activity of the company, including information relating to environmental and personnel matters.

(iii) A description of the main risks and uncertainties facing the company.

(iv) Where relevant to the valuation of its assets, liabilities, financial position, and profit or loss, the indications of its objectives and policy regarding hedging; this applies to each main category of planned transactions for which hedge accounting is used, as well as on the company's exposure to price, credit, liquidity, and cash flow risks. These indications include the company's use of financial instruments.

A nonfinancial performance statement is inserted in the management report when the balance sheet total or the turnover and the number of employees exceed the thresholds set by decree of the *Conseil d'Etat* (CC Art. L225-102-1). The undertakings included in the scope of the provision are those that exceed two of the following three thresholds: a balance sheet total of 20 M€, a net turnover of 40 M€, and an average number of 250 permanent employees (Decree 2017-1265 of August 9, 2017).

Commercial undertakings that are small businesses are exempted from the obligation to issue a management report (CC Art. L232-1 (IV)). Small undertakings are those which do not bypass two of the three following thresholds: a total balance sheet of 4 M€, net revenues of 8 M€, and an average number of 50 employees (see Table 1). Those thresholds are applied at each year-end. France has not used the option in the Directive, Article 23 (2), to exempt medium-sized groups.

3.3.3 The Statement of Cash Flow (Tableau des flux de trésorerie)

In France, according to Directive 2013/34/EU and as it was the case before, the statement of cash flow is not compulsory for individual accounts, as shown in Table 3 (ANC 2014-03). However, the notes of the developed system include a uses-resources table (PCG 2023 Art. 810-7).

3.3.4 Consolidated Financial Statements and Reports (États financiers et rapports consolidés)

In the EU directive, Chapter 6, articles 21 to 29, presents consolidated financial statements and reports. In France, the accounting regulations for listed consolidated companies are based on IFRS. The accounting regulations for unlisted consolidated companies that do not opt for IFRS are exposed in the CC Art. L233-16 to 233-28 and R233-3 to R233-16 (regulatory part of the CC) and in the ANC regulation 2020-01 (previously CRC 99-02). French regulations on consolidated accounts are very detailed, much more than those appearing in the European directive. A major difference relates to the size of firms consolidated.

The thresholds are different for medium-sized groups in France. It applies to any group of companies that outruns one of the following two thresholds: more than 250 employees, a balance sheet of more than 24 M€, and/or a turnover of more than 48 M€ (CC R233-16).

The group's accounting methods are defined in the ANC 2014-03 regulations and provision: the benchmark methods provided for in ANC 2014-03 regulation relating to the general chart of accounts are benchmark methods for the preparation of consolidated accounts, unless this regulation provides otherwise (ANC 2020-01 Art. 271-3). For entities under significant influence, the equity method must be used (ANC 2020-01 Art. 221-1). The proportional consolidation method is not authorized in the case of significant influence in France.

In ANC 2020-10, Section 8, the statement of cash flow, presents general principles (Art. 282-41) and methods of presentation for the statement of cash flow (Art. 282-42). Two statements of cash flow models (ANC 2020-10) are available: a statement of cash flow model based on the net income of consolidated entities (Art. 282-43) and a statement of cash flow presentation model based on the operating result of consolidated entities (Art. 282-44). Those are the indirect and direct methods.

Information relating specifically to the consolidated management report can be found in the French Commercial Book 2 Title 3, Chapter 3, Section 3, for consolidated accounts (Art. L233-16 to L233-28). Its content is specified in Article L225-100-1-II. When the company draws up consolidated financial statements, the consolidated management report gives an account of the information for all the companies included in the consolidation.

3.4 *Simplifications for Small- and Medium-Sized Entities and Exemptions for Micro-undertakings*

3.4.1 General Provisions

The European directive is based on the "think small first principle" and "should ensure that the requirements for small undertakings are to a large extent harmonised throughout the Union" (para. 10). Moreover, directive precises "It should be possible for Member States to exempt micro-undertakings from certain obligations applying to small undertakings that would impose excessive administrative burdens on them" (para. 13).

Some entities are exempted from the publication of financial statements. Those are the companies whose turnover (excluding taxes, adjusted, if necessary, in proportion to the operating time during the reference year) of the preceding calendar year or the penultimate year, does not exceed:

(i) 188,700 € in the case of companies whose main business is to sell goods, objects, supplies, and foodstuffs to take away or consume on site or to provide accommodation, excluding direct rental or indirect residential premises furnished or intended to be rented furnished, other than those mentioned in 2° and 3° of III of Article 1407

(ii) 77,700 € in the case of other companies

Companies with no employee and in process of ceasing their activities benefit from the same exemption. However, they have to keep a "light accounting" including: a quarterly estimation of their revenues, a cash receipts book, chronologically recorded, track of the amount, and origin of receipts (identity of the client or the agent company and of the method of payment (check, cash, or others) and references of supporting documents (numbering of invoices, notes). Merchants and retailers must also keep a record of purchase, chronologically summarized by year with the details of the purchase information: method of payment (check, cash, etc.) and references of supporting documents (invoices, notes, etc.).

3.4.2 Simplifications and Exemptions of the Required Layouts May Be Made Available

Small businesses may, under conditions set by a regulation of the Accounting Standards Authority, adopt a simplified presentation of their annual accounts (CC Art. L123-16). Medium-sized companies may, under conditions set by a regulation of the Accounting Standards Authority, adopt a simplified presentation of their profit and loss account (CC Art. L123-16). The current condition is set in CC Art. D 123-200 (see Table 1).

Micro-undertakings may declare that the annual accounts they file will not be made public (CC Art. L232-25). Small businesses can request that the profit and loss account not be made public (CC Art. L232-25). Medium-sized companies may request that only a simplified presentation of their balance sheet and their notes be made public (CC Art. L232-25).

3.4.3 Simplifications and Exemptions of the Notes to the Financial Statements

Legal persons having the status of merchant and placed on option or automatically under the simplified tax regime may submit abridged notes (CC Art. L123-25 and PCG 2023 Art. 831-1). An abridged model for legal persons subject to the simplified tax system is proposed in PCG 2023 Art. 831-1 and 831-2 with information in the form of tables.

Micro-undertakings (. . .) are not required to draw up notes (CC Art. L123-16-1). The micro-undertakings may not draw up notes to their annual accounts. Information is to be provided following their balance sheet (PCG 2023 Art. 810-9).

Small businesses may, under conditions set by a regulation of the Accounting Standards Authority, adopt a simplified presentation of their annual accounts

(CC Art. L123-16), and medium-sized undertakings may request that only a simplified presentation of their balance sheet and their notes be made public (CC Art. L232-25).

The publication requirements are summarized in Table 5, except for the micro-undertakings under the threshold and for listed companies employing IFRS. It exposes the legal form that companies are required to complete according to their situation. All those certified forms are freely available online.

4 Valuation Approaches

There is no such thing as the definition of measurement bases in France. There are however multiple potential approaches to valuation. This is reflected in the fact that the concept of measurement bases in the directive is translated to "valuation approaches" in the French translation. The various approaches to value provide with the conventional vocabulary here below, where defined terms appear in bold characters:

- The **gross value** *(valeur brute)* of an asset is its entry value when recognised in the balance sheet or its revaluation value.
- The **net book value** *(valeur nette comptable)* of an asset corresponds to its gross value less accumulated depreciation and impairment.
- An asset is impaired when its current value is inferior to its net book value. The **current value** *(valeur actuelle)* is the higher of the market value or the value in use.
- The **market value** *(valeur de marché)* is the amount that could be obtained, on the closing date, from the sale of an asset during a transaction concluded under normal market conditions, net of exit costs.
- The **value in use** *(valeur d'usage)* of an asset is the value of the future economic benefits expected from its use and disposal. These more likely correspond to the estimate of the discounted net cash flows. For activities where the expected cash flows alone do not reflect the expected future economic benefits, relevant additional elements are taken into account.

The cost approach is prevalent in initial valuations, with the exceptions of bartered assets or specific arrangements such as life annuity rents (PCG, 2023, Chapter 1, CC 233-22). Most fixed assets are initially recognized at costs, which include acquisition costs or production costs. However, when there is no acquisition (free or bartered asset), market value is the compulsory reference value. Acquisition costs also designate, for goods and securities received as contributions in kind by the beneficiary company, the values appearing in the contribution agreement. Such contributions are treated as exchanges (barter). However, the recognition is conditional to the fact that the transaction must bear some commercial substance, which exists when it impacts future cash flows. When a fixed asset cannot be valued at

Table 5 Conditions for producing a simplified version of accounts, and their specific forms, designated by a number as by French law

	Large non-listed undertakings	Medium undertakings	Small undertakings	Micro-undertakings
Max. total balance sheet		20,000,000 €	6,000,000 €	350,000 €
Max. revenues		40,000,000 €	12,000,000 €	700,000 €
Av. nb of employees		250	50	10
System to apply	**Basic system**	**Simplified system**	**Simplified system**	**Simplified system**
Balance sheet—form required				
Assets	Form N° 2050	2033 A	2033 A	2033 A
Liabilities	2051	2033 A	2033 A	2033 A
Profit and loss account—form required				2033 B
Revenues and expenses	2051 and 2053	2033 B	2033 B	
Notes—form required				
Table of fixed assets, sales, and acquisitions	2054	2033 C	2033 C	
Fixed asset, variation in values	2054 BIS			
Fixed assets: depreciation and impairment	2055	2033 C	2033 C	
Provisions	2056	2033 D	2033 D	
Statement of maturities of debts, receivables, and payables	2057			
Net income to taxable income	2058 A	2033 D (derogatory depreciation)	2033 D (derogatory depreciation)	
Carry back	2058 B	2033 D	2033 D	
Allocation of income	2058			
Gain and loss and sales	2059 A			
Short-term gain on sales and in M&A	2059 B			
Long-term value losses	2059 C			
Special reserve for long-term capital gains	2059 D			
Added value of the year	2059 E	2033 E	2033 E	
Social capital	2059 F	2033 F	2033 F	
Table of subsidiaries and equity interests	2059 G	2033 G	2033 G	
Possibility to request confidentiality on			Profit and loss account	All accounts

(continued)

Table 5 (continued)

	Large non-listed undertakings	Medium undertakings	Small undertakings	Micro-undertakings
		Simplified balance sheet and notes		
Developed system				
Table of performance indicator	Optional			
Cash flow estimation	Optional			
Uses and resources table (vertical or horizontal)	Optional			
Management report	CC L225-100	CC 232-1		
Nonfinancial performance statement	Required	Required	Thresholds are those of Table 1	
Other reports				
Report of the supervisory board	SA			
Report on internal control	SA et SCA			
5Y earnings	SA et SCA			

market value, it is estimated at net book value of the sold asset. In any case, subsidies have no incidence on the estimated costs.

In general, an **acquisition cost** includes the purchase costs, taxes, tariffs, and all attributable costs and decommissioning costs (for fixed assets). It is permitted to include loan cost. Costs are allocated to the value of the asset from the date at which the management made the decision to acquire or produce it. The recognition of cost related to the effective use of the asset or its reuse is prohibited. Nevertheless, maintenance expenditures subject to multi-year major maintenance programs or major overhauls pursuant to laws, regulations, or consistent practices of the entity must be accounted for from the outset as a separate component of fixed assets. This supposes that no provision for major maintenance or major overhauls has been recorded.

In general, assets are depreciated or amortized. The base amount is the gross value minus the residual value. The **residual value** is the amount, net of expected disposal costs, that an entity would obtain from the disposal of the asset on the market at the end of its use. It is a fictious value that has no other use than the calculation of the depreciation. Depreciation of an asset begins on its first usage date, which generally corresponds to the commissioning of the asset. Depreciation methods must be consistent across similar assets and must reflect the consumption of the expected economic benefits. Linear depreciation is the default method, but small undertakings can adopt the useful life defined in the Tax Code.

Unless for goodwill for which it is systematic, an impairment test is conducted when there is an indication of a value loss (PCG 2023, Art. 214-15). When it is the case, the impairment test consists in comparing the net book value to the present value of the benefits expected to be generated by the asset. If the former is superior to the latter, a depreciation is recorded that is equal to the difference in the two values. Indications of loss in value can be externally driven (market value, important changes, interest rate, yield rate, etc.) or internally driven (obsolescence, physical alteration, change in usage modes, performance below expectations, etc.) (Art. 214-16). An exception is that of inventories, for which a latent loss leads to the recognition of a provision (Art. 214-21). For those assets, there is no possible profit from revaluation because, in general, French accounting law is very attached to the principle of prudence. Therefore, in the case of a revaluation, potential gains are not recorded, whereas potential losses are. It is different when financial assets are concerned and in the case of occasional revaluations.

Fixed securities follow the same rules as those applied to nonfinancial assets, unless they equate the value of a partial transfer of asset, in which case their value is that written in the transfer report. In case of transactions, the first in, first out method is applied. Assets that are neither tangibles nor intangibles or inventories are revaluated on yearly basis and depreciated even when the change is reversible. Equity interest (representing more than 10% of the equity) is revaluated at their usage value. Securities that provide control are evaluated as a portion of equity (before distribution and elimination of intercompany transfers), plus the portion of the goodwill. The gain or loss on sales on equity and investment securities are respectively recorded as revenues or expenses. Other securities that are neither fixed nor equity interests are kept at their purchase price, and their sale equates a reduction in equity. Non-listed securities are recorded at their negotiation value. However, a temporary loss on other securities than equity or fixed interest securities may remain unrecognized when compensated by gain on sales. Instruments used for hedging are not subject to impairment tests.

Art. 214-27 of the PCG 2023 authorizes an important exception. Adjustments to value of fixed tangible and financial assets are occasionally possible, under the will of the entity, or in order to comply with regulation. In the case of such revaluation, the difference between the present value and the net book value is not recorded in the profit and loss account, but it directly affects shareholders' equity. The value differential can compensate losses only if it has been previously integrated in the capital. This possibility is applicable to individual and consolidated statements (CC Art. L123-18). There are however two requirements: (1) depreciation and amortization schemes must be adjusted to the revaluated amounts, and (2) the revaluation must apply to all noncurrent tangible and financial assets. The revaluation of intangible assets is prohibited. In consolidated statement, this includes leased assets. Also, if the revaluation applies to consolidated statements, it does not have to be applied to individual statements. However, within the consolidation process, the revaluation should apply to all consolidated entities. Notably, there is no clear definition of what is an occasional revaluation, and recurrent revaluations are possible. Finally, this article has not been intended to match the directive; it was already existing as Chapter 5, par. 350-1 of PCG 1999.

In individual statements, revaluations affect taxes because revaluations are recorded in form 2058-A (line WQ), where they increase the taxable earnings or reduce the existing tax credit. This is not the case for consolidated statements that are neutral to tax. Nevertheless, when the practice is different in individual and consolidated statements, a differed tax is recorded. An exception to the law was a provision of the *Loi des finances 2020-1721*, which allowed to neutralize the taxation of value differentials in case of revaluations. The aim was to improve shareholders' equity and applied to all revaluations conducted between December 31, 2020, and December 31, 2022. The charges have to be equally spread between 5 and 15 years, depending on the kind of depreciable asset concerned. The valuation differential is then recorded in shareholders' equity (account 1052). The remaining value becomes immediately taxable if it is sold. Interestingly, the valuation differential can be transferred to distributable reserves (1) immediately after the sale of the corresponding asset or (2) at the pace of the depreciated amounts. In any case, it is part of the basis of calculation for employee participation and to assess the threshold of half of the social capital.

Table 6 provides an overview of the accounting methods available in the PCG for various assets and liabilities.

5 Conclusion

French accounting is contrasted like France is. On the one hand, the French accounting standard-setting process is a state issue in a centralized country, having sought uniformity of trading practices since the seventeenth century. On the other hand, major contributions of French accounting have been conducted to answer the pressures exercised by citizens on the government. Two revolutions characterize it, the second still being in process.

The first revolution in French accounting was the issuance of the Commercial Code, as a companion to the Civil Code; it made people (economic actors) equal in front of law. The method to reach its goal was codification. The second revolution started 50 years ago and has taken an important step recently with the PACTE law (2019). It placed human beings at the center of a society, and companies as participants, to avoid any endeavor to free ride a society and its environment. This makes social accounting a hallmark of French accounting (Mattessich, 2008 p.11).

In between those two revolutions, much effort was invested in building a "master chart of accounts," the Plan Comptable Général (PCG). As Mattessich would describe it: when not concentrating on changing their world (to make it a better place) and building accounting theories for that purpose, French standard-setters concentrated on theories of accounts. This is the category of debates where Directive 2013/34/EU belongs, which was not perceived as being very different from the fourth and the seventh directives which it superseded (FEE, 2014). Nevertheless,

Table 6 The accounting methods available in the PCG for various assets and liabilities

Item	Value at initial recognition	Value adjustments and location of their recognition	Comments/ forthcoming changes model/method used
Assets	213-1 and sub. Acquisition cost or production cost or market value (free of charge or bartered assets 213-3 and 213-4) with attributable costs (incl. loan) Price stipulation (life annuity assets) or estimation (life annuity assets) 213-5	212-7 Constantly renewed assets can be kept at a fixed value 214-1 When useful life is defined: depreciation and impairment 214-2 When indefinite useful life: impairment only 214-15 Impairment if there is evidence of a loss of value 214-19 Impairment reversals are permitted, except for goodwill 214-27 Revaluation of tangible and financial asset is possible, through equity but cannot compensate losses. Revenues from gains on sales are distributable	212-5 Leasing is expensed during the contract, recognized after exercise of the option 212-6 Nonmaterial assets must be expensed When put out of action, fixed assets 213-3 Barter is recognized unless the exchange transaction does not have commercial substance, or the market value of the asset received or the asset given cannot be measured reliably Price stipulation is calculated in reference to a legal index 214-9 Non-dissociable assets are recognized together and depreciated as one
Intangible assets	213-22 Acquisition cost and attributable costs 213-27 Production and preparation costs, internally generated asset	Profit and loss account	Recognition is permitted, under conditions identical to those of IFRS. It is the reference method PCG 212-3. Installation costs: Permitted but expensed is the reference method
Software	611-2 and subs/production costs (conception, code, tests, and notice)	Profit and loss account	611-2 Software for commercial use are recognized if their profitability can be demonstrated
Internet sites	612-2 Cost of development and production is the reference method	Profit and loss account	
Development costs	213-22 Acquisition cost and attributable costs 213-27 Production and preparation costs, internally generated asset	214-3 Amortized according to project life. When project life is unknown, default horizon is 5 years	Recognition is permitted, under conditions identical to those of IFRS, but unlike IFRS recognition is not

(continued)

Table 6 (continued)

Item	Value at initial recognition	Value adjustments and location of their recognition	Comments/ forthcoming changes model/method used
		Goodwill has an indefinite useful life. If refuted, amortization over 10 years. The latter is also the simplified method for all goodwill of small undertakings When useful life is indefinite, an impairment test is conducted yearly, even in the absence of evidence of loss of value Profit and loss (operating depreciation and impairment) No upward revaluation	compulsory. It is the reference method PCG 212-3-1. Development costs that cannot be separated from research are expensed PCG 212-3-2 Acquired goodwill as "commercial ground" is recognized PCG 212-3-3 Non-separable assets (brands, mastheads, etc.) are excluded CC R123-188 Extractive activities development costs (as of Mining Code L111-1) are treated as development costs
Internally generated intangible assets	213-22 Acquisition cost and attributable costs (acquired assets) Inclusion of loan costs permitted (213-28)	Profit and loss (operating depreciation and impairment) No upward revaluation	213-27 Historical costs The cost of an internally generated intangible asset that qualifies for recognition under Section 212-3/1 includes all directly attributable expenditures that are necessary to create, produce, and prepare the asset for its intended use by management
Acquired goodwill	Acquisition costs (out of business combinations)	Has an indefinite useful life but this can be refuted. An amortization is that of usage time or 10 years. The latter is also the simplified method for small undertakings. When useful life is indefinite, an impairment test is conducted yearly, even in the absence of evidence of loss of value	Required, PCG 212-3-2

(continued)

Table 6 (continued)

Item	Value at initial recognition	Value adjustments and location of their recognition	Comments/ forthcoming changes model/method used
Fees paid for the transfer of a sport player	613-3 Book value of the asset (acquired assets)	Maximum useful life of 5 years Yearly impairment test comparing market value to book value In the absence of market value, a usage value is permitted	613-3 The market for sport player transfer is not considered as an active market The transfer has no impact on P&L Contract renewal is between the player and the club and cannot be recognized 613-9 Perceived fees are revenues
GHG emissions quotas and recognized energy efficiency certificates	*Acquisition cost*: acquired quotas and certificates (stocks) Null value: quotas allocated by state *Production costs*: certificates obtained or to be obtained	214-22 Prices and sales projections are forecasted to estimate the need for an impairment Gain or loss on sales is recognized in operating profit 616-18 An asset (stock) is recognized if the energy savings achieved are greater than the energy savings obligations.	615-4 and 616-2 and subs. Obligation is recognized as a liability
Tangible/fixed assets	213-8 Acquisition costs and attributable costs, decommissioning costs Inclusion of loan costs permitted (213-9) Production costs (capitalized production) Inclusion of share of depreciation permitted Acquisition cost: attributable share to depths (quarries)	Profit and loss Impaired like tangible assets (quarries)	Inclusion of attributable costs starts when the purchase decision has been made (213-10) Production cost calculation is similar to those of inventories Tangible or fixed assets acquired for security reasons or related to environment do not comply with the definition of an asset (because they do not generate future benefits)but they are recognized because they create an underlying condition for other assets.
Inventories	213-31 Acquisition cost	214-22 Prices and sales projections are	213-33 Non-fungible stocks are estimated

(continued)

Table 6 (continued)

Item	Value at initial recognition	Value adjustments and location of their recognition	Comments/ forthcoming changes model/method used
	Production cost If the two above are not relevant, market value Loan costs may be included 617-3 Acquisition cost: attributable share to material (quarries)	forecasted to estimate the need for an impairment 613-7 Forward-looking value based on material production costs (quarries)	individually 213-34 Allowed cost formulas for fungible stocks: weighted average costs or FIFO LIFO is forbidden 213-35 Production costs can use either standard cost method or retail price method and include SG&A and fixed costs 214-22 Revaluation unit by unit, category by category. Hedging is excluded from valuation Potential losses are the object of provisions for risks
Payment entitlements (agriculture)	618-3 Null value: attributed payments 618-4 Acquisition cost: acquired rights		618-5 Out of balance sheet accounting
Issued or acquired tokens	Subscription price: 619-3 Issued tokens are like financial assets, recognized as debts or income collected in advance Book value: in case of transfer of a token as intangible asset	Market value 619-8 and 619-12 Valuation difference for a debt is recorded as a payable (if negative) or a receivable (if positive) Adjustment in the P&L: cancellation	Tokens without obligations are accounted as revenues Some tokens have financial assets characteristics and follow the same principles Other tokens are intangible assets When associated to a bundle of rights, an analysis dictates the specific rights recognition Token issuers have specific notes requirements
Public service concession (exclusive right)	621-6 Book value in concessionaire's accounts	Technical and nullity depreciation	The asset value is recognized in equity
Long-term contract	622-2 Completion method of % of completion method	Potential losses are provisioned	

(continued)

Table 6 (continued)

Item	Value at initial recognition	Value adjustments and location of their recognition	Comments/ forthcoming changes model/method used
Financial asset			
Fixed securities Financial assets	221-1 like 213-1 to 213-8	In comparison with market value (listed) or probable negotiation value (not listed)	The entry cost of the securities received in return for a partial contribution of assets by the contributing company must be equal to the value of the contributions retained in the contribution agreement 221-7 In the case of a temporary and abnormal loss, depreciation is not required. Hedging assets are excluded
Equity interests above 10% of share capital (listed or not)	Acquisition cost or market value	221-3 Value in use In comparison with market value (listed) or probable negotiation value (not listed)	
Investment titles	Transferor side: selling price Assignee side: acquisition price	222-1 Gain and losses in P&L (derogatory)	
Forward financial instruments	Market value or model	Hedging: profit and loss account Isolated open position: potential losses as assets, potential gains as liabilities Only potential gains are not in profit and loss account	Cash payment, margin calls, and security deposits are recognized The nominal amounts of contracts, whether or not they are intended to be settled over time, are not recognized in the balance sheet.
Transactions involving entities under common control	Book value if no change in control Acquisition cost or book value (entities under common control)	General provisions	
Transactions involving entities under distinct control	Book value if reverse operations Book value and market value otherwise	General provisions	
New entity in the perimeter of consolidation: identifiable assets	Entry value Possible sale value (assets held for sale)	Complies with group accounting method	The entry value corresponds to the price that the acquiring entity would have agreed to pay if it had acquired the assets and liabilities identified separately

(continued)

Table 6 (continued)

Item	Value at initial recognition	Value adjustments and location of their recognition	Comments/ forthcoming changes model/method used
Insurance contracts portfolio	Technical provisions minus NPV of acquired rights and existing obligations (NPV at fair value)		
Equity interests with exclusive control	Book value Fair value	A global impairment is recorded when equivalent value is inferior to acquisition price Value in use	The equity value of the securities of a company under exclusive control is equal to the share of equity corresponding to the securities, increased by the amount of the goodwill attached to these securities Forward-looking values are not authorized
Provisions	321-5 and 323-2 Best estimation of the present value of the expected future outflows required to settle the obligation, before effect on corporate tax	Profit and loss	313-1 Regulated provisions are refined by higher law

Directive 2013/34/EU adopted some elements of language like "measurement bases" similar to that of IFRS that were not object of a straightforward translation, because there is no equivalent concept in France. For the inventors of the metric system, the concept of balance sheet items measurement is hardly thinkable. By reference to the international system of units of measurement, measurements are defined by constants.

However, complying with Directive 2013/34/EU is not a menial engagement, as France has continuously and actively participated in the construction of Europe and the subsequent harmonization and convergence of accounting systems that critical sizes require. Even though some issues in the directive may affect the traditional and long-lived representations French people have of companies, as it modifies the categories, names, and definitions and also the views on control in the consolidation process, the harmonization is conducted.

It may be too early to understand the impact of the recent changes in regulations, but small- and medium-sized companies have experienced a reduction in their obligations, including the possibility not to consolidate. This was wished to safeguard a dynamic fabric of SMEs within a sovereign legal system of equal rights and obligations. Like in many other European countries, sovereignty is preserved with two sets of national GAAPS, one for individual companies and another for consolidation, which converge toward Directive 2013/34/UE and IFRS, respectively. With upcoming changes moving toward entity theory rather than proprietary theory, and extending accounting scope to social, environmental, and governance issues, the best in European directives and their impact on national accounting is yet to come.

Bibliography

AMF publications are available at: https://www.amf-france.org/en/

ANC. (2022). Principes sous-jacents à l'élaboration par l'ANC des normes comptables françaises (comptes annuels et comptes consolidés). Available at: https://www.anc.gouv.fr/files/live/sites/anc/files/contributed/ANC/1_Normes_françaises/Recommandations/RECO2022/Principes-elaboration-des-normes-comptables.pdf

ANC 2014-03. (2019). Available at: https://www.anc.gouv.fr/files/live/sites/anc/files/contributed/ANC/1_Normes_fran%c3%a7aises/Reglements/Recueils/PCG_Janvier2019/PCG_2019.pdf

ANC 2020-01. (2020). Available at: https://www.anc.gouv.fr/files/live/sites/anc/files/contributed/ANC/1_Normes_françaises/Reglements/2020/Reglt_2020_01/Reglt_2020_01_version_recueil.pdf

Burlaud, A., & Colasse, B. (2011). International accounting standardisation: Is politics back? *Accounting in Europe, 8*(1), 23–47. https://EconPapers.repec.org/RePEc:taf:acceur:v:8:y:2011:i:1:p:23-47

Chatriot, A. (2012). La réforme de l'entreprise : Du contrôle ouvrier à l'échec du projet modernisateur. *Vingtième Siècle. Revue d'histoire, 114*, 183–197. https://doi.org/10.3917/vin.114.0183

Code de commerce available at: https://www.legifrance.gouv.fr/codes/id/LEGITEXT000005634379/

Coquery, N., & Praquin, N. (2008). Règlement des faillites et pratiques judiciaires. *Histoire & mesure, XXIII-1*, 43–83.

de Cambourg, P. (2019). Garantir la pertinence et la qualité de l'information extra-financière des entreprises: une ambition et un atout pour une Europe durable. Rapport remis au ministère en charge de l'économie en mai 2019. https://www.anc.gouv.fr/cms/news/rapport-de-cambourg-sur-les-informations-extra-financieres%2D%2Dde-cambourg

Décret n° 2008-1354 du 18 décembre 2008 relatif aux critères permettant de déterminer la catégorie d'appartenance d'une entreprise pour les besoins de l'analyse statistique et économique. https://www.legifrance.gouv.fr/loda/id/JORFTEXT000019961059?init=true&page=1&query=2008-1354&searchField=ALL&tab_selection=all

Décret n° 2015-903 du 23 juillet 2015 relatif aux obligations comptables des commerçants. https://www.legifrance.gouv.fr/jorf/id/JORFTEXT000031644717?init=true&page=1&query=2015-903&searchField=ALL&tab_selection=all

Décret n° 2017-1265 du 9 août 2017 pris pour l'application de l'ordonnance n° 2017-1180 du 19 juillet 2017 relative à la publication d'informations non financières par certaines grandes entreprises et certains groupes d'entreprises. https://www.legifrance.gouv.fr/loda/id/JORFTEXT000035401863?init=true&page=1&query=2017-1265&searchField=ALL&tab_selection=all

Décret n° 2019-539 du 29 mai 2019 portant application de l'article 47 de la loi n° 2019-486 du 22 mai 2019 relative à la croissance et la transformation des entreprises. https://www.legifrance.gouv.fr/loda/id/JORFTEXT000038529289?init=true&page=1&query=2019-539&searchField=ALL&tab_selection=all

Décret n° 2020-101 du 7 février 2020 fixant les modalités de calcul du seuil d'effectif salarié dans le code de comme. https://www.legifrance.gouv.fr/loda/id/JORFTEXT000041547677?init=true&page=1&query=2020-101+&searchField=ALL&tab_selection=all

Directive 2006/43/EC of the European Parliament and of the Council of 17 May 2006 on statutory audits of annual accounts and consolidated accounts, amending Council Directives 78/660/EEC and 83/349/EEC and repealing Council Directive 84/253/EEC (Text with EEA relevance). https://eur-lex.europa.eu/legal-content/EN/TXT/?uri=CELEX%3A32006L0043&qid=1658055114721

Directive 2013/34/EU of the European Parliament and of the Council of 26 June 2013 on the annual financial statements, consolidated financial statements and related reports of certain types of undertakings, amending Directive 2006/43/EC of the European Parliament and of the Council and repealing Council Directives 78/660/EEC and 83/349/EEC Text with EEA relevance. https://eur-lex.europa.eu/legal-content/EN/TXT/?uri=CELEX%3A32013L0034&qid=1658055071346

Directive 2014/95/EU of the European Parliament and of the Council of 22 October 2014 amending Directive 2013/34/EU as regards disclosure of non-financial and diversity information by certain large undertakings and groups Text with EEA relevance. https://eur-lex.europa.eu/legal-content/EN/TXT/?uri=CELEX%3A32014L0095

FEE Federation of European Accountants. (2014). Factsheet: the June 2013 Directive.

Fourth Council Directive 78/660/EEC of 25 July 1978 based on Article 54 (3) (g) of the Treaty on the annual accounts of certain types of companies. https://eur-lex.europa.eu/legal-content/FR/ALL/?uri=celex:31978L0660

Garnier, P. (1947). *La comptabilité, algèbre du droit et d'observation des sciences économiques*. Dunod. 216 pages.

INSEE. (2021). Recovery, but with constraints Economic outlook, Mesurer pour comprendre, https://www.insee.fr/en/statistiques/6010586?sommaire=6010594

Lamrani, E. (2013). Comptabilité politique ou le droit comptable au service de l'intérêt général. *Vie & sciences de l'entreprise, 195-196*, 77–98. https://doi.org/10.3917/vse.195.0077

Le Manh, A. (2017). The role and current status of IFRS in the completion of national accounting rules—Evidence from France. *Accounting in Europe, 14*(1/2), 94–101.

Loi n° 77-769 du 12 juillet 1977 relative au bilan social de l'entreprise. https://www.legifrance.gouv.fr/loda/id/JORFTEXT000000339023?init=true&page=1&query=77-769+&searchField=ALL&tab_selection=all

Loi n° 2001-420 du 15 mai 2001 relative aux nouvelles régulations économiques. https://www.legifrance.gouv.fr/loda/id/JORFTEXT000000223114?init=true&page=1&query=2001-420&searchField=ALL&tab_selection=all

Loi n° 2008-776 du 4 août 2008 de modernisation de l'économie. https://www.legifrance.gouv.fr/loda/id/JORFTEXT000019283050/

Loi n° 2009-967 du 3 août 2009 de programmation relative à la mise en œuvre du Grenelle de l'environnement. https://www.legifrance.gouv.fr/loda/id/JORFTEXT000020949548?init=true&page=1&query=2009-967+&searchField=ALL&tab_selection=all

Loi n° 2010-788 du 12 juillet 2010 portant engagement national pour l'environnement. https://www.legifrance.gouv.fr/loda/id/JORFTEXT000022470434?init=true&page=1&query=2010-788%2C+&searchField=ALL&tab_selection=all

Loi n° 2019-486 du 22 mai 2019 relative à la croissance et la transformation des entreprises. https://www.legifrance.gouv.fr/loda/id/JORFTEXT000038496102/

Loi n° 2022-171 du 14 février 2022 tendant à abroger des lois obsolètes pour une meilleure lisibilité du droit. https://www.legifrance.gouv.fr/loda/id/LEGIARTI000045168380/2022-02-16/

Marteau, D., & Morand, P. (2009). Normes comptables et crise financière. *Report to the French Minister of Economy, Industry and Employment*.

Mattessich, R. (2008). *Two hundred years of accounting research*. Taylor & Francis.

Monéger, J. (2004). De l'ordonnance de Colbert de 1673 sur le commerce au code de commerce français de Septembre 2000 : Réflexion sur l'aptitude du droit économique et commercial à la codification. *Revue internationale de droit économique, XVIII*(2), 171–196. https://doi.org/10.3917/ride.182.0171

Nobes, C. W. (1983). A judgmental International Classification of Financial Reporting Practices. *Journal of Business, Finance and Accounting, Spring, 10*(1), 1–19.

Obert, R. (2016). La construction du droit comptable. http://robert.obert.pagespersoorange.fr/La_construction_du_droit_comptable_2016.pdf

Ordonnance n° 2015-900 du 23 juillet 2015 relative aux obligations comptables des commerçants. https://www.legifrance.gouv.fr/loda/id/JORFTEXT000030920982?init=true&page=1&query=2015-900+&searchField=ALL&tab_selection=all

Ordonnance n° 2017-1180 du 19 juillet 2017 relative à la publication d'informations non financières par certaines grandes entreprises et certains groupes d'entreprises. https://www.legifrance.gouv.fr/loda/id/JORFTEXT000035250851?init=true&page=1&query=+2017-1180+&searchField=ALL&tab_selection=all

Rossignol, J.-L. (1999). Comptabilité et fiscalité : chronique d'une relation impérieuse. *Comptabilité-Contrôle-Audit, 5*(2), 5–24.

Seventh Council Directive 83/349/EEC of 13 June 1983 based on the Article 54 (3) (g) of the Treaty on consolidated accounts. https://eur-lex.europa.eu/legal-content/en/ALL/?uri=CELEX%3A31983L0349

Sudreau, P. (1975). *Rapport du Comité d'étude pour la réforme de l'entreprise, présidé par Pierre Sudreau*. la Documentation française.

Italy

Francesco Giunta and Michele Pisani

1 National Accounting Scenario

In Italy, all companies are required to draw up an annual report. To this end, preparers of such reports should abide by specific rules. As Italy is a country with a civil law system, most of these rules are established by the Civil Code (CC), in particular clauses 2423–2435 ter. These clauses apply to limited companies only, which run industrial, commercial, or service production activities. Banks and, in general, financial companies must comply with a specific regulation, as must assurance companies.

As annual report preparation is a technical issue, the legal regulation is complemented by a set of generally accepted accounting principles (GAAP) issued by the national standard setter, the Italian Accounting Standard Body called *Organismo Italiano di Contabilità* (OIC), established in 2001. In 2014, the OIC's activity was officially recognized by the Italian law (116/2014), which states that the OIC is entrusted to interpret and integrate the law when the law is too generic or does not provide for a specific accounting issue (Avi, 2020).

Annual reports are also important for fiscal administration. The Italian fiscal law is not concerned with financial statement preparation but with the calculation of taxable profits. In this respect, in Italy, the relationship between taxable profit and

F. Giunta
University of Florence, Florence, Italy
e-mail: francesco.giunta@unifi.it

M. Pisani (✉)
University of L'Aquila, L'Aquila, Italy
e-mail: michele.pisani@univaq.it

A. Incollingo, A. Lionzo (eds.), *The European Harmonization of National Accounting Rules*, SIDREA Series in Accounting and Business Administration,
https://doi.org/10.1007/978-3-031-42931-6_5

Table 1 Number of active companies at the end of the financial year 2021: ISTAT Census 2021

Employees	Total	%
Total	4,540,634	
0–9	4,314,961	95.1
10–49	196,855	4.3
50–249	24,526	0.5
250 and more	4292	0.1

accounting profit is based on a logic wherein the former depends on the latter—i.e., the elements represented in the financial statements are relevant for filing tax returns. Simply put, taxable profit depends on accounting profit. Against this backdrop, the income statement hogs the spotlights in the fiscal law, as only income and expenses properly recognized in this statement can be used to compute the taxable profit and taxes to be paid. However, some income and expenses should be adjusted to achieve a specific fiscal administration's purposes. In any case, these adjustments should be carried out in the tax return—that is, outside the income statement (and the annual report in general terms) so as not to affect the accounting results by prematurely revealing its information. In this regard, Italy represents an interesting case study among European countries, with the domestic GAAP oriented toward creditor protection and characterized by a close connection between financial and tax accounting (Gavana et al., 2013).

With regard to the economic and financial reporting system, at the end of the financial year 2021, 4.5 million companies were registered in Italy (ISTAT Census 2021). Table 1 gives an overview of the number of active companies and their employees as per December 31, 2021.

2 Evolution of Accounting Regulations

Growing economic globalization has pushed companies to compete all over the world. Therefore, accounting regulation has developed, becoming more and more supranational owing to IFRS activity. In Italy, alongside a set of domestic accounting principles, IFRS has also caught on, owing to Law 38/2005, which implements EU Regulation 1606/2002 (Adamo et al. 2018; Adamo et al., 2020; Canziani, 2016).

Due to this regulation, listed companies, banks, financial companies, and companies that issue securities traded on the public markets must prepare consolidated as well as separate financial statements according to the international accounting standards. Other companies can apply these standards—for example, subsidiary companies whose parent company prepares their annual reports using IFRS, the companies that draw up the consolidated statements, and the companies included in those statements. Non-listed companies may apply the IFRS standards if their size parameters are above two of the three thresholds provided for by clause 2435 bis of the Italian Civil Code—i.e., when a company's total assets are higher than Euro

Table 2 Size bounds for financial statement simplifications according to the Italian Civil Code

	Small- and medium-sized entities	Micro-entities
Net revenues	EUR 8,800,000	EUR 350,000
Total assets	EUR 4,400,000	EUR 175,000
Average number of employees	50	5

Table 3 The annual report contents for limited companies of different sizes

	Large entities	Small- and medium-sized entities	Micro-entities
Balance sheet	X	X[a]	X[a]
Profit and loss statement	X	X[a]	X[a]
Cash flow statement	X		
Notes	X	X[a]	
Management report	X		
Accounting policies	X	X[a]	X[a]

[a]With simplifications

Table 4 Number of active limited companies on December 31, 2021

Total	1,519,233
Non-listed companies that can apply Italian Civil Code or IFRS	555,803
Non-listed companies that must apply Italian Civil Code and may apply the simplifications of article 2435 bis	963,430
Non-listed companies that must apply Italian Civil Code and may apply the simplifications of article 2435 ter	517,494

4,400,000, sales revenues are higher than Euro 8,800,000, and, on average, during the financial year, employees are higher than 50.

Non-listed companies that fall under two of the three parameters set forth in article 2435 bis (small- and medium-sized entities) must apply the Civil Code and may prepare financial statements with certain simplifications. Further simplifications are provided for the financial statements of micro-entities, which fall under two of the three parameters set forth in article 2435 ter of the Civil Code—i.e., when a company's total assets are lower than Euro 175,000, sales revenues are lower than Euro 350,000, and, on average, during the financial year, employees are lower than 5. Table 2 provides an overview of accounting classes and size limits.

Table 3 provides an overview of annual report contents for businesses that apply the Italian Civil Code, according to their size.

Table 4 provides updated information about the number of active limited companies in the Italian economy classified by the three given parameters.

Considering this evolution, two sets of rules for financial statement preparation coexist in Italy—on the one hand, the Civil Code with domestic GAAP and, on the other hand, IFRS. The empirical analyses have thrown into relief some discrepancies between Italian GAAP and IFRS in the accounting treatment of intangible assets, income taxes, and business combinations with reference to both net income and equity (Cordazzo, 2013). Therefore, the rules to determine taxable profit differ for companies that apply the IFRS standards.

Most Italian limited companies prepare their financial statements referring to the Civil Code and domestic GAAP. Nevertheless, this set of rules has become increasingly closer to IFRS. In fact, during the last 10 years, the Civil Code has changed in order to be more consistent with IFRS. In particular, the implementation of the European Directive 34/2013 has modified the Civil Code clauses dealing with financial statement preparation. As the domestic GAAP are strictly intertwined with the law, they have also been changed consistent with the law's novelties. It is not by chance that the OIC is entrusted not only to work out domestic accounting standards but also to contribute to the elaboration of the international standards adopted in Europe, given its relationships with the *European Financial Reporting Advisory Group* (EFRAG) and the accounting bodies of other countries.

Nevertheless, the effects of this convergency are disputed. In fact, some research has shown that the mandatory adoption of IFRS, in a typical code-law country such as Italy, has brought about an overall increase in the value relevance of accounting information. In the period surrounding IFRS adoption, research has also provided evidence of changes in some Italian country-specific factors that may contribute to an improvement in accounting quality (Paglietti, 2009). These results are consistent with the previous literature, supporting the idea that accounting quality depends not only on the quality of accounting standards but also on the country's complex institutional setting. On the contrary, another piece of research has shown that IFRS adoption has not improved reporting quality among private companies in Italy. In particular, assuming that entities controlled by listed companies could switch to IFRS to comply with the parent company's requirements and/or to simplify their financial reporting process, researchers have found signs of earnings quality deterioration in subsidiaries' financial statements (Cameran et al., 2014).

In any case, the existence of two models of financial statements affects both preparers and users. As mentioned above, many companies have the opportunity to choose the model they wish to adopt, taking into account their communication aims, the markets in which they compete, and the capital providers they address. This reality can prevent users from effective comparisons if they do not pay extremely close attention to the differences that still persist, in spite of the convergence process, between the two accounting systems (Incollingo & Lionzo, 2018).

In addition to this, IFRS adoption has also affected the issue of book-tax conformity. In Italy, research has shown that IFRS and tax reporting have a high degree of disconnection, while Italian GAAP, in line with the accounting tradition of most continental European countries, are more closely related to tax rules. However, a rapidly evolving situation has been documented, with connections between accounting systems and taxation becoming tighter, mainly because of the changes in the tax law introduced during the last few years (Di Pietra, 2017; Gavana et al., 2013).

3 Implementation of the EU Directive 2013/34

In the Italian Civil Code, there are two tiers of regulations. First, there are the *postulates*, so called because they are overriding rules. Postulates comprise a frame with which to interpret and apply the *specific criteria*, which are rules focused on particular aspects of financial statement preparation. The specific criteria operationalize the postulates. Hierarchically, the postulates have a higher position than the other rules, which means that the specific rules, when interpreted and applied, cannot contrast the postulates, i.e., the general principles. If it were the case, the postulates would be useless.

All the rules mentioned above, alongside the *bases of measurement* (see §4), are used in preparing the following four main financial statements: balance sheet, income statement, cash flow statement, and notes. These documents are complemented by the management discussion and analysis report. In Italy, the implementation of the European Directive 2013/34 has affected all these strands of the annual report to varying degrees (Provasi & Sottoriva, 2015).

3.1 General Clauses and Bases for Preparations

When a specific rule is lacking and other rules cannot be analogically applied, the preparers of financial statements need to refer to the pillars upon which the accounting system is based. This is the role played by the *postulates*, which comprise a set of rules organized into two levels—general clauses and bases of preparation. Three are *general clauses*: transparency, truth, and accuracy. Regarding *transparency*, the financial statements should be prepared in order for the users to clearly understand the nature and the meaning of the different line items, in addition to how the amounts have been measured. The *truth* also has two facets: objective and subjective. An *objective truth* implies that preparers abide by the facts, meaning that they cannot recognize elements related to facts that did not happen or cannot omit elements caused by facts that have already happened. The *subjective* facet of truth is concerned with the fact that most line items' monetary amount is measured by resorting to estimates and guesswork. As a consequence, these values cannot be true in absolute terms. They can be held true with respect to some assumptions that have been worked out.

Nevertheless, estimates and assumptions should not be arbitrary. On the contrary, they should be rational, in that they should be the result of an organized and rigorous assessment process. In this case, the line items affected by this process can be deemed *credible*. Furthermore, there are two strands of the general *accuracy* clause. First, there is a *technical* strand, which means that whoever prepares the financial statements should know the rules stated by the Civil Code and the GAAP and should also be able to apply them without making mistakes. In addition to this, there is a matter of professional ethics, i.e., of *fairness*. When applying the rules, the preparers should feel they have an accurate understanding of the meaning of these rules, without resorting to literal interpretations of convenience. Otherwise, the other two clauses would be an empty shell.

The general rules, to be effective, are put into practice by means of a set of rules with a narrower focus—the *bases of preparation*. Examples of these rules are the going concern assumption, the accrual principle, the prudence or conservatism approach, and the substance over form criterion. In the Italian Civil Code, over time, these rules have been deeply affected by some European Directives, which have impinged, in particular, on the conservative approach and the substance over form principle.

An Italian legislator interprets prudence differently than IFRS, which presents prudence as a mere accounting behavior according to which, when you measure the line items' value, you must act carefully, paying attention not to jeopardize the company as a going concern. On the contrary, in the Italian system, prudence is interpreted and applied considering the *disparity* principle, which provides that losses, even if they are only prospective, should be recognized, while gains should not be recognized until they are actually realized (Fox et al., 2013; Zeff, 2013).

The substance over form principle, which has always been part of the international GAAP, has gradually taken root in Italian accounting regulation. A first definition was due to the implementation of the European Directive 51/2003, which reads: "assets and liabilities should be measured taking into account their economic function." Owing to European Directive 34/2013, this definition has been clarified and simplified, reading as follows: "the elements of the financial statements should be presented taking into account the substance of the operation or of the contract that they follow on from." Italian Accounting Standard 11 elaborates on this principle, referring to *substantial representation*. However, the full implementation of this principle involves the following two fundamental issues concerning financial statement preparation: what should be presented in the financial statements and what the aim of those reports is. On the first issue, the contents of the balance sheet are crucial, as this document should represent the resources at a company's disposal to run its future activity and the obligations to settle. The choice between a legal and formal approach, on the one hand, and an economic and substantial one, on the other hand, deeply affects the representation of a company's financial position. In fact, according to the latter approach, assets and liabilities should be defined and recognized without referring to legal constructs. For example, to recognize some resources as an asset, it is not necessary for a company to have legal possession of those resources. Unfortunately, the Italian Civil Code imposes the substance over form principle but does not complement this principle with a clear definition of an asset or a liability. The domestic accounting principles do not tackle this issue either. Therefore, the principle has not been fully implemented thus far (De Luca & Di Berardino, 2018).

The pillars of the accounting system are also important when a company has to waive some specific rules set by the Civil Code. In fact, even if these rules are highly prescriptive, a company's features can be so particular that they cannot be properly represented by applying rigid accounting standards and templates. For this reason, the legislator itself provides for exceptions to its rules in three specific cases:

- When not applying the rules has an effect that could be deemed as not relevant
- When applying some rules could prevent the company from presenting a *true and fair view* of its performance
- When a company, in order to present a true and fair view of its performance, decides to change the accounting principles previously applied

The Civil Code qualifies the abovementioned situations as *extremely rare circumstances* that can affect the quality of the information conveyed to users through the financial statements.

In these circumstances, a preparer is compelled to resort to other rules, different from those set by the legislator, which are usually represented by generally accepted accounting standards and courts' judgments. Nevertheless, the newly adopted accounting principles should not collide with the general aims upon which the legislator desires the financial statements to be based. To this end, the general principles play an overriding role, acting as a north star that traces the path for the selection and application of other accounting principles (Van Hulle, 1997).

The legislator also requires companies to explain the reason for their "diversion" alongside the effects on the net worth and the income statement balance. In particular, if some earnings are generated, they should be earmarked in a specific reserve, which is not distributable as long as they are not actually realized. The reserve at hand must be created without recognizing earnings in the income statement and then allocating them in the reserve.

In order to restore comparability, the domestic GAAP provide that the representation of the cumulative effects caused by the new accounting principle adopted is carried out using the *retrospective* approach. Consequently, the opening balance of net worth should be adjusted. The comparative information should also be retroactively modified, recalculating the balances of all the items affected by the change as if the new principles had always been applied.

3.2 Presentation of Financial Statements

The contents and the structure of the primary financial statements are strictly disciplined by the Civil Code, which leaves preparers very limited room to maneuver when drawing up their annual reports. In particular, looking at the balance sheet, assets and liabilities are shown in a statement with two sections, providing for specific line items and the order in which they should be presented. Assets are split into current and fixed, according to the *destination criterion*, which implies that all the assets destined to be used in the long run should be classified as fixed assets. Regarding the liabilities, no specific classification exists, apart from a distinction between provisions and debt.

The balance sheet structure reveals another key to understanding that the legislator offers the users. Apart from receivables to shareholders, which is the first-line item of the asset side section, the other assets are presented moving from fixed assets to liquidity, passing through current assets. The liabilities are also presented, beginning with equity and ending with "other debt." This presentation reveals an additional classification based on *order of liquidity*. The attention reserved for this information is reinforced by the legislator when it requires an entity to disclose the amount expected to be recovered or settled after more than 12 months for each asset and liability line item that combines amounts expected to be recovered or settled, as follows: (a) no more than 12 months after the reporting period and (b) more than 12 months after the reporting period.

Looking at the income statement, line items are also presented following a rigid template. Different from the balance sheet, this statement should be prepared using a multistep format. A multistep income statement is more detailed than a simple income statement and is conceived to compute some disaggregated results. Even if the format provided for by the legislator does not show an explicit *operating profit*, this is the subtotal the legislator refers to when it states to show the difference between the *value of production* and the *costs of production*. With this choice, the Italian legislator is in line with the academic research that has established that users of financial statements view operating profit as a useful measure of entity performance (Barton et al., 2010; Chen & Wang, 2004; Isidro & Marques, 2015). Specifically, the academic evidence has shown that operating profit is value relevant—associated with stock prices and returns—and has predictive ability for future entity performance. To the extent that it enhances comparability, including operating profit as a subtotal in the statement of profit and loss is likely to benefit investors, analysts, auditors, and the reporting entities.

To present the operating margin, the Italian legislator has chosen a cost classification based on the nature of expenses. The *function of expense* method is not allowed. Expenses should be detailed on the face of the statement, without resorting to notes, according to experimental research suggesting that information presented in the financial statements is reflected in individuals' judgments and decisions to a greater degree than when information is located in the notes (Sami & Schwartz, 1992).

After the operating margin, financial income and expenses should be presented, alongside the impairment losses of financial assets and possible reversals of these losses. In this way, the Italian income statement structure is in keeping with what much research has highlighted, i.e., investors break down a company's performance into two components—the operating markets, in which goods and services are traded, and the financial markets, in which financial claims are traded (Barker, 2010). It is also worth mentioning that, based on evidence in the academic literature, Staff Paper 21E issued by IFRS has stated that the operating-financing distinction in financial reporting is useful for investors' decision-making, as it corresponds to the conceptual distinction between *value generation* and *value distribution* activities in a given firm. In this regard, IFRS has been working on staff proposals to improve the level of aggregation and disaggregation of line items in the primary financial statements and notes.

The summation of both sections, operating and financial, represents a company's earnings before income taxes. By deducting the overall amount of current and deferred taxes, the profit of the financial year is obtained, comprising the final balance of the income statement. As provided for by European Directive 34/2013, the template at hand does not show any *extraordinary* or not-repeatable item; companies are required to comment on these items, if any, in the notes, presenting their nature and amount when the amount is *material*. This choice seems to be based on academic studies confirming that, to forecast a company's future earnings, investors should be able to detect items that are largely transitory in nature and have limited predictive value. Nevertheless, presentation on the face of the income statement would have been better, as there is also some evidence showing that the more prominent presentation of special items (in the income statement as opposed to disclosure in the notes) is associated with lower managerial reasons to opportunistically classify a persistent item as a special item (Cready et al., 2010; Riedl & Srinivasan, 2010).

Complying with suggestions coming from research and standard setters, the Italian legislator has also included the cash flow statement among the primary statements that companies are required to present. Different from the balance sheet and the income statement, a specific format is not provided for. Only a few key pieces of information should be shown in this statement. First, Italian law indicates that cash and cash equivalents are the financial resources for which the statement should account. Different from what is provided for in IAS 7, some specific liabilities such as bank overdrafts are not included. However, according to the abovementioned accounting standard, cash inflows and outflows must be classified as due to operating, investing, and financing activities. Therefore, a multistep presentation is required, as it allows for the highlighting of some financial subtotals that measure a company's financial needs, as well as how these needs have been met.

Focusing on the operating area, the legislator has not stated if the cash flows coming from a company's current activities should be computed by resorting to the direct or the indirect method. The national standard setter complements the legislator, clearly opting for the use of the latter method—a choice that deflects from what IFRS recommends. Analogously, the Italian legislator has not tackled another key issue—the classification of interest paid in the statement of cash flow. According to the domestic accounting standards (OIC 11), most companies classify interest paid in the cash flows from operating activities (Baik et al., 2016).

The contents of the three main primary financial statements are contingent on a company's size. In fact, *small* companies are allowed to present an abridged version of these statements. In this regard, a company's size is measured in terms of sales revenue, total assets, and number of employees. A simplified approach to the statement entails the elimination of the cash flow statement and, in some cases, the management discussion and analysis. In particular, the balance sheet contents can be shortened, including fewer line items. The measurement of some financial assets and liabilities can also be simplified, as companies' managers are not required to apply the *amortized cost method*.

By the same token, the Italian law also homes in on micro-companies, i.e., businesses whose sales revenue, assets, and number of employees are particularly low. In these cases, companies can also avoid presenting notes, provided some pieces of information are shown in the balance sheet footnotes. Regarding the measurement of assets and liabilities, micro-companies enjoy some preferential treatment, as they are not required to measure derivatives at *fair value* nor to give supplementary information if, in extremely rare circumstances, the company does not apply the accounting principles provided by the law.

4 Valuation Approaches

Because of the EU Directive 2013/34, Italian accounting rules have moved toward the international accounting standards and their framework, contents, and methods. In addition to the strict and detailed regulation of the balance sheet and the income statement formats, the main differences among national rules and IFRS are represented by the measurement rules (Di Pietra, 2017).

The basic valuation principle is historical cost. This is clearly set out in the 2426 clause of the Civil Code, devoted to the valuation criteria. According to the historical cost principle, assets are recognized at the value of the financial resources used at the time of the acquisition of the asset. Liabilities, on the other hand, are recognized at the amount of money received for the obligations or considering the amount of resources to settle the obligation under normal operating conditions (Alexander & Servalli, 2011).

Historical cost is consistent with the going concern assumption and prudence because it uses information derived from the price of the transaction or other event that gave rise to the asset or liability. If an entity acquires an asset in a market transaction, the entity expects that the asset will provide sufficient economic benefits to recover the cost of the asset. Similarly, if a liability has been incurred as a result of a market transaction, an entity expects that the amount of economic resources to settle the obligation will normally be no more than the value of the consideration received minus transaction costs (IASB, Framework).

The amount expected to be recovered from an asset measured at historical cost must be at least equal to its carrying amount. Therefore, the historical cost must be reduced to reflect the asset consumption and any loss of its recoverable amount. Similarly, the value of economic resources to settle an obligation should not exceed the liability's carrying amount, and therefore the historical cost of a liability should be increased when it becomes onerous.

The recoverable amount depends on the assets to be valued. For non-current assets such as property, plant and equipment, and intangible assets, the recoverable amount is the higher of its fair value less costs of disposal and its value in use, i.e., the present value of the future cash flows expected to be derived from an asset. For inventory, the recoverable amount is the net realizable value, i.e., the estimated selling price in the ordinary course of business less the estimated costs of completion and the estimated selling costs. In some circumstances, the replacement cost of materials may be the best available measure of the net realizable value.

Italian legislation provides for certain exceptions to the cost principle as follows:

- Equity investments can be valued, under certain circumstances, at the equity method.
- For construction contracts, an entity may recognize as sales revenue the amount of the transaction price.
- Foreign currency monetary items may be translated using the closing rate.
- Derivative financial instruments shall be measured at fair value. Italian legislation also refers to fair value for financial fixed assets. If these assets are presented in the financial statements at a value higher than their fair value (with the exclusion of investments in subsidiaries and associated companies and investments in joint ventures), the notes must disclose their fair value, as well as the reasons the book value has not been reduced, including the substantial elements on which the belief that this value can be recovered is based.

Table 5 shows an overview of bases of measurement as provided for by the Italian Civil Code.

The introduction in the Italian accounting system of the fair value measurement is one of the main contributions made by Directive 34/2013. Fair value is used for different purposes—first, as a basis of the measurement of financial instruments (Corbella et al., 2013). It is also used to determine the recoverable amount to run the impairment test of fixed assets. In fact, the net realizable value upon which the recoverable amount is based is a market value. When there is no active market, the value in use calculation represents a fair value. However, in this case, there is a difference that IAS 36 (§53A) clearly indicates when it states that "fair value reflects the assumptions market participants would use when pricing the asset," while "value in use reflects the effects of factors that may be specific to the entity and not applicable to entities in general."

5 Conclusions

The implementation of the European Directive 34/2013 has sped up the renewal process of the regulation of financial statements in Italy. Consistent with the main features of the European Directive, the overlap between the domestic rules and the typical IFRS approach has increased. This fact is the consequence of a general harmonization process between, on the one hand, the sets of rules applied in the European countries and, on the other hand, the IFRS system. However, some peculiarities of the Italian context can be detected.

First, looking at the general principles, the Italian accounting environment interprets and applies prudence according to the disparity principle, i.e., an asymmetric

Table 5 Measurement bases of assets and liabilities

Asset/liability	Measurement bases	Value adjustments recognized in...
Intangible assets	Historical cost	Profit and loss (impairments)
Tangible fixed/non-current assets	Historical cost	Profit and loss (impairments)
Investment property	Historical cost	Profit and loss (impairments)
Investments in subsidiaries (parent company financial statements)	Historical cost Net asset value/ equity method	Profit and loss (impairments) Profit and loss
Investments in associates	Historical cost Net asset value/ equity method	Profit and loss (impairments) Profit and loss
Investments in joint ventures and joint operations	Historical cost Net asset value/ equity method	Profit and loss (impairments) Profit and loss
Shares with no significant influence	Historical cost	Profit and loss (impairments)
Investments in debt instruments—hold to maturity or loans and receivables	Amortized cost Historical cost	Profit and loss (impairments)
Investments in debt instruments—trading	Historical cost	Profit and loss
Derivative financial instruments, including contracts to buy and sell nonfinancial items that can be settled net (no hedge accounting)	Historical cost Fair value	Profit and loss Profit and loss
Inventories	Historical cost	Profit and loss (impairments)
Financial liabilities	Amortized cost Nominal value	N/A

approach, where unrealized losses should be recognized, while unrealized gains should not. As mentioned above, this stance differs from that provided for by the IFRS Conceptual Framework. In fact, §2.16 of the Conceptual Framework reads:

> Prudence is the exercise of caution when making judgements under conditions of uncertainty. The exercise of prudence means that assets and income are not overstated, and liabilities and expenses are not understated. Equally, the exercise of prudence does not allow for the understatement of assets or income or the overstatement of liabilities or expenses. Such misstatements can lead to the overstatement or understatement of income or expenses in future periods.

Briefly, IFRS considers prudence as a mere call to responsibly manage the "wiggle room" that preparers benefit from when they have to measure some elements of financial statements. In this regard, the European Parliament's Committee on Economic and Monetary Affairs (ECON) put forward some interesting observations more in step with the Italian approach to prudence. In 2019, the Committee stated that the IFRS interpretation of prudence is not in keeping with what the Court of Justice of the European Union (CJEU) has ruled and for which the Accounting Directive provides.

Furthermore, in Italy, the *prevalence of the substance over form* principle struggles to be fully applied. In fact, the legislator and the domestic accounting standards have not worked out a definition of the elements of the financial statements, causing doubt and misinterpretation. These effects are blatant in the case of lease accounting. The Civil Code establishes the principle of the prevalence of substance over form but imposes the recognition of lease contracts in the financial statements of the user as a rental. Only in the notes should the substantial lease effects be shown, drawing up a report that illustrates what would have been the effects on the balance sheet and the income statement of a lease accounting based on the economic substance of the operation. In order to cope with this issue, it is necessary for the legislator and national GAAP to deal with the definition of the elements of the financial statements, hopefully referring to what is stated in the IFRS Conceptual Framework.

Finally, fair value has been adopted with great caution. Even if Directive 34/2013 provides for the use of fair value as a basis of measurement of various assets and liabilities (as an option or as a requirement), the Italian legislator has chosen to use fair value only to measure derivative financial instruments. In this case, for the definition of fair value (of financial instruments and derivative financial instruments) and for its application, Italian law explicitly refers to "internationally recognized accounting standards compatible with the relevant European Union regulations." This choice is clearly inspired by the national accounting tradition, where prudence and historical cost still prevail.

Overall, Directive 34/2013 has enriched the financial information that Italian small- and middle-sized companies communicate to the markets. This is a result of paramount importance for the development of these companies. Indeed, growth requires capital that in part can only be provided by banks, which still have a predominant role in financing the Italian productive system. Companies, therefore, must open up to financial markets, not only the domestic one, offering quality information according to the logic of international accounting principles.

References

Adamo, S., Alexander, D., & Fasiello, R. (2020). Time and accounting in the middle ages: An Italian-based analysis. *Accounting History, 25*(1), 53–68.

Adamo, S., Fellegara, A. M., Incollingo, A., & Lionzo, A. (a cura di). (2018). *La "nuova" informativa di bilancio. Profili teorici e criticità applicative dopo il D. Lgs. 139/2015 e i nuovi principi OIC*. FrancoAngeli.

Alexander, D., & Servalli, S. (2011). Economia Aziendale and financial valuations in Italy: Some contradictions and insights. *Accounting History, 16*(3), 291–312.

Avi, M. S. (2020, November). Accounting standard in Italy: Interpreting and essential integrating instruments of the law about financial reporting but... *European Journal of Economics, Finance and Administrative Sciences*, issue 107.

Baik, B., Cho, H., Choi, W., & Lee, K. (2016). Who classifies interest payments as financing activities? An analysis of classification shifting in the statement of cash flows at the adoption of IFRS. *Journal of Accounting and Public Policy, 35*(4), 331–351.

Barker, R. (2010). The operating-financing distinction in financial reporting. *Accounting and Business Research, 40*(4), 391–403.

Barton, J., Hansen, T. B., & Pownall, G. (2010). Which performance measures do investors around the world value the most and why? *The Accounting Review, 85*(3), 753–789.

Cameran, M., Campa, D., & Pettinicchio, A. (2014). IFRS adoption among private companies: Impact on earnings quality. *Journal of Accounting, Auditing & Finance, 29*(3), 278–305.

Canziani, A. (2016). *Italy.* The transition to IFRS in Italy and elsewhere, or from *Code Napoléon* to the devolution of sovereignty. In D. Bensadon & N. Praquin (Eds.), *IFRS in a global world.* Springer.

Chen, S., & Wang, Y. (2004). Evidence from China on the value relevance of operating income vs. below-the-line items. *The International Journal of Accounting, 39*(4), 339–364.

Corbella, S., Florio, C., & Rossignoli, F. (2013). IFRS adoption in Italy: Which effects on accounting figures and subjectivity? *Accounting and Finance Research, 2*(4), 130–148.

Cordazzo, M. (2013). The impact of IFRS on net income and equity: evidence from Italian listed companies. *Journal of Applied Accounting Research, 14*(1), 54–73.

Cready, W., Lopez, T. J., & Sisneros, C. A. (2010). The persistence and market valuation of recurring nonrecurring items. *The Accounting Review, 85*(5), 1577–1615.

De Luca, F., & Di Berardino, D. (2018). Evolution of the substance over form principle in the Italian GAAP from a comparative and international perspective. *International Journal of Critical Accounting, 9*(4).

Di Pietra, R. (2017). The role and current status of IFRS in the completion of national accounting rules—Evidence from Italy. *Accounting in Europe, 14*(1–2), 121–130.

Fox, A., Hannah, G., Helliar, C., & Veneziani, M. (2013). The costs and benefits of IFRS implementation in the UK and Italy. *Journal of Applied Accounting Research, 14*(1), 86–101.

Gavana, G., Guggiola, G., & Marenzi, A. (2013). Evolving connections between tax and financial reporting in Italy. *Accounting in Europe, 10*(1), 43–70.

Incollingo, A., & Lionzo, A. (2018). Il bilancio che cambia alla ricerca di identità. In S. Adamo, A. M. Fellegara, A. Incollingo, & A. Lionzo (a cura di) (Eds.), *La "nuova" informativa di bilancio. Profili teorici e criticità applicative dopo il D. Lgs. 139/2015 e i nuovi principi OIC* (pp. 360–390). FrancoAngeli.

Isidro, H., & Marques, A. (2015). The role of institutional and economic factors in the strategic use of non-GAAP disclosures to beat earnings benchmarks. *European Accounting Review, 24*(1), 95–128.

Paglietti, P. (2009). Investigating the effects of the EU mandatory adoption of IFRS on accounting quality: Evidence from Italy. *International Journal of Business and Management, 4*(12), 3–18.

Provasi, R., & Sottoriva, C. (2015, June). Preliminary considerations about the transposition of Directive 2013/34/EU into Italian accounting system. *Journal of Modern Accounting and Auditing, 11*(6), 302–312.

Riedl, E. J., & Srinivasan, S. (2010). Signalling firm performance through financial statement presentation: An analysis using special items. *Contemporary Accounting Research, 27*(1), 289–332.

Sami, H., & Schwartz, B. (1992). Alternative pension liability disclosure and the effect on credit evaluation: an experiment. *Behavioural Research in Accounting, 4*, 49–62.

Van Hulle, K. (1997). The true and fair view override in the European Accounting Directives. *European Accounting Review, 6*(4), 711–720.

Zeff, S. A. (2013). The objectives of financial reporting: a historical survey and analysis. *Accounting and Business Research, 43*(4), 262–327.

Spain

Ana Gisbert and Araceli Mora

1 The National Accounting Scenario

1.1 The Role of the Company Law and the Accounting Rules

The Spanish Company Regulation is enshrined in two key legal sources: (a) Code of Commerce (*Código de Comercio*) and (b) Company Law (*Ley de Sociedades de Capital*). Both legal documents incorporate the general accounting principles and fundamental accounting valuation concepts that are developed in depth along rules enacted at different levels of authority [1] either as laws, royal decrees, ministerial orders, resolutions, and circulars. The most relevant rule which includes in detail the Spanish Generally Accepted Accounting Principles (GAAP) is known as "General

[1] The royal decree is placed in the order of precedence of legal norms immediately after the norms with the rank of law and before the ministerial order. Its difference with the former is that it emanates from the executive power and not from the legislative power. Its difference is that the royal decree requires the approval of the Council of Ministers exclusively for its adoption, while the ministerial order can be established by a single minister. Resolutions are nonregulatory decisions or guidelines issued by a public authority, and circulars are communications issued by a public authority to be applied mandatorily by subordinates (i.e., Bank of Spain Circulars for financial institutions).

A. Gisbert
Universidad Autonoma de Madrid, Madrid, Spain
e-mail: ana.gisbert@uam.es

A. Mora (✉)
Universitat de València, Valencia, Spain
e-mail: araceli.mora@uv.es

A. Incollingo, A. Lionzo (eds.), *The European Harmonization of National Accounting Rules*, SIDREA Series in Accounting and Business Administration,
https://doi.org/10.1007/978-3-031-42931-6_6

Accounting Plan" (*Plan General de Contabilidad*—PGC). The *PGC* is issued by the Accounting and Auditing Institute, (*Instituto de Contabilidad y Auditoría de Cuentas—ICAC*), a body dependent on the Ministry of Economy and Finance, through the legal form of "royal decree." The ICAC also serves as an interpretation committee. This role has two lines of action. On the one hand, the ICAC prepares and issues what is known as "resolutions," which are detailed guidance on complex issues.[2] On the other hand, the ICAC prepares interpretations at the request of preparers and auditors, which are publicly available.

The *PGC* is applied to all types of companies independently of their industry [3] (with a few exceptions, being the most remarkable the exception of financial entities). There have been three past PGCs (*PGC-1973, PGC-1990,* and *PGC-2007,* with some amendments through the time). Since 2007 there has also been a simplified version for small- and medium-sized entities (SMEs). The current *PGC* was issued in 2021 (*PGC-2021*).

The *PGC* has four sections: (1) conceptual framework, (2) recognition and measurement standards, (3) financial statement formats and content of the notes to the financial statements, and (4) chart of accounts. Everything is enclosed in one single document, and all parts are compulsory, except for the chart of accounts.

The first *PGC* (*PGC-1973)* was very close to the French GAAP at that time and was highly influenced by the tax law. However, the entrance of Spain into the European Economic Community (EEC) forced the incorporation of the Fourth and Seventh Directives and therefore the reform of the Code of Commerce (Law 19/1989), the issuance of an auditing law (19/1988), and the issuance of a new PGC (*PGC-1990*) (Royal Decree 1643/1990). All these changes implied an absolute shift in the paradigm of the Spanish financial reporting system.

The reform accomplished in 1990 was a significant step toward a clear distinction between tax and accounting information, so the tax and accounting relationship experienced an absolute revolution from a tax-accounting-dependent system until 1990 to a cooperation relationship between both disciplines. Since then, Spain can be considered one of the EU countries where there is more independence between accounting and tax regulation. There is indeed a nexus between the two disciplines since income before taxes calculated under the Spanish GAAP is the key basis to proceeding with the calculation of the income tax. However, all changes in the accounting regulation are always settled under the "true and fair view" principle, whereas the tax regulation adapts to the changes in accounting regulation establishing the adjustments required to implement the fiscal policies. Differences between taxable income and accounting income imply the recognition of deferred assets and liabilities. The regulatory changes did not only imply a clear separation

[2]These *resolutions* deal with specific matters such as revenue recognition, intangible assets, financial instruments, income tax, production costs, impairment of assets, or emission rights. They are all publicly available at the ICAC website.

[3]There are specific industry adaptations of the PGC mostly issued before 2007. They are in force in everything that does not oppose the current legislation. In most cases, this leaves a little more than a few account designations and formats of the annual accounts.

between tax and accounting rules but also increased the overall institutional concern about the relevance of financial information and the disclosure requirements for listed and non-listed companies. It also implied the introduction of the mandatory independent audit of financial statements of larger entities (Law 19/1988) and the issuance of rules for the consolidation of financial statements in company groups (Royal Decree 1815/1991).

After all these significant changes were accomplished at the beginning of the 1990s, the second major change in the Spanish accounting regulatory framework arrived 17 years later. It was forced by the international framework and more specifically by the new accounting strategy adopted in the EU (COM 2000/359) to adopt the International Financial Reporting Standards (IFRS) to prepare consolidated financial statements across EU-listed companies. The issuance of Regulation EC 1606/2002 led to a new set of significant changes in the Company Law and the issuance in 2007 of a new *PGC*. Spain decided to align its national accounting regulation to the content of the IFRS. Instead of allowing non-listed companies to use directly the IFRS as enforced in the EU, the accounting regulators decided to adapt the content of the *PGC* to embrace the IFRS principles. The adoption of this new accounting regulation in 2007 was a great challenge for all non-listed firms, particularly for the smaller entities, as it implied an absolute change of paradigm in the principles and objectives of financial reporting. It was then that two different versions of the *PGC* were issued: full version, PGC-2007 (Royal Decree 1514/2007), and a simplified version, PGC-SMEs-2007 [4] (Royal Decree 1515/2007) for small- and medium-sized entities. To ensure that the 2007 accounting reform did not pose a problem when it came to tax settlement (e.g., due to the introduction of the fair value of certain financial instruments), an amendment to the tax law itself was issued.

This *PGC* 2007 had two significant later amendments. In 2010 it was amended to adapt the rules on consolidation to the IAS 27 on Separate Financial Statements and IFRS 3 on Business Combinations, adopted by the EU (Royal Decree 1159/2010). In 2016 it was amended again due to the adaptation of the PGC and PGC for SMEs to the 2013/34/EU Directive (Royal Decree 602/2016).

The latest reform took place in 2021 (Royal Decree 1/2021) to adapt to some, but not all, of the most relevant changes introduced in IFRS in the previous years. The current PGC is mostly aligned with IFRS 9 on Financial Instruments and fully aligned with IFRS 15 on Revenue from Contracts with Customers. However, changes in IFRS 16 on Leases were not considered (the recognition criteria for leasing transactions remained as in IAS 17).

Financial entities follow the Central Bank of Spain *(Banco de España)* accounting rules (*circulares*) since 1991. The Bank of Spain adapted the accounting rules for financial entities to IFRS principles in 2004 (Circular 4/2004), and after several modifications in subsequent years, a new circular (Circular 4/2017) was issued to incorporate the latest IFRS changes, particularly those related to IFRS 9.

[4]In 2007, SMEs were considered those companies with assets <2.85 million €, revenues <5.7 million €, and n°. employees <50.

The most recent changes in company reporting regulation have been those related to nonfinancial disclosure after the issuance of Directive 2014/95/UE. The content of this Directive, which affected the larger companies, has been incorporated through Royal Decree 17/2017 and Law 11/2018.

1.2 The Accounting Standard-Setting Bodies

The issuance of accounting regulation in Spain has been mainly a public administration issue, with scant input from the private sector, at least formally. The main official Spanish Standard Setter, as mentioned, is the Institute of Accounting and Auditing (*Instituto de Contabilidad y Auditoría de Cuentas—ICAC*), which is a governmental body.

There are other institutions with delegated functions to regulate accounting matters: The Bank of Spain (*Banco de España—BdeE*), the Stock Exchange Commission (*Comisión Nacional del Mercado de Valores—CNMV*), and the General Directorate of Insurance and Mutual Funds (*Dirección General de Seguros y Fondos de Pensiones—DGSFP*). However, any of the rules enacted by these institutions cannot be inconsistent with the general accounting standards (PGC) and must be ultimately approved by the ICAC. There is also a private organization, the Spanish Association of Accounting and Business Administration (*Asociación Española de Contabilidad y Administración de Empresas—AECA*), whose influence and indirect role in the standard-setting process have always been very significant.

1.2.1 The ICAC

The *ICAC* was created in 1988 [5] with two key objectives: (a) to issue the Spanish accounting and auditing regulation and (b) to oversight the auditing profession. The *ICAC* structure is composed of a president (proposed by the government) and, consistent with its two roles, an Auditing Committee and an Accounting Board.

Both the Accounting Board and the Auditing Committee are chaired by the *ICAC*'s president and composed of representatives of different governmental and private institutions linked to economic, tax, legal matters, and the accounting and auditing profession. [6] Neither the Accounting Board nor the Auditing Committee has

[5]The former body was called *Instituto de Planificación Contable*, founded in 1976.

[6]The members of the Accounting Board belong to the following institutions: the Stock Exchange Commission, Ministry of Treasury, Central Bank of Spain, and General Directorate of Insurance and Mutual Funds. Each institution has one representative. The members of the Auditing Committee belong to the following institutions: Public Audit Board, Ministry of Treasury, Ministry of Justice, State Legal Service, Central Bank of Spain, the Stock Exchange Commission, the General Directorate of Insurance and Mutual Funds, the Institute of Certified Public Accountants, and the General Economists Association. Each institution has one representative except for the audit profession representatives of the Institute of Certified Public Accountants and the General Economists Association. Each of these institutions has two representatives on the Auditing Committee.

executive powers. Academics and practitioners are represented in the Accounting Advisory Committee that plays a role as a second-tier advisor.

There is not a formal "due process" in the Spanish accounting regulatory process. The *ICAC* is responsible for the preparation, amendment, and issuance of any accounting or auditing regulation. However, when *ICAC* undertakes relevant changes, it usually organizes unofficial working groups or specific advisory committees in which there are auditors, preparers, and academics.

1.2.2 Other Standard Setters

The Bank of Spain, unlike the banking regulators in most countries, has delegated authority for accounting regulation and, since 1991, has issued accounting "circulars" (*circulares*) to be applied in the elaboration of the financial statements of financial entities, both individual and consolidated accounts.[7]

The *DGSFP*, an agency of the Ministry of Economy, apart from supervising and controlling insurance companies, also has the power to issue regulations related to the preparation of financial statements in the insurance industry.

The *CNMV* is the body in charge of supervising the Spanish securities markets and the activities of all those involved in them. The *CNMV* is also the enforcer of accounting standards for listed companies. It issues circulars, guidance, and recommendations related to its functions. Some of them are related to accounting matters and nonfinancial disclosure. It also issues accounting rules and requirements for some regulated entities, such as investment entities.

AECA is a private association with a great diversity of members from different backgrounds, mainly accounting professionals (auditors, preparers) and a great percentage of accounting academics. It was established in 1979 and does not have any formal authority, but its influence on national accounting rules and practices has always been quite significant, particularly since the first reform in the 1990s. AECA has a Committee of Accounting Principles which has been issuing accounting principles as well as opinions since its foundation. It has helped greatly in disseminating the IFRS culture in Spain. It is also worth mentioning the influence of its Committee of Corporate Social Responsibility, responsible for issuing documents on integrated and nonfinancial reporting that have been highly significant not only for guiding the nonfinancial disclosure practice across companies but also has served as a reference for official guides and regulations on these issues.

[7] According to Regulation (EC) 1606/2002, the Bank of Spain should not have any authority to regulate accounting for consolidated accounts of listed entities. However, it does regulate, and all entities follow *BdeE* rules in their consolidated accounts. Even the *Circular* 4/2004, which was supposed to be aligned with IFRS, is not fully in line with IAS 39, at least in the loan impairment model. Also, the Spanish Government issued direct impairment rules for the financial industry in 2012 (Royal Decree-Law 2/2012 and 18/2012) not aligned with IFRS and overriding the Bank of Spain Circular 4/2004. See details in Giner and Mora (2021) and Ucieda and Gonzalo (2019).

Table 1 Number of active companies on January 1, 2020

Employees	Total	%
Total	3,404,428	
0	1,912,010	56
1–2	907,192	27
3–5	305,986	9
6–9	125,472	4
10–19	81,298	2
More than 20	72,470	2

Source: National Institute of Statistics (INE)

1.3 The Economic System: Large-Sized Companies vs. SMEs

SMEs in Spain are the core of the economy. Table 1 provides updated information about the number of active companies in the Spanish economy classified by the number of employees. [8] Aggregated data reported in Table 1 shows that 92% of the Spanish companies have less than five employees and, therefore, can be classified as micro-entities. This significant percentage remains in most sectors (Panel B), except for the industry sector where this percentage drops to 76%.

The number of companies with more than 1000 employees is very limited. The Bank of Spain database counts a total of 1356 companies with more than 250 employees, where only 32% of these companies (431) have more than 1000 employees. [9]

2 The Evolution of the Spanish Regulation

2.1 The Role of IFRS

As mentioned in the first section, the influence of the IFRS on the Spanish accounting rules has been very significant, even when IFRS were not in the landscape of financial accounting rules in Europe. [10] Spain was a pioneer in the incorporation of the world's leading international accounting standards from IASC, especially those requiring the capitalization of financial leasing and deferred taxes, in its first reform of the *PGC* in 1990.

---

[8] The data are available on the website of the Spanish National Institute of Statistics (www.ine.es).

[9] These data are available in the Bank of Spain Database. Banco de España—Central de Balances (https://www.bde.es/bde/es/areas/cenbal/).

[10] See Cañibano and Gisbert (2007), Cañibano and Ucieda (2004), Giner (2003), Gonzalo (2014), Mora (2017), or Ucieda and Gómez (2020) for more details.

Table 2 Accounting rules in Spain

	Individual accounts	Group accounts
Listed companies	National GAAP	IFRS
Non-SMEs (non-listed)	National GAAP	IFRS or national GAAP (optional)
SMEs	National GAAP for SMEs	–

When the accounting harmonization in Europe underwent the significant change of adopting the IFRS system through the EC Regulation 1606/2002, member states had to decide whether non-listed companies should require or allow IFRS or continue using each national GAAP. Like most countries in Europe, Spain adopted the latter, requiring non-listed companies to use the national GAAP.

Table 2 summarizes the accounting regulation to be used for the preparation of either individual or group accounts. IFRS is only required across listed companies to prepare group accounts. Individual accounts must be always prepared under the Spanish PGC

However, the Spanish strategy was different from that of its peers, and as mentioned, Spain decided to adapt the national GAAP to the IFRS, avoiding (or minimizing) noncomparability between the financial information of listed and non-listed companies.

When the strategy of adopting IFRS in the EU was announced (COM 2000/359), the *ICAC* created a working group of experts. Members of the working group were accounting academics, auditors, preparers, and regulators' representatives. They issued in 2002 the *White Book of the Spanish Accounting Reform* where they raised two key recommendations: (1) to adapt the Spanish GAAP to the content of the IFRS regulation and (2) to give the option for non-listed companies to prepare consolidated accounts based on either IFRS standards or the new national GAAP. The direct application of IFRS was never considered, as it would imply a loss of sovereignty. After the issuance of the working group report, the first significant legislative changes arrived with the enactment of Law 62/2003, which introduced the first changes in the Company Law to adapt its content to the near-future changes later included in the *PGC*-2007. For instance, the law introduced the "fair value" concept, which did not previously exist.

Embracing the IFRS philosophy and content in the Spanish *PGC* was an absolute challenge for regulators. On top of that, certain issues incorporated in the IFRS standards and therefore in the *PGC*-2007 introduced a significant complexity in a business context where, as reported in Table 1, small companies are the core of the economy. Consequently, the ICAC also issued the *PGC-SME-2007*. It allowed smaller companies to report in a more condensed form or even to provide less information about certain issues. The significant differences were: (a) the exemption to prepare the cash flow statement; (b) the elimination of the recognition of gains and losses associated with financial instruments in equity (there is no statement of other comprehensive income—OCI); (c) the elimination of the concept of cash-generating units; and (d) the omission of the accounting treatment for several transactions that are not presumably linked to SMEs such as hedge accounting, business combinations and goodwill, financial derivatives with non-quoted equity instruments as underlying assets, noncurrent assets held for sale, and the analysis of the functional currency.

2.2 The 2013/34/EU Directive: Accounting for SMEs

The key goals of the 2013/34/EU were twofold: (a) to reduce the information requirements and administrative burdens across SMEs and (b) to promote the internationalization of SMEs facilitating funding, harmonizing, and simplifying the financial reporting requirements across the EU. This Directive led to the introduction of additional changes in the Spanish accounting and auditing legislation. Those changes were introduced through the 22/2015 Auditing Law, which incorporated a set of accounting changes to be included in the Company Law and Code of Commerce. But the most relevant change was the issuance of the Royal Decree 602/2016, to update the content of the PGC to the postulates of the Directive, as detailed later.

2.3 The 2014/95/EU Directive: Nonfinancial Disclosure

Since 2011, the European Commission has always placed great emphasis on the need to improve and harmonize nonfinancial information about social and environmental matters across companies, particularly across larger entities. The European Parliament also recognized this need and required the Commission to prepare several legislative initiatives that led to the issuance of the 2014/95/EU Directive to reinforce the requirements about nonfinancial information that were already incorporated in the 2013/34/EU Directive.

According to the 2013/34/EU Directive, the management report and the consolidated management report should provide "non-financial performance indicators including information relating to environmental and employee matters." The 2014/95/EU Directive extends the content of the 2013/34/EU Directive focusing on the specific additional nonfinancial information requirements to be incorporated into the "nonfinancial statement." Companies should provide an understanding of the business development, performance, position, and impact of its activity relating to environmental, social, and employee matters, respect for human rights, and anti-corruption and bribery matters. This information is required to be included in the management report for large companies which are considered public interest entities (PIEs) with more than 500 employees.

The content of this Directive was transposed into the Spanish regulation through the Royal Decree 17/2017 and Law 11/2018 about nonfinancial information and diversity.[11] This latest legislative development reduces the size limits included in the Directive and therefore extends the nonfinancial information requirements to non-PIE groups of companies that for 2 consecutive years comply with two out of the following limits: (a) have more than 250 employees, (b) consolidated revenues > EUR 4,000,000, and (c) consolidated assets > EUR 20,000,000. Although many listed companies already provided nonfinancial information within the annual Corporate Social Responsibility Report or in their Integrated Annual Reports, this legislation increased the amount of information to be disclosed.

Consistent with the Directive, Law 11/2018 promotes the use of the different national and international frameworks and guidelines to prepare nonfinancial information, particularly those from some well-known international organizations, [12] as well as the Spanish Stock Exchange Commission (CNMV) Guidelines or the AECA Integrated Reporting Framework.

3 Implementation of the EU Directive 2013/34

3.1 General Provisions and Principles

As previously stated, the entrance of Spain into the European Economic Community (EEC) forced the incorporation of the Fourth and Seventh Directives and therefore the reform of the Code of Commerce, the issuance of an auditing law, and the issuance of a new PGC (*PGC-1990*). All these changes implied an absolute shift in the paradigm of the Spanish financial reporting system with the introduction of the "true and fair view" principle.

After all these significant changes were accomplished at the beginning of the 1990s, the second major change in the Spanish accounting regulatory framework arrived nearly two decades later. The issuance of Regulation 1606/2002 led to the issuance in 2007 of a new set of Spanish Generally Accepted Accounting Principles (PGC 2007) in order to adapt the existent Spanish accounting regulation to the content of the IFRS. The adoption of these accounting regulations implied an

[11]Royal Decree-Law 18/2017 and Law 11/2018 amended the Code of Commerce, the Company Law, and the Auditing Law in matters of nonfinancial information and diversity.

[12]The Eco-Management and Audit Scheme (EMAS) incorporated to the Spanish legislation in the Royal Decree 239/2013, the United Nations Global Compact for sustainable development, the Paris Agreement on Climate Change, the UN Guiding Principles on Business and Human Rights, the OECD Guidelines for Multinational Enterprises, the Sustainability Reporting Standards of the GRI, the United Nations Sustainable Development Goals, the EU Commission Guidelines (2017/C 215/01; 2019/C 209/01), the ISO standard 26000, the (SA) 8000 on International Corporate Social Responsibility, or the Tripartite Declaration of Principles concerning Multinational Enterprises and Social Policy (International Labor Organization).

absolute change of paradigm in the principles and objectives of financial reporting for all types of companies: listed vs. non-listed. As explained before, two different versions of the *PGC* were issued: a full version of the PGC-2007 and a simplified version of PGC-SMEs-2007 for small- and medium-sized entities.

Therefore, the implementation of Directive 2013/34/EU in the Spanish legislation did not imply significant changes in the regulation. The reason is that the *PGC-2007* and its simplified version *PGC-SMEs-2007* were already underpinned in the content of the superseded IASC conceptual framework. Therefore, both PGCs already incorporated the same financial reporting principles and general provisions included in the 2013/34/EU Directive: (a) going concern, (b) accrual, (c) consistency, (d) conservatism, (e) non-compensation of assets and liabilities (setoff), and (f) materiality. All principles are equally relevant. None of them prevails over the others. Disapplication of any of these principles in exceptional cases [13] (i.e., when there is a conflict between accounting principles) is only feasible (as in IFRS) to ensure the true and fair view principle in the presentation of the equity and financial position and results of the company.

Together with the accounting principles, the *PGC-2007* conceptual framework had already incorporated in the Spanish accounting regulation: (1) the "true and fair view principle"; (2) the qualitative characteristics of the accounting information: relevance, reliability, comparability, and understandability; (3) the components of the financial statements; (4) the recognition criteria; and (5) the valuation principles, particularly fair value. The enactment of Law 16/2007 updated the Spanish legislation (Code of Commerce and Company Law) to embrace the following relevant issues: (1) the new set of financial statements, incorporating the statement of changes in equity; (2) the importance of the economic substance over the legal form of the transaction; (3) the euro as the presentation currency; (4) the definition of the elements of the financial statements; (5) the incorporation of new valuation principles, such as amortized cost and fair value; (6) the introduction of the concept of impairment loss for assets, particularly goodwill impairment; and (7) the straightforward recognition in equity of certain gains and losses.

[13] As IFRS, the PGC gives flexibility and allows disapplication under justified circumstances. However, this is rarely applied in practice, and any noncompliance with a standard must be previously approved by the regulator. A relevant example was the case of bank mergers in 2010, where the Bank of Spain authorized the application of the "fresh starting" method and, therefore, no acquiring company was identified, and all companies applied fair value in the interests of a "true and fair view."

Table 3 Size limits for companies according to the Spanish accounting regulation

	PGC-2021 Limits to prepare abridged BS	*PGC-2021* Limits to prepare abridged PL	Limits to use PGC-SMEs-2021	Micro-entities[a] according to the Spanish regulation
Net turnover	EUR 8,000,000	EUR 22,800,000	EUR 8,000,000	EUR 2,000,000
Total assets	EUR 4,000,000	EUR 11,400,000	EUR 4,000,000	EUR 1,000,000
Average number of employees	50	250	50	10

[a]The Spanish accounting regulation also considers micro-entities and recognizes for this set of undertakings an additional simplification of the accounting treatment that is applied in leasing transactions and income taxes. Under these exemptions for micro-entities, financial leasing is not considered, and therefore all leasing transactions are considered as an operating renting expense. Similarly, income tax resulting from the annual liquidation from tax authorities is registered as an operating expense, and therefore no differed tax assets or liabilities are considered

3.2 Financial Statement Formats: Balance Sheet and Profit and Loss Account, Simplifications for Small- and Medium-Sized Entities

Before the issuance of the 2013/34/EU Directive, the Spanish Company Law had already defined a set of limits to classify a company as SMEs and, therefore, to be eligible to present abridged financial statements. Therefore, these limits were already introduced since the issuance of the *PGC-1990*.

Table 3 shows the current limits, aligned with the ones established in the 2013/34/EU Directive. Consistent with its content, the Spanish accounting regulation requires small companies as defined in the 2013/34/EU Directive to present an abridged version of the balance sheet and the notes to the financial statements. They are also allowed to use the *PGC* for SMEs. The company must comply with at least two of the three limits shown in Table 3 for 2 consecutive financial years. When the content of the simplified version of the notes to the financial statements or the use of the *PGC* for SMEs is not enough to represent the "true and fair view" of the financial situation and performance, the company should provide any necessary additional information to comply with this core financial reporting principle.

Regardless of the size, companies considered public interest entities (PIEs) are not allowed to use the *PGC* for SMEs. The limits for the company to be eligible to present an abridged profit and loss account (PL) are more conservative under the *PGC* compared to the Directive. In addition, companies under this medium-sized category are not allowed to use the *PGC* for SMEs.

The 2013 Directive adopts two different formats to prepare each of the two required financial statements. The balance sheet (BS henceforth) can be prepared with either a horizontal (A = E + L) or vertical structure (A – L = E), whereas the profit and loss account (PL henceforth) can be prepared either by nature or by function.

The Spanish PGC and the PGC for SMEs adopt the horizontal layout for the BS and the PL account by nature of the expense. The main difference in the BS arises in the classification of subscribed capital unpaid and formation expenses considered in the 2013 Directive as part of the asset structure, while the Spanish GAAP classifies both categories in the equity structure.

Regarding the PL account, there are two remarkable differences: firstly, the recognition in the Spanish PGC of a separate line for discontinued operations, in line with the IFRS standards, and, secondly, the clear identification of operating income and financial income in separate lines.

The Spanish Company Law has traditionally required companies to prepare the management report and provides the guidelines of the content that should be included, fully aligned with the 2013/34/EU Directive. Therefore, this requirement is not new for Spanish companies. As in the Directive, it also includes the exemption from the obligation to prepare the management report to those companies that comply with the size limits to elaborate abridge balance sheet (Table 3). Similarly, small- and medium-sized companies are not required to prepare nonfinancial information.

3.3 Amendments to National Rules

The reform of the auditing law (Law 22/2015) was the means to incorporate the Directive. The main changes introduced because of the Directive were as follows:

3.3.1 For Small- and Medium-Sized Entities (SMEs)

For SMEs, the obligation to issue the statement of changes in equity for small companies is eliminated (the cash flow statement was never required). Consequently, the Code of Commerce and the Company Law, which previously did require it, are amended.

Second, the content of the notes to the annual accounts has been reduced compared to previous requirements in the Code of Commerce and Company Law and the requirements settled in *PGC*-2007. The Directive sets out the maximum amount of information that the company is required to provide (without prejudice to the information which may be required by law or which is necessary to give a true and fair view). These fewer requirements were incorporated accordingly in *PGC*-SMEs-2021. Table 4 contains the list of notes to the financial statements included in the *PGC*-2021 and *PGC*-2021 for SMEs.

Table 4 Notes to the financial statements: information requirements established in the PGC-2021 and PGC-SMEs-2021

PGC-2021 notes to the financial statements	PGC-SMEs-2021 notes to the financial statements
1. Activity of the company 2. Basis of preparation of the financial statements 3. Net income distribution 4. Recognition and measurement standards 5. Tangible assets 6. Property, plant, and equipment 7. Intangible assets 8. Leasing transactions 9. Financial instruments 10. Inventory 11. Foreign currency transactions 12. Taxes 13. Revenues and expenses 14. Provisions and contingencies 15. Environmental information 16. Long-term employee benefits 17. Share-based transactions 18. Grants, donations, and legacies 19. Business combinations 20. Joint ventures 21. Noncurrent assets held for sale 22. Events after the balance sheet date 23. Related party transactions 24. Other information (i.e., audit fees, number of employees) 25. Segment information	1. Activity of the company 2. Basis of preparation of the financial statements 3. Recognition and measurement standards 4. Property, plant, and equipment, intangible assets, and investment property 5. Financial assets 6. Financial liabilities 7. Equity 8. Taxes 9. Related party transactions 10. Other information (i.e., number of employees)

3.3.2 For All Companies Regardless of the Size

The Code of Commerce is amended in the following issues: First, it is allowed that any asset and liability might be measured at fair value if a European standard requires it. Until then, just financial instruments classified as trading portfolio or available for sale and derivatives (in accordance with IAS 39) were required to be measured at fair value. This amendment facilitated the adaptation to IFRS 9 in *PGC-2021*. Second, it is specified that if the useful life of intangible assets cannot be reliably estimated, intangible assets will be amortized over 10 years, unless another legal or regulatory provision indicates otherwise. Therefore, the possibility of considering an indefinite useful life is abandoned. Concerning goodwill, and in line with the provisions established for intangible assets, it is presumed that unless there is evidence to the contrary, the useful life is 10 years. The notes to the financial statements must disclose the useful life of intangible assets. In addition, the rules on impairment were revised in the latest *PGC-2021* to adapt them to the new amortization criteria for these assets.

3.3.3 Changes in Consolidated Financial Statements

The Code of Commerce is amended to introduce a change to the size exemption. The size limits are kept as in the Directive. However, it is assumed that if any company within the group is qualified as a public interest entity (previously it was required to issue securities admitted to trading on a regulated market), in any case, the group must consolidate regardless of the size of the group in which they are included as subsidiaries based on the nature of their activity, size, or number of employees.

In addition, a new exemption from the obligation to prepare consolidated financial statements is included when (1) in extremely rare cases in which the information necessary to prepare the consolidated financial statements is not available, (2) when the sole purpose of holding the shares of this company is for subsequent disposal, and (3) when severe and lasting restrictions hinder the exercise of control by the parent company over this subsidiary. The 2013/34/EU Directive exception to consolidating for those groups in which the parent company only participates in subsidiaries that do not have a significant impact on the true and fair view of the group was already incorporated into the Spanish consolidation rules.

4 Valuation Approaches

Since the issuance of *PGC*-2007 and PGC-SMEs-2007, the following valuation approaches are considered: (a) historical cost, (b) fair value, (c) net realizable value, (d) present value, (e) value in use, (f) cost to sell, and (g) amortized cost. In addition, the PGC describes the concept of residual value, net book value, and transaction costs for financial assets and liabilities. These valuation approaches are mostly aligned with IFRS. The most significant differences in the recognition and measurement with IFRS nowadays are:

(i) Cost model is required, and revaluation is not allowed for PPE and intangible assets.
(ii) Cost is required for investment property and fair value is not allowed.
(iii) Cost is required for investment in subsidiaries, and associated entities and the fair value option and equity method are not allowed.
(iv) Goodwill for noncontrolling interest recognition is not allowed.
(v) Research cost can be capitalized under some circumstances.
(vi) Indefinite useful life is not considered for intangible assets, and therefore goodwill must be amortized (because of the 2013/34/EU Directive).
(vii) Operating leasing is not recognized in the balance sheet (the current *PGC*-2021 does not embrace the content of the IFRS 16).

Following the content of the Directive, the most significant change in valuation approaches was related to goodwill. The initial valuation approach for goodwill was aligned with the content of the IFRS 3 and IAS 36 and, therefore, omitted

Table 5 The content of annual reports for the various types of companies

	Micro-entities	SMEs	Large	Listed companies
Management report			X	X
Nonfinancial disclosures[a]			X	X
Disclosure of adopted accounting policies	X	X	X	X
Profit and loss/balance sheet statements	X	X	X	X
Possibility of abridged balance sheet	X	X		
Possibility of abridged profit and loss statement	X	X		
Cash flow statement			X	X
Statement of changes in equity			X	X
Notes to the financial statements (increasing requirements depending on the type of company)	X	X	X	X

[a]Nonfinancial information requirements apply also to non-PIE groups of companies that for 2 consecutive years comply with two out of the following limits: (a) have more than 250 employees, (b) consolidated revenues > EUR 4,000,000, and (c) consolidated assets > EUR 20,000,000. Otherwise, companies are exempt from this requirement

amortization as a measurement criterion after initial recognition. Impairment as considered in IAS 36 and IFRS 3 was therefore adopted approach for goodwill and other intangible assets with an indefinite useful life. The *PGC*-2007 and even the *PGC*-SMEs-2007 considered that goodwill and intangible assets with an indefinite useful life should be annually tested for impairment.[14]

Although it is allowed by the 2013/34/EU Directive, asset revaluation has been never allowed under the *PGC*, unless it was authorized by law,[15] nor has the LIFO method for inventory.

Table 5 summarizes the main valuation approaches adopted in the current Spanish GAAP. The differences between the *PGC*-2021 and the *PGC*-SMEs-2021 are scarce. The *PGC*-SMEs_2021 does not include the valuation criteria for goodwill nor noncurrent asset held for sale, share-based transactions, or long-term employee benefits. In addition, it simplifies the revenue recognition criteria. Regarding financial instruments, the *PGC*-SMEs-2021 omits the category of other financial assets at fair value with changes in equity (Tables 6, 7, 8, and 9).

[14]Additionally, to preserve the equity value of the company and to avoid potential goodwill or intangible asset miss valuations, the *PGC*-2007 required a non-distributable reserve for an amount equal to 10% of the goodwill amount.

[15]The latest government authorizations to revalue assets took place in 1996.

Table 6 Measurement bases and accounting methods used in the Spanish PGC-2021 for various assets and liabilities (part I)

Asset/ liability	Measurement bases allowed	Model/ method used	Value adjustments recognized in	Comments
Intangible assets	Acquisition cost Production cost	Cost model	Profit and loss (impairment and amortization)	Intangible assets are considered to have a definitive useful life. If useful life cannot be estimated, the PGC establishes a maximum of a 10-year period (i.e., goodwill)
	Fair value (i.e., business combinations, grants)	Revaluation model is not permitted	*Impairment reversals* are permitted with the same limit as in IAS 36, except for goodwill impairments	
Research and development	Acquisition cost Production cost	Cost model	Profit and loss (impairment and amortization)	*Research expenditures*: capitalization is **permitted** when the capitalization requirements are met *Development expenditures*: capitalization **required** when the capitalization requirements are met
	Fair value (i.e., business combinations)	Revaluation model is not permitted	*Impairment reversals* are permitted with the same limit as in IAS 36	
Tangible fixed/ noncurrent assets	Acquisition cost Production cost	Cost model	Profit and loss (impairments and amortization)	*Noncurrent assets held for sale*, must be classified as **current assets** and valued at the highest of its NBV or fair value less cost to sale
	Fair value (i.e., business combinations)	Revaluation model is not permitted	*Impairment reversals* are permitted with the same limit as in IAS 36	
Investment property	Acquisition cost	Cost model	Profit and loss (impairments and amortization)	Classification in a separate category in the balance sheet
	Fair value (i.e., business combinations)	Revaluation model is not permitted	*Impairment reversals* are permitted with the same limit as in IAS 36	

5 Conclusions

Spanish accounting regulation is ultimately determined by a governmental body (*ICAC*), although the influence of academics and practitioners can be considered significant. The national GAAP (*PGC*) has been clearly inspired by the IFRS principles since the early 1990s. However, Spain has not given up its sovereignty in the accounting standard-setting process after the change in the EU strategy to adopt IFRS standards. Spain has chosen to consolidate a dual model where the

Table 7 Measurement bases and accounting methods used in the Spanish PGC-2021 for various assets and liabilities (part II)

Asset/liability	Measurement bases allowed	Model/method used	Value adjustments recognized in	Comments
Inventories	Acquisition cost Production cost Net realizable value	Cost model Inventory must be measured at the lowest of its cost or net realizable value	Profit and loss (impairments) Impairment reversals are permitted	Allowed cost formulas: FIFO and weighted average cost
Leasing	Fair value Present value	Operating lease (lessee): expense recognition Finance lease (lessee): assets and liabilities for an amount equal to the lower of fair value of the asset or the present value of the lease payments	Profit and loss (operating leases) Asset and liabilities (finance leases)	Separation between finance and operating lease as in IAS 17 (superseded) Sale and lease back transactions do not lead to the recognition of gains and losses
Provisions	Present value	Initial recognition: present value of the expected future outflows required to settle the obligation	Profit and loss	
Investments in subsidiaries, jointly controlled companies, and associates (parent company financial statements)	Acquisition cost	Cost model	Profit and loss (impairments)	
Investments in subsidiaries, jointly controlled companies, and associates (consolidated financial statements)	Acquisition cost	*Subsidiaries*: full consolidation *Jointly controlled*: proportional consolidation and equity method *Associates*: equity method		

national GAAP coexists with IFRS with both accounting regulations highly harmonized, even when they are applied to SME entities.

The implementation of Directive 2013/34/EU in the Spanish legislation did not bring significant changes. Leaving aside the move from the impairment to the amortization model for goodwill and other intangibles, the main change for the

Table 8 Measurement bases and accounting methods used in the Spanish PGC-2021 for various assets and liabilities (part III)

Asset/liability	Measurement bases allowed	Model/method used	Value adjustments recognized in	Comments
Investments in joint operations (financial statements of the investor)	Acquisition cost Proportion of joint venture's assets and liabilities	Cost model	Profit and loss: proportion of joint venture's revenues and expenses	
Investments in joint operations (financial statements of the investor)	Acquisition cost Proportion of joint venture's assets and liabilities	Cost model	Profit and loss: proportion of joint venture's revenues and expenses	
Investments in joint ventures and joint operations (consolidated financial statements)		*Joint ventures*: proportional consolidation and equity method *Joint operations*: proportion of joint venture's assets and liabilities		
Financial assets (1): held-for-trading financial assets, financial derivatives, and hybrid financial assets	Fair value	Fair value model	Profit and loss (impairment)	Hedging rules similar to IFRS 9
Financial assets (2): long-term receivables and credits; held to maturity investments	Amortized cost Nominal value (short-term)	Amortized cost	Profit and loss (impairment) Impairment is estimated as the difference between the present value of the future expected cash flows and the book value of the asset	

SMEs was a reduction of some disclosure requirements in the notes and the elimination for SMEs of the obligation to issue the statement of changes in equity.

The latest reform to revise the national GAAP through the issuance of the current *PGC*-2021 to be aligned with the last changes in IFRS moves a step backward in the traditional strategy of minimizing the differences in the recognition and valuation criteria between national GAAP and IFRS. While *PGC*-2021 is mostly aligned with IFRS 9 (Financial Instruments) and aligned with IFRS 13 (Fair Value) and IFRS 15 (Revenue Recognition), the fact of rejecting the alignment to IFRS 16 (Leases)

Table 9 Measurement bases and accounting methods used in the Spanish PGC-2021 for various assets and liabilities (part IV)

Asset/liability	Measurement bases allowed	Model/ method used	Value adjustments recognized in	Comments
Financial assets (3): residual category for financial assets that cannot be considered in the previous categories	Fair value	Fair value model	Profit and loss (impairment) Equity (comprehensive income), only changes in value not linked to impairments, interests, or changes in currency values	Acquisition costs can be added to the fair value at initial recognition
Financial assets (4): investments in equity where fair value cannot be estimated reliably	Acquisition cost	Cost model	Profit and loss (impairment)	
Financial liabilities (1): trade payables and loans	Amortized cost Nominal value (short-term)	Amortized cost model	Profit and loss	Short-term payables with no contractual interest rate, will be recognized at its nominal value
Financial liabilities (2): held-for-trading liabilities	Fair value	Fair value model	Profit and loss. All changes in value are recognized in P&L	The PGC does not incorporate the IFRS 9 option to recognize in equity all changes in the liability's fair value associated with the company's credit risk

will increase the differences between the individual and consolidated accounts over the next few years, at least in the case of many listed entities and non-listed groups adopting IFRS for consolidated accounts. However, complexity for smaller entities will be undoubtedly avoided.

References

Cañibano, L., & Gisbert, A. (2007). El proceso de armonización contable internacional, la estrategia europea y la adaptación de la normativa contable en España. *Contaduría, 1*, 11–40.

Cañibano, L., & Ucieda, J. L. (2004). Accounting and financial reporting in Spain. In L. Cañibano & A. Mora (Eds.), *Readings in European accounting* (pp. 19–55). AECA.

Giner, B. (2003). Accounting in Spain. In P. Walton, A. Hallen, & B. Raffounier (Eds.), *International accounting* (pp. 253–260). Thomson.

Giner, B., & Mora, A. (2021). Political interference in private entities' financial reporting and the public interest: evidence from the Spanish financial crisis. *Accounting Auditing & Accountability Journal, 34*(7), 1581–1607.

Gonzalo, J. A. (2014). La Reforma Contable Española: un balance. *Spanish Accounting Review, 17*(2), 183–200.

Mora, A. (2017). The role and the current status of IFRS in the completion of national accounting rules—Evidence from Spain. *Accounting in Europe, 14*(1-2), 199–206.

Ucieda, J. L., & Gómez, P. (2020). *Accounting regulation & business reporting in Spain*. AECA.

Ucieda, J. L., & Gonzalo, J. A. (2019). The financial crisis impact on institutions and accounting practices in Spain. In V. Krivogorsky (Ed.), *Institutions and accounting practices after the financial crisis international perspective* (pp. 180–210). Routledge/Taylor & Francis.

Denmark

Frank Thinggaard

1 Introduction: The National Accounting Scenario

1.1 The Role of Civil Code (Company Law)

The Danish legal system resembles the continental European law tradition in the sense that the central legal source is most often written legislation passed by parliament. However, law scholars usually describe the civil law tradition in Denmark as a special Scandinavian/Nordic form. One of the characteristics is that the preparatory work for new laws has a very special status. In particular, Danish law attaches great importance to the explanatory notes that accompany a bill as these notes contribute to ensuring that the overall objectives of the bill and the content of the individual provisions are interpreted correctly (Blume, 2011). In Denmark, the EU accounting directives and regulations for nonfinancial companies are transposed into one Act, the Danish Financial Statements Act (the "Aarsregnskabsloven"). The Act is supplemented with a statutory order (the "IFRS-bekendtgørelsen"), which identifies (relatively few) sections in the Act that are still applicable for the companies that mandatorily or voluntarily prepare consolidated or individual financial statements in accordance with IFRS. The first Danish Financial Statements Act was adopted in 1981, but the Act has subsequently been revised on numerous occasions.

F. Thinggaard (✉)
Department of Economics and Business Economics, Aarhus University, Aarhus, Denmark
e-mail: fth@econ.au.dk

A. Incollingo, A. Lionzo (eds.), *The European Harmonization of National Accounting Rules*, SIDREA Series in Accounting and Business Administration,
https://doi.org/10.1007/978-3-031-42931-6_7

1.2 The Role of Professional Standard-Setting Bodies (Accounting Standards)

In 2001, a new section (Section 136) was inserted in the Financial Statements Act, which authorized the Danish Commerce and Companies Agency (today the Danish Business Authority) to issue standards that must, to the extent necessary, complete and supplement the Act. According to the section, the Business Authority has the option to delegate the work to an independent organization. So far, however, no such standard-setting body has been set up. This means that there is no official accounting standard setter in Denmark similar to those found in many other countries (e.g., the FRC in the UK or the DRSC (ASCG) in Germany). But on an ad hoc basis, the Danish Business Authority issues interpretations and guidelines that clarify the accounting issues that arise in relation to the provisions of the Financial Statements Act. The main reason for not having a separate Danish standard-setting body is Denmark's positive attitude and orientation toward IFRS.

Notwithstanding that there is no official standard-setting organization, a collaboration with the Danish Organization of Approved Auditors (FSR - danske revisorer) at the helm began issuing accounting standards in 1998. For a period of time, those standards were mandatory for issuers of shares at the Copenhagen Stock Exchange according to the listing rules. However, since 2005, when the international accounting standards took over for the listed companies in the consolidated financial statements, these standards have not had any formal status in the regulatory hierarchy.

1.3 The Role of Tax Regulation

Until 1970, financial statements from Danish companies were strongly influenced by the tax rules for the recognition and measurement of income, expenses, assets, and liabilities. Thereafter, under the influence of developments in the UK and the USA, the larger Danish companies, in particular, developed financial statements purely with the aim of providing a true and fair view of the companies' economic activities (Erhvervs- og Selskabsstyrelsen, Erhvervsministeriet, 1999, p. 15). As the first country in the EC, Denmark adopted a separate Financial Statements Act in 1981 based on the Fourth Council Directive (78/660/EEC). The Directive did not preclude assets from being measured at tax values in the financial statements (cf. Article 35 (1) d and Article 39 (1) e) — similar to Article 17 (1) b in the current Directive), but Denmark decided not to incorporate these rights in the Financial Statements Act (Folketinget, 1981, p. 3006). In fact, the Financial Statements Act of 1981 formally severed all ties to the tax rules. So in Denmark there is no authoritative principle similar to the German "Massgeblichkeitsprinzip"—the principle of congruence (see, e.g., Alexander & Nobes, 2020, Section 5.3.4). However, in practice many of the rules are identical for the two sets of reports, and the taxable income of a company is

Table 1 Number of active companies at the end of the financial year 2020

Employees	Total	%
Total	292,335	
0[a]	175,143	60
1–2	69,640	24
3–5	16,866	6
6–9	9970	3
10–20	9522	3
More than 20	11,194	4

Source: Data received from the Danish Business Authority based on XBRL filings in the Central Business Register

[a]Includes both companies that positively stated 0 employees and companies without registrations

obtained by adjusting the financial statements for the differences that remain. In this situation, the tax return is therefore not an actual account that can stand alone but only a number of adjustments to the operating accounts (Erhvervs- og Selskabsstyrelsen, Erhvervsministeriet, 1999, p. 224).

1.4 Economic and Financial Reporting System

Table 1 provides information based on the 2020 financial statements about the number of active companies in the Danish economy classified by the number of employees.

Aggregated data reported in Table 1 clearly shows that the Danish business environment is dominated by small- and micro-sized companies. Thus, 90% of the Danish companies have five or less employees.

The Danish Financial Statements Act is structured as a building block system with four accounting classes A, B, C, and D. The building block system basically means that the set of rules that each company is bound to follow in the preparation of its annual report primarily depends on the size of the company. However, there are two accounting classes A and D that are based on the entity's legal form of organization or stock exchange listing status without regard to the size. Accounting class A contains commercial entities that do not have limited liability such as sole proprietorships and partnerships. They are not required to submit an annual report to the Business Authority. However, if they prepare an annual report, which is not solely for its own internal use, then they have to follow the—rather broad—rules in accounting class A. Accounting class D is reserved for listed companies and state-owned public companies, and it has the most demanding accounting requirements. Table 2 provides an overview of the accounting classes and the size limits.

Accounting rules for a "lower" accounting class apply to companies in a "higher" accounting class if no new provisions are inserted for the "higher" accounting class. In this respect, the law was an early application of the "think small first principle" that was advanced by the European Commission in 2008 (European Commission,

Table 2 Size limits for companies according to the Danish Financial Statements Act

	Accounting class A	Accounting class B		Accounting class C		Accounting class D
	Sole proprietorships, partnerships, etc.	Micro	Small	Medium-sized	Large	Listed + state-owned public companies
Total assets		0–0.36m EUR	0–6m EUR	6.01m–21m EUR	>21m EUR	
Net revenue		0–0.72m EUR	0–12m EUR	12.01m–42m EUR	>42m EUR	
Average number of employees		0–10	0–50	51–250	>250	

Source: The Danish Financial Statements Act, Sections 7 and 22a translated into Euros

2008). The building block system formally has four general accounting classes: A, B, C, and D. In reality, however, accounting class C consists of two accounting classes with slightly differentiated requirements for medium-sized and large companies, and with the adoption of Directive 2013/34 accounting class B was split into two subgroups: micro-entities and small companies. As regards the size criteria, Denmark has a long tradition of exploiting the size limits in the Accounting Directive (currently Article 3) for micro, small, medium, and large undertakings to the maximum. According to Section 7 (5) in the Financial Statements Act, companies are allowed to apply some or even all of the rules from a "higher" accounting class if they wish to do so, provided that this is done in a systematic and consistent way.

Table 3 shows a distribution according to accounting class of the 2020 financial reports filed in the central company register.[1] The table is not fully complete since the table is based on XBRL filings, and a number of reports are missing in the table due to technical problems encountered by the Danish Business Authority when downloading the data (an estimate by the Business Authority suggests approximately 5000 observations). However, the table gives an indication of the distribution of companies with limited liability in Denmark, and it illustrates the use of the building block system in the Financial Statements Act.

Table 3 shows that less than three percent of the reportable companies belong to the group of medium or large companies (accounting class C) or listed or state-owned public companies (accounting class D). At the end of the year 2021, a total of 126 companies were listed on the Nasdaq Copenhagen Stock Exchange. Before dismissing this number as unimportant, the Danish population of just 5.8 million

[1] Annual reports on an individual basis are available free of charge from the Central Business Register: https://datacvr.virk.dk/ (search by company name or by use of the company number available on the companies' websites). The Danish word for financial report is "regnskab."

Table 3 Financial reports for the financial year 2020 filed with the Danish Business Authority, distributed according to accounting classes

	Separate financial statements	Consolidated financial statements	Total	Percentage
Financial statement year 2020				
Accounting class A	73	0	73	0.03
Accounting class B—micro	35,748	0	35,748	12.28
Accounting class B—small	247,434	217	247,651	85.10
Accounting class C—medium	3094	1973	5067	1.74
Accounting class C—large	1013	983	1996	0.69
Accounting class D (not IFRS)	12	15	27	0.01
Accounting class D + others (IFRS)	0	433	433	0.15
Total	287,374	3621	290,995	100

Source: Data received from the Danish Business Authority based on XBRL filings in the Central Business Register

should be taken into consideration. The number of listed companies per million inhabitants in Denmark is thus significantly higher than in, e.g., Germany and France.[2] Nonetheless, Denmark has an extremely high number of companies relying on bank financing as their most important source of finance.

2 The Evolution of Accounting Regulations

2.1 The Danish Financial Statements Act: Background and Orientation

The first Danish Financial Statements Act was adopted in 1981 and was based on the Fourth Council Directive (78/660/EEC). Before that time, financial reporting was regulated by very few sections in the Companies Act. In 2001, a major revision of the Danish Financial Statements Act was carried out. One of the purposes was to modernize the law. Among other things, the legislators wanted to exploit the space and flexibility provided by the Accounting Directives to follow the changes in the international accounting standards that had been made since the 1981 law was passed and to align the law more clearly with the conceptual basis used by the international accounting standard setters (Folketinget, 2001).

[2] https://data.worldbank.org/indicator/CM.MKT.LDOM.NO?most_recent_year_desc=false.

The 2001 revision laid the foundation for the Financial Statements Act in force today. However, the law is changed and adapted on a continuous basis. The Danish Business Authority is an agency under the Ministry of Business entrusted with the task to participate in the legislative process and prepare draft legislation within the business area and to be involved in the governmental supervision and enforcement of regulations within the business area. They report that in the period 2001–2019, there have been no less than 34 large and small amendments to the law. The incorporation of the Accounting Directive 2013/34/EU in 2015 is one of the more significant changes.

2.2 EU Directive 2013/34 Transposition

The Danish Business Authority is the driving force in the preparation of new accounting legislation—sometimes triggered by initiatives from the Government in power or initiated by the need to change the national legislation due to changes in the EU regulations. When major changes to the Financial Statements Act are considered, a thorough due process will start. This involves consulting with the Business Authority's accounting advisory body (the "Regnskabsrådet"), sending the draft bill to a large number of interest groups for commenting, etc. However, the changes in the 2013/34/EU Accounting Directive were considered so important that the Business Authority additionally conducted a survey among potential users of financial statements from smaller entities about the value and use of information in the financial report (Damvad, 2014), and the Parliament invited representatives of various stakeholders to a public hearing. The law was passed by the Danish Parliament on June 1, 2015. It also included the amendments of the Directive 2014/95/EU on the publication of nonfinancial information and information on diversity for certain large companies and groups. However, in 2018, the Danish Business Authority realized that some provisions of the Accounting Directive had not been fully implemented in the Danish Financial Statements Act or that the requirements were implemented in an inappropriate manner (Folketinget, 2018, p. 9), and the Act was consequently changed again.

2.3 The Level of IFRS Adoption and the Level of Convergence of Local GAAP to IFRS

Thinggaard (2017) has analyzed the role and current status of IFRS in the completion of the Danish accounting rules. His analysis shows that the provisions in the Act are aligned with the IFRS to a great extent. It also shows that the Danish legislators extensively refer to IFRS in the explanatory notes that accompany a bill and hence that they consider the IFRS to be the source to use for completing the national rules.

Table 4 Use of IAS/IFRS in consolidated and individual financial statements in Denmark

	Use of IAS/IFRS in the consolidated financial statements	Use of IAS/IFRS in the individual financial statements
Listed companies	Mandatory from January 1, 2005 (Regulation (EC) No 1606/2002)	Mandatory from January 1, 2009, if the reporting entity only prepares individual financial statements (Financial Statements Act, Section 137 (2)) Optional for all other entities
Non-listed companies	Optional for all (Financial Statements Act, Section 137 (1))	Optional for all (Financial Statements Act, Section 137 (1))

The following quote from the legislators' notes to the draft bill from 2018 illustrates this fact:

> When the Financial Statements Act was amended in 2015, as many conflicts as possible between the Financial Statements Act and IFRS were eliminated. However, certain conflicts could not be removed due to requirements in the Accounting Directive. The Danish Financial Statements Act is a frame law, and there is therefore a need for reference to interpretations in relation to how the framework is to be filled in. Here, it has been found most appropriate that the interpretation is based on international standards. (Folketinget, 2018, p. 11)

Table 4 shows the extent to which Denmark requires or permits IFRS in consolidated and individual financial statements.

Table 4 clearly shows the positive Danish attitude toward IFRS. A listed company needs to produce at least one financial report based on IFRS. If it is the parent company of a group, then the consolidated financial statements must, of course, be based on IFRS, and if it is a listed, single company with no subsidiaries or if the company for other reasons does not produce consolidated financial statements, then the individual financial statements will have to be prepared in accordance with IFRS. For all other companies—listed or non-listed—the use of EU-endorsed IFRS instead of the provisions in the Financial Statements Act is optional.

2.4 *Nonfinancial Disclosure Evolution*

Table 5 provides information about the nonfinancial disclosure requirements in force in Denmark and the group of companies to which they apply.

Denmark introduced CSR reporting rules in the Financial Statements Act Section 99a in 2009, i.e., long before the EU amended the Accounting Directive with Directive 2014/95/EU in 2014 as regards disclosure of nonfinancial and diversity information. The purpose of the regulation in 2009 was to encourage the largest Danish companies, listed companies, and state-owned public limited

Table 5 Nonfinancial disclosure requirements in Denmark

	Accounting class C		Accounting class D			PIE
Disclosure requirement (section in the Danish Financial Statements Act)	Medium > 6/12/50 ≤ 21/42/250[a]	Large > 21/42/250	Listed	State-owned public companies	Large listed > 21/42/250	> 21/42/500
Nonfinancial statement ("CSR statement") Based on Directive 2014/95/EU, Article 19a (99a)		X	X	X		
Target figure for the proportion of the underrepresented gender in the top management body + policy to increase the proportion Partly based on Directive 2014/95/EU Article 20 paragraph 1 (99b (1))		X	X	X		
A description of the policy applied in order to increase the proportion of the underrepresented gender in other management levels (national requirement) (99b (3))		X If more than 50 employees	X If more than 50 employees	X If more than 50 employees		
A description of the diversity policy applied in relation to the undertaking's administrative, management, and supervisory bodies Based on Directive 2014/95/EU Article 20 paragraph 1 (107 d)				X	X	
Report on payments to governments. Based on Directive 2013/34/EU Chapter 10 (99c)		X If active in the extractive industry	X If active in the extractive industry	X If active in the extractive industry		

Statement on data ethics (national requirement) (99d)		X	X	X		
Statement on corporate governance. Based on Directive 2013/34/EU Article 20 (107b and 107c)			X	X		
Information on how and to what extent the undertaking's activities are associated with economic activities that qualify as environmentally sustainable Based on Regulation 2020/852/EU Article 8 (2)						X

[a]Numbers refer to the size criteria for total assets/net revenue/average number of employees

companies, to actively consider how they could contribute to solving societal challenges (Folketinget, 2008, Section 3).

In 2014 the other EU countries caught up with the adoption of the Non-financial Reporting Directive 2014/95/EU. Denmark decided to keep the scope from the original rules, i.e., all large companies together with all listed and state-owned public companies were required to follow the rules and not just public interest entities as required by the Non-financial Reporting Directive.

In addition to the requirements arising from EU regulation, Denmark has some national requirements. In 2012 a new section (now Section 139c) was introduced in the Companies Act that requires all large companies, listed companies, and state-owned public companies to set a target figure for the proportion of the underrepresented gender in their top management body as well as to draw up a policy to increase the proportion of the underrepresented gender at the other management levels of the company. Simultaneously, a new section (Section 99b) was introduced in the Financial Statements Act that requires that the companies from fiscal years beginning on January 1, 2013, report annually about their targets and policies in the management's report in the annual report or on the company's website (to be referred to in the management report).

In 2020 Denmark introduced yet another national nonfinancial reporting requirement in the Financial Statements Act (Section 99 d). For fiscal years beginning on January 1, 2021, or later, all large companies, listed companies, and state-owned public companies are required to disclose in the management report or on the company's website (to be referred to in the management report) information about their data ethics. Companies that have a policy for data ethics must disclose information about the policy and about the way in which the company works with the policy. If the company does not have a policy for data ethics, then it has to explain the reasons for this (i.e., "comply or explain"). The Danish legislators emphasize that data ethics covers more than meeting applicable requirements for data and privacy protection in the narrow sense. According to guidance from the Danish Business Authority, data ethics is about "the company's ethical considerations in relation to how the company's use of data, its development and use of artificial intelligence, etc. affect our society" (Erhvervsstyrelsen, 2020, Section 1.1).

3 The Implementation of the EU Directive 2013/34

3.1 General Provisions

3.1.1 True and Fair View

In accordance with Article 4 (3) in Directive 2013/34, the Danish Financial Statements Act includes (in Section 11 (1)) an overarching objective (the "general clause") for the financial statements: they must give a true and fair view of the company's assets, liabilities, financial position, and profit or loss. The Financial

Statements Act supplements with an objective for the management report: it shall give a true and fair account of the matters to which the report relates. The Financial Statements Act Section 11 (3) contains the "true and fair override provision" from the Directive Article 4 (4). The general view is that application of the specific provisions in the Act will lead to financial statements that give a true and fair view. Hence, derogations from the provisions of the law in order to obtain a true and fair view (i.e., the true and fair override provision) will only come into play as a rare exception, not least because most issues can be solved by providing additional information. The decision to derogate must be based on a balancing of the qualitative characteristics, relevance and reliability (Folketinget, 2001, p. 3273). Rare exceptions could, for instance, be related to specific circumstances in the reporting entity or specific circumstances in the economic environment in which the reporting entity operates. It is difficult to find specific examples, but a hypothetical example could perhaps be the application of the reclassification rules for financial assets which the IASB introduced during the financial crisis in 2008. In 2008 the Financial Statements Act was based on IAS 39, and IAS 39 prohibited the reclassification of financial instruments into or out of the fair value through profit and loss category. However, in October 2008, with an extremely short notice, the IASB permitted certain nonderivative financial assets to be reclassified from the fair value through profit and loss category to categories measured at amortized cost (Fiechter, 2011; International Accounting Standards Board, 2008). Here a company could perhaps argue that application of the original rules would not provide a true and fair view of the company's affairs since this would entail measuring financial assets at fair value in a situation where they clearly are no longer held for the purpose of selling or repurchasing it in the near term, whereas the amended rules would give a true and fair view (note that this argument can be contested (Fiechter, 2011)). Notwithstanding, should the situation arise, then Danish companies are instructed by the legislators' notes to the 2015 draft bill only to choose an accounting solution that is in accordance with IFRS:

> It is unlikely that disapplication of specific provisions in the law can be made if companies make other choices for recognition and measurement than those permitted under IFRS. The reason is that the law is based on the same fundamental framework as the IFRS. Considerable resources are spent on continuous development of IFRS including a global dialogue with companies, financial statement users, authorities and auditors. It is consequently very unlikely that a company has such a special situation that this has not been taken into account by the IFRS. . . . The IFRS contain a large number of detailed provisions that are developed and changed more frequently than the Financial Statements Act. Consequently, there will be cases where the IFRS will take account of new situations—for example the consequences of a financial crisis—before the Act. In these cases it can be relevant for companies to derogate from the Act and apply a specific methodology from the IFRS . . . . (Folketinget, 2015, p. 47)

Again, this note stresses the important role that the Danish legislators attribute to the international accounting standards in the completion of the Danish accounting rules. However, the notes explain that this is not an open invitation to disapply the specific provisions in the Financial Statements Act simply because the companies prefer an IFRS solution:

> However, if a specific provision in an IFRS was adopted at the time when the Financial Statements Act adopted a different provision for a similar transaction, then the provision in the Act cannot be disapplied by arguing that the IFRS rules give a more true and fair view. Here the legislators have specifically decided to implement a regulation that deviates from the IFRS regulation of the similar transaction. (Folketinget, 2015, p. 47)

The use of a statement of other comprehensive income (IAS 1.81A) in addition to the profit and loss statement and the non-amortization of intangible assets with an indefinite useful life (IAS 38.107) are examples of IFRS solutions for which the true and fair override provision cannot be applied because the Danish legislators decided on—or were forced by the Accounting Directive to choose—a different provision at the adoption of the law.

3.1.2 General Financial Reporting Principles

Section 13 of the Danish Financial Statements Act contains the general financial reporting principles from Articles 6 (and 4) in the Directive 2013/34 worded as follows (non-authoritative translation from Danish by the Karnov Group[3] and emphasis added):

Section 13 (1). The annual report must be based on the following basic assumptions:

1. It must be prepared in a clear and well-arranged manner (*clarity*).
2. It must consider facts rather than formalities with no real contents (*substance*).
3. All relevant matters must be included in the annual report, unless such matters are insignificant (*materiality*). Where several insignificant matters are deemed to be significant when combined, such matters must be included.
4. The operation of an activity is assumed to continue (*going concern*), unless such activity is not to continue or is assumed not to be capable of continuing. If an activity is discontinued, classification and presentation as well as recognition and measurement must be adjusted accordingly.
5. Recognition and measurement must be carried out on a *prudent* basis, and, for example, all accounting estimates must be well founded and *neutral*. All value adjustments must be recognized, whether the result of the financial year is a profit or a loss.
6. Transactions, events, and changes in value must be recognized as they occur, regardless of the time of payment (*accruals basis*).
7. Recognition methods and measurement bases must be uniformly applied to the same categories of matters (*consistency*).
8. Each transaction, event, and change in value must be separately recognized and measured, and individual matters must not be offset against each other (*gross presentation*).

[3] https://pro.karnovgroup.dk/document/7000876463/1#LBKG2019838EN_P13.

9. The opening balance sheet for the financial year must be equivalent to the closing balance sheet for the previous financial year (*formal continuity*).

Section 13 (2): The financial year, the presentation and classification, the consolidation method, the recognition method and measurement basis, and the monetary unit applied must not change from year to year (*real continuity*). However, a change may take place if a more true and fair view is therefore obtained or is necessary to comply with new rules when transitioning to a new accounting class, statutory amendments, new rules or regulations laid down under Danish legislation, or new standards issued under Section 136.

The wording in the Danish Financial Statements Act is not a direct adoption of the wording in the Directive. Note, for instance, number 5 about the principle of prudence (sometimes referred to as conservatism). Only at the adoption of the EU Directive 2013/34 did the Danish Financial Statements Act include prudence/conservatism in the list of general financial reporting principles. Until then the concept of neutrality was thought to represent prudence. However, the Danish Business Authority realized that the Financial Statements Act needed to include this principle in order to reflect the Directive. In spite of this, the wording of the provision in the Financial Statements Act clarifies that neutrality is part of prudence, and the explanatory notes to this section in the draft bill still emphasize that these two concepts are not considered to be in conflict with each other when preparing annual reports (Folketinget, 2018, p. 20). So in line with the IASB conceptual framework (2018, paragraph 2.17), the Danish interpretation of the principle of prudence does not imply a systematic need for asymmetry. Note, for instance, that Section 13 (1) No. 5 mentions that "any" value adjustment shall be recognized, whereas Article 6 (1) (c) (iii) in Directive 2013/34 only mentions that all "negative" value adjustments shall be recognized. The Danish legislators acknowledge that the principle of prudence is embodied in specific provisions in the Danish Financial Statements Act, e.g., that write-downs on tangible fixed assets are mandatory, whereas revaluations are optional, but according to the explanatory notes to the draft bill: "The application of the principle of prudence pursuant to the Danish Financial Statements Act must not deviate from the principles in IFRS, as in substance there is a close connection between preamble No. 22 to the Accounting Directive and the IASB's conceptual framework" (Folketinget, 2018, p. 20). All in all, the essence of the Danish interpretation of prudence is that financial statement preparers must exercise caution when making judgments under conditions of uncertainty.

3.2 The Content of the Annual Report

Table 6 gives an overview of the elements that the annual report must include for the various accounting classes.

The annual report consists of the financial statements, the management statement, the management report, and any supplementary, voluntary reports (e.g., intellectual

Table 6 The content of the annual report for the various accounting classes

	A	B (micro)	B (small)	C (medium)	C (large)	D
Management statement	X	X	X	X	X	X
Management report		(X)[a]	(X)[a]	X	X	X
Disclosure of adopted accounting policies	X		X	X	X	X
Profit and loss and balance sheet statements	X	X	X	X	X	X
Cash flow statement				X	X	X
Statement of changes in equity				X	X	X
Notes (increasing requirements depending on accounting class)	X	X	X	X	X	X

[a]Accounting class B: the management report only has to describe the company's main activities and explain significant changes in the company's activities and financial conditions (if any)

capital statements, etc.). The term financial statements covers the profit and loss and balance sheet statements, the cash flow statement (if any), the statement of changes in equity (if any), and notes including the disclosure of adopted accounting policies.

Table 6 shows that almost all companies must include a management statement in the financial report. The management's statement is a statement in which the management, with its signature(s), states that it is responsible for the annual report and that the annual report, in the management's opinion, gives a true and fair view. Companies in accounting classes A–C are, however, exempted if the responsible management body only consists of one member.

All companies except firms in accounting class A must include a management report in which the management reviews the development and performance of the undertaking's business and of its position, together with a description of the principal risks and uncertainties that it faces. However, the requirements vary according to accounting class, for instance, as regards CSR disclosures (see Table 5).

As the only category, the micro-entities are exempted from disclosing in the notes the accounting policies adopted. This is one of only four disclosure exemptions that the Danish legislators specifically implemented in 2015 for micro-entities, based on the Directive Article 36 (this is elaborated on later in this chapter).

In accordance with the Directive, all companies must present a balance sheet and a statement of profit and loss. However, the requirements for a cash flow statement and a complete statement of changes in equity are purely national requirements. Table 6 shows that in Denmark this requirement applies to accounting class C and upward.

Note disclosures need to be provided by all companies, but the requirements are increasing with the accounting class (cf. later).

3.3 Balance Sheet and Profit and Loss Formats

The Danish Financial Statements Act provides the companies with a choice between two balance sheet forms, both of which are in the horizontal layout. The first form distinguishes between fixed assets and current assets, where fixed assets are defined in accordance with Article 2 (4) as assets that are intended for use on a continuing basis for the undertaking's activities. Liabilities on the credit side are divided into long-term and short-term liabilities, based on whether or not they are due within 1 year after the end of the financial year. Moreover, there is a separate category for provisions. The second form was introduced in 2015. The motivation for the introduction was the desire to adapt the Danish Financial Statements Act to international developments in the field of accounting (Folketinget, 2015, p. 124). This form is thus inspired by IFRS. Here the asset side distinguishes between current and noncurrent assets. Current assets are defined as in IAS 1.66, i.e., as assets that are expected to be realized or held for sale or consumption as part of the company's normal operating cycle, assets held primarily for the purpose of trading, assets that the company expects to realize within 12 months after the balance sheet date, or assets that are cash and cash equivalents that are not subject to any restrictions on negotiability. On the liability side, we find the same distinction between long-term and short-term liabilities as in the first form, as the Directive does not allow the Financial Statements Act to make the same distinction as in IAS 1.69. In this balance sheet form, there is—similar to IFRS—no separate category for provisions.

As regards the profit and loss statement, the Danish Financial Statements Act provides a choice between the two formats in Article 13 in the Directive, i.e., a layout based on expenses by nature and a layout based on expenses by function. As a result of the implementation of Directive 2013/34, extraordinary items are no longer part of the profit and loss statement. In return, a requirement was introduced that companies must disclose in a note the size and nature of income and expense items that are special due to their size or nature.

The balance sheet and profit and loss forms are almost the same for all limited liability companies regardless of size, i.e., accounting classes B, C, and D (see below for a review of discontinued operations and the option for small- and medium-sized companies to combine the first items in the layout of the profit and loss statement). Accounting class A, which contains sole proprietorships and partnerships that have no obligation to submit an annual report to the Business Authority but which can voluntarily choose to submit one, has more flexibility. During the deliberations in relation to the implementation of Directive 2013/34, the Danish Business Authority together with its accounting advisory board considered allowing micro-entities to prepare abridged balance sheet and profit and loss information (cf. Article 36 (2) in the Directive). A number of German examples were scrutinized. However, such significantly abridged financial statements were deemed as having too little usefulness for the financial statement users.

In connection with the amendment of the Danish Financial Statements Act in 2015, an obligation was introduced for companies in accounting classes C and D to present separately in the income statement and balance sheet, respectively, the activities that must be divested, closed, or abandoned according to an overall plan, unless they cannot be separated from the other activities. This is in accordance with the concept of discontinued operations in IFRS 5 and in the legislators' opinion something that can be accommodated within the requirements of the Articles 9 (2) and (3) in the Directive.

3.4 Simplifications and Exemptions for Micro-undertakings and Small- and Medium-Sized Entities

In addition to the exemption from presenting discontinued operations separately, companies in accounting class B are allowed to combine the first items in the layout of the profit and loss statement, and they are consequently exempt from disclosing the company's net revenue. This exception also applies to medium-sized companies in class C (Sections 32 and 81 of the Danish Financial Statements Act).

The Danish Financial Statements Act contains a number of important recognition and measurement simplifications and exemptions for micro-sized and small companies in accounting class B. The Financial Statement Act exploits, for instance, the surprising lack of detail in the Directive as regards the recognition of income and exempts micro-sized and small companies from the requirement to recognize income over time according to the degree of completion. In other words, companies in accounting class B, but not the medium-sized and large companies in accounting class C, nor the listed and state-owned public companies in accounting class D, are exempt from recognizing income in accordance with the percentage of completion method (Financial Statements Act, Section 49 (1)). The explanatory notes to the draft bill point to the international accounting standards for guidance on when and how to apply the percentage of completion method, and since 2018, after the issuance of IFRS 15, the notes specifically allow the companies a choice between using IFRS 15 and the old standards IAS 18 and IAS 11. The reason for allowing a choice between two solutions was that when the law was revised in 2018, it was considered too burdensome for the companies solely to follow IFRS 15 (Folketinget, 2018, p. 33).

Another exemption for the micro-entities and the small companies in accounting class B is that they do not have to recognize assets that they do not own from a legal viewpoint (i.e., leased assets/right-of-use assets and the corresponding lease liabilities) even though such assets meet the definition of assets in the Act (Financial Statements Act, Section 33 (1)). Here the Financial Statements Act uses the option in the Directive Article 6 (3) to exempt undertakings from the substance over form principle. The notes to the draft bill explain that those companies that are either required to recognize such assets (accounting classes C and D) or voluntarily decide to recognize such assets (accounting classes A and B) have a choice between using IFRS 16 or the old rules in IAS 17. This choice is considered an accounting policy choice that must be clearly stated in the disclosure of adopted accounting policies.

Article 12 (11) and annexes III and IV in the Directive state that national law may authorize the inclusion of costs of development under "Assets." Denmark has decided that large companies in accounting class C, and hence also companies in accounting class D, must recognize development costs (Financial Statements Act, Section 83), whereas all companies in accounting class B together with medium-sized companies in accounting class C are exempted (Financial Statements Act, Section 33).

The Financial Statements Act (Section 82) requires all companies in accounting classes C and D to include in the cost price of manufactured goods a reasonable proportion of fixed and variable overhead costs indirectly attributable to the production of the goods (cf. the Directive, Articles 2 (7) and 6 (1) (i)). However, all micro-sized and small companies in accounting class B are exempted from this requirement and consequently only have to include the costs directly attributable to the goods in inventory (Section 44 (1)). As regards fixed/noncurrent assets manufactured for the company's own use, all companies in accounting classes B, C, and D have the option, but not the obligation, to include indirectly attributable overhead costs.

As regards note disclosures, it follows from Article 4 (5) and Article 16 (3) of Directive 2013/34 that for small companies no information can be required in the annual accounts other than the information that follows from the Directive ("maximum harmonization"). Article 16 (1) contains the note disclosures that are required by all companies except micro-entities. In accordance with Article 16 (2), the member states are also allowed to require five additional note disclosures for small companies—all of which are mandatory for medium-sized and large companies.[4] However, Denmark does not require any of these disclosures for the small companies.

Article 36 of the Directive provides a number of exemptions for micro-entities, but Denmark chose only to implement a partial exemption as regards the notes to the financial statements in accordance with Article 16 of the Directive. Thus, the Financial Statements Act (Section 22 B) exempts micro-entities from four note disclosures required for other companies. These exemptions are (1) the requirement to disclose in the note the accounting policies adopted, (2) the requirement to disclose the amount of liabilities that are due more than 5 years after the balance sheet date, (3) the requirement to disclose special items, and (4) the requirement to disclose the average number of employees employed in the financial year. Thus, micro-entities will have to meet all the other requirements that apply to small companies in accounting class B. Micro-entities are defined in accordance with the size criteria in Article 3 (1) of the Directive, respecting the restrictions in Article 36 (7) for investment undertakings or financial holding undertakings. However, Denmark added an additional restriction: the exemptions for micro-entities cannot

[4]The additional note disclosures are (1) a specification of the changes from the beginning to the end of the financial statement year for fixed assets, (2) information about the closest undertaking that includes the company as a subsidiary in its consolidated financial statements, (3) the nature and business purpose of the company's significant arrangements that are not included in the balance sheet, (4) events after the balance sheet date, and (5) and transactions with related parties.

be used by companies that are parties to derivative financial instrument contracts. The reason for this additional restriction is the prohibition in Article 36 (3) of the Directive against being able to measure derivative financial instruments at fair value, which the Danish legislators find inappropriate (Folketinget, 2015, p. 53).

The bulk of the note disclosures that the companies must provide is included in the part of the Financial Statements Act that covers medium-sized companies in accounting class C. Large companies have only a few additional note disclosure requirements compared to medium-sized companies, e.g., the distribution of net revenue on activities and geographical markets, and disclosure of the fees paid to the audit firm that performs the statutory audit, and companies in accounting class D have yet another few additional note requirements.

That said, some exemption options in the Directive have not been used. For instance, as regards the obligation to draw up consolidated financial statements and a consolidated management report, Denmark has not used the option in the Directive, Article 23 (2), to exempt medium-sized groups. That is, only small groups are exempted (Financial Statements Act, Section 110). In the calculation of the size limits, the Danish Financial Statements Act offers the companies a choice between calculating the limits before or after the elimination of internal group transactions (cf. the Directive, Article 3(8)). In the former case, the standard size limits are increased by 20%.

4 Valuation Approaches

Table 7 provides an overview of the measurement bases and accounting methods available in the Danish Financial Statements Act for various assets and liabilities. From an overall perspective, the cost model is very widespread within the group of assets that do not generate cash flows independently of other assets such as intangible assets and property, plant, and equipment. The fair model, on the other hand, is very widespread within the group of financial instruments used for trading, shares without significant influence, derivatives, investment property, and assets and liabilities that qualify as hedged items in a fair value hedge. Overall, Table 7 clearly shows that the Danish legislators certainly are not opposed to the use of fair values—fair value is an optional measurement basis even for many nonfinancial assets. However, few companies use fair value measurements for nonfinancial assets, specifically because the positive fair value adjustments will never be recognized in profit and loss, and companies' net income will be negatively affected by higher depreciations when the revaluation model is used. A count among the more than 290,000 companies that have filed their financial statements for the financial year 2020 in the central business register shows that less than 5000 companies have a revaluation reserve under capital and reserves in the balance sheet. Table 7 also shows the positive Danish attitude toward following the IFRS. Denmark has, for example, implemented the option in Article 8 (6) of the Directive and permits the recognition, measurement, and disclosure of financial instruments in conformity

Table 7 Measurement bases and accounting methods used in the Danish Financial Statements Act for various assets and liabilities

Asset/liability	Measurement bases allowed (section in the Financial Statements Act)	Model/ method used	Value adjustments recognized in....	Comments
Intangible assets	Historical cost (36) Fair value if obtained from an active market (41)	Cost model Revaluation model	Profit and loss (impairments) Revaluation reserve	Revaluation model similar to IAS 16 except no use of comprehensive income
Tangible fixed/ noncurrent assets	Historical cost (36) Fair value (41)	Cost model Revaluation model	Profit and loss (impairments) Revaluation reserve	Revaluation model similar to IAS 16 except no use of comprehensive income
Investment property	Historical cost (36) Fair value (38) Fair value (41)	Cost model Fair value model Revaluation model	Profit and loss (impairments) Profit and loss Revaluation reserve	Revaluation model similar to IAS 16 except no use of comprehensive income
Investments in subsidiaries (parent company financial statements)	Historical cost (36) Fair value (41) Proportion of subsidiary's equity (43a)	Cost model Revaluation model Equity method	Profit and loss (impairments) Revaluation reserve Profit and loss (investee's direct transactions through equity are also recognized through equity by the investor)	Revaluation model similar to IAS 16 except no use of comprehensive income
Investments in associates (consolidated financial statements)	Proportion of associate's equity (119)	Equity method	Profit and loss (investee's direct transactions through equity are also recognized through equity by the investor)	
Investments in associates (financial statements of the investor)	Historical cost (36) Fair value (41) Proportion of associate's equity (43a)	Cost model Revaluation model Equity method	Profit and loss (impairments) Revaluation reserve Profit and loss (investee's direct transactions through equity are also recognized through equity by the investor)	Revaluation model similar to IAS 16 except no use of comprehensive income

(continued)

Table 7 (continued)

Asset/liability	Measurement bases allowed (section in the Financial Statements Act)	Model/ method used	Value adjustments recognized in. . . .	Comments
Investments in joint ventures and joint operations (consolidated financial statements)	Proportion of joint arrangement's equity (119)	Equity method	Profit and loss (investee's direct transactions through equity are also recognized through equity by the investor)	
	Proportion of joint arrangement's assets and liabilities (124)	Pro rata method	Profit and loss (investee's direct transactions through equity are also recognized through equity by the investor)	
Investments in joint ventures (financial statements of the investor)	Historical cost (36) Fair value (41) Proportion of joint venture's equity (43a)	Cost model Revaluation model Equity method	Profit and loss (impairments) Revaluation reserve Profit and loss (investee's direct transactions through equity are also recognized through equity by the investor)	Revaluation model similar to IAS 16 except no use of comprehensive income
Investments in joint operations (financial statements of the investor)	Historical cost (36) Fair value (41) Proportion of joint operation's equity (43a)	Cost model Revaluation model Equity method	Profit and loss (impairments) Revaluation reserve Profit and loss (investee's direct transactions through equity are also recognized through equity by the investor)	Revaluation model similar to IAS 16 except no use of comprehensive income
	Proportion of joint operation's assets and liabilities	Pro rata method	Profit and loss (investee's direct transactions through equity are also recognized through equity by the investor)	Pro rata method based on the principle of substance of the arrangement

(continued)

Table 7 (continued)

Asset/liability	Measurement bases allowed (section in the Financial Statements Act)	Model/ method used	Value adjustments recognized in....	Comments
Shares with no significant influence	Fair value (37 (1)) Historical cost if not traded on an active market (37 (4)) Option to use IFRS 9 instead of provisions in the Act (37 (5))	Fair value model Cost model	Profit and loss Profit and loss (impairments)	
Investments in debt instruments—hold to maturity or loans and receivables	Adjusted historical cost (37 (2)) Option to use IFRS 9 instead of provisions in the Act (37 (5))	Amortized cost model	Profit and loss	
Investments in debt instruments—trading	Fair value (37 (1)) Option to use IFRS 9 instead of provisions in the Act (37 (5))	Fair value model	Profit and loss	
Derivative financial instruments incl. contracts to buy and sell nonfinancial items that can be settled net	Fair value (37 (1)) Option to use IFRS 9 instead of provisions in the Act (37 (5))	Fair value model	Profit and loss	Hedging rules similar to IAS 39 apply if option to apply IFRS 9 is not used
Inventories	Historical cost (36)	Cost model	Profit and loss (impairments)	Allowed cost formulas (45): FIFO and weighted average cost
Financial liabilities —non-trading	Adjusted historical cost (37 (2)) Option to use IFRS 9 instead of provisions in the Act (37 (5))	Amortized cost model	Profit and loss	

(continued)

Table 7 (continued)

Asset/liability	Measurement bases allowed (section in the Financial Statements Act)	Model/ method used	Value adjustments recognized in. . . .	Comments
Financial liabilities —trading	Fair value (37 (1)) Option to use IFRS 9 instead of provisions in the Act (37 (5))	Fair value model	Profit and loss	

with international accounting standards adopted in accordance with Regulation (EC) No. 1606/2002 instead of the provisions in the Financial Statements Act (even though the provisions and their completion in the Financial Statements Act are based on the old IAS rules in IAS 39).

5 Conclusions

The following are the main characteristics or features of the Danish accounting regulation based on Directive 2013/34/EU:

The Directive has been transposed into one Act: The Financial Statements Act (in Danish: Aarsregnskabsloven). There is no official standard setter in Denmark, but occasionally the Danish Business Authority issues interpretations and guidelines that clarify the accounting issues that arise in relation to the provisions of the Financial Statements Act. According to the special Scandinavian/Nordic law tradition, the explanatory notes that accompany a bill are given great importance in Danish law, as they contribute to ensuring the correct understanding of the bill's overall objectives and of the content of the individual provisions. IFRS standards play a decisive role and have strong legitimacy in Denmark. The Danish legislators refer extensively to IFRS in the notes that accompany a bill and consider the IFRS to be the source to use for completing the national rules. In addition, both listed and non-listed companies have the option to apply (full) IFRS in the consolidated, individual, or both sets of financial statements instead of using the provisions of the Financial Statements Act. The Financial Statements Act contains the "true and fair override provision" from the Directive, but even here the importance of IFRS is very clear, as the legislators stress that it is unlikely that disapplication of specific provisions in the law can be made if companies make other choices for recognition and measurement than those permitted under IFRS. The Financial Statements Act contains the general financial reporting principles from the Directive, but in line with IFRS, the Danish interpretation of the principle of prudence is that financial statement preparers must exercise caution when making judgments under conditions of uncertainty rather than implying a need for asymmetry.

The Financial Statements Act is structured as a building block system with the four accounting classes A, B, C, and D. The building block system basically means that the set of rules which each company is bound to follow in the preparation of its annual report primarily depends on the size of the company. As regards the size criteria, Denmark has a long tradition of exploiting the size limits in the Accounting Directive for micro, small, medium, and large undertakings to the maximum. A vast majority of reportable Danish companies are micro-sized or small.

Denmark has a progressive attitude to CSR/ESG reporting in the annual report. New provisions have been added to the Financial Statements Act before EU regulations required such information, and whenever the EU has caught up, Denmark has often decided on an expanded scope. Currently, Denmark has a national requirement for all large companies, listed companies, and state-owned public companies to disclose in the management report or on the company's website (to be referred to in the management report) information about their data ethics.

There are a number of important recognition and measurement simplifications and exemptions for micro-sized and small companies in accounting class B. These simplifications include the following: companies in accounting class B are exempt from recognizing income over time as the work is carried out; they do not have to recognize leased assets/right-of-use assets and the corresponding lease liabilities; they do not have to include fixed and variable overhead costs indirectly attributable to the production of the goods in the cost price of manufactured goods; and they do not have to prepare cash flow statements and consolidated financial statements. Moreover, all companies in accounting class B (together with medium-sized companies in accounting class C) are exempted from recognizing development costs as assets, they do not have to disclose their net revenue, and they have far fewer note disclosure obligations than accounting classes C and D due to the maximum harmonization principle in the Accounting Directive. The Financial Statements Act provides only limited additional exemptions for micro-sized entities.

As regards measurement bases, the Financial Statements Act clearly demonstrates that the Danish legislators certainly are not opposed to the use of fair values; fair value is often mandatory for financial assets and an optional measurement basis for many other financial and even nonfinancial assets.

References

Alexander, D., & Nobes, C. (2020). *Financial accounting: An international introduction*. Pearson.

Blume, P. (2011). *Legal method in Danish law*. Djøf.

DAMVAD. (2014). *Brugen af årsrapporter for mindre virksomheder—Analyse udarbejdet af DAMVAD for Erhvervsstyrelsen—The use of the annual report for smaller entities—An analysis by DAMVAD for the Danish Business Authority*. DAMVAD.

Erhvervs- og Selskabsstyrelsen, Erhvervsministeriet. (1999). *Regnskabsrådets rapport om revision af årsregnskabsloven (Report of The Danish Business Authority's financial accounting advisory*

board about amendments to the Financial Statements Act). Erhvervs- og Selskabsstyrelsen, Erhvervsministeriet.
Erhvervsstyrelsen. (2020). *Vejledning om lovpligtig redegørelse for dataetik*. Erhvervsstyrelsen.
European Commission. (2008). COM(2008) 394: "Think Small First"—A "Small Business Act" for Europe—Communication from the Commission to the Council, the European Parliament, The European Economic and Social Committee and the Committee of the regions. Commission of the European Communities.
Fiechter, P. (2011). Reclassification of financial assets under IAS 39: Impact on European banks' financial statements. *Accounting in Europe, 8*, 49–67.
Folketinget. (1981). Lovforslag nr. L 116: Forslag til Lov om visse selskabers aflæggelse af årsregnskab m. v. Folketinget (Ed.), L116. Copenhagen.
Folketinget. (2001). L138: Forslag til Lov om erhvervsdrivende virksomheders aflæggelse af årsregnskab m.v. (årsregnskabsloven). Folketinget (Ed.).
Folketinget. (2008). 2008/1 LSF 5: Forslag til ændring af årsregnskabsloven—Redegørelse for samfundsansvar i større virksomheder.
Folketinget. (2015). L117: Forslag til lov om ændring af årsregnskabsloven og forskellige andre love -Reduktion af administrative byrder, tilpasning til de internationale regnskabsstandarder, gennemførelse af det nye regnskabsdirektiv og af ændringer til gennemsigtighedsdirektivet m.v. Folketinget (Ed.).
Folketinget. (2018). L 99: Forslag til lov om ændring af årsregnskabsloven, revisorloven og lov om anvendelsen af visse af Den Europæiske Unions retsakter om økonomiske forbindelser til tredjelande m.v. L99.
International Accounting Standards Board (IASB). (2008). *Reclassification of financial assets—Amendments to IAS 39 financial instruments: Recognition and measurement and IFRS 7 financial instruments: disclosures*. The International Accounting Standards Board.
International Accounting Standards Board (IASB). (2018). *Conceptual framework for financial reporting*. IFRS Foundation.
Thinggaard, F. (2017). The role and current status of IFRS in the completion of national accounting rules—Evidence from Denmark. *Accounting in Europe, 14*, 67–79.

Sweden

Niclas Hellman and Tomas Hjelström

1 Introduction

Different factors have contributed to the development of financial accounting in Sweden over time. The decades around the mid-1900s were characterized by creditor protection and accounting prudence, low transparency, and political influence through tax and corporate governance systems. This phase culminated in the 1970s, as illustrated by the Nobes (1983, p. 7) classification where Sweden was assigned to a class of its own at one of the extreme positions (characterized by prudence, tax and government influence, flexibility in use of provisions, etc.). A differentiation gradually took place from the 1980s and onward, where different accounting systems emerged for different entities. Swedish multinationals began to cross-list in the United States, and US GAAP reconciliations pointed at the need for consolidated financial statements prepared in accordance with high-quality standards. Accordingly, the International Accounting Standards (IASs) were gradually translated in 1990–2002 and adopted into Swedish GAAP for listed groups, followed by mandatory IFRS adoption in 2005 as Sweden had become a member of the European Union in 1995. However, legal-entity accounting developed

Niclas Hellman is associate professor and acting holder of the Handelsbanken Chair in Accounting at the Stockholm School of Economics. Tomas Hjelström is assistant professor at the Stockholm School of Economics and member of the Expert Panel of the Swedish Financial Reporting Standards Council (Rådet för finansiell rapportering).

N. Hellman (✉) · T. Hjelström
Stockholm School of Economics, Stockholm, Sweden
e-mail: niclas.hellman@hhs.se; Tomas.Hjelstrom@hhs.se

A. Incollingo, A. Lionzo (eds.), *The European Harmonization of National Accounting Rules*, SIDREA Series in Accounting and Business Administration,
https://doi.org/10.1007/978-3-031-42931-6_8

differently; major efforts were made to develop a Swedish version of IFRS for SMEs, and the resulting standard (K3) has been in force since 2014. In addition to requiring IFRS to be applied by listed companies, Sweden today (2023) has one accounting system for consolidated financial statements in privately held groups (K3-consolidated), one system for large limited-liability legal entities (K3-legal entity), one system for small limited-liability legal entities (K2), and one system for sole proprietorships (K1). There are links between financial accounting and tax in the legal entities, where smaller firms are expected to benefit from more tax-aligned financial accounting systems (K1 and K2).

1.1 The Role of Company Law and Accounting Legislation

The first edition of the Swedish Companies Act (*Aktiebolagslagen*, ABL) was issued in 1848 with new versions in 1895, 1910, 1944, 1975, and 2005. Creditor protection was emphasized in ABL throughout the 1900s, and according to Jönsson (1991), the adopted view was that the dividend restrictions and mandatory profit retentions were needed to (p. 529) "protect the company from shareholders [. . .] that could threaten the existence of the company." Today, ABL prescribes two criteria to consider when determining dividends:

(i) *Amount restriction*; dividends may not exceed the amount of nonrestricted equity.[1]
(ii) *Prudence restriction*; notwithstanding the amount restriction, the size of dividends should be based on an evaluation of the nature, the size, and the risks of the business and the company's capital needs, liquidity, and financial position.

The 2005 version of ABL reduced creditor protection (af Sandeberg, 2006). One change concerned the amount restriction, which for parent companies in the 1975 version was expressed as the lower of nonrestricted equity in the parent company and the group, respectively. In the 2005 version, the amount restriction no longer applies at the group level (only the amount of nonrestricted equity in the parent matters); however, the prudence restriction applies both to legal entities and at the group level. Another change was that the mandatory retention of profits (transfer from nonrestricted to restricted equity) was abolished. A third change was that the share-premium part in connection with a new issue of shares is treated as nonrestricted equity in the 2005 version. Earlier, such owner contributions were classified as restricted equity.

Let us now turn to the role of accounting legislation. An overview is provided in Fig. 1.

[1] Shareholders' equity in a Swedish limited-liability legal entity (*aktiebolag*, AB) is divided into restricted equity (not possible to distribute as dividends to shareholders) and nonrestricted equity (available for dividend distribution).

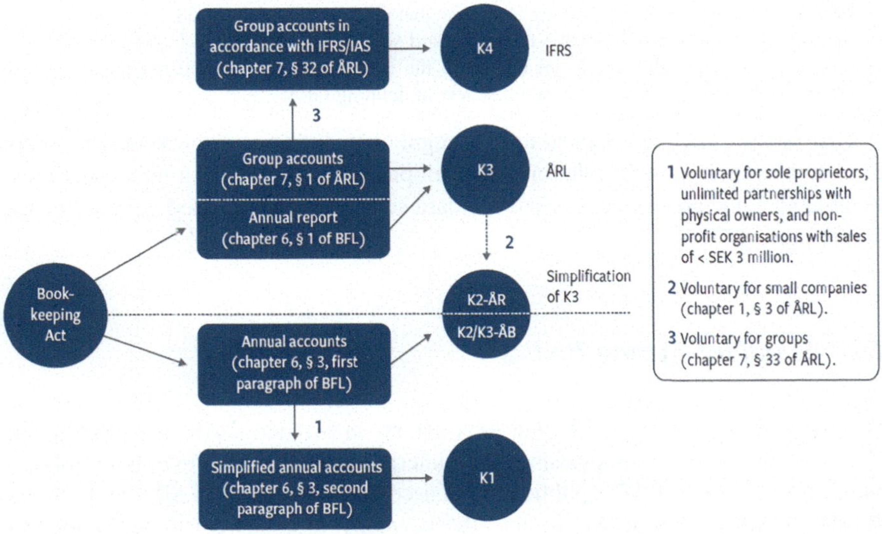

Fig. 1 Swedish accounting regulation for non-listed entities. Source: Figure 1.7 in Hellman et al. (2020) *Principle-based Accounting*. Studentlitteratur

As indicated in Fig. 1, Sweden has two accounting laws: the Bookkeeping Act (*Bokföringslagen*, BFL) and the Annual Accounts Act (*Årsredovisningslagen*, ÅRL).[2] BFL regulates the bookkeeping practices to be followed by all businesses. In addition, BFL regulates how the closing of books shall be made, depending on legal form and firm size. BFL states that a limited-liability company must prepare an annual report according to ÅRL, whereas sole proprietors only need to prepare annual accounts (*årsbokslut*). Annual reports are publicly available, whereas annual accounts are not. Listed parent companies must apply EU-endorsed IFRS in their consolidated financial statements, whereas privately held groups may choose either full IFRS or the so-called K3 standard, which is an adaptation of IFRS for SMEs adjusted to Swedish conditions (Sigonius, 2019). This will be further discussed below.

ÅRL can be characterized as framework legislation, where reporting formats, classification, recognition, measurement, and disclosures are regulated at a general level. As regards more detailed application of the law, ÅRL refers to the concept of "good accounting practice" (*god redovisningssed*, GRS). Marton (2017, p. 207) describes GRS as follows:

> [. . .] GRS has a specific – legally defined – meaning, as the accounting principles that are followed by a 'qualitatively representative sample of firms'. The term 'qualitatively representative' is traditionally interpreted as large and economically important firms. Laws must be followed. Pronouncements from standard setters must be followed to the extent that they are implemented by important (qualitatively representative) firms. Pronouncements are then

[2]There are also specific accounting laws for financial institutions.

> backed up by the law, as accounting laws state that GRS must be followed [. . .] In practice, firms tend to implement guidance from standard setters, so normally such guidance does represent GRS. In addition, in an update to the law in 1999, the Swedish government emphasized the importance of standard setters in defining GRS.

Historically, GRS has opened for self-regulation, and two private standard setters came to play an important role for the development of GRS in the 1980s and 1990s. In the 2000s, the government-based standard setter gradually gained more influence in interpreting GRS.

1.2 Standard-Setting Bodies

The Association of Certified Public Accountants in Sweden (FAR) was founded in 1923 and has played an important role in interpreting GRS over time, both through auditing and through FAR's publication of accounting guidance (FAR Standards are denoted RedR in Swedish). In the 1980s, many large Swedish multinationals acquired subsidiaries in other countries, and the accounting diversity gradually increased in the consolidated financial statements. In particular, accounting practice in the area of business combinations was flexible and inconsistent (Hellman, 1993, 2011b). This concerned areas like application of the pooling method, accounting for negative goodwill, accounting for restructuring reserves, and various methods used for accounting for goodwill: direct write-off, capitalization and amortization over different maximum periods of useful life, and linear and progressive amortization. The prevailing standards were not satisfactory, and in 1989 the profession (FAR), the preparers, and the government jointly founded a new private standard-setting body, the Swedish Financial Accounting Standards Committee (*Redovisningsrådet*, RR). In order to reduce accounting diversity, the Stockholm Stock Exchange required, in the listing contract, all listed firms to apply the RR Standards. RR developed a large number of standards during 1991 to 2002 by translating most of the International Accounting Standards (IASs) to Swedish. Some adaptations to the Swedish context were made beyond simply translating the IAS Standards. The enforcement was, however, weak as the RR Standards had a "comply or explain" feature. Hellman (2011b) refers to the voluntary IAS adoption in Sweden 1991–2002 as a "soft adoption," a concept introduced by Ordelheide (1990). The "softness" refers to the Swedish adaptations made in connection with the voluntary adoption of IAS Standards via the RR Standards and to the weak enforcement institutions.

Since 2005, listed Swedish companies are required to apply EU-endorsed IFRS Standards in their consolidated financial statements. Privately held groups have an option to adopt EU-endorsed IFRS Standards in their consolidated financial statements (see Fig. 1). As a result of the IFRS adoption, RR was closed; however, a new private body was founded, the Swedish Financial Reporting Standards Council (*Rådet för finansiell rapportering*, RFR). This body has issued one standard concerning Swedish group accounting requirements beyond IFRS (RFR 1) and one standard concerning accounting requirements for the Swedish listed parent company of the group applying IFRS (RFR 2).

Finally, there is one government-based standard setter called the Swedish Accounting Standards Board (*Bokföringsnämnden*, BFN), founded in 1976 with the objective to support the development of GRS. The BFN board members are formally appointed by the Swedish government, but the board structure follows a stakeholder model where, for example, the accounting profession, Swedish tax authorities, Swedish industry, banks, IT experts, academia, and the Swedish Economic Crime Authority may be represented. During the 1980s and the 1990s, BFN focused primarily on individual entities (not groups) and had to position its standards in relation to the standards issued by FAR and, subsequently, the RR Standards. As the RR Standards were designed for listed companies, BFN tried to develop standards that were less demanding; however, this resulted in significant flexibility and cherry-picking opportunities among the non-listed companies (see Hellman et al., 2022). Private firms could choose, on an item-by-item basis, whether to follow the BFN Standard or the RR Standard. In case there was not yet a BFN Standard issued in an area, there was a general exemption from having to apply the RR Standard, i.e., the preparer would make its own interpretation of what constitutes GRS.

This situation was not satisfactory, and, in 2004, BFN put forward a new strategy where entities would primarily be classified according to size: K1 (small sole proprietorships), K2 (small entities), K3 (large entities), and K4 (listed firms). In turn, each category would have its own package of standards, to be followed comprehensively. The K1 Standard was issued in 2006 and was developed in close cooperation with the Swedish tax authorities so that all accounting numbers prepared under K1 are also accepted for taxation purposes. In response to political pressure at the time, the purpose of the so-called simplified annual accounts prepared under the K1 Standard was to lower cost and complexity for small businesses. This was also a main driver behind the K2 Standard (BFNAR 2008:1; current version is BFNAR 2016:8 including updates until November 12, 2021), i.e., to try to simplify the accounting and minimize the differences between financial accounting and tax accounting. As an example of the emphasis on simplification, the K2 Standard has a chapter on operating expenses (Chapter 7) that allows for deviations from accrual accounting to avoid work with interim receivables and interim liabilities. The K3 Standard (BFNAR 2012:1; current version including updates until November 12, 2021) was a bigger project, comprising both consolidated financial statements and annual reports for legal, nonfinancial entities domiciled in Sweden. The K3 Standard must be applied by privately held groups when preparing consolidated financial statements (unless the entity opted for full IFRS) and in the individual financial statements prepared by large companies. Small companies are allowed to choose between the K2 and K3 Standards.[3]

[3]Please note that K3 is the general standard and, accordingly, allows for all ÅRL options and provides comprehensive guidance. K2 offers simplifications but also restricts certain ÅRL options;

The K3 Standard sets out to be principle-based and guided by IFRS for SMEs (same chapter structure), but substantial adaptations were made in the development of the standard. In her PhD thesis, Sigonius (2019) identifies three contextual factors that influenced the adaptation: accounting legislation, the link between accounting and taxation, and the differential reporting framework (the different K-categories). Sigonius concludes (p. 222):

> In the evaluation of prospective models, the standard-setter [BFN] analysed the consequences in relation to all three contextual factors. Evaluating IFRS for SMEs' potential as a primary model for K3, the standard-setter found that incompatibilities with accounting legislation and the link between accounting and taxation were manageable through adaptation. That standard's differential reporting fit made it appropriate to use as K3's primary model. Thus, considerations related to contextual factors influenced the selection of the primary model [IFRS for SMEs]. Later, the extent to which the model was compatible with contextual factors in turn influenced the extent to which adaptations followed.

A key solution for how to adapt to the legislation was the text structure of the standard. A hierarchy was used where law text has the highest status, followed by the standard setter's general advice and finally the standard setter's commentary text, all drawn together in one document (Sigonius, 2019, pp. 219–220).

The K3 Standard was issued in 2012, and in 2014 BFN removed all old BFN Standards and the RR Standards so that firms had to adopt K3 (or any of the options available: K2 for small firms, full IFRS for groups). A PhD thesis by Seger (2018) reports that the accounting profession played an important role in guiding small firms in choosing between K2 and K3 and points at the challenges for the accounting profession to live up to professional and commercial expectations when providing this guidance.

1.3 The Role of Tax Regulation

It is a common view that the link between tax rules and financial accounting varies internationally. In Europe, countries like Germany, France, and Italy are viewed as having strong tax-accounting links, whereas this is not the case in the United Kingdom (Alexander & Nobes, 2020, p. 250). Even though country differences exist, they are, arguably, differences in emphasis—there will always be differences between taxable income and financial accounting profit, and it will be difficult for countries to have completely decoupled systems. In Sweden, the basic presumption in corporate tax legislation is that all business revenues are taxable, and all business expenses are tax-deductible, but then this presumption does not always apply. First, the *scope of tax legislation* differs to some extent from the accounting regulation. This pertains to various expenditures (fines, entertainment, certain capital losses)

for example, capitalization of development costs is not allowed under K2. Thus, a small firm that wishes to capitalize development costs must apply the K3 Standard.

where the tax-legislation scope is narrower which means that such business expenses will never become tax-deductible, so-called permanent differences. Second, the Swedish Income Tax Act (*Inkomstskattelagen*) 14:2 states (translated from Swedish):

> Taxation shall be based on good accounting practice [GRS] unless there is an explicit tax rule

This is the legal link between financial accounting and tax accounting in Sweden. Please note that if more than one accounting treatment is in line with GRS, the chosen treatment will apply also for taxation purposes. R&D expenditure is an example of such a case, as the accounting legislation opens for both immediate expensing and capitalization. On the other hand, if there is an explicit tax rule, the taxable profit is unaffected by the financial accounting treatment. In that case there will be a (temporary) difference between accounting values and tax values. Under K3, deferred tax will be reported for most temporary differences, while deferred tax accounting is not allowed under K2.

This direct impact of accounting standards (via the GRS link) on taxation is normally not set out as clearly in other countries (Knutsson et al., 2012, p. 107). Another aspect of interest in this context is how the Swedish accounting-tax system handles disputes between tax subjects (firms) and the Swedish tax authorities. If such a dispute reaches the highest court level, the Swedish Supreme Administrative Court (*Högsta Förvaltningsdomstolen*) may request a statement from BFN on what constitutes GRS in the disputed case. It is not uncommon that the court also rules in accordance with this statement, which implicitly gives the standard setter much influence on the establishing of precedents. According to Knutsson et al. (2012, p. 107), this practice is unique compared to other countries (see also Marton, 2017).

1.4 Swedish Economic Context

1.4.1 Accounting and Corporate Governance

In a study by Cooke (1989), it was noted that Sweden has a disproportionate number of multinational enterprises (p. 113). One explanatory factor is the so-called Swedish corporate governance model. Sweden has several ownership spheres that execute management control over large companies through networks of loyal CEOs and board members (Collin, 1993). The spheres also execute financial control through sphere banks and shares with different voting power. The most famous sphere is the Wallenberg sphere (e.g., Carlsson, 2003). The strong influence of spheres was possible due to support from the political sector and the trade unions. The stability of the spheres and their focus on retaining capital in the companies to finance long-term industrial development and growth was well in line with the interests of the Social Democrats (the party in power over several decades after the end of World War II) and the unions (see Henrekson & Jacobsson, 2003). The accounting system played a role in this context in that it provided room for managers to smooth income through hidden reserves and provisions (see Hellman, 2011a).

1.4.2 Company Structure

An overview of the company structure in Sweden is provided in Table 1.

Table 1 shows the distribution of legal entities across different size variables (average number of employees, net turnover, and total assets). All industries are well represented across different size categories (not tabulated).

2 Development of Accounting Regulation

2.1 Introduction

BFL applies to all businesses and the current law is from 1999. It is a framework law, i.e., preparers need further guidance to apply the law. Accordingly, in 2013, BFN issued a bookkeeping standard (BFNAR 2013:2) with comprehensive guidance within nine areas: basic concepts, bookkeeping during the accounting period, time spans for bookkeeping, fixed-asset registers, verifications, accounting information, archiving, and systems documentation. There is an ongoing discussion regarding modernization of the Bookkeeping Act so that digital solutions related to verifications and archiving can be utilized to a greater extent.

ÅRL was developed in response to Sweden becoming a member of the EU in 1995. One change was the introduction of provisions as a separate category in the balance sheet. Another notable change was the introduction of the "true and fair view" concept, included in the Fourth Directive in the 1970s, following pressure from Anglo-Dutch countries. Table 2 shows the definitions of different categories referred to in ÅRL.[4]

The Swedish accounting laws have tended to focus on the accounting in legal entities, whereas standards and practices for consolidated financial statements have traditionally been developed by the accounting profession and self-regulation bodies. Swedish group accounting for listed companies started to develop in a capital-market-oriented direction in the 1980s, followed by the RR Standards issued in 1991–2002 (required via the stock exchange listing contract) and finally the IFRS requirement from 2005 and onward via legislation at the EU level.

2.2 ÅRL Requirements

Table 3 provides an overview of the reporting requirements set by ÅRL for the different categories in Table 2.

[4]The category "Mini-micro" has been included in Table 2 to indicate the minimum mandatory audit requirement, i.e., mini-micro firms are not subject to mandatory audits.

Table 1 Overview of companies domiciled in Sweden in 2020

Panel A: average number of employees							
Employees (avg. no.)	0	1–2	3–5	6–9	10–19	>19	Total
Firm distribution	206,033	179,113	47,685	23,617	18,960	18,394	493,802
Panel B: total assets (SEK thousand)							
Total assets (kSEK)	0–999	1000–9999	10,000–99,999	100,000–999,999	1,000,000–9,999,999	>=10,000,000	Total
Firm distribution	182,683	214,728	76,988	15,520	2674	373	492,966
Panel C: net turnover (SEK thousand)							
Net turnover (kSEK)	0–999	1000–9999	10,000–99,999	100,000–999,999	1,000,000–9,999,999	>=10,000,000	Total
Firm distribution	261,466	169,055	52,904	8598	994	71	493,088

Source: the database Serrano

Table 2 Definitions of different company categories in Sweden

	Definition	Net turnover	Total assets	Average number of employees
"Mini-micro"	Meeting more than one of the criteria to the right for 2 years in a row	$\leq$ MSEK 3.0	$\leq$ MSEK 1.5	≤ 3
Small	Not meeting the definition of a large company			
Large	Listed or meeting more than one of the criteria to the right for 2 years in a row	$>$ MSEK 80	$>$ MSEK 40	> 50
Very large	Listed or meeting more than one of the criteria to the right for 2 years in a row	$>$ MSEK 350	$>$ MSEK 175	> 250
Public	Companies allowed to raise capital from the public			
Voluntary IFRS	Parent companies that voluntarily decided to apply IFRS for the preparation of consolidated financial statements			
Listed	Companies that have issued securities traded on a regulated market			

Table 3 Annual report and audit requirements for different legal entities in Sweden

	Mini-micro	Small	Large	Very large
Management report—all-firm requirements	X	X	X	X
Management report—large			X	X
Sustainability information—small and mini-micro	X	X		
Sustainability information—large			X	
Sustainability report—very large				X
Disclosure of adopted accounting policies	X	X	X	X
Comparison year in connection with changed accounting principles			X	X
Profit or loss and balance sheet statements	X	X	X	X
Abridged profit or loss and balance sheet statements	X	X		
Cash flow statement			X	X
Statement of changes in equity (or table in the management report)	X	X	X	X
Notes—all-firm requirements	X	X	X	X
Notes—large			X	X
Mandatory audit		X	X	X

2.2.1 Financial Statement Format

Starting with the format of the financial statements, small companies are allowed to abridge the profit or loss statement so that the reported top line is gross income (a net of revenue and certain costs). Small companies are also allowed to abridge items within different balance sheet categories (assets, equity, provisions, liabilities).

In cases of changed accounting principles, small firms are not required to make retrospective adjustments of the comparison year in income statements and balance sheets, and pending users are informed about the lack of comparability.

2.2.2 Notes

As regards the information provided in notes, there are minimum requirements that apply to all companies. In addition, large companies shall:

- Specify significant interim receivables and payables
- Specify significant "other provisions"
- Provide details about fixed assets (capitalized interest costs, accumulated depreciation, etc.)
- Provide details about current assets (capitalized interest costs, inventory value adjustments)
- Provide fair-value-related information about financial instruments
- Report shares of intragroup sales and purchases (applies to large firms which are part of a group)
- Provide information about entities in which the company has owner interests
- Inform about loans given to board members, the CEO, or such persons in other group companies
- Provide information about convertible debt
- Provide information about the share capital (number, quota value, different voting rights)
- Propose suggested treatment of the net profit for the financial year
- Provide details about recognized deferred tax items
- Report gender distribution across employees and management team
- Report salaries, wages, and social security contributions, including pensions, across different employee categories, including former board members and CEOs (some further details are required for large, public companies)
- Report pension obligations to current and former board members and current and former CEOs or corresponding position (some further details are required for large, public companies)
- Report severance pay agreements with board members and members of the management team
- Report details regarding the highest-level company in the group that prepares consolidated financial statements (in case this is a foreign entity, information

should be provided about where the consolidated financial statements can be found)

- Report pledged assets
- Report, if relevant, distribution of net turnover across business lines and markets
- Report size and distribution of fees paid to auditors

2.2.3 Management Report

The management report has certain minimum requirements that apply to all companies. They comprise:

- Provide an overview of business development, results, and financial position, in particular conditions outside the financial statements that are important for understanding business development, results, and financial position.
- Present significant events during the financial year.
- Companies with business activities that influence the environment in a way that require legal notice or permission must report its business impact on the environment.
- Show changes in equity in the management report or in a separate statement.

Furthermore, there are management report requirements that apply only to large firms:

- Present expected future development, including a description of important risks and uncertainties.
- Report R&D activities.
- Report foreign branches.
- Report detailed information about share repurchases.
- Report, if significant, exposure to price risk, credit risk, liquidity risk, and cash flow risk; and policies used manage risks, including hedging policy.
- Report entity-specific sustainability information necessary to understand business development, results, and financial position, including environmental and employee-related aspects.

Finally, there are special requirements in ÅRL for management reports produced by listed companies:

- Report remuneration guidelines.
- Report details regarding different classes of shares.
- Report restrictions in buying or selling shares due to legislation or bylaws.
- Report significant owners (10% or more).
- Report employee ownership through pension foundations or similar.
- Report any limitations regarding how many votes an owner may control at the Annual General Meeting (AGM).
- Report known shareholder agreements that may involve limitations in buying or selling shares.

- Report bylaws information about appointing and dismissing board members and how to change the bylaws.
- Report on permissions given by the AGM to the board regarding issuing and repurchasing shares.
- Report significant agreements (and their effects) that influence corporate control in case of a public takeover offer.
- Report agreements with board members and employees regarding consequences in case of termination due to dismissal or public takeover offer.
- Provide a corporate governance report.
- For groups: describe internal control and risk management system.

2.2.4 Sustainability Information

Very large companies must produce a sustainability report that contains sustainability information necessary to understand company developments, results, financial position, and business consequences, including environmental-, social-, human rights-, and employee-related aspects. The sustainability report shall comprise the following (somewhat abbreviated list):

- The company's business model.
- Sustainability policy, including conducted controls.
- Results from implementing the sustainability policy.
- Significant entity-specific risks, including, when relevant, business relationships, products, or services likely to have negative effects.
- How the above risks are managed.
- Key performance indicators that are relevant to the company.
- If suitable, the report shall refer to and explain other numbers presented in the annual report.
- If certain guidelines have been applied, this shall be stated.

As regards companies that are not "very large," see Sect. 2.6.

2.2.5 Related-Party Transactions

Large companies shall provide disclosure about nonmarket term related-party transactions (excluding intragroup transactions). Small public firms shall also provide such disclosures if the transactions pertain to large owners or board members.

2.3 EU Directive 2013/34 Transposition

To deal with the changes required by Directive 2013/34/EU, a committee was formed with government officials and accounting experts. The instructions from the government were: "(1) investigate changes to Swedish law that is required based on the Directive, (2) consider information needs of financial statement users, and (3) simplify the reporting process for preparers" (Marton, 2017, p. 209). The committee investigated these matters and wrote two reports, SOU 2014:22 and SOU 2015:8. The first report formed the bass for the changes in ÅRL triggered by Directive 2013/34/EU. These changes were given priority as the directive had to be implemented in Swedish law by December 2015. The implemented changes are described in Sect. 3.

2.4 *Other Relevant Aspects of Swedish GAAP*

As referred to earlier, an interesting feature of Swedish GAAP is the K-project. The decision to create comprehensive standards for each of four different categories of companies was a big and costly reform. Requiring application of K2 and K3, while at the same time removing all old standards at one point in time (2014), stands out as a unique regulatory event. An empirical study of Swedish privately held groups before and after K3 adoption finds that the accounting quality improved in some dimensions following K3 adoption (Hellman et al., 2022). In addition, economic benefits in terms of lowered cost of debt were observed (ibid.).

2.5 *IFRS Adoption*

Since 2005, Swedish companies with securities listed on regulated markets must apply EU-endorsed IFRS Standards in their consolidated financial statements. In addition to the EU regulation, national regulation (RFR 1) requires some specific disclosures at the consolidated level (e.g., number of full-time equivalent employees).

Using a size threshold of SEK 1 billion (about EUR 100 million), Hellman (2011b) identified 132 Swedish listed firms that adopted IFRS in 2005. It may also be noted that state-owned groups are required by the Swedish government to apply EU-endorsed IFRS in their consolidated financial statements. In addition, privately held groups may voluntarily apply EU-endorsed IFRS in their consolidated financial statements. According to Hellman et al. (2022), 1068 privately held groups adopted K3 in their consolidated financial statements in connection with the regulatory change in 2014. Seventy-six firms chose instead to voluntarily adopt full IFRS in their consolidated financial statements.

What about legal entities? Legal entities must apply either K2 or K3 as described earlier; however, additional regulation applies to legal entities belonging to groups that apply EU-endorsed IFRS Standards in their consolidated financial statements. First, parent companies in this category apply a standard called RFR 2 in their individual financial statements. Marton (2017, p. 212) describes RFR 2 as follows:

The structure of RFR 2 is entirely based on IFRS. For each individual standard and interpretation, RFR 2 lists exceptions for Swedish companies. Most of these exceptions are related to tax issues.

Subsidiaries belonging to groups that apply EU-endorsed IFRS Standards in their consolidated financial statements can choose between RFR 2 and K3 (and K2 if they are small) when preparing their individual financial statements.

2.6 *Nonfinancial Disclosures*

As reported in Sect. 2.2 and Table 3, ÅRL requires companies of different categories to provide sustainability information. First, all companies with business activities that influence the environment in a way that require legal notice or permission must report this business impact in a sustainability report. Second, large companies must report entity-specific sustainability information necessary to understand business development, results, and financial position, including environmental and employee-related aspects. Third, very large companies must produce a *sustainability report* (see Sect. 2.2 for a description of the requirements).

In addition to sustainability information, there are ÅRL requirements for different firm categories concerning presentation of business developments in general and in various topic areas, such as corporate governance, top management remuneration, R&D activities, and internal control and risk management. See Sect. 2.2 for a detailed description.

2.7 *Summary*

Having now covered relevant Swedish accounting regulation in this chapter, Table 4 provides an overview of what regulation applies to different company categories.

In sum, although full IFRS and IFRS for SMEs influence the preparation of legal entities' financial statements via RFR 2 and K3, respectively, the influence of IFRS on legal entities is still somewhat limited due to Sweden-specific restrictions (e.g., accounting-taxation links). For a comprehensive overview of differences between IFRS and Swedish accounting, see Marton (2017).

3 Implementation of EU Directive 2013/34

EU Directive 2013/34 introduced "full harmonization" for small companies, implying equal application of some rules within all EU countries. Thus, when "full harmonization" applies, EU member states cannot require either more or less from

Table 4 Overview of the regulation that applies to companies domiciled in Sweden

		Non-listed	
	Listed	Voluntary IFRS	Swedish, non-IFRS
Consolidated level	IFRS/RFR 1	IFRS/RFR 1	ÅRL/K3
Parent company	ÅRL/RFR 2	ÅRL/RFR 2	ÅRL/K3 (or K2)
Subsidiary	ÅRL/choice of RFR 2 or K3 (or K2)	ÅRL/choice of RFR 2 or K3 (or K2)	ÅRL/K3 (or K2)
Separate legal entity	ÅRL/RFR 2	N.A.	ÅRL/K3 (or K2)

Note: small legal entities can choose K2 instead of K3
Source: Marton (2017)

these small entities. This led to lower disclosure requirements for small Swedish companies. Some examples of disclosures no longer required:

- Employee costs (salaries, employer contributions for national security purposes, pension costs)
- Gender distribution of full-time employees
- Information about subsidiaries
- Information about intragroup sales and purchases
- Number of shares and the distribution of shares across different share categories
- Information about what balance sheet items pledged assets pertain to

There were also a few changes regarding where in the annual report certain information was provided. Significant events after the closing date were moved from the management report to a note, whereas changes in shareholders' equity were to be reported in the management report.

EU Directive 2013/34 further introduced a requirement related to R&D activities; companies capitalizing development costs should create a "development cost fund" as part of restricted equity. This would prevent companies from being able to distribute dividends corresponding to capitalized development costs. Under Swedish GAAP, this had no effect on K2 firms as K2 does not allow for capitalization of development costs. Under K3, firms make a policy choice between the "expense model" (immediate expensing) and the "capitalization model." Companies opting for the latter model had to apply the new EU requirement and create a development cost fund as part of restricted equity.

3.1 General Provisions and Principles

The implementation of EU Directive 2013/34 and international developments led to certain changes in terminology related to owner interests, joint control, and joint arrangements (ÅRL, 1.4, 1.5. 1.5a). Another change concerned the increased emphasis on materiality. Marton (2017) describes the considerations made, as follows (p. 211):

> There are a few areas and standards with many references in the SOU, such as general regulation, consolidation (IFRS 3 and IFRS 10), IFRS 11, IAS 1, IAS 24, IAS 31, and IAS 37. The references to regulation in general mostly relate to the IAS/IFRS Regulation in the EU and to the increasing importance of IFRS over time. The reference to particular standards refers to specific discussions in the SOU. It is clear that the committee producing the SOU refers to and uses IFRS to analyze terminology that is not defined or explained in the directive. As such, IFRS is an important source of reference for the committee. There are several examples of this. Beginning with examples from SOU 2014:8, the new term 'jointly controlled entity' is introduced in ÅRL, based on an analysis of terms in IFRS 11 and IAS 31. The meaning of 'materiality' – which is included in the Directive – is analyzed with reference to IAS 1 [. . .] several respondents – e.g. FI (the financial supervisory authority), the Swedish tax authority, BFN, the lawyers' association, and FAR (the accounting profession's association) – point out that materiality should be based on the definition in IFRS to achieve international harmonization. The University of Gothenburg agrees, and points to the work currently done by the IASB, such as the issuance of a draft practice statement on materiality.

As described by Marton (2017), the Swedish committee frequently referred to IFRS regulation when discussing the EU Directive matters. It illustrates an increasing impact of IFRS on Swedish accounting legislation and standard-setting over time.

3.2 Simplifications for Small- and Medium-Sized Entities/Exemptions for Micro-undertakings

As described earlier, simplifications have been a guiding principle in the K-project, including both simplified annual accounts (K1) and simplified annual report (K2). The K3 Standard was not primarily guided by simplifications, but there were regulatory requirements imposing simplifications (disclosures, cash flow statement) and pragmatic decisions made in the name of simplicity (valuation of pension obligations).

4 Valuation Approaches

4.1 Valuation Approaches Adopted

Historical cost has been the dominating valuation approach in Swedish accounting over time. However, other approaches are also allowed or required. Table 5 shows the valuation approaches applied according to ÅRL (and the K3 standard in cases where further guidance is needed).

Table 5 Measurement bases and accounting methods used in *Årsredovisningslagen* (ÅRL, Swedish Annual Accounts Act) and *BFNAR 2012:1 (K3)* for various assets and liabilities

Assets/ liabilities	Measurement bases at first balance sheet recognition (ÅRL § or K3 reference)	Model/method used during subsequent periods (ÅRL § or K3 reference)	Value adjustments recognized in... (ÅRL § or K3 reference)	Comment
Intangible assets	Historical cost (4.3)	Cost model	Profit or loss (amortization, impairment)	Revaluations are not made on a regular basis; no use of comprehensive income
		Voluntary revaluation (4.6)	Revaluation reserve (restricted equity) (4.6)	
Tangible fixed assets	Historical cost (4.3)	Cost model	Profit or loss (depreciation, impairment)	Revaluations are not made on a regular basis; no use of comprehensive income
		Voluntary revaluation (4.6)	Revaluation reserve (restricted equity) (4.6)	
Investment property	Historical cost (4.3)	Cost model	Profit or loss (depreciation, impairment)	Revaluations are not made on a regular basis; no use of comprehensive income; K3 requires fair value disclosure
		Voluntary revaluation (4.6)	Revaluation reserve (restricted equity) (4.6)	
Shares in subsidiaries (parent company financial statements)	Historical cost (4.3)	Cost model	Profit or loss (impairment)	
		Voluntary revaluation (4.6)	Revaluation reserve (restricted equity) (4.6)	Revaluations are not made on a regular basis; no use of comprehensive income; ÅRL 4.14b third paragraph refers to firms choosing application of full IFRS
	Fair value (4.14b, third paragraph)	Fair value model	Profit or loss	
Shares in associates (consolidated financial statements)	Historical cost (7.25)	Equity method	Profit or loss (unrealized value increases classified as restricted equity)	
Investments in associates (financial statements of the investor)	Historical cost (4.3)	Cost model	Profit or loss (impairment)	
		Voluntary revaluation (4.6)	Revaluation reserve	Revaluations are not made on a regular basis; no use of

(continued)

Table 5 (continued)

Assets/ liabilities	Measurement bases at first balance sheet recognition (ÅRL § or K3 reference)	Model/method used during subsequent periods (ÅRL § or K3 reference)	Value adjustments recognized in... (ÅRL § or K3 reference)	Comment
			(restricted equity) (4.6)	comprehensive income; ÅRL 4.14b third paragraph refers to firms choosing application of full IFRS
	Fair value (4.14b, third paragraph)	Fair value model	Profit or loss	

Assets/liabilities	Measurement bases at first balance sheet recognition (ÅRL § or K3 reference)	Model/ method used during subsequent periods	Value adjustments recognized in...	Comment
Investments in joint arrangements (consolidated financial statements)	Proportion of joint arrangement's equity (7.30)	Equity method	Profit or loss (unrealized value increases classified as restricted equity)	
	Proportion of joint arrangement's assets and liabilities (7.30)	Proportionate consolidation method	Profit or loss	
Investments in joint ventures (financial statements of the investor)	Historical cost (4.3)	Cost model	Profit or loss (impairment)	
		Voluntary revaluation (4.6)	Revaluation reserve (restricted equity) (4.6)	Revaluations are not made on a regular basis; no use of comprehensive income; ÅRL 4.14b third paragraph refers to firms choosing application of full IFRS
	Fair value (4.14b, third paragraph)	Profit or loss	Profit or loss	
Investments in joint operations (financial statements of the investor)	Proportion of joint arrangement's assets and liabilities (K3 15.7)	Proportionate method	Profit or loss	
Shares with no significant influence	Historical cost (4.3; K3 12.19)	Cost model (Ch. 11)	Profit or loss (impairment)	Policy choice between cost-based (K3: Chapter 11) and fair-value-based accounting (K3: Chapter 12)
		Lower of cost and fair value less costs to sell (Ch. 11)	Profit or loss (impairment)	

(continued)

Table 5 (continued)

Assets/liabilities	Measurement bases at first balance sheet recognition (ÅRL § or K3 reference)	Model/ method used during subsequent periods	Value adjustments recognized in. . .	Comment
		Voluntary revaluation ((4.6) and Ch. 11)	Revaluation reserve (restricted equity) (4.6)	Revaluations are not made on a regular basis; no use of comprehensive income
		Fair value model (Ch. 12)	Profit or loss, or fair value fund (nonrestricted equity)	
Investments in debt instruments —hold to maturity or loans and receivables	Historical cost (K3 11.16; K3 12.19)	Amortized cost model with impairment test	Profit or loss (impairment)	Policy choice between cost-based (K3: Chapter 11) and fair-value-based accounting (K3: Chapter 12); revaluations are not made on a regular basis; no use of comprehensive income
		Voluntary revaluation (Ch. 11)	Revaluation reserve (restricted equity)	

Assets/ liabilities	Measurement bases at first balance sheet recognition (ÅRL § or K3 reference)	Model/method used during subsequent periods	Value adjustments recognized in. . .	Comment
Investments in debt instruments —trading	Historical cost (K3 11.16)	Lower of cost and fair value less costs to sell (Ch. 11)	Profit or loss (impairment)	Policy choice between cost-based (K3: Chapter 11) and fair-value-based accounting (K3: Chapter 12)
	Fair value (K3 12.19)	Fair value model (Ch. 12)	Profit or loss, or fair value fund (nonrestricted equity)	
Derivative financial instruments	Historical cost; no or insignificant cost (K3 11.8)	Positive values: lower of cost and fair value less costs to sell (Ch. 11)	Profit or loss (impairment)	Policy choice between cost-based (K3: Chapter 11) and fair-value-based accounting (K3: Chapter 12)
		Negative values: the value most advantageous to the firm if the obligation is transferred on the closing date (Ch. 11)	Profit or loss	

(continued)

Table 5 (continued)

Assets/ liabilities	Measurement bases at first balance sheet recognition (ÅRL § or K3 reference)	Model/method used during subsequent periods	Value adjustments recognized in...	Comment
	Fair value (K3 12.19)	Fair value model (Ch. 12)	Profit or loss, or fair value fund (nonrestricted equity)	
Inventories	Historical cost (4.9)	Lower of cost and fair value less costs to sell (Ch. 11)	Profit or loss	Allowed cost formulas (ÅRL 4.11): FIFO, weighted average, or similar
Financial liabilities—non-trading	Historical cost (K3 11.16; K3 12.19)	Amortized cost model (Ch. 11, Ch. 12)	Profit or loss	Policy choice between cost-based (K3: Chapter 11) and fair-value-based accounting (K3: Chapter 12)
Financial liabilities—trading	Historical cost (K3 11.16)	Amortized cost model (Ch. 11)	Profit or loss	Policy choice between cost-based (K3: Chapter 11) and fair-value-based accounting (K3: Chapter 12)
	Fair value (K3 12.19)	Fair value model (Ch. 12)	Profit or loss, or fair value fund (nonrestricted equity)	

4.2 *Historical Cost Approach*

Historical cost is still the dominating approach in Sweden (see Table 5). When RR translated all IASs to Swedish, three standards were not included: IAS 39, IAS 40, and IAS 41. These standards require or allow for fair value accounting, and this was considered controversial in the Swedish context at the time. However, the transition to IFRS for consolidated financial statements prepared by listed companies (and voluntary adopters) has made the use of fair values more acceptable over time (see Table 5).

4.3 *Valuation Approaches Different from the Historical Cost*

4.3.1 Value Higher Than the Historical Cost (Unrealized Gains; Revalued Amount)

One interesting feature of Swedish GAAP is the use of revaluations (see Table 5). ÅRL allows companies to make revaluations of fixed assets if certain criteria are met (substantial value increase above the carrying amount; not a temporary value increase; reliable measurement of the estimated fair value). Revaluations are made in the legal entity and affect the consolidated financial statements accordingly. The unrealized revaluation gain is not recognized in the income statement but booked as restricted equity (revaluation reserve) as part of the legal entity's shareholders' equity. Swedish GAAP does not make use of the concepts "other comprehensive income" and "comprehensive income," neither in the legal entity nor in the consolidated financial statements.

4.3.2 Value Lower Than the Historical Cost (Write-Downs)

Write-downs have been made extensively by Swedish companies in the past. As referred to in the introduction of this chapter, there was a period in the 1950s, 1960s, and 1970s where "over-prudence" was accepted in terms of creating hidden reserves and making arbitrary provisions (e.g., Davidson & Kohlmeier, 1966). Such "over-prudence" appears to have decreased over time; however, the use of arbitrary write-downs is still subject to debate, for example, in relation to application of the expected credit loss model for banks under IFRS 9 (e.g., Andersson & Hellman, 2019). Regarding goodwill, the K3 Standard prescribes a dual model with amortization combined with an impairment test in case a further value decrease is indicated. Originally, the maximum goodwill amortization period was 10 years, but in 2016 this limitation was removed and replaced with a requirement to provide specific evidence supporting any amortization period longer than 5 years. Two examples of indications of a value decrease below the carrying amount are: increased interest rates and reported equity above the estimated fair value of the company. If such indicators trigger an impairment test, the test procedure is similar to IAS 36 (Chapter 27 in K3). Shares in associated companies including goodwill will also be tested for impairment pending indication of a value decrease below the carrying amount. The K3 Standard includes a chapter on provisions (Chapter 21), which is similar to the requirements in IAS 37.

4.3.3 Fair Value

As referred to above, RR never issued Swedish standards corresponding to the fair value standards IAS 39, IAS 40, and IAS 41. In the K3 Standard, fair value accounting for financial instruments was introduced by offering preparers a policy choice between historical-cost-based accounting (Chapter 11 in K3) and fair-value-based accounting (Chapter 12 in K3). Companies are not allowed to mix the two different chapters. For illustrations of how the two chapters differ, see Table 5. As regards investment property, K3 prescribes the cost model (including fair value disclosure in a note, as in IAS 40), but the fair value model is not allowed under K3. This issue was revisited by the committee dealing with the EU Directive 2013/34. Marton (2017, p. 211) reports:

> There is also a discussion about allowing fair value for investment property in agreement with IAS 40, but the committee decided to not propose it due to taxation issues (because of the link between financial reporting and taxation in Sweden). However, two of the accounting specialists on the committee – representing the accounting profession and the association of businesses – have a dissenting opinion in the report. They would like fair value to be allowed to harmonize with IAS 40.

Thus, investment property continues to be valued based on historical cost under Swedish GAAP.

4.3.4 Alternative Measurement Basis

The K3 Standard includes a separate chapter on accounting in foundations and similar entities (Chapter 36). A foundation receives donations and spends funds in accordance with its objectives. There are no owners of the foundation, so it cannot be sold or pay dividends. These entities may own assets that are not generating positive net cash flows but must be continuously owned because of donation terms. This is consistent with foundations not having profit generation as a key characteristic. BFN decided to exempt such assets from the regular impairment tests prescribed by K3, where an impairment loss is recognized when the carrying amount is lower than the recoverable amount. Instead, K3 prescribes in Chapter 36 that the carrying amount shall be compared with the deprival value, i.e., the lower of the recoverable amount and the replacement cost. The deprival value may be determined as the insurance value. Before K3, the deprival-value concept had not been used in Swedish accounting standards.

5 Conclusions

Swedish accounting is differentiated depending on the type of entity concerned. Consolidated financial statements for listed entities developed in a capital-market-oriented way during the 1980s and 1990s, followed by IFRS adoption in 2005, a decade after Sweden became a member of the European Union in 1995. However, a strong focus on the accounting-tax link has remained for the legal entities. This has resulted in standards with more emphasis on accounting with tax alignment (K1 and K2) and standards more oriented toward the capital markets through IFRS for SMEs (K3) and full IFRS. Recent empirical research suggests that the adoption of the K3 Standard by Swedish privately held groups have positive effects in terms of lower cost of debt and increased financial statement comparability (Hellman et al., 2022).

References

Alexander, D., & Nobes, C. W. (2020). *Financial accounting – An international introduction* (7th ed.). Pearson Education.

Andersson, H., & Hellman, N. (2019). Analysis of changing regulatory conditions, new accounting policies and the global financial crisis: The case of Swedish banks. In V. Krivogorsky (Ed.), *Institutions and accounting practices after the financial crisis: International perspective* (pp. 154–179). Routledge.

Carlsson, R. H. (2003). The benefits of active ownership. *Corporate Governance, 3*(2), 6–31.

Collin, S.-O. (1993). The brotherhood of the Swedish sphere. *International Studies of Management and Organization, 23*, 69–86.

Cooke, T. E. (1989). Disclosure in the corporate annual reports of Swedish companies. *Accounting and Business Research, 19*(74), 113–124.

Davidson, S., & Kohlmeier, J. M. (1966). A measure of the impact of some foreign accounting principles. *Journal of Accounting Research, 4*(2), 183–212.

Hellman, N. (1993). A comparative analysis of the impact of accounting differences on profits and return on equity – differences between Swedish practice and US GAAP. *European Accounting Review, 2*(3), 495–530.

Hellman, N. (2011a). Analysis of changing institutional environments, new accounting policies and corporate governance practices in Sweden. In V. Krivogorsky (Ed.), *Law, corporate governance, and accounting: European perspectives* (pp. 210–229). Routledge.

Hellman, N. (2011b). Soft adoption and reporting incentives: a study of the impact of IFRS on financial statements in Sweden. *Journal of International Accounting Research, 10*(1), 61–83.

Hellman, N., Nilsson, H., Tylaite, M., & Vural, D. (2022). The impact of an IFRS for SMEs-based standard on financial reporting properties and cost of debt financing: Evidence from Swedish private firms. *European Accounting Review, 31*(5), 1175–1205

Hellman, N., Tagesson, T., Öhman, P., & Grönlund, A. (2020). *Principle-based Accounting*. Studentlitteratur.

Henrekson, M., & Jacobsson, U. (2003). *The Swedish model of corporate ownership and control in transition* (IUI Working Paper Series No. 593). The Research Institute of Industrial Economics

Jönsson, S. (1991). Role making for accounting while the state is watching. *Accounting, Organizations and Society, 16*(5/6), 521–546.

Knutsson, M., Norberg, C., & Thorell, P. (2012). *Redovisningsfrågor i skattepraxis [How accounting matters are dealt with in Swedish taxation practice]* (3rd ed.). Iustus Förlag AB.

Marton, J. (2017). The role and current status of IFRS in the completion of national accounting rules evidence from Sweden. *Accounting in Europe, 14*(1–2), 207–216.

Nobes, C. W. (1983). A judgmental international classification of financial reporting practices. *Journal of Business Finance & Accounting, 10*(1), 1–19.

Ordelheide, D. (1990). Soft-transformations of accounting rules of the 4th directive in Germany. *Les Cahiers Internationaux de la Comptabilité, 3*, 1–15.

af Sandeberg, C. (2006). *Aktiebolagsrätten [Corporate Law]*. Studentlitteratur.

Seger, K. (2018). *Institutional logics and accounting professional: The Case of K2 and K3*. Doctoral Thesis. Örebro Studies in Business 11.

Sigonius, T. (2019). *Accounting standard-setting through adaptation: Models and contextual factors in the case of the Swedish Standard K3*. Doctoral Thesis. Stockholm School of Economics.

The Netherlands

Martin Hoogendoorn

1 Introduction

1.1 The Role of Company Law[1]

The legal basis for corporate reporting in the Netherlands is provided in Book 2, Title 9, of the Dutch Civil Code ('Dutch Law, DL'). DL gives basic measurement, presentation and disclosure rules for the preparation of financial statements, management report and certain required other accompanying information and also addresses the audit requirements. DL is applicable to a wide range of legal entities that exercise commercial activities, both profit and non-profit. In addition to DL, further legislation on specific topics is provided in a number of decrees, the most important of which are the decree financial statement models, which prescribe the layout of the primary statements, and the decree current value, which details the application of the current value model to specific types of assets and liabilities.

DL, Article 362.1, provides the overriding principle that underlies the preparation of financial statements:

Martin Hoogendoorn is a professor of corporate reporting at the Erasmus University Rotterdam, former chairman of the DASB and former partner of EY.

[1]This section and Sects. 1.2 and 2.2 are based on Brouwer and Hoogendoorn (2017).

M. Hoogendoorn (✉)
Erasmus University Rotterdam, Rotterdam, Netherlands
e-mail: hoogendoorn@ese.eur.nl

A. Incollingo, A. Lionzo (eds.), *The European Harmonization of National Accounting Rules*, SIDREA Series in Accounting and Business Administration,
https://doi.org/10.1007/978-3-031-42931-6_9

> The financial statements provide, in accordance with principles that are considered generally acceptable in society,[2] such an insight that a sound judgment can be made regarding the equity and the result as well as, insofar as the nature of financial statements permit, of the solvency and liquidity of the entity.

This overriding principle on 'required insight' can be summarized by the requirement that financial statements give a true and fair view. Following this overriding principle, an entity must provide additional information beyond the information required by law when this is necessary to provide the required insight (DL, Article 362.4). Furthermore, an entity must even deviate from the specific rules set out in DL when this is necessary for giving the true and fair view (i.e. a true and fair view override).

1.2 The Dutch Accounting Standards Board

DL only stipulates the key requirements that an entity must comply with and certain exemptions in 55 articles (approximately 15,000 words), plus specific sections for banks and insurance companies. There are no requirements to apply specific accounting standards. The only reference is that financial statements should be prepared in accordance with principles that are generally acceptable in society. Therefore, a key aspect of the preparation and audit process is the identification of the accounting principles that are considered generally acceptable in the Netherlands. This process is driven by the Dutch Accounting Standards Board (DASB), which develops the Dutch Accounting Standards (DAS). The DASB is a private standard setter and consists of representatives of the preparers, users and auditors of financial statements. The DASB therefore represents the stakeholders that have an interest in financial reporting. The DAS provide more detailed guidance as it comes to recognition, measurement and disclosure within the context of DL. They contain 56 individual standards addressing topics that can apply to each type of entity and 11 standards that apply to specific types of entities or entities that operate in a specific industry.

Although DL does not explicitly refer to the DAS, the DAS are considered to be the authoritative guidance in the Netherlands as regards generally acceptable accounting principles. This is, among others, signified by the reference that was made to DAS during the process of adopting the EU Accounting Directive and by the fact that representatives of the Ministry of Justice attend the DASB meetings. Furthermore, the Enterprise Court ('Ondernemingskamer'), the court that rules in financial statement procedures, confirmed in a number of cases that an entity

[2] Although it is not specifically mentioned in the first sentence of DL Article 362.1, the generally accepted principles that are referred to are accounting principles generally accepted in the Netherlands.

applying DAS will generally give a true and fair view in accordance with DL. The Supreme Court has confirmed this view.

This does not mean that an entity is obliged to apply all the specific requirements included in DAS. As an element of true and fair override, the DASB states that there may be sound reasons to deviate from its specific standards. Also, the Enterprise Court makes it clear that the application of the DAS is not the only way that an entity can provide the required insight. A deviation from a specific standard might occur when there is an entity-specific situation where the application of the standard would not result in a true and fair view. Another situation where a deviation might occur is applying the US GAAP treatment by a subsidiary of a US-based parent, although that would not be allowed according to specific Dutch standards. Furthermore, an entity might apply a new standard in an earlier year than is formally allowed. In summary, we conclude that Dutch GAAP is very much principle-based.

1.3 Tax Regulation

The role of tax regulation in the Netherlands is, on a formal basis, very limited. Taxable income needs to be calculated in accordance with sound business practices. What these sound business practices are is determined by way of court decisions. There is no such thing as a DASB for tax purposes. Formally, the calculation of accounting income and tax income is fully separated. However, from a practical point of view, there are some linkages:

- The sound business practice finds its basis in business economics, as does the idea of a true and fair view. Many views in accounting are also applied in calculating taxable income.
- Estimates are neutral in the sense that it is difficult to argue that for tax purposes estimates are different than for accounting purposes, unless tax authorities allow specific tax facilities like accelerated depreciation by allowing shorter useful lives.

Furthermore, there is one specific link. For small entities and micro-entities, it is allowed to calculate their accounting income based on tax rules instead of accounting rules (DL, Articles 395a:7 and 396:6).

1.4 Economic System

The Netherlands, being a small country with 17.5 million inhabitants, has traditionally been very much focused on international business. There are many multinational companies based in the Netherlands, and the stock market plays an important role.

Table 1 Number of active companies on the 1 April 2022

Employees	Total	%
Total	2,086,670	
1	1,660,015	79.6%
2–49	411,315	19.7%
50–249	11,925	0.6%
250–499	1755	0.1%
500 and more	1660	0.1%

Source: Centraal Bureau voor de Statistiek (CBS)

At the end of 2021, 2.1 million companies have been registered in the Netherlands[3] (the main types being companies in business services, trade and construction). There are less than 100 listed companies and a little more than 3000 large companies. The number of SME companies with more than one employee is around 425,000. The remaining 80% are one-employee companies (self-employed without employees).

Table 1 gives an overview of the number of active companies and their employees as of 1 April 2022.

2 The Evolution of Accounting Regulation

2.1 Implementing the Accounting Directive (EU Directive 2013/4 34)

The starting point in implementing the Accounting Directive has been that only changes would be made in DL where they result from differences between the Accounting Directive on the one hand and the Fourth and Seventh EU Directives (including later amendments) on the other hand. Therefore, there has been no redeliberation on aspects of financial accounting and reporting that did not arise from changes at the EU level. I will discuss the main changes made.

As a general remark, the Netherlands shows a rather permissive attitude in implementing the Accounting Directive, as it did in implementing the Fourth and Seventh Directives. This means that the options allowed by the Directive are generally used.

In Chapter 3, we will discuss the specific issues of implementation.

[3] https://www.kvk.nl/download/KVK_Bedrijvendynamiek_jaaroverzicht_2020_tcm109-495721.pdf.

Table 2 Accounting rules in the Netherlands

	Individual Accounts	Group Accounts
Listed companies	IFRS or national GAAP (optional)	IFRS
Non-listed companies	IFRS or national GAAP (optional)	IFRS or national GAAP (optional)

Note: the combination of national GAAP for individual accounts and IFRS for consolidated accounts is allowed (as well as national GAAP or IFRS for both), but not the combination of national GAAP for consolidated accounts and IFRS for individual accounts

2.2 *The Level of IFRS Adoption*

DL is positive towards IFRS:

- IFRS may be used by all entities for both the individual and the consolidated accounts or the consolidated accounts only.
- There is a specific legal option for entities using IFRS in the consolidated financial statements to apply an IFRS-friendly version of DL in their separate financial statements (using the IFRS measurement rules, while measuring participating interests at net asset value in order to keep equality between individual and consolidated equity and net result).
- IFRS for SMEs can be used by non-listed and non-regulated companies in combination with DL.

In Table 2, an overview of the accounting rules in the Netherlands is given.

In the process of making changes to DL, alignment with IFRS is generally considered, although limited (implicit or explicit) references are made to IFRS. This can be explained by the starting point in the adoption process that only discussions have been raised that were necessary as a result of changes at the EU level, not by a reduced interest in IFRS. The limited explicit reference to IFRS in DL is also explained by the relatively broad nature of DL that relies to a large extent on the development of generally accepted principles in practice and specifically by the DASB, whereby the DASB has a history of considering IFRS when developing DAS.

For DAS, a change in strategy has occurred from 2005 on, where the policy of implementing IFRS was replaced by a policy of considering the relevance of IFRS for DAS. This new policy has mostly resulted in including the IFRS option as one of the options in Dutch GAAP and adding one or more additional optional treatments considered suitable for non-listed companies. An example is accounting for financial instruments, where DAS leaves more room for measuring at historical cost. The number of major differences between Dutch GAAP and IFRS is relatively limited, with only a few differences that cannot be avoided by an entity when preparing financial statements under Dutch GAAP. The main example is goodwill accounting (amortization is required under Dutch GAAP). In some cases, DAS is contrary to IFRS, but DAS allows the application of the specific IFRS as an alternative within Dutch GAAP. The main example is pension accounting, where Dutch GAAP applies the general requirements for provisions to the measurement of pension liabilities, but also allows to fully apply IAS 19 as part of Dutch GAAP. That alternative is attractive for companies that are subsidiaries of parents reporting under IFRS (and therefore have to prepare IFRS-based information for the group accounts), but that choose to apply local GAAP for their own statutory financial statements.

In practice, IFRS is only applied by all listed and many large entities. SME entities apply local GAAP. IFRS for SME is not applied at all (or maybe in incidental cases).

2.3 Non-Financial Disclosure Evolution

According to DL, Article 391:1, the management report shall contain a balanced and complete analysis of the situation on the balance sheet date, the development during the year and the results. If necessary for a good understanding, the analysis comprises both financial and non-financial performance indicators, including environmental and employee matters. This requirement is obligatory for all large- and medium-sized entities (small and micro-entities are not required to prepare a management report).

As a result of implementing the EU Non-Financial Reporting Directive (Directive 2014/95/EU), in addition to DL, Article 391:1, a specific degree has been published: the Decree Disclosure of Non-Financial Information. The requirements in the decree only apply to large public interest entities (with generally more than 500 employees). According to the decree, a non-financial statement needs to be included in the management report, containing the following information:

a. A brief description of the business model of the entity.
b. A description of the policies, including the applied due diligence procedures, and the results of this policy with regard to the following themes:
   (i) Environmental, social and human affairs.
   (ii) Human rights respect.
   (iii) Corruption and bribery.
c. The main material risks with regards to the topics mentioned in sub b related to the activities of the entity including where relevant and proportional, the business relations, products or services of the entity likely to have adverse effects on these subjects and how the entity manages these risks.
d. Non-financial performance indicators that are relevant to the specific business activities of the entity.

Large subsidiaries are exempted when the ultimate parent includes the non-financial information for the entire group.

In providing this information, the entity may make use of several frameworks like those of the Global Reporting Initiative (GRI), the International Integrated Reporting Council (IIRC) and the Guidance for Social Reporting, published by the DASB. The use of a framework needs to be disclosed in the non-financial statement, with the entity having a responsibility to verify whether the use of the framework comprises the information required by the decree.

3 Implementation of EU Directive 2013/34

3.1 Introduction

In this section, we will first discuss the major changes that were made in implementing the Accounting Directive and some general requirements. The changes in valuation issues will be discussed in Sect. 4.

3.2 General Provisions and Principles

Article 6 of the EU mentions the general financial reporting principles. These are reflected in DL as follows:

(a) Going Concern. The valuation of assets and liabilities shall be based on the assumption that all the activities of the entity are to be continued, unless that assumption is incorrect or its accuracy is subject to reasonable doubt. If so, this will be clarified, mentioning the impact on equity and results (DL, Article 384: 2). According to DAS 170, in case of reasonable doubt, the financial statements will still be prepared on a going concern basis. Only when discontinuity is inevitable, the financial statements will be prepared on a liquidation basis.
(b) Consistency. The balance sheet and the profit and loss account shall be prepared on a consistent basis (DL, Article 362: 3 and 4).
(c) Prudence. In applying the valuation principles, prudence is observed. Profits are only recognized when they are realized on the balance sheet date. Liabilities shall be recognized if they became known prior to the preparation of financial statements. Foreseeable liabilities and potential losses that originate from an event prior to the end of the financial year may be taken into account if they became known prior to the preparation of financial statements (DL, Article 384: 2; EU, Article 6:5). The DASB interprets these legal requirements in a way that prudence is applied as in IFRS: prudence is the exercise of caution when making judgements under conditions of uncertainty. The exercise of prudence means that assets and income are not overstated and liabilities and expenses are not understated (DASB, Conceptual Framework, para 37). For example, it is not allowed to use prudence as an argument not to capitalize on development expenses of deferred tax assets or to recognize provisions when there is no legal, contractual or constructive obligation.

   DL uses the option to deviate from the principle that profits are only recognized when they are realized for financial instruments, other investments and agriculture produce measured at fair value (EU, Article 8; DL, Article 384:7): unrealized profits may be recognized in the profit and loss account for these assets (see Sect. 4.2).

(d) Accrual basis. The income and expenses over a financial year shall be included in the financial statements, regardless of whether they have actually led to receipts or expenditures in that year (DL, Article 362:5).

(e) Opening balance shall correspond to the closing balance for the preceding year. This principle is not explicitly stated in DL, probably because it is self-evident.

(f) Separate valuation of assets and liabilities. Assets and liabilities shall be valued separately when needed for the true and fair view (DL, Article 385:1).

(g) No netting. Where assets and liabilities or revenues and expenses have to be included as separate items, it is not allowed to show them on a net basis (DL, Article 363:2).

(h) Substance over form. This basic principle is not explicitly reflected in DL, but is considered to be a self-evident component of the true and fair view. The DASB, however, does explicitly mention this principle: in order to give a true and fair view of transactions and events, it is required to recognize them in accordance with their substance and not just their form (DAS 110.116).

(i) Historical cost principle. We discuss this principle in Sect. 4.

(j) Materiality. It is not necessary to disclose an item separately if that item is of negligible importance for the true and fair view (DL, Article 363:3). There is no requirement to include in the consolidated figures data of subsidiaries that, on a combined basis, are negligible (DL, Article 407:1a). There is no legal general materiality requirement regarding recognition, measurement and presentation, probably because they are considered a logical element of the true and fair view requirement. In general, the principle of materiality is prevalent in the DAS, where materiality is defined based on the IASB Conceptual Framework (para 2.11): information is material if omitting, misstating or obscuring it could reasonably be expected to influence decisions that the users of the financial statements make (DAS 115.207). This is equal to the definition of materiality in EU 2:16, except for the addition of 'obscuring' in the DAS (and IFRS) definition.

3.3 Components of Financial Statements and Layouts

3.3.1 Balance Sheet and Profit and Loss Account

The EU Accounting Directive mentions three components of financial statements: the balance sheet, the profit and loss account and the notes (EU, Article 4:1). In DL, no additional components are identified, but the DASB does.

Compared to the Fourth Directive, the Accounting Directive contained some limited changes in the layout of the balance sheet and the profit and loss account

(EU, Articles 9–14). These changes have been implemented in the Decree on the Layout of Financial Statements.

One of the more principal changes is the removal of two of the four profit and loss layouts (the horizontal statements with debit and credit) and of the extraordinary items. This has led to corresponding changes in DL.

Several options on the layout have been included in the Fourth Directive. An important option is the horizontal or vertical layout of the balance sheet (EU, Article 10). In DL, both layouts are included for entities to choose from. The option of Article 11 of the EU to present items on the basis of a distinction between current and non-current items has not been used. Furthermore, for the profit and loss account, the option of Article 13:2 of the EU to present a statement of performance instead of the presentation of profit and loss has not been used either. However, we refer to the discussion below of the statement of comprehensive income.

For other main options, DL has made the following choices:

- 'Subscribed capital unpaid' is not included as an asset (but deducted from equity).
- 'Formation expenses' is not a separate item, but is included as the first item under 'Intangible assets'.
- 'Own shares' is not included as an asset (but deducted from equity).
- 'Prepayments and accrued income' is not a separate item, but is included in 'Debtors'.
- 'Accruals and deferred income' is not a separate item, but is included in 'Creditors'.

3.3.2 Other Components of Financial Statements

The DASB requires a consolidated cash flow statement for all large- and medium-sized entities (DAS 360). Only if no consolidated accounts have been prepared, an individual cash flow statement is required. The structure of the cash flow statement is equal to that of IAS 7, distinguishing operating activities, investing activities and financing activities. The specific requirements are mostly identical with some minor exceptions, of which the most significant is the definition of cash and cash equivalents. In IAS 7, bank overdrafts that are repayable on demand and form an integral part of an entity's cash management are included as a (negative) component of cash and cash equivalents (IAS 7:8). The DASB does not permit this (DAS 360.102).

Another component identified by DAS 265 is the consolidated statement of comprehensive income, combining the net result (the bottom line of the profit and loss account) with items of income and expenses that are directly recognized in equity ('other comprehensive income' in the IASB terminology, IAS 1:81A). The statement of comprehensive income is only required for large entities. There are three alternatives in presenting the statement of comprehensive income:

- As a separate statement.
- Combined with the profit and loss account.
- Combined with the reconciliation statement of equity (see below).

The IASB only allows for the first two alternatives.

One of the other components of IFRS is the statement of changes in equity (IAS 1:10). Although not specified in the Accounting Directive, under DL it is required to include in the individual accounts a reconciliation statement of movements in equity, revealing the amount of each equity item at the beginning of the year, additions to and reductions in each item over the year (distinguished by nature) and the amount of each item at the end of the year. This reconciliation statement is not a primary statement, as in IFRS, but is included as part of the notes.

3.4 *Exemptions for Non-Large Entities*

3.4.1 Micro-Entities

One of the major changes is the introduction of a special optional regime for micro-entities (DL, Article 2:395a BW2). They are defined in the Accounting Directive (EU, Article 3:1), as entities that, on their balance sheet date, do not exceed the limits of at least two of the three following criteria:

(a) Balance sheet total: EUR 350,000.
(b) Net turnover: EUR 700,000.
(c) Average number of employees during the financial year: 10.

Following EU, Article 36, micro-entities are allowed to

- Only draw up an abridged balance sheet and profit and loss account.
- Only publish the abridged balance sheet.

Furthermore, they are exempted from:

- Preparing consolidated accounts.
- Presenting notes to the financial statements (with a few exceptions).
- Presenting and recognizing prepayments and accrued income as well as accruals and deferred income.
- Preparing a management report.

Following the requirement in the Accounting Directive, micro-entities are not allowed to use the alternative measurement basis of fair value. They may, however, use tax accounting rules, as small entities were already allowed to do so before the implementation of the Accounting Directive (see Sect. 1.3). Neither the Accounting Directive nor its predecessors do explicitly mention the option to use tax accounting rules.

3.4.2 Other Small Entities

In defining a small entity, the Accounting Directive sets new thresholds regarding balance sheet total, net turnover and average number of employees (Article 3:2). These new thresholds are as follows:

(a) Balance sheet total: minimum EUR 4 million; maximum EUR 6 million.
(b) Net turnover: minimum EUR 8 million; maximum 12 million.
(c) Average number of employees during the financial year: 50.

The Netherlands (DL, Article 396:2) has chosen to apply the maximum amounts, increasing the balance sheet total threshold from € 4.4 million to EUR 6 million and the net turnover threshold from EUR 8.8 million to 12 million. The main reason for choosing the maximum thresholds is to enable as many entities as possible to enjoy relatively lower administrative expenses.

The Fourth Directive did not prescribe on what basis the thresholds needed to be calculated: an individual basis or a consolidated basis. In DL, the requirement has been to calculate the thresholds on a consolidated basis. The starting point for the Accounting Directive is calculation on an individual basis. However, using a consolidated basis may also be required (EU, Article 3: 12). This has not led to a change in DL, so the consolidated basis of calculating the thresholds remains, not only for small entities, but for all (DL, Articles 395a:2, 396:2 and 397:2). For both micro-entities and small entities, which are not required to prepare consolidated reports, this is somewhat in contrast to the idea of lower administrative expenses. To calculate the thresholds, they need to follow an 'as, if' approach: what would the balance sheet total, net turnover and number of employees have been when they were required to prepare consolidated financial statements? The approach does, however, correspond to the policy of making no change in law when not required to do so.

The Fourth and Seventh Directives did not require one set of disclosures in small entity financial statements for all EU countries. This has changed in the Accounting Directive. As a result, changes have been made in DL to limit the disclosures to those stated in the Accounting Directive.

Some member state options remain: drawing up an abridged balance sheet and profit and loss account (EU, Article 14), exempting small entities from the obligation to prepare management reports (EU, Article 19:3) and exempting them from the obligation to publish their profit and loss accounts (EU, Article 31:1). These options were also maintained in DL. Furthermore, the Dutch legislator maintained the option not to prepare consolidated accounts and not to require an audit for small entities.

3.4.3 Medium-Sized Entities

Also, the thresholds for defining a medium-sized entity have been changed and correspond to the maximum levels in the Accounting Directive (EU, Article 3:3; DL, Article 397:1):

(a) Balance sheet total: EUR 20 million (was EUR 17.5 million).
(b) Net turnover: EUR 40 million (was EUR 35 million).
(c) Average number of employees during the financial year: 250 (unchanged).

Medium-sized entities, compared to large entities, have exemptions in preparing a limited profit and loss account and limited publishing requirements.

An exception to the principle that the Netherlands adopts options in the EU Directive as much as possible in its law is the requirement to prepare consolidated reports by medium-sized entities. The Accounting Directive, as well as the Seventh Directive, gives member states the options not to oblige medium-sized entities to prepare consolidated accounts. This option was and still is not used in DL (DL, Articles 397 and 406:1).

3.4.4 Overviews

Table 3 gives an overview of the size limits for companies.

In Table 4, we have included an overview of content of the annual report for the different companies according to size.

Table 3 Size limits for companies according to the Dutch Civil Code

	Medium-sized entities	Small entities	Micro-entities
Net turnover	EUR 40,000,000	EUR 12,00,000	EUR 700,000
Total assets	EUR 20,0000	EUR 6,000,000	EUR 350,000
Average number of employees	250	50	10

Table 4 Content of the annual report for the different companies according to size

	Micro-entities	Small entities	Medium-sized entities	Large entities
Management report			X	X
Balance sheet	X[a]	X[a]	X	X
Profit and loss statement	X[a,b]	X[a,b]	X[c]	X
Consolidated financial statements			X[c]	X
Cash flow statement			X	X
Disclosure of accounting policies		X	X	X
Other notes (increasing requirements depending on accounting class)		X	X	X

[a]Only abridged
[b]Only drawing up, no requirement to publish
[c]With a few exemptions in presenting separate items

3.5 *Notes to the Financial Statements*

A new requirement in the Accounting Directive is that notes shall be presented in the order in which items are presented in the balance sheet and in the profit and loss account. This requirement is quite contrary to the liberal attitude in the Netherlands towards a free format in presenting the notes, with the general requirement of a true and fair view as a basic concept. The Accounting Directive leaves no option in this regard, so the requirement is included in DL, Article 363:1. However, in the explanatory memorandum, it is made clear that priority should be given to the overall requirement of a true and fair view. This would probably mean that Dutch entities are not prevented from:

- Putting the most important information at the beginning of the notes section.
- Combining notes when this is adequate, like those regarding deferred tax assets, deferred tax liabilities and tax expenses.

To stay in accordance with DL, it might be necessary to apply the order of the items presented, while using references to other notes for (more) content.

Some of the new disclosure requirements in DL introduced as a consequence of the Accounting Directive are as follows:

- The name of the entity (EU, Article 5; DL, Article 380b).
- The amount of contingent assets and liabilities (EU, Article 16:1 (d); DL, Article 381:1).
- The amounts of advances and credits granted to members of the administrative, managerial and supervisory boards that are written off or waived (EU, Article 16: 1(e); DL, Article 383:2).
- The amounts and nature of individual items of income and expenditure that are of exceptional size or incidence (EU, Article 16:1(f); DL, Article 377:8).

Furthermore, some information has been replaced from a separate section outside the financial statements ('Other data') to the notes (DL, Articles 380a, c, d): events after the balance sheet date, profit distribution and the existence of profit certificates.

4 Valuation Approaches

4.1 *Historical Cost*

The basic EU measurement principle for assets and liabilities in the balance sheet is that of historical cost (purchase price, production cost; EU, Article 6:1(i)). Article 384:1 of DL generally describes that in choosing a measurement principle, giving a true and fair view should be the dominant guidance. Historical cost (purchase cost or production cost) and current value are mentioned as basic principles. The application of these principles can be found in the decree on current value.

The historical cost principle (including amortized costs for financial instruments) is required for:

- Intangible assets when there is no liquid market (applicable to the far majority of intangible assets).
- Inventories with the exception of agricultural produce.
- Loans and bonds acquired that are held until maturity.
- Debtors, unless they are held for trading.
- Creditors, unless they are held for trading.

For all other assets and liabilities, there is a principal choice between historical cost and current value, with two remarks:

- Participating interests where the entity has a significant influence need to be measured at net asset value (which is the equity method, without the goodwill component), with some limited exceptions.
- Provisions need to be measured at their best estimate, using discounting when the cash flows are expected to flow out after more than 1 year.

4.2 Alternative Measurements

An alternative to historical cost is the current value. In DL, current value is a collective term, encompassing measurements such as fair value, fair value less costs of disposal, net realizable value, current cost, replacement value and value in use. For different assets and liabilities, different interpretations of current value might be applicable.

The EU introduced two alternative measurements:

- Revalued amounts for fixed assets (EU, Article 7)
- Fair value (EU, Article 8).

Based on the Fourth Directive, it was possible to measure fixed assets and inventories at replacement value. This measurement basis is no longer allowed in the Accounting Directive. For fixed assets, the new current value measurement concept is that of current cost, as an interpretation of EU, Article 7.

The current cost is defined as either the current purchase price, including additional costs, or the current production cost, both reduced by depreciation (DL, decree current value). A difference with the replacement value is that the current cost is not defined by the costs of replacing the asset, but by its own costs of acquiring or producing the asset.

Intangible fixed assets may only be measured at the current cost in the case of a liquid market for the asset, which will only be in exceptional cases (emission rights being an example).

Upward changes in current cost need to be recognized in a revaluation reserve. The revaluation reserve is reduced by downward price changes and upon realization by depreciation or sale of the asset. In case of realization, DL allows two alternatives: to transfer the realized amount to the other reserves or to recycle them in profit and loss (DL, Article 390:3-4). Note that the alternative of recycling is not allowed by IAS 16.

For inventories, measurement at the current value is no longer allowed (with the exception of agricultural produce).

Regarding fair value, no changes have been made in DL. Measurement at fair value is allowed for most financial instruments and investment properties, while agricultural produce may be measured at fair value less costs of disposal.

Measuring financial instruments at fair value is required for those in the trading portfolio, for investments in listed shares and for derivatives based on listed shares. It is an option for derivatives used in hedging, derivatives not based on listed shares, loans and bonds acquired that are not held to maturity and investments in non-listed shares.

How to recognize changes in the fair value of financial instruments depends on the nature of the financial instrument. Two alternatives of recognition are identified (DAS 290.5):

- Immediate recognition in profit and loss. This is required for financial instruments in the trading portfolio and derivatives (when not used for hedging). It is an option for investments in listed shares and for loans and bonds acquired that are not held to maturity. When there are no frequent market listings for the financial instrument, is it required to recognize a revaluation reserve for unrealized gains? For this purpose, there is a within-equity transfer from other (free) reserves to the revaluation reserve (and back when unrealized gains diminish).
- First recognition in a revaluation reserve, with recycling to profit and loss upon realization. This is an option for investments in listed shares and for loans and bonds acquired that are not held to maturity.

In case of recognition in the revaluation reserve, there is no option not to recycle. The revaluation reserve may not be negative. Impairments need to be recognized in profit and loss at all times (as in valuation on amortized cost).

In case of hedging, the DASB allows three hedge accounting models: the two models as in IFRS 9 (cash flow hedge accounting and fair value hedge accounting) and a model of cost price hedge accounting. That model is based on measuring derivatives at cost. When using cost price hedge accounting, a downward valuation because of a value below cost is not recognized, as a corresponding upward valuation will exist regarding the hedged item.

For investment property measured at fair value, immediate recognition in profit and loss is required (DAS 213.504). There is no option to include unrealized gains in a revaluation reserve first. However, as with financial instruments for which there are no frequent market listings, a revaluation reserve needs to be recognized for these unrealized gains by a within-equity transfer.

Changes in the fair value of agricultural produce are recognized in the revaluation reserve, with recycling (DAS 220.402/404). However, in case of frequent market listings, it is also allowed to recognize the changes in profit and loss (DL, Article 384:7).

4.3 Write-Down for Impairment Losses

Next to the systematic depreciation or amortization of fixed assets (EU, Article 12: 5), Article 12:6 treats the accounting for impairments ('value adjustments') of fixed assets. There is one explicit option: member states may permit or require value adjustments to be made in respect of financial fixed assets, so that they are valued at the lower figure to be attributed to them at the balance sheet date. In DL, such value adjustments are permitted (DL, Article 387:3).

Further requirements are as follows:

- Value adjustments are taken into account regardless of the result of the financial year (DL, Article 387:1).
- Value adjustments of fixed assets are only to be taken into account when it is to be expected that the value decrease will be permanent (DL, Article 387:4).
- Value adjustments are recognized in profit and loss as far as they have not been recognized as a reduction of the revaluation reserve (in case of valuing fixed assets at current cost) (DL, Article 387:5).
- Value adjustment needs to be reversed as soon as the decrease in value has ceased to exist, except for goodwill (DL, Article 387:5).

The Accounting Directive leaves in the middle how the value adjustments of fixed assets should be calculated, as does DL. The DASB has included extensive requirements in DAS 121, which are based on IAS 36. Estimations of an impairment loss are made when there is an indication of impairment (different from IAS 36, this also holds for goodwill and all intangible assets, as amortization is always required) (DAS 121.202). An impairment loss is the amount by which the carrying amount of the asset or a cash-generating unit exceeds its recoverable amount (DAS 121.401). The recoverable amount of an asset or a cash-generating unit is the higher of its fair value less cost of disposal and its value in use (DAS 121.0). An impairment loss shall first be allocated to reduce the carrying amount of any goodwill allocated to the cash-generating unit and then to the other assets of the unit on a pro rata basis (DAS 121.520).

For current assets, EU Article 12:7 requires that value adjustments shall be made to show them at the lower market value or, in particular circumstances, another lower value. This has been implemented in DL, Article 387:2, where 'market value' has been replaced by 'current value'. The DASB has specified that 'current value' is the 'fair value less costs of disposal' (220.322). It has not identified situations where 'another lower value' might be relevant.

EU Article 12:7 further states that measurement at the lower value may not continue if the reasons for which value adjustments have been made no longer apply. This is reflected in DL, Article 387:4.

4.4 Goodwill

Under DL, there were three options to recognize goodwill:

- Capitalization in the balance sheet, with an amortization period of five years, unless the useful life was significantly longer.
- Immediate deduction from equity (other reserves).
- Immediately recognition in profit and loss.

EU, Article 12:11, no longer accepts the last two alternatives. Goodwill is required to be capitalized in the balance sheet. The Accounting Directive states that in exceptional cases where the useful life of goodwill cannot be reliably estimated it shall be written off within a maximum period that is not shorter than five years and does not exceed 10 years. In DL, the maximum period of 10 years has been elected (DL, Article 386:3). An explanation of the period over which goodwill is written off will be provided in the notes.

Another change in goodwill accounting is the restriction on the reversal of an impairment. As in the Fourth Directive, reversals of impairments are required for fixed assets: as mentioned above, EU Article 12:6 (d) states that measurement at the lower of values may not continue if the reasons for which the value adjustments were made have ceased to apply. A new requirement is that such a reversal is no longer allowed in the case of goodwill (DL, Article 387:5).

4.5 Other Changes in Measurement

Changes in DL were made on two specific measurement topics:

- The requirement on goodwill, that in exceptional cases where the useful life cannot be reliably estimated it shall be written off within a period not exceeding 10 years, also applies to capitalized development cost (DL, Article 396:3).
- The legal possibility to capitalize on research costs (which was not allowed by the DASB) has been abolished.
- An exceptional value adjustment of current assets, which is expected after the balance sheet date, is no longer allowed.

4.6 Income Taxes

Accounting for income taxes is very much in line with IAS 12, however, in a simplified version. Deferred tax liabilities shall be recognized for taxable temporary differences (DAS 272.301). Deferred tax assets shall be recognized for deductible temporary differences to the extent that it is probable that the asset will be realized by future taxable profit (DAS 272.306). A difference with IAS 12 is that deferred tax may be discounted (DAS 272.404).

4.7 An Overview

In Table 5, an overview is given of the measurement bases in Dutch GAAP for various assets and liabilities. In this table, recycling means that upon realization of the upward value adjustment (by depreciation/amortization or by selling the asset) the value adjustment will be included in profit or loss. For those unrealized changes in value that are immediately recognized in profit and loss and for which no frequent market listings exist, a revaluation reserve needs to be presented within equity (as a transfer from other reserves). A revaluation reserve is a legal reserve, from which it is prohibited to pay dividends to shareholders.

5 Conclusions

Nobes and Parker (2008) classified accounting systems in developed Western countries in their book on Comparative International Accounting. Already in their first edition in 1981, they considered the Netherlands as a 'sui generis', a case apart. The accounting system in the Netherlands was characterized as commercially driven (as opposed to government-driven of tax-driven), based on business economics and highly judgemental. In the refined classification of 1998, Dutch accounts are still a separate category, in the family of 'Strong equity', as IFRS, UK GAAP and US GAAP.

I would say that in substance the 1981 characterization still holds, 40 years later. In implementing the EU Accounting Directive and earlier the Fourth and Seventh EU Directives, the Dutch legislator has mostly chosen to include the options given, which shows a rather liberal attitude. Furthermore, DL does not contain any explicit obligation to apply the DAS, nor any reference to it, which makes it different from IFRS, UK and USA.

However, the true and fair view (or the required insight) is a rather dominant feature in DL and DAS. That makes it less liberal, because the apparent 'free choice' is limited by reference to this true and fair view. This makes Dutch accounting very much principles-based. The 'rules' as given in DL and in the DASB are no strict rules: it is possible or even required to deviate from the 'rules' when the true and fair view would require so. An entity may not defend its accounting policy choice by just referring to the 'rule', and it should be the true and fair view. Of course, the DAS are considered to be an application of the true and fair view principle, and applying the DAS will in most cases result in giving a true and fair view, but not as an automatism, not by just filling in the checklist. Professional judgement is needed

Table 5 Measurement bases in Dutch GAAP for various assets and liabilities

Asset/liability	Measurement bases allowed or required	Value adjustments recognized in. . . .
Intangible assets	Historical cost Fair value if obtained from an active market	Profit and loss (impairments) Revaluation reserve (option to recycle to profit and loss)
Tangible fixed/non-current assets	Historical cost Current cost	Profit and loss (impairments) Revaluation reserve (option to recycle to profit and loss)
Investment property	Historical cost Fair value	Profit and loss (impairments) Profit and loss
Investments in subsidiaries (parent company financial statements)	Net asset value/ equity method	Profit and loss (investee's direct transactions through equity are also recognized through equity by the investor)
Investments in associates (financial statements of the investor)	Net asset value/ equity method	Profit and loss (investee's direct transactions through equity are also recognized through equity by the investor)
Investments in joint ventures and joint operations (consolidated financial statements)	Net asset value/ equity method Proportional consolidation	Profit and loss (investee's direct transactions through equity are also recognized through equity by the investor) N/A
Investments in joint ventures and joint operations (financial statements of the investor)	Net asset value/ equity method	Profit and loss (investee's direct transactions through equity are also recognized through equity by the investor)
Shares with no significant influence	Historical cost Fair value (required for listed shares) Fair value (option for non-listed shares)	Profit and loss (impairments) Profit and loss Revaluation reserve (with recycling to profit or loss); reserve may not be negative
Investments in debt instruments—hold to maturity or loans and receivables	Amortized cost	Profit and loss (impairments)
Investments in debt instruments—trading	Fair value	Profit and loss
Derivatives on listed shares	Fair value	Profit and loss
Other derivative financial instruments including contracts to buy and sell non-financial items that can be settled net (no hedge accounting)	Historical cost Fair value	Profit and loss (impairments) Profit and loss
Inventories	Historical cost	Profit and loss (impairments)

(continued)

Table 5 (continued)

Asset/liability	Measurement bases allowed or required	Value adjustments recognized in. . . .
Agricultural inventories with frequent market listings	Historical cost Fair value less costs of disposal	Profit and loss (impairments) Profit and loss or revaluation reserve (with recycling)
Other agricultural inventories	Historical cost Fair value less costs of disposal	Profit and loss (impairments) Revaluation reserve (with recycling)
Financial liabilities—non-trading	Amortized cost	N/A
Financial liabilities—trading	Fair value	Profit and loss

to see whether deviations from the 'rules' are required or whether additional disclosures would be necessary that have not been included in the DAS.

Having a final look at the content of the Dutch accounting system, we see that the DASB follows IFRS closely, with sometimes additional options and with less disclosure requirements (taking into account the cost and benefits for non-listed entities). The Netherlands has been one of the founders of current value accounting, with the replacement value theory of Theodore Limperg in the thirties, based on principles of business economics (see Zeff et al., 1992). Also, from this perspective, it is not surprising that the Dutch legislator has adopted the current value alternative measurement options in the EU Directives. True and fair view, business economics, accounting principles and professional judgement are still the cornerstones of current Dutch accounting.

References

Brouwer, A., & Hoogendoorn, M. (2017). The role and current status of IFRS in the completion of national accounting rules – evidence from the Netherlands. *Account Europe, 14*(1–2), 137–149.

Dutch Accounting Standards Board , Richtlijnen voor de jaarverslaggeving, yearly editions

Nobes, C., & Parker, R. (2008). *Comparative international accounting* (10th ed.). Prentice-Hall.

Zelff, S. A., van der Wel, F., & Camfferman, K. (1992). *Company financial reporting, a historical and comparative study of the Dutch regulatory process*. North Holland.

Part II
Cross-cutting Issues

Objectives, Overriding Principles and Relevance

Cristian Carini, Alberto Quagli, and Claudio Teodori

1 EU Directive 2013/34 on General Provisions and Financial Reporting Standards

In this chapter, we analyse how the European Directive 2013/34 (hereafter, the "Accounting Directive" or the "Directive") was transposed in some European countries with reference to general provisions and general financial reporting principles. The scope of this Directive should be principle-based, and Paragraphs 9, 16, 17, 18, 19 and 42 present these principles.

In Chapter 2, Articles 4 and 6, the Directive cites the general provisions and principles. The principle of the relevance is considered in the "Whereas" and not in the articles.

These principles show only light differences with the text of IV Directive of 1978. The general objective remained "the true and fair view of the undertaking's assets, liabilities, financial position and profit or loss". The true and fair view (TFV hereafter) is so relevant that the general principle of drawing up "in accordance with the provisions of this Directive" can be overridden in both senses. Indeed, it is required the disapplication of a provision of the Directive if incompatible with the TFV (par. 5), and, in the other sense, the addition in the Notes of further information necessary to gain the TFV, if the provisions of the Directive are not sufficient.

Compared with the old text, the new Directive specifies that the further information necessary to TFV shall be placed in the Notes, and, most of all, it imposes a

C. Carini (✉) · C. Teodori
Università degli Studi di Brescia, Brescia, Italy
e-mail: cristian.carini@unibs.it; claudio.teodori@unibs.it

A. Quagli
Università degli Studi di Genova, Genoa, Italy
e-mail: quaglia@economia.unige.it

A. Incollingo, A. Lionzo (eds.), *The European Harmonization of National Accounting Rules*, SIDREA Series in Accounting and Business Administration,
https://doi.org/10.1007/978-3-031-42931-6_10

limitation to the power of Member States of adding further disclosure for small enterprises. It is worth to remind that the Accounting Directive stems from the general approach of "think small first" approved in Lisbon treaty,[1] according to which the new class of "micros" is now exempted from many mandated information in their financial statements.

In the chapter, only the Directive and the articles of the national regulations will be commented on. For the United Kingdom, a country with a common law vocation, GAAP was also used as references.[2]

2 Overriding Principles

The Accounting Directive sets the objectives and the general principles of the financial statement in Chapter 2, Article 4, as the following paragraphs:

1. The annual financial statements shall constitute a composite whole and shall for all undertakings comprise, as a minimum, the balance sheet, the profit and loss account and the notes to the financial statements. Member States may require undertakings other than small undertakings to include other statements in the annual financial statements in addition to the documents referred to in the first subparagraph.
2. The annual financial statements shall be drawn up clearly and in accordance with the provisions of this Directive.
3. The annual financial statements shall give a true and fair view of the undertaking's assets, liabilities, financial position and profit or loss. Where the application of this Directive would not be sufficient to give a true and fair view of the undertaking's assets, liabilities, financial position and profit or loss, such additional information as is necessary to comply with that requirement shall be given in the notes to the financial statements.
4. Where in exceptional cases the application of a provision of this Directive is incompatible with the obligation laid down in paragraph 3, that provision shall be disapplied in order to give a true and fair view of the undertaking's assets, liabilities, financial position and profit or loss. The disapplication of any such provision shall be disclosed in the notes to the financial statements together with an explanation of the reasons for it and of its effect on the undertaking's assets, liabilities, financial position and profit or loss. The Member States may define the

[1]Commission Communication entitled "Think Small First – Small Business Act for Europe", adopted in June 2008 and revised in February 2011, "*recognises the central role played by small and medium-sized enterprises (SMEs) in the Union economy and aims to improve the overall approach to entrepreneurship and to anchor the 'think small first' principle in policy-making from regulation to public service*" (premise 1 of Directive 34/2013).

[2]The reference is to the Financial Reporting Standards (FRSs) published by the Financial Reporting Council.

exceptional cases in question and lay down the relevant special rules, which are to apply in those cases.

5. Member States may require undertakings other than small undertakings to disclose information in their annual financial statements, which is additional to that required pursuant to this Directive.
6. By way of derogation from paragraph 5, Member States may require small undertakings to prepare, disclose and publish information in the financial statements, which goes beyond the requirements of this Directive, provided that any such information is gathered under a single filing system and the disclosure requirement is contained in the national tax legislation for the strict purposes of tax collection. The information required in accordance with this paragraph shall be included in the relevant part of the financial statements.
7. Member States shall communicate to the Commission any additional information they require in accordance with paragraph 6 upon the transposition of this Directive and when they introduce new requirements in accordance with paragraph 6 in national law.
8. Member States using electronic solutions for filing and publishing annual financial statements shall ensure that small undertakings are not required to publish, and in accordance with Chapter 7, the additional disclosures required by national tax legislation, as referred to in paragraph 6.

This article specifies the fundamental characteristics that the annual financial statements must have. First, these statements shall be compliant with the prescriptions of the Directive (.2), as a sort of affirmation of the primacy of written EU rules on any other accounting standard, guidance or practice.

Second, they have to give the true and fair view of the company's situation, the basic principle around which the overriding principle (.4 see Alexander, 2001) and the need of supplementary information (.3) are posed.

Third, the information deriving from the EU rules is the minimum level that companies should provide, considering that Member States can establish additional requirements.

The other points concern administrative simplifications for small enterprises (.6, .7 and .8).

Thus, among the objectives and the general principles of the financial statement, the most relevant is true and fair view, to which the following section is dedicated.

3 True and Fair View Still Resists!

After 40 years, the TFV objective still resists, even if it is not more a passionate issue for accounting scholars. The TFV was codified as a good European exercise of wording compromise in the Directive, in the period around 1970, between the approach of the German commercial law, based on mandatory detailed valuation and presentation rules, and the British approach, more oriented to the tradition of common law, and the relevance of practice (Sordini, 1982, p. 7; Incollingo, 1999, p. 11). In the UK Company Act (1948), there were no specific financial reporting rules, but the general request to provide users a true and fair view in the financial statements (Art. 149 UK Company Act) and in accounting records (Art. 147 UK Company Act). TFV appeared for the first time in the UK in the 1844 Joint Stock Companies Registration and Regulation Act (McGregor, 1992). Even if the real meaning remained overall uncertain (Walton, 1993, p. 49; Incollingo, 1999; Evans, 2003), the TFV was an expression appreciated for the implicit call for the necessary flexibility for companies in valuations and disclosure (Alexander, 1993) and the consequent primacy of self-regulation of the professional practice (Hopwood, 1990; Hamilton & Ó hÓgartaigh, 2009). Thus, the original TFV concept is rooted in all the practical rules and conventions, which, inductively and incrementally, over time composed "a solid basis with an undoubted practical consistency" (Sordini, 1982, p. 15).

Thus, the overriding principle (Art.4, par. 4) was aimed at giving companies the possibility to balance the coexistence of application of mandatory specific rules (Art.4, par. 2) and the general objective of TFV.

To circumscribe the possible strong impact of the overriding principle, the Directive both in the old and in the new text allows Member States "to define such exceptional cases and to lay down the relevant special rules which are to apply in those cases. Those exceptional cases should be understood to be only very unusual transactions and unusual situations and should, for instance, not be related to entire specific sectors".

The overriding principle found different applications in Europe. In the UK experience, for example, there have been cases of application of the overriding rule, preferring professional standards to Directive's rules (Incollingo, 1999, p. 163; Livne & McNichols, 2009; Nobes, 2009; Alexander & Grottke, 2016). Oppositely, in the German translation of the Directive, the overriding rule was limited to disclosure only (Ordelheide, 1993), demonstrating that divergence within the member countries on one of the main principle of financial statements still remains (Alexander & Eberhartinger, 2009; Alexander & Jermakowicz, 2006).

For the main European Countries, the TFV is clearly codified in their national rules, as shown by the following Table 1 (in the footnotes the corresponding text in the original language).

We can observe a substantial similitude among national transpositions of the Directive in Denmark, France, Netherlands, Spain, Sweden and Italy. In the UK, the TFV is defined as the general postulate, but the overriding principle is not codified at the same level, remaining implicitly resumed in the true and fair view. In Germany, the TFV is replaced by the expression "factually accurate view.. in accordance with generally accepted accounting principles" and the overriding principle can only bring additional disclosure in the notes, remaining excluded the possibility of not applying the existing rules. Denmark allows the use of the overriding principle and alternative criteria of recognition, measurement, presentation and disclosure only if the solutions come from the IAS/IFRS.

Table 1 True and fair view

DenmarkConsolidation Act 2015-12-10 No. 1580 the Financial Statements Act, Art.11, Chapter 3	(1) The financial statements and the consolidated financial statements, if any, must give a fair presentation of the enterprise's and group's assets, equity and liabilities, financial position and profit or loss for the year. The management commentary must give a fair review of the matters under review. (2) Where the application of the provisions of this Act is not sufficient to give a fair presentation as mentioned in subsection (1), further disclosures must be made in the financial statements or the consolidated financial statements, as the case may be. (3) If, in special cases, the application of the provisions of this Act conflicts with the requirement in subsection (1), first sentence, such provisions must be departed from to allow compliance with this requirement. Each year such departure must be disclosed in the notes, and specific and adequate grounds for the departure must be given, stating the effect, including, if possible, the monetary effect, of the departure on the enterprise's or group's assets, equity and liabilities, financial position and profit or loss for the year.[a,b]
France **Code de Commerce** **Art. L 123-14** **(see also Plan Comptable, Art. 121-1 and 121-3)**	The annual accounts shall be honest and truthful and shall ensure a fair representation of the assets, financial situation and results of the undertaking. When the application of an accounting requirement is not sufficient to ensure the fair representation indicated in this article, additional information must be provided in the annex. If, in an exceptional case, the application of an accounting requirement proves to be unsuitable in order to ensure a fair representation of the assets, financial situation or results, an exception must be made to this. This exception shall be indicated in the annex and duly reasoned, with an indication of its effect on the assets, financial situation and results of the undertaking.[c]
Germany **Handelsgesetzbuch** **§ 243 Principle of preparation** **§ 264 Duty to prepare; exemption**	**§ 243** (1) Annual financial statements have to be prepared in accordance with generally accepted accounting principles. (2) Annual financial statements have to be clearly arranged and easy to comprehend. (3) The annual financial statements have to be prepared within a time period consistent with a proper conduct of business. **§ 264** (2) 1—The annual financial statements of

(continued)

Table 1 (continued)

	a corporation have to give a factually accurate view of the net asset, financial position and results of operations of the corporation in accordance with generally accepted accounting principles. 2—In case that, as a result of special circumstances, the financial statements do not give a factually accurate view within the meaning of sentence 1, additional disclosures have to be provided in the notes.[d]
Italy **Codice Civile** **Article 2423**	The administrators shall prepare the financial statement composed of balance sheet, profit and loss account, cash flow statement and the notes. Financial statement shall be prepared with clarity and shall show in a truly and fair way the patrimonial and financial position of the company and the income of the period. If the information required by the provisions of law is not enough to guarantee a true and fair view, the administrators shall add the necessary complementary information. It is not compulsory to respect the provisions of recognition, measurement, presentation and disclosure if their application has no material effect on the true and fair view. If in exceptional cases the application of a following provision is incompatible with the true and fair view, the provision shall be not applied. In the notes, the deviation shall be motivated and explained, together with the disclosure of its impact on the financial position. Profits deriving from the deviation cannot be distributed until they are realized and an equity reserve shall be created.[e]
Netherlands **Burgerlijk Wetboek** **Article 362 Insight in financial position; used accounting standards**	1. The annual accounts shall provide, on the basis of generally accepted accounting principles, such an insight that an informed assessment can be made about the legal person's property (assets and liabilities) and result and, insofar as the nature of annual accounts permits so, about its solvency and liquidity. . . . 2. The balance sheet and explanatory notes thereto shall fairly, clearly and consistently show the size and composition of the property at the end of the financial year, expressed in assets and liabilities. . . . 3. The profit and loss account and explanatory notes shall fairly, clearly and consistently show the profit amount for the financial year and how it is deduced from the income and expenditure items. 4. If necessary in order to provide the insight as

(continued)

Table 1 (continued)

	meant in paragraph 1, the legal person shall disclose in the annual accounts data in supplementation of what is required under the specific statutory provisions of and pursuant to the present title (Title 2.9). If necessary in order to provide such insight, the legal person shall depart from these statutory provisions; the reason for such depart is explained in the notes, where necessary with mention of the impact thereof on the property (assets and liabilities) and result.[f]
Spain **Codigo de Comercio** **Artículo 34** **(official translation by Ministerio de Justicia)** **(see also Plan General de Contabilidad, Art. 1 and Art. 2)**	1. At the year end, the trader must draw up the annual accounts of his business that shall include the balance sheet, the profit and loss accounts and a statement of the changes in the net assets during the business year, a cash flow statement and the annual report. These documents shall form a unit. The cash flow statement shall not be obligatory when this is established by a legal provision. 2. The annual accounts must be drafted clearly and provide a true image of the assets, financial situation and results of the company, pursuant to the legal provisions. To that end, accounting for the operations shall attend to their financial reality and not just to their legal format. 3. When the application of the legal provisions is not sufficient to provide a true image, the necessary complementary information shall be provided in the annual report to achieve that result. 4. In exceptional cases, if the application of a legal provision on matters of accounting were to be incompatible with the true image the annual accounts must provide, that provision shall not be applicable. In these cases, the annual report must state that it is not applied, provide sufficient motives and explain its influence on the assets, financial situation and results of the company.[g]
Sweden **Annual Accounts Act (1995:1554)** **2.3**	Balance sheet, income statement and notes, established as a whole and give a true and fair view of the company's financial position and results of operations. If it is needed for a fair presentation to be given, shall be supplementary information.If the deviation is made from what follows from general advice or recommendations from regulatory agencies, shall discloseThis, and of the reasons for the departure, is disclosed in the notes on the accounts. Law (1999:1112).[h,i]

(continued)

Table 1 (continued)

United Kingdom **Companies Act** **Art. 289—Accounts to give true and fair view**	(1) The directors of a company shall not approve financial statements for the purposes of this part unless they are satisfied that they give a true and fair view of the assets, liabilities and financial position, as at the end of the financial year, and profit or loss, for the financial year

[a]Original text in Danish:
11. Årsregnskabet og et eventuelt koncernregnskab skal give et retvisende billede af virksomhedens og koncernens aktiver og passiver, finansielle stilling samt resultatet. Ledelsesberetningen skal indeholde en retvisende redegørelse for de forhold, som beretningen omhandler.
Stk. 2. Hvis anvendelsen af bestemmelserne i denne lov ikke er tilstrækkelig til at give et retvisende billede som nævnt i stk. 1, skal der gives yderligere oplysninger i årsregnskabet, henholdsvis koncernregnskabet.
Stk. 3. Hvis anvendelse af bestemmelserne i denne lov i særlige tilfælde vil stride mod kravet i stk. 1, 1. pkt., skal de fraviges, således at dette krav opfyldes. En sådan fravigelse skal hvert år oplyses i noterne, hvor den skal begrundes konkret og fyldestgørende med oplysning om, hvilken indvirkning, herunder så vidt muligt den beløbsmæssige indvirkning, fravigelsen har på virksomhedens henholdsvis koncernens aktiver og passiver, finansielle stilling samt resultatet.
Stk. 4. Kravene i stk. 1-3 gælder tilsvarende, når der anvendes standarder, der er udstedt inden for rammerne af denne lov, jf. § 136.
[b]In Denmark, as clearly reported by F. Thinggaard in Chapter 8 of this book, the Danish Financial Statements Act in section 11 (1) declares the TFV as "general clause" for the financial statements. Regarding the overriding principle, "the general view is that application of the specific provisions in the Act will lead to financial statements that give a true and fair view. Hence, derogations from the provisions of the law in order to obtain a true and fair view (i.e. the true and fair override provision) will only come into play as a rare exception, not least because most issues can be solved by providing additional information. Notwithstanding, should the situation arise, then Danish companies are instructed by the legislators' notes to the 2015 draft bill only to choose an accounting solution that is in accordance with IFRS. It is unlikely that disapplication of specific provisions in the law can be made if companies make other choices for recognition and measurement than those permitted under IFRS. The reason is that the law is based on the same fundamental framework as the IFRS".
[c]Original text in French:
Les comptes annuels doivent être réguliers, sincères et donner une image fidèle du patrimoine, de la situation financière et du résultat de l'entreprise. Lorsque l'application d'une prescription comptable ne suffit pas pour donner l'image fidèle mentionnée au présent article, des informations complémentaires doivent être fournies dans l'annexe. Si, dans un cas exceptionnel, l'application d'une prescription comptable se révèle impropre à donner une image fidèle du patrimoine, de la situation financière ou du résultat, il doit y être dérogé. Cette dérogation est mentionnée à l'annexe et dûment motivée, avec l'indication de son influence sur le patrimoine, la situation financière et le résultat de l'entreprise
[d]Original text in German:
§ 243 Aufstellungsgrundsatz
(1) Der Jahresabschluß ist nach den Grundsätzen ordnungsmäßiger Buchführung aufzustellen.
(2) Er muß klar und übersichtlich sein.
(3) Der Jahresabschluß ist innerhalb der einem ordnungsmäßigen Geschäftsgang entsprechenden Zeit aufzustellen.
§ 264 Pflicht zur Aufstellung; Befreiung
(2) Der Jahresabschluß der Kapitalgesellschaft hat unter Beachtung der Grundsätze ordnungsmäßiger Buchführung ein den tatsächlichen Verhältnissen entsprechendes Bild der Vermögens-, Finanz- und Ertragslage der Kapitalgesellschaft zu vermitteln. Führen besondere Umstände dazu, daß der Jahresabschluß ein den tatsächlichen Verhältnissen entsprechendes Bild

(continued)

im Sinne des Satzes 1 nicht vermittelt, so sind im Anhang zusätzliche Angaben zu machen. Die Mitglieder des vertretungsberechtigten Organs einer Kapitalgesellschaft, die als Inlandsemittent (§ 2 Absatz 14 des Wertpapierhandelsgesetzes) Wertpapiere (§ 2 Absatz 1 des Wertpapierhandelsgesetzes) begibt und keine Kapitalgesellschaft im Sinne des § 327a ist, haben in einer dem Jahresabschluss beizufügenden schriftlichen Erklärung zu versichern, dass der Jahresabschluss nach bestem Wissen ein den tatsächlichen Verhältnissen entsprechendes Bild im Sinne des Satzes 1 vermittelt oder der Anhang Angaben nach Satz 2 enthält. Macht eine Kleinstkapitalgesellschaft von der Erleichterung nach Absatz 1 Satz 5 Gebrauch, sind nach Satz 2 erforderliche zusätzliche Angaben unter der Bilanz zu machen. Es wird vermutet, dass ein unter Berücksichtigung der Erleichterungen für Kleinstkapitalgesellschaften aufgestellter Jahresabschluss den Erfordernissen des Satzes 1 entspricht.

[e]Original text in Italian:

Gli amministratori devono redigere il bilancio di esercizio, costituito dallo stato patrimoniale, dal conto economico, dal rendiconto finanziario e dalla nota integrativa.

Il bilancio deve essere redatto con chiarezza e deve rappresentare in modo veritiero e corretto la situazione patrimoniale e finanziaria della società e il risultato economico dell'esercizio.

Se le informazioni richieste da specifiche disposizioni di legge non sono sufficienti a dare una rappresentazione veritiera e corretta, si devono fornire le informazioni complementari necessarie allo scopo.

Non occorre rispettare gli obblighi in tema di rilevazione, valutazione, presentazione e informativa quando la loro osservanza abbia effetti irrilevanti al fine di dare una rappresentazione veritiera e corretta. Rimangono fermi gli obblighi in tema di regolare tenuta delle scritture contabili. Le società illustrano nella nota integrativa i criteri con i quali hanno dato attuazione alla presente disposizione.

Se, in casi eccezionali, l'applicazione di una disposizione degli articoli seguenti è incompatibile con la rappresentazione veritiera e corretta, la disposizione non deve essere applicata. La nota integrativa deve motivare la deroga e deve indicarne l'influenza sulla rappresentazione della situazione patrimoniale, finanziaria e del risultato economico. Gli eventuali utili derivanti dalla deroga devono essere iscritti in una riserva non distribuibile se non in misura corrispondente al valore recuperato.

[f]Original text in Dutch:

1- De jaarrekening geeft volgens normen die in het maatschappelijk verkeer als aanvaardbaar worden beschouwd een zodanig inzicht dat een verantwoord oordeel kan worden gevormd omtrent het vermogen en het resultaat, alsmede voor zover de aard van een jaarrekening dat toelaat, omtrent de solvabiliteit en de liquiditeit van de rechtspersoon. Indien de internationale vertakking van zijn groep dit rechtvaardigt kan de rechtspersoon de jaarrekening opstellen naar de normen die in het maatschappelijk verkeer in een van de andere lidstaten van de Europese Gemeenschappen als aanvaardbaar worden beschouwd en het in de eerste volzin bedoelde inzicht geven.

2- De balans met de toelichting geeft getrouw, duidelijk en stelselmatig de grootte van het vermogen en zijn samenstelling in actief- en passiefposten op het einde van het boekjaar weer. De balans mag het vermogen weergeven, zoals het wordt samengesteld met inachtneming van de bestemming van de winst of de verwerking van het verlies, of, zolang deze niet vaststaat, met inachtneming van het voorstel daartoe. Bovenaan de balans wordt aangegeven of daarin de bestemming van het resultaat is verwerkt.

3- De winst- en verliesrekening met de toelichting geeft getrouw, duidelijk en stelselmatig de grootte van het resultaat van het boekjaar en zijn afleiding uit de posten van baten en lasten weer.

4- Indien het verschaffen van het in lid 1 bedoelde inzicht dit vereist, verstrekt de rechtspersoon in de jaarrekening gegevens ter aanvulling van hetgeen in de bijzondere voorschriften van en krachtens deze titel wordt verlangd. Indien dit noodzakelijk is voor het verschaffen van dat inzicht, wijkt de rechtspersoon van die voorschriften af; de reden van deze afwijking wordt in de toelichting uiteengezet, voor zover nodig onder opgaaf van de invloed ervan op vermogen en resultaat.

[g]Orginal text in Spanish:

(continued)

Las cuentas anuales deben redactarse con claridad y mostrar la imagen fiel del patrimonio, de la situación financiera y de los resultados de la empresa, de conformidad con las disposiciones legales. A tal efecto, en la contabilización de las operaciones se atenderá a su realidad económica y no sólo a su forma jurídica.
3. Cuando la aplicación de las disposiciones legales no sea suficiente para mostrar la imagen fiel, se suministrarán en la memoria las informaciones complementarias precisas para alcanzar ese resultado.
4. En casos excepcionales, si la aplicación de una disposición legal en materia de contabilidad fuera incompatible con la imagen fiel que deben proporcionar las cuentas anuales, tal disposición no será aplicable. En estos casos, en la memoria deberá señalarse esa falta de aplicación, motivarse suficientemente y explicarse su influencia sobre el patrimonio, la situación financiera y los resultados de la empresa
[h]Original text in Swedish:
Rättvisande bild
3 § Balansräkningen, resultaträkningen och noterna skall upprättas som en helhet och ge en rättvisande bild av företagets ställning och resultat. Om det behövs för att en rättvisande bild skall ges, skall det lämnas tilläggsupplysningar.
Om avvikelse görs från vad som följer av allmänna råd eller rekommendationer från normgivande organ, skall upplysning om detta och om skälen för avvikelsen lämnas i en not.
Lag (1999:1112).
[i]In Sweden (Levin, 2006), the requirement for the annual accounts to be prepared to give a true and fair view of the company's situation is established in 2:3 ÅRL (the Swedish Annual Accounts Act). The Swedish legislator has chosen to keep GAAP as legal standard as opposed to the concept of a true and fair view, which is the legal standard of the EC Directives. In EC law, this is an overriding concept. The Swedish legislator, however, considered the content of the concept to be uncertain and prohibited deviations from explicit rules in ÅRL even though such actions would be motivated by the requirement of providing a true and fair view. The rules in 2:4 ÅRL have been interpreted by the ECJ as secondary to the requirement of a true and fair view. This implies that the true-and-fair-view concept overrides the fundamental principles of accounting. It can indeed be considered awkward that the concept of a true and fair view is prohibited to override a specific rule of law but allowed to deviate from the principles of which the rules are based. The ground for the decision by the Swedish legislator to refrain from implementing the overriding concept was the assessment that it would be wrong if a company, which has prepared its accounts according to ÅRL, would feel insecure of the compliance of the preparation

In summary, Directive 34/2013 has not changed the TFV principle and some relevant differences among Member Countries still remain, depending on the specificity of local contexts.

Even if the TFV is the best example of "principle prevailing on rules", on a substantial point of view, we outline an inherent contrast between rules and principles in the Directive. The Directive clearly affirms in Premise (6) that "should be principles-based", and the presence of TFV seems to confirm it, but, at the same time, the Directive prescribes "that annual financial statements shall be drawn up... in accordance with the provisions of this Directive", and those provisions include detailed regulations that "look like" rules. In the Spanish Plan General de Contabilidad, (Primera parte—Marco conceptual de la contabilidad—1° Cuentas anuales. Imagen fiel), we can find an elegant attempt to compose the above inherent contrast. The Spanish principle says that financial statements shall be prepared with clarity, so the information reported is understandable and useful for the users' economic decisions, since it shall show the true view of the financial position, income and net assets, according to legal provisions. The systematic and regular application of the legal provisions shall drive to show the true and fair view. In other words, the adoption of the legal rules will result (automatically) in a true and fair view. This axiom (application of legal provisions = TFV) is in substance the position accepted in many EU countries, even if the Article 4 (4) of the Directive, allowing "the disapplication of any such provision" to reach the true and fair view, still supposes that TFV is a concept not coincident with the respect of legal rules, but only "in exceptional cases".

4 The Materiality Concept in the New Directive and Its Transposition in Member Countries

A relevant change in the new Directive is the appearance of users (*addressees*) of financial statements and the concept of materiality. The old text was silent on it. There are two relevant premises in the Directive 34/2013:

> 4. Annual financial statements pursue various objectives and do not merely provide information for investors in capital markets but also give an account of past transactions and enhance corporate governance. Union accounting legislation needs to strike an appropriate balance between the interests of the addressees of financial statements and the interest of undertakings in not being unduly burdened with reporting requirements

> 17. The principle of materiality should govern recognition, measurement, presentation, disclosure and consolidation in financial statements. According to the principle of materiality, information that is considered immaterial may, for instance, be aggregated in the financial statements. However, while a single item might be considered to be immaterial, immaterial items of a similar nature might be considered material when taken as a whole. Member States should be allowed to limit the mandatory application of the principle of materiality to presentation and disclosure. The principle of materiality should not affect any national obligation to keep complete records showing business transactions and financial position.

In Premise 4, the Directive tackles the question of the general aim of financial statements saying that they serve not only as an informational basis for investors' decisions but also as instruments to convey stewardship and effective corporate governance. This point seems to echo in a light polemical way the IASB Conceptual Framework where still remains the primacy of the informational role of financial reports. At the same time, the Directive introduces the need of balancing information benefits of the users and the costs for preparers. The point opens to Premise 17 where the principle of materiality is introduced, allowing to aggregate information considered immaterial. This opening to materiality and its potential effects on *recognition, measurement, presentation, disclosure and consolidation* is prudentially circumscribed giving Member States the power to limit the application of principle.

The principle is defined in Art. 2 of the Directive:

> (16) *"material" means the status of information where its omission or misstatement could reasonably be expected to influence decisions that users make on the basis of the financial*

> *statements of the undertaking. The materiality of individual items shall be assessed in the context of other similar items*

and operationalized in the Art. 6, (j):

> *(j) the requirements set out in this Directive regarding recognition, measurement, presentation, disclosure and consolidation need not be complied with when the effect of complying with them is immaterial.*

In the rest of the Directive, the specific examples of this principle regard only some points in the notes. This should not surprise us, considering the principle-based nature of the Directive.

Member States applied in different ways this principle.

In France, the principle is not applied in the Code de Commerce but in the Plan Comptable General. Article 810-1 says that the financial statements shall evidence any relevant facts able to influence the users. There is no specific reference to what aspect it could regard, even if it seems to regard only presentation and disclosure.[3]

In the Netherlands, the principle is transposed in the Commercial Code clearly establishing its effect on presentation and disclosure:

> *Article 2:363 Arrangement of data in the annual accounts and notes*
>
> *- 3. It is not necessary to disclose an item separately if that item, within the annual accounts as a whole, is of negligible importance for obtaining the legally required insight. Disclosures to be made pursuant to the present Title (Title 2.9) may be omitted if these, as well on their own as together with similar disclosures, would be of negligible importance for obtaining that insight. Disclosures to be made pursuant to Articles 2:378, 2:382 and 2: 383 may not be omitted.*

In Denmark, Section 13 (1), 3, of the Danish Financial Statements Act contains the general principle that the annual report must be based on the basic assumption of materiality. *All relevant matters must be included in the annual report, unless such matters are insignificant (materiality). Where several insignificant matters are deemed to be significant when combined, such matters must be included.* In general, the Danish law says that (3) the annual report must be prepared in a manner disclosing information on matters that are normally relevant to the users of financial statements (Section, 12, 3).

In Italy (Art. 2423/4 Civil Code) and Spain (Art. 38 of the Commercial Code, see also Plan General de Contabilidad, Art. 6—*Importancia relativa*), there are very similar transposition, allowing companies the departure from the codified accounting principles when their application is not material. The scope of their rules seems to embrace all the aspects of the accounting process (from recognition to disclosure) and not only presentation and disclosure, but some wording differences in their legal text exist. For example, the Spanish Code allows to avoid *aplicacion estricta* of

---

[3]- *Art. 810-1: Les documents de synthèse, qui comprennent nécessairement le bilan, le compte de résultat et une annexe mettent en évidence tout fait pertinent, c'est-à-dire susceptible d'avoir une influence sur le jugement que leurs destinataires peuvent porter sur le patrimoine, la situation financière et le résultat de l'entité ainsi que sur les décisions qu'ils peuvent être amenés à prendre.*

accounting principles according to materiality principle (strict application), whereas in Italy there is no specific limitation.[4]

Germany has not standardized the principle of materiality centrally (Müller-Burmeister & Velte, 2016) even if it appears in several individual sections, especially referred to disclosure of risks.

UK too has not standardized the principle of materiality. In the Companies Act, there are specific references to disclose only material information but for specific issues.

Thus, the principle of materiality, functional to the general aim of the financial reports' information role, finds different applications within the EU. In general, a certain cautiousness in introducing it emerges, maybe for its potential impacts. Italy seems to acknowledge that principle more than other countries, but we have no notice of its real application in the companies' annual accounts.

5 General Financial Reporting Principles

General financial reporting principles are presented in Article 6 of the Directive as follows.

Article 6—general financial reporting principles

1. Items presented in the annual and consolidated financial statements shall be recognized and measured in accordance with the following general principles:

   (a) The undertaking shall be presumed to be carrying on its business as a going concern.
   (b) Accounting policies and measurement bases shall be applied consistently from one financial year to the next.
   (c) Recognition and measurement shall be on a prudent basis, and in particular:

      (i) Only profits made at the balance sheet date may be recognized.
      (ii) All liabilities arising in the course of the financial year concerned or in the course of a previous financial year shall be recognized, even if such liabilities become apparent only between the balance sheet date and the date on which the balance sheet is drawn up.

---

[4]Art. 2423/4 Italian Civil Code: *Non occorre rispettare gli obblighi in tema di rilevazione, valutazione, presentazione e informativa quando la loro osservanza abbia effetti irrilevanti al fine di dare una rappresentazione veritiera e corretta. Rimangono fermi gli obblighi in tema di regolare tenuta delle scritture contabili. Le società illustrano nella nota integrativa i criteri con i quali hanno dato attuazione alla presente disposizione.*

Art. 38 Spanish Commercial Code: i*) Se admitirá la no aplicación estricta de algunos principios contables cuando la importancia relativa de la variación que tal hecho produzca sea escasamente significativa y, en consecuencia, no altere la expresión de la imagen fiel del patrimonio, de la situación financiera y de los resultados de la empresa.*

    (iii) All negative value adjustments shall be recognized, whether the result of the financial year is a profit or a loss.

(d) Amounts recognized in the balance sheet and profit and loss account shall be computed on accrual basis.
(e) The opening balance sheet for each financial year shall correspond to the closing balance sheet for the preceding financial year.
(f) The components of asset and liability items shall be valued separately.
(g) Any set-off between asset and liability items, or between income and expenditure items, shall be prohibited.
(h) Items in the profit and loss account and balance sheet shall be accounted for and presented having regard to the substance of the transaction or arrangement concerned.
(i) Items recognized in the financial statements shall be measured in accordance with the principle of purchase price or production cost.
(j) The requirements set out in this Directive regarding recognition, measurement, presentation, disclosure and consolidation need not be complied with when the effect of complying with them is immaterial.

2. Not with standing point (g) of paragraph, Member States may in specific cases permit or require undertakings to perform a set-off between asset and liability items, or between income and expenditure items, provided that the amounts that are set off are specified as gross amounts in the notes to the financial statements.
3. Member States may exempt undertakings from the requirements of point (h) of paragraph 1.
4. Member States may limit the scope of point (j) of paragraph 1 to presentation and disclosures.
5. In addition to those amounts recognized in accordance with point (c)(ii) of paragraph 1, Member States may permit or require the recognition of all foreseeable liabilities and potential losses arising in the course of the financial year concerned or in the course of a previous financial year, even if such liabilities or losses become apparent only between the balance sheet date and the date on which the balance sheet is drawn up.

The following section will comment on the individual principles, with a degree of detail related to possible differences in transposition in the various countries.

5.1 Going Concern

Going concern is the first of the General Financial Reporting Principles to be referred to in Article 6 of the Directive: "*the undertaking shall be presumed to be carrying on its business as a going concern*" *(Art. 6.a).*

On closer inspection, even before being a General Financial Reporting Principles, going concern is the necessary premise without which there would not even be annual financial statements prepared according the Directive. In the absence of the going concern requirement, in fact, the financial statements must be prepared with a view to the dissolution of the entity.

The Directive also recalls how the going concern informs both the recognition and measurement principles (p. 16) and the disclosure in the notes (p. 24). To about: "*To ensure the disclosure of comparable and equivalent information, recognition and measurement principles should include the going concern, the prudence, and the accrual bases*" (16); "*Disclosure in respect of accounting policies is one of the key elements of the notes to the financial statements. Such disclosure should include, in particular, the measurement bases applied to various items, a statement on the conformity of those accounting policies with the going concern concept and any significant changes to the accounting policies adopted*" (24).

The going concern is present in all the laws of the countries examined, without any difference.

5.2 *Prudence (Conservatism)*

Prudence (or conservatism) is a general principle of financial reporting present in all European legislations and has its basis in Directive 34/2013 no. 9 where it is clarified that annual financial statements should be prepared on a prudent basis and should give a true and fair view of an undertaking's assets and liabilities, financial position and profit or loss.

Again, in Directive 34/2013 no. 16, it is made explicit that: "*To ensure the disclosure of comparable and equivalent information, recognition and measurement principles should include the going concern, the prudence, and the accrual bases*". It follows that prudence is a pervasive principle of the European and national legislative system that is mentioned even before the true and fair view and jointly with the going concern and the accrual basis.

Prudence is linked to situations of uncertainty that arise in the circumstances in which the recognition and measurement of some items in financial statements are based on estimates, judgements and models rather than exact depictions. As a result of the uncertainties inherent in business activities, certain items in financial statements cannot be measured precisely but can only be estimated. Estimation involves judgements based on the latest available reliable information. The use of estimates is an essential part of the preparation of financial statements (Maltby, 2000; Sterling, 1967; Watts, 2003a, 2003b; Zhong & Li, 2017). This is especially true in the case of provisions, which by their nature are more uncertain than most other items in the balance sheet. Estimates should be based on a prudent judgement of the management of the undertaking and calculated on an objective basis, supplemented by experience of similar transactions and, in some cases, even reports from independent experts. The evidence considered should include any additional evidence provided by events after the balance sheet date.

In the EU Directive, recognition and measurement shall be on a prudent basis, and in particular: (i) only profits made at the balance sheet date may be recognized; (ii) all liabilities arising in the course of the financial year concerned or in the course of a previous financial year shall be recognized, even if such liabilities become apparent only between the balance sheet date and the date on which the balance sheet is drawn up; and (iii) all negative value adjustments shall be recognized, whether the result of the financial year is a profit or a loss.

This approach is made explicit in the laws of some countries, such as Italy, while in various other circumstances these principles coexist with the more or less significant influence exercised by the International Accounting Standards/International Financial Reporting Standards (IASs/IFRSs).

The Netherlands and the UK specify that the exercise of prudence means that assets and income are not overstated and liabilities and expenses are not understated (DASB, Conceptual Framework, para 37 and FRS 102 par. 2.9). FRS 102 of UK adds that bias is not allowed. In this sense, prudence recalls neutrality, through which reliability is realized. Financial statements are not free from bias (i.e. not neutral) if, by the selection or presentation of information, they are intended to influence the making of a decision or judgement in order to achieve a predetermined result or outcome.

The link between prudence and neutrality is also underlined in the Danish legislation where it is specified that recognition and measurement must be carried out on a prudent basis, and all accounting estimates must be neutral. All value adjustments must be recognized, whether the result of the financial year is a profit or a loss. As analysed in detail in Chapter 8 (Denmark), the Danish interpretation of the principle of prudence does not imply a systematic need for asymmetry. Section 13 (1) no. 5 of the Danish Financial Statements Act mentions that "any" value adjustment shall be recognized, whereas Article 6 (1) (c) (iii) in Directive 2013/34 only mentions that all "negative" value adjustments shall be recognized. This approach is supported by the will not to deviate Danish Financial Statements Act from the principles in IFRS and impact the assessment of assets and liabilities. Referring to the chapters on country analysis for the appropriate in-depth analysis, as regards the purpose of the paragraph, for instance that Danish legislator (and also the UK system) is not opposed to the use of fair values as an optional measurement basis even for many non-financial assets. However, in the Danish legislation according to Directive UE 34/2013 the positive fair value adjustments will never be recognized in profit and loss (differently in the UK where changes in fair value have to be recognized through other comprehensive income).

In summary, at a European level prudence (and neutrality) has been implemented in a different way, but influence exercised by the IASs/IFRSs is limited by the principle that only profits made at the balance sheet date may be recognized.

5.3 Accrual Basis

The accrual principle provides that an economic transaction should be recorded in the time period in which they occur, regardless of the actual timing of their associated cash flows.

The accrual principle is incorporated in all legislations and given its relevance it could not be otherwise (Superti Furga, 1988; Adamo et al., 2018). On the other hand, as seen in other situations, the general principles form the framework of the financial statement rules and, as such, must be present.

What may change, as seen in the other chapters, is how they are implemented in practice: for example, the competence may be severely limited by prudence, depending on the extent of its scope, e.g. broad in Italy and narrower in Sweden. The description of the principle is not very extensive, precisely because of its diffusion and knowledge: in some cases, it is referred to as the matching principle where appropriate.

5.4 Substance Over the Legal Form of the Transaction

This principle is not always explicitly reflected but is a self-evident component of the true and fair view (i.e. the Netherlands and Spain).

This principle, in addition to its own relevance, is fundamental to achieving the fair presentation of a company's equity, financial position and results. For example, the prevalence of substance over form affects the recognition of certain financial instruments, which should be accounted for as liabilities when, a priori, and from a strictly legal perspective, they appear to be equity instruments. The same reasoning applies to leasing, repo transactions and others.

However, its definition is not always followed by a specific accounting regulation for its application: emblematic, in Italy, is the case of leasing, where accounting is not based on financial criterion. For this reason, the principle is only partially applied in Italy because the Italian Civil Code imposes the substance over form principle but does not complement this principle with a clear definition of what an asset or a liability is.

Always with regard to lease, FRS 102 establishes a distinction between finance leases and operating leases. To qualify as a finance lease, all the risks and rewards of ownership need to be transferred to the lessee: for finance leases a depreciable asset and finance lease liability are recognized at the lower of fair value of the leased asset or the present value of the minimum lease payments on the balance sheet of the lessee; for operating leases, recurring payments are expensed in the income statement of the lessee.

5.5 *Consistency*

In Directive 34/2013, the principle of consistency is twofold treated.

From one side, recognition methods and measurement bases (in addition to monetary unit applied and consolidation method in the case of Consolidated Financial Statements) must be consistently applied from one financial year to the other (Barth, 2013; Schipper, 2003). This kind of consistency is also known as "real continuity" principle. However, a change may take place if a truer and fair view is thereby obtained, or is necessary to comply with new rules when transitioning to a new accounting class, statutory amendments, new rules or regulations laid down under national legislation or new standards issued.

From the other side, the opening balance sheet shall correspond to the closing balance sheet for the preceding financial year. This consistency principle is also defined as "formal continuity".

This dual mode of interpretation of consistency is explicated in the legislation of the Netherlands, Denmark and France. In other countries, however, the focus is exclusively on "real continuity" being formal continuity self-evident.

Also, in the UK system consistency principle is present and it is treated as "comparability" in the FRS 102, Chapter 2, "*Concepts and Pervasive Principles*". Consistency setting is not only an internal issue of the entity. Comparability is also a matter among companies in the perspective of user's needs: "*the measurement and display of the financial effects of like transactions and other events and conditions must be carried out in a consistent way throughout an entity and over time for that entity, and in a consistent way across entities*". This approach complies with the IASs/IFRSs perspective in which "*Users' decisions involve choosing between alternatives, for example, selling or holding an investment, or investing in one reporting entity or another. Consequently, information about a reporting entity is more useful if it can be compared with similar information about other entities and with similar information about the same entity for another period or another date*" (IFRS Conceptual Framework for Financial Reporting, par. 2.24).

5.6 *Measurement Basis*

The aim of the paragraph is to analyse the measurement basis, highlighting the relationships with the principles of accrual basis and prudence (ICAEW, 2006; Milburn, 2012; Filip et al., 2017). We refer to part 2 as regards the measurement basis applied to the items recognized in the financial statements.

Directive 34/2013 is based on the purchase price or production cost to measure items recognized. Historical cost ensures the reliability of information contained in financial statements (par. 18 and Art. 6.1 i)). Historical cost is an entry price. In detail:

- Purchase price is the price payable and any incidental expenses minus any incidental reductions in the cost of acquisition.
- Production cost is the purchase price of raw materials, consumables and other costs directly attributable to the item in question. Member States shall permit or require the inclusion of a reasonable proportion of fixed or variable overhead costs indirectly attributable to the item in question, to the extent that they relate to the period of production. Distribution costs shall not be included.

While historical cost is the cornerstone of the Directive, it is not the only measurement basis as:

- Member States should be allowed to permit or require undertakings to revalue fixed assets in order that more relevant information may be provided to the users of financial statements: it is the alternative measurement basis of fixed assets at revalued amounts (Art. 7).
- Member States shall or may permit or require alternative measurement basis of fair value to (i) financial instruments, including derivative financial instruments and (ii) specified categories of assets other than financial instruments. Fair value shall or may permitted or required to all undertakings or any classes of undertaking, other than micro-undertakings making use of the exemptions provided by the Directive, in respect of both annual and consolidated financial statements or, if a Member State so chooses, in respect of consolidated financial statements only (Art. 8).

While both the revalued model for fixed assets and fair value are considered alternative measurement basis of historical cost, the Directive provides insights limited to the measure of fair value in the case of financial instruments only. In details, Article 8.7 states that fair value (Alexander & Archer (2000), Chastney (1975), Kirk (2006), Ruch & Taylor (2015), Walton (1991), Zeff, Buijink & Camfferman (1999) shall be determined by reference to one of the following values: (i) in the case of financial instruments for which a reliable market can readily be identified, the market value and, where the market value is not readily identifiable for an instrument but can be identified for its components or for a similar instrument, the market value may be derived from that of its components or of the similar instrument; (ii) in the case of financial instruments for which a reliable market cannot be readily identified, a value resulting from generally accepted valuation models and techniques, provided that such valuation models and techniques ensure a reasonable approximation of the market value; (iii) financial instruments that cannot be measured reliably by any of the methods described in points (i) and (iii) of the first subparagraph shall be measured in accordance with the principle of purchase price or production cost in so far as measurement on that basis is possible. It is a perfectly overlapping approach with that indicated in IFRS 13—Fair value.

Referring to Directive Article 16.1.c. related to disclosure, fair value determined in this way is applicable also to alternative measurement basis related to other specified categories of assets other than financial instruments.

By the way, from the literal wording of the Directive, the measurement (i.e. the assessment) of alternative bases of the revalued model for fixed assets remains undetermined, except to specify that value adjustments "*shall be calculated each year on the basis of the revalued amount*" (Art. 7.3).

The setting of the Directive allows us to make some considerations.

Firstly, the Directive distinguishes the alternative bases from historical cost not so much looking at the measurement (i.e. the assessment) but with reference to the scope of application. It proposes two (actually three) accounting models or methods, where the focus is on recognition and disclosure other than the assessment of revalued amount or fair value amount: (i) an accounting alternative method for fixed assets, (ii) an accounting alternative method for financial instruments and (iii) an accounting alternative method for other specified categories of assets other than financial instruments (and logically other than fixed assets).

Secondly, to understand the use (i.e. the assessment) of alternative measurement bases other than historical cost, we have to refer to single national legislation. In this regard, it should be understood that fair value is the basis for measuring the categories of fixed assets too and of other assets other than financial instruments.

Some examples of alternative measurement bases other than historical cost are as follows.

Looking at Denmark examples alternative measurement bases other than historical cost refers to intangible assets, tangible fixed/non-current assets, investment property, investments in subsidiaries, in associates, in joint venture and in joint operations, investments in debt instruments and financial liabilities held for trading and derivative financial instruments. In the case of Sweden, examples are for tangible assets, financial fixed assets and financial instruments. The Netherlands provides alternative measurement bases other than historical cost, for example fixed assets and intangible assets, financial instruments and property investments. As regards Spain, we detected alternative measurement bases other than historical cost for example to non-current assets held for sale and some categories of financial assets and financial liabilities, as well leasing. In France, examples of alternative measurement bases other than historical cost are asset acquired in a non-monetary exchange and equity interests with exclusive control and in Italy are derivative financial instruments. In the UK examples of alternative measurement bases other than historical cost are to property, plant and equipment; investment property; intangible assets; leases; financial instruments; and investments in associates and in joint ventures. In Germany, historical cost is the main accounting convention and generally no revaluations are allowed. Alternative measurement bases other than historical cost are applied with few exceptions as pension obligations or comparable long-term liabilities and when a business combination is carried out.

In conclusion, the alternative measurement basis of fixed assets at revalued amounts and the alternative measurement basis of fair value differ from each other not so much for the assessment but for the recognition and disclosure.

Looking at the recognition, applying alternative measurement basis of fixed assets at revalued amounts, the amount of the difference with the purchase price or production cost shall be entered in the balance sheet in a revaluation reserve of the equity. This reserve cannot be distributed but may be capitalized in whole or in part at any time (Art. 7.2.1). Looking at the alternative measurement basis of fair value, Member States may permit or require a change in the value of an available for sale financial asset, other than a derivative financial instrument, to be included directly in a fair value reserve. As regards assets other than financial instruments measured at fair value, Member States may permit or require, in respect of all undertakings or any classes of undertaking, that a change in the value be included in the profit and loss account.

Moving on to disclosure, where fixed assets are measured at revalued amounts, in the notes must be provided information on (i) movements in the revaluation reserve in the financial year, with an explanation of the tax treatment of items therein, and (ii) the carrying amount in the balance sheet that would have been recognized had the fixed assets not been revalued (Art. 16.1.b). Where financial instruments and/or assets other than financial instruments are measured at fair value an entity must provide in the notes: (i) the significant assumptions underlying the valuation models and techniques where fair values have been determined; (ii) for each category of financial instrument or asset other than financial instruments, the fair value, the changes in value included directly in the profit and loss account and changes included in fair value reserves; (iii) for each class of derivative financial instrument, information about the extent and the nature of the instruments, including significant terms and conditions that may affect the amount, timing and certainty of future cash flows; and (iv) a table showing movements in fair value reserves during the financial year (Art. 16.1.c).

Since the alternative valuation bases are based on the exit price, prudence and the general principle of competence undergo changes, as well as requiring adequate coordination with the objectives pursued by Directive 34/2013.

In fact, Directive 34/2013 arises with respect to a pool of users and uses that do not coincide with those of the IASs/IFRSs and among others the most significant are the following:

- *Annual financial statements pursue various objectives and do not merely provide information for investors in capital markets but also give an account of past transactions and enhance corporate governance. Union accounting legislation needs to strike an appropriate balance between the interests of the addressees of financial statements and the interest of undertakings in not being unduly burdened with reporting requirements* (par. 4).
- *The scope of this Directive should include certain undertakings with limited liability such as public and private limited liability companies* (par. 5).
- *The Directive is based on the "think small first" principle in order to avoid disproportionate administrative burdens* (par. 10).

With reference to prudence, the revalued amounts and the fair value require greater attention to the estimation situations. As noted, prudence is linked to situations of uncertainty due to estimates, judgements and models, which are high in the case of the two alternative measurement bases. In these cases, conservatism requires disclosure:

- *Where national law provides for the revaluation basis of measurement, it shall define its content and limits and the rules for its application* (Art. 7.1).
- The content of the notes to the financial statements relating to all undertakings includes the *significant assumptions underlying the valuation models and techniques where fair values have been determined (Art. 16. c. (i)).*

With reference to the accrual basis, the revalued amounts and the fair value modifies the *revenue and expense view* by considering assets as a priority over income components, the so-called *asset and liability view*. Assets are considered stand alone for their *cash-generating ability*.

In addition, the use of an alternative measurement basis requires advanced and specialized skills, on the part of the preparers, but also of the users, who certainly must be "sophisticated users".

Finally, from the analysis of the Directive and its transpositions into the regulations of the countries examined, a certain heterogeneity of the measurement basis emerges, which reveals an atomistic vision of the measurement principles—differentiated by items—rather than a general principle.

Concluding, it should be noted that the Directive does not expressly refer to the amortized cost, since it is a criterion that falls within the context of the historical cost, applied to financial assets and liabilities. Directive Art. 2.6 specifies that: "*purchase price means the price payable and any incidental expenses minus any incidental reductions in the cost of acquisition*", which refers to the setting of IASs/IFRSs. In the newest version of Conceptual Framework (2018), it is noted that: "*One way to apply a historical cost measurement basis to financial assets and financial liabilities is to measure them at amortised cost. The amortised cost of a financial asset or financial liability reflects estimates of future cash flows, discounted at a rate determined at initial recognition. For variable rate instruments, the discount rate is updated to reflect changes in the variable rate. The amortised cost of a financial asset or financial liability is updated over time to depict subsequent changes, such as the accrual of interest, the impairment of a financial asset and receipts or payments*" (par. 6.9).[5]

Looking at the cross-cutting, all the countries examined envisage the use of amortized cost in the accounting for financial assets and liabilities.

[5]Reference is to the version of the CF 2018 although the Directive was issued before, due to the clarity of CF with regards amortised cost. In any case, the amortized cost was already present in the version of the International Accounting Standards and International Financial Reporting Standards in force at the time of the preparation of the Directive.

References

Adamo, S., Fellegara, A. M., Incollingo, A., & Lionzo, A. (a cura di) (2018). La "nuova" informativa di bilancio. Profili teorici e criticità applicative dopo il D. Lgs. 139/2015 e i nuovi principi OIC, FrancoAngeli, 1–410.

Alexander, D. (1993). A European *true and fair* view? *European Accounting Review, 2*(1), 59–80.

Alexander, D. (2001). The over-riding importance of internationalism: A reply to Nobes. *Accounting and Business Research, 31*(2), 145–149.

Alexander, D., & Archer, S. (2000). On the myth of "Anglo-Saxon" financial accounting. *International Journal of Accounting, 35*(4), 539–557.

Alexander, D., & Eberhartinger, E. (2009). The *True and fair* view in the European Union. *European Accounting Review, 18*(3), 571–594.

Alexander, D., & Grottke, M. (2016). A *true and fair* view on harmonisation in accounting in the European Union. In *Paper at Accounting and Regulation workshop*, July 2016.

Alexander, D., & Jermakowicz, E. (2006). A *True and fair* view of the principles/rules debate. *Abacus, 42*(2), 132.

Barth, M. E. (2013). Global comparability in financial reporting: What, why, how, and when? *China Journal of Accounting Studies, 1*(1), 2–12.

Chastney, J. G. (1975). *True and fair* view: History, meaning and impact of fourth directive. *Research Committee Occasional Paper No. 6,* ICAEW.

Evans, L. (2003). The *true and fair* view and the "fair presentation" override of IAS 1. *Accounting and Business Research, 33*(4), 311–325.

Filip, A., Hammami, A., Huang, Z., Jeny, A., Magnan, M., & Moldovan, R. (2017). Literature Review on the Effect of Implementation of IFRS 13 Fair Value Measurement, International Accounting Standard Board's public January 2018 meeting and referenced as Agenda Paper 7C.

Hamilton, G., & Ó hÓgartaigh, C. (2009). The third policeman: 'The *true and fair* view', language and the habitus of accounting. *Critical Perspectives on Accounting, 20*(8), 910–920.

Hopwood, A. G. (1990). Ambiguity, knowledge and territorial claims: Some observations on the doctrine of substance over form. *British Accounting Review, 22*(1), 79–87.

Incollingo, A. (1999). *L'applicazione del principio di "true and fair view" nel bilancio di esercizio.* Giuffrè.

Institute of Chartered Accountants in England & Wales (ICAEW). (2006). Measurement in financial reporting, 1–75.

Kirk, N. (2006). Perceptions of the *true and fair* view concept: An empirical investigation. *Abacus, 42*(2), 205–235.

Livne, G., & McNichols, M. F. (2009). An empirical investigation of the *True and fair* Override. *Journal of Business, Finance and Accounting, January/March*, 1–30.

Maltby, J. (2000). The origins of prudence in accounting. *Critical Perspective on Accounting, 11*(1), 51–70.

McGregor, W. (1992). *True and fair* view – An accounting anachronism. *Australian Accountant, 62*(1), 68–71.

Milburn, J. A. (2012). Toward a measurement framework for financial reporting by profit-oriented entities. *The Canadian Institute of Chartered Accountants*, 1–152.

Müller-Burmeister, C., & Velte, P. (2016). Increased materiality judgments in financial accounting and external audit. *International Journal of Critical Accounting, 8*(3/4), 227–245.

Nobes, C. (2009). The importance of being fair: An analysis of IFRS regulation and practice – A comment. *Accounting and Business Research, 39*(4), 415–427.

Ordelheide, D. (1993). *True and fair* view – A European and a German perspective. *European Accounting Review, 2*(1), 81–90.

Ruch, G. W., & Taylor, G. (2015). Accounting conservatism: A review of the literature. *Journal of Accounting Literature, 34*, 17–38.

Schipper, K. (2003). Principles-based accounting standards. *Accounting Horizons, 17*(1), 61–72.

Sordini, M. (1982). *Il bilancio d'esercizio secondo la IV Direttiva CEE*, Giuffré.

Sterling, R. R. (1967). Conservatism: The fundamental principle of valuation in traditional accounting. *Abacus, 3*(2), 109–132.

Superti, F. F. (1988). Passato e presente del bilancio d'esercizio verso un bilancio intellegibile. *Rivista dei Dottori Commercialisti*, 1035–1063.

Walton P. J. (1991). The *true and fair* view: A shifting concept. *Occasional Research Paper No. 7.* ACCA.

Walton, P. J. (1993). Introduction: The *true and fair* view in British accounting. *European Accounting Review, 2*(1), 49–58.

Watts, R. L. (2003a). Conservatism in accounting part I: Explanations and implications. *Accounting Horizons, 17*(3), 207–221.

Watts, R. L. (2003b). Conservatism in accounting part II: Evidence and research opportunities. *Accounting Horizons, 17*(4), 287–301.

Zeff, S. A., Buijink, W., & Camfferman, K. (1999). '*True and fair*' in the Netherlands: inzicht or getrouw beeld? *European Accounting Review, 8*(3), 523–548.

Zhong, Y., & Li, W. (2017). Accounting conservatism: A literature review. *Australian Accounting Review, 81/27*(2), 195–213.

Financial Statement Layouts

Michele Bertoni and Ugo Sostero

1 Introduction: Categories of Undertakings and Financial Statement Layouts According to the Accounting Directive

Article 3 of EU Directive 34/2013 (also known as the "accounting directive") defines different categories of undertakings and groups to which Member States can apply different financial reporting requirements. For this chapter, the analysis will focus only on annual financial statements. One of the aims of the Directive was to ease the financial reporting requirements for small entities and micro-entities to increase their productivity.[1] For this purpose, Article 3 of the Directive identifies four size classes: micro-undertakings, small undertakings, medium-sized undertakings and large

[1] The premise to the Directive 2013/34/EU recalls the Commission Communication entitled "Single Market Act", adopted in April 2011, which proposed to simplify the Fourth and Seventh Directives regarding financial information obligations and to reduce administrative burdens, particularly for SMEs. "The Europe 2020 Strategy" for smart, sustainable and inclusive growth, also recalled in the premise of Directive 2013/34/EU, aimed to reduce administrative burdens and improve the business environment, particularly for SMEs, and to promote the internationalisation of SMEs. The European Council of 24 and 25 March 2011 also called for the overall regulatory burden, particularly for SMEs, to be reduced at both the European Union and national levels and suggested measures to increase productivity, such as the removal of red tape and the improvement of the regulatory framework for SMEs.

M. Bertoni (✉)
Università degli Studi di Trieste, Trieste, Italy
e-mail: michele.bertoni@deams.units.it

U. Sostero
Università Ca' Foscari Venezia, Venezia, Italy
e-mail: sostero@unive.it

A. Incollingo, A. Lionzo (eds.), *The European Harmonization of National Accounting Rules*, SIDREA Series in Accounting and Business Administration,
https://doi.org/10.1007/978-3-031-42931-6_11

undertakings.[2] The different thresholds described by the Directive are summarised in Table 1, along with those chosen by the countries selected for this analysis, which will be commented on in the following paragraph.

The goal of the Directive was to enable companies to adopt a level of complexity in their financial reporting proportionate to their size and the information needs of the users of their financial statements.[3] In particular, the new micro-undertaking category was intended to provide these companies with at least the same level of protection from the complexities of financial reporting as the one offered to small undertakings, leaving each Member State the option to expand this simplified application of the financial reporting requirements. However, the simplifications and exemptions set out by the Directive for smaller entities do not apply to public-interest entities,[4] which should be treated as large undertakings regardless of their net turnover, balance sheet total or number of employees (Art. 40).

The accounting directive states that for all undertakings the annual financial statements should comprise, as a minimum, the balance sheet, the profit and loss account and the notes to the financial statements (Art. 4, par. 1). Member States can impose companies other than small undertakings to prepare additional statements or disclose information that is not required by the Directive (Art. 4, par. 1 and 5), unless financial reporting and tax information are gathered under a single filing system and additional disclosure is required for the strict purpose of tax collection (Art. 4, par. 6).

The Directive provides two alternative formats for the balance sheet and two for the profit and loss account. Member States can choose one of the formats for each financial statement or allow companies to adopt either format. The formats provided for the balance sheet are the so-called "horizontal" and "vertical" layouts set out in Annexes III and IV of the accounting directive. The horizontal layout distinguishes between fixed and current assets, depending upon the purpose for which they are held by the entity (Art. 12, Section 3), while liabilities on the credit side are divided into long-term and short-term liabilities, based on whether or not they are due within one year after the end of the financial year. Provisions are reported in a separate category. The vertical layout aims to report the net current assets by subtracting the current operating liabilities from the current assets; both categories must be reported and detailed in the balance sheet. The balance sheet prepared according to this layout must also report the amount of net assets calculated by subtracting noncurrent liabilities from the sum of fixed assets and net current assets. Since neither of the formats allows the determination of the amount of current and noncurrent assets and liabilities without further reclassification, the Directive permits Member States to

[2] The Directive also introduces the definition of middle-sized and large groups, not examined in this chapter.

[3] See https://ec.europa.eu/commission/presscorner/detail/de/MEMO_13_540.

[4] Public-interest entities are defined as follows: (a) companies listed on any EU-regulated market; (b) credit institutions; (c) insurance companies; and (d) any entities designated as public-interest entities by Member States. See Art. 2, section 1, of the Directive.

Table 1 Categories of undertakings (at least two of the three following criteria)

	Directive 34/2013/ EU	Germany	United Kingdom	France	Italy	Spain	Denmark	Sweden	The Netherlands
Large undertakings	(a) BST> € 20 million (b) NT > € 40 million (c) n.E > 250	In accordance with the Directive	(a) BST> £ 18 million (b) NT > £ 36 million (c) n.E > 250	In accordance with the Directive	(a) BST > € 4,4 million (b) NT > € 8,8 million (c) n.E > 50	(a) BST > € 11,4 million (b) NT > € 22,8 million (c) n.E > 250	(a) BST > DKK 156 million (b) NT >DKK 313 million (c) n.E > 250	(a) BST> SEK 40 million (b) NT > SEK 80 million (c) n.E > 50 + Listed companies[c]	In accordance with the Directive
Medium-sized undertakings	(a) BST≤ € 20 million (b) NT ≤ € 40 million (c) n.E ≤ 250	In accordance with the Directive	(a) BST≤ £ 18 million (b) NT ≤ £36 million (c) n.E ≤ 250	In accordance with the Directive		(a) BST≤ € 11,4 million (b) NT ≤ € 22,8 million (c) n.E ≤ 250[b]	(a) BST≤ DKK 156 million (b) NT ≤ DKK 313 million (c) n.E ≤ 250		In accordance with the Directive
Small undertakings[a]	(a) BST≤ € 4 million (b) NT ≤ € 8 million (c) n.E ≤ 50	(a) BST≤ € 6 million (b) NT ≤ € 12 million (c) n.E ≤ 50	(a) BST< £ 5.1 million (b) NT ≤ £10.2 million (c) n.E ≤ 50	(a) BST< € 6 million (b) NT ≤ € 12 million (c) n.E ≤ 50	(a) BST≤ € 4,4 million (b) NT ≤ € 8,8 million (c) n.E ≤ 50	(a) BST≤ € 4 million (b) NT ≤ € 8 million (c) n.E ≤ 50	(a) BST≤ DKK 44 million (b) NT ≤ DKK 89 million (c) n.E ≤ 50	(a) BST≤ SEK 40 million (b) NT ≤ SEK 80 million (c) n.E ≤ 50	a) BST≤ € 6 million (b) NT ≤ € 12 million (c) n.E < 50

(continued)

Table 1 (continued)

	Directive 34/2013/ EU	Germany	United Kingdom	France	Italy	Spain	Denmark	Sweden	The Netherlands
Micro-undertakings	(a) BST≤ € 350 000 (b) NT ≤ € 700 000 (c) n.E ≤ 10	In accordance with the Directive	(a) BST≤ £316 000 (b) NT ≤ £632 000 (c) n.E ≤ 10	In accordance with the Directive	(a) BST≤ € 175 000 (b) NT ≤€ 350 000 (c) n.E ≤ 5	(a) BST≤ € 1 million (b) NT ≤ € 2 million (c) n.E ≤ 10	(a) BST≤ DKK 2.7 million (b) NT ≤ DKK 5.4 million (c) n.E ≤ 10	(a) BST≤ SEK 1.5 million (b) NT ≤ SEK 3 million (c) n.E ≤ 3	In accordance with the Directive

BST = balance sheet total; *NT* = net turnover; *n.E* = number of employees

[a]Member States may define thresholds exceeding the thresholds in points (a) and (b). However, the thresholds shall not exceed EUR 6 million for the balance sheet total and EUR 12 million for the net turnover

[b]Spanish regulations do not consider medium-sized companies as a separate category; instead, they provide specific dimensional thresholds for drawing up abridged PLs

[c]Sweden considers an undertaking to be "very large" when: (a) BST> SEK 175 million, (b) NT > SEK 350 million and (c) n.E > 250

introduce an alternative presentation of the balance sheet based on the distinction between current and noncurrent items (Art. 11). The directive does not provide a specific layout for this alternative presentation; it simply notes that the information provided must be at least equivalent to that included in the standard layouts.

For the presentation of the profit and loss account, the Directive prescribes two layouts. The first, where expenses are classified by their nature (Annex V), leads to the "total output" or "value of production" profit and loss account (although the accounting directive does not require highlighting this item in its layout). The second layout, where expenses are classified by function, is also known as the "cost of goods sold" format (Annex VI). Article 13 of the Directive allows Member States to deviate from the two layouts and to permit or require a "statement of performance", provided that the information given is at least equivalent to the content of the official layouts. As we will illustrate in this chapter, this particular provision is the least applied among the countries analysed for this study.

Article 19 describes the content of the management report, which should include a fair review of the development and performance of the business, along with a description of the principal risks and uncertainties. The report should include financial and nonfinancial performance indicators, including information relating to environmental and employee matters. Article 30 of the accounting directive requires the publication of annual financial statements no later than 12 months after the balance sheet date.

Article 14 of the accounting directive introduces some simplifications for small and medium-sized entities. According to the Directive, Member States can permit small undertakings to draw up abridged balance sheets, reporting only the items preceded by letters and roman numerals in the layouts. Small and medium-sized undertakings can prepare an abridged profit and loss account, grouping different items[5] under the label "gross profit or loss".

Small undertakings can be exempted from the obligation to prepare a management report as long as they provide information about the acquisition of their own shares in the notes (Art. 19). Small and medium-sized undertakings can also be exempted from disclosing nonfinancial indicators. Member States may exempt small undertakings from the obligation to publish their management reports and profit and loss accounts (Art. 31, par. 1). Medium-sized undertakings may be allowed to publish an abridged balance sheet and abridged notes to their financial statements (Art. 31, par. 2).

Article 36 introduces further simplifications for micro-undertakings, which can be exempted from presenting specific balance sheet items (i.e. accruals and prepayments), drawing up notes to the financial statements, preparing a management report and publishing annual financial statements (provided that the balance sheet

[5]Items 1 to 5 for the total output layout (net turnover, variation of stocks in finished goods, work performed by the undertaking and capitalised, other operating income, raw materials and other expenses) and items 1, 2, 3 and 6 for the cost of goods sold layout (net turnover, cost of sales, gross profit or loss from sales and other operating income).

information is duly filed with at least one competent national authority). Micro-undertakings, moreover, can be allowed to draw up abridged balance sheets and profit and loss accounts (Art. 36, par. 2).

2 Categories of Undertakings and Composition of Annual Financial Statements in the Jurisdictions Analysed

All the information reported in this chapter and the following paragraphs refers to non-public-interest companies (i.e. private companies other than banks and insurance companies). Table 1 reports the different categories of undertakings identified in the eight jurisdictions analysed.

In January 2020, the United Kingdom ceased to become a member of the European Union. Therefore, the information reported in this chapter refers to UK domestic law (Companies Act 2006), according to which non-public-interest companies can choose between UK GAAP and IFRS for both their individual and consolidated accounts[6] (IFRS, 2022).

As shown in Table 1, Italy and Sweden do not separate medium-sized undertakings from large undertakings. Spain provides specific thresholds for this class of reporting entities for the sole scope of drawing up an abridged profit and loss account. In defining small undertakings, Germany, the United Kingdom, France, Denmark and the Netherlands increased the quantitative thresholds for total assets and net turnover compared with those stated by the accounting directive[7]; a similar decision, but for micro-undertakings, was made by Spain. On the other hand, the thresholds for micro-undertakings in Italy have decreased.

Table 2 summarises the composition of annual financial statements in the different jurisdictions. It is interesting to observe how all the jurisdictions analysed, except France, decided to require the presentation of a statement of cash flows, at least for large companies. Germany, the United Kingdom, Spain and Denmark require, in addition, a statement of changes in equity.

The United Kingdom is the only jurisdiction requiring large companies adopting UK GAAP[8] to prepare a statement of comprehensive income, either as a single statement or as a separate statement from the profit and loss account. In fact, the UK Financial Reporting Standard 102, from which this obligation stems, is based on the

[6] Listed companies domiciled in the United Kingdom must adopt UK-endorsed IFRS for their consolidated financial statements but can choose between IFRS and UK GAAP for their individual accounts. See Chap. 4 (the United Kingdom).

[7] Member States may define thresholds exceeding those indicated by the accounting directive. However, the thresholds shall not exceed EUR 6 million for the balance sheet total and EUR 12 million for the net turnover.

[8] As opposed to IFRS, in which the presentation of statement of comprehensive income is mandatory (IAS 1:10).

Table 2 Annual financial statements comprise, as a minimum

	Directive 34/2013/EU	Germany	United Kingdom	France	Italy	Spain	Denmark	Sweden	The Netherlands
Large undertakings	BS PL Nt	As provided by the Directive. Only listed firms (if not obliged to draw up consolidated financial statements): + SCF + SCEq	In accordance with UK-adopted international accounting standards ("IAS individual accounts") or according to UK GAAP, i.e. FRS 102 (based on IFRS for SMEs): BS, PL (single statement of comprehensive income or separate profit and loss account and separate statement of comprehensive income), SCEq, SCF, Nt.	As provided for in the Directive	As provided for in the Directive + SCF	As provided for in Directive + SCF + SCEq	As provided for in Directive + SCF + SCEq	As provided for in Directive + SCF + SCEq	As provided for in Directive + SCF
Medium-sized undertakings		BS Abridged PL Simplified Nt It is mandatory to publish only abridged BS and simplified Nt		BS Abridged PL Nt		BS Abridged PL Nt SCF SCEq	As provided for in Directive + SCF + SCEq		As provided for in Directive + SCF

(continued)

Table 2 (continued)

	Directive 34/2013/EU	Germany	United Kingdom	France	Italy	Spain	Denmark	Sweden	The Netherlands
Small undertakings	Member States may permit to draw up abridged BS and abridged PL and simplified Nt[a]	Abridged BS Abridged PL Simplified Nt It is mandatory to publish only BS and simplified Nt	Abridged BS, abridged PL, simplified Nt	Abridged BS Abridged PL Simplified Nt	Abridged BS Abridged PL Simplified Nt	Abridged BS Abridged PL Simplified Nt	BS Abridged PL Nt	Abridged BS Abridged PL SCEq Simplified Nt	Abridged BS Abridged PLs Simplified Nt
Micro-undertakings		Abridged BS Abridged PL It is not mandatory to publish any document	Abridged profit and loss account (costs classified by nature), abridged BS (vertical or horizontal layout) with Nt included at the foot of the statement (FRS 105)	Abridged BS Abridged PL	Abridged BS Abridged PL	Abridged BS Abridged PL Simplified Nt	BS Abridged PL Abridged Nt	Abridged BS Abridged PL SCEq Simplified Nt	Limited BS Limited PLs

BS = balance sheet; *PL* = profit and loss account; *Nt* = notes; *SCF* = statement of cash flows; *SCEq* = statement of changes in equity
[a]Member States may exempt small undertakings from the obligation to publish their PLs

IFRS for Small and Medium-Sized Entities standard, with significant modifications (IFRS, 2022).

The statement of cash flows is required for medium-sized entities in Spain, Denmark and the Netherlands[9] but not in Germany (Italy and Sweden do not differentiate between large and medium-sized companies). No jurisdiction requires a statement of cash flows for small or micro-companies. Simplifications for small undertakings generally consist of abridged balance sheets and profit and loss accounts, accompanied by simplified notes. In some cases, there are differential publication requirements, such as in France,[10] Germany[11] and the Netherlands,[12] where small undertakings can choose not to make their profit and loss accounts public. This benefit extends to all financial statements in the case of micro-undertakings in France and Germany. In addition to being generally allowed to adopt an abridged version of their financial statements, micro-undertakings are exempted from preparing notes in Germany, France, Italy and the Netherlands. Micro-entities in Sweden have the same financial reporting obligations as small undertakings but are exempted from mandatory audit requirements.[13]

As reported in Table 3, all jurisdictions require large and medium-sized companies to accompany their financial statements with a management report (known as a strategic report in the United Kingdom). Sweden and Denmark require a simplified management report for small companies, but in the remaining jurisdictions, it is not mandatory. Requirements for micro-undertakings are the same as those for small companies as far as the presentation of the management report is concerned.

---

[9] A cash flow statement is required for medium-sized and large companies based on the Dutch Accounting Standard 360.104. The cash flow statement is however not mentioned in the Dutch Civil Code as a primary financial statement. The Dutch Accounting Standard 360.101 states that the cash flow statement is part of the financial statements. Given the definition of financial statements in the Dutch Civil Code (Art. 361-1), it could be argued that the cash flow statement forms part of the notes to the financial statements. However, in practice, medium-sized and large companies present the cash flow statement together with the balance sheet and the profit and loss account, as a third primary financial statement. There are exemptions for wholly owned subsidiaries under certain conditions, for 100% intermediate holding companies and for legal entities applying Section 2:403 of the Dutch Civil Code.

[10] Small undertakings in France can ask that the profit and loss account they file should not made public. Micro-undertakings enjoy a similar right, extended to their complete financial statements. Medium-sized undertakings may request that only a simplified version of their balance sheet and notes is made public (French Code de commerce, Art. L232-25).

[11] See Chap. 3 (Germany).

[12] Small undertakings in the Netherlands are allowed to draw up abridged PLs but are not required to publish them. Micro-undertakings are allowed to draw up limited PLs but are not required to publish them. They are exempted from presenting notes to the financial statements (with a few exceptions). See Chap. 10 (The Netherlands).

[13] See Chap. 9 (Sweden).

Table 3 Management reports

	Directive 34/2013/EU	Germany	United Kingdom	France	Italy	Spain	Denmark	Sweden	The Netherlands
Large undertakings	The MR [and the consolidated MR] are important elements of financial reporting	The FSs must be accompanied by an MRs	The FSs must be accompanied by a directors' report and by a strategic report	The FSs must be accompanied by an MR	The FSs must be accompanied by an MR	The FSs must be accompanied by an MR	The FSs must be accompanied by an MR and by a management statement concerning the adherence to a true and fair view.	The FSs must be accompanied by an MR	The FSs must be accompanied by an MR
Medium-sized undertakings	Member states may exempt small and medium-sized undertakings from the obligation to include nonfinancial information[a]	The FSs must be accompanied by an MR		The FSs must be accompanied by an MR		The FSs must be accompanied by an MR	The FSs must be accompanied by an MR and by a management statement		The FSs must be accompanied by an MR
Small undertakings	Member States may exempt small undertakings from the obligation to prepare MRs[b]	Not mandatory	Strategic report not mandatory. Simplified Directors' report	Not mandatory	Not mandatory	Not mandatory	Management statement, abridged MR.	Simplified MR	Not mandatory

Micro-undertakings		Not mandatory	Strategic report not mandatory. Simplified Directors' report	Not mandatory	Not mandatory	Not mandatory	Management statement, abridged MR	Simplified MR	Not mandatory

FSs = financial statements; *MR* = management report

[a]Directive 34/2013/EU, Art. 19.4 Member States may exempt small and medium-sized undertakings from the obligation set out in the third subparagraph of paragraph 1 in so far as it relates to nonfinancial information

[b]Directive 34/2013/EU, Art. 19.3 Member States may exempt small undertakings from the obligation to prepare management reports, provided they require the information referred to in Article 24(2) of Directive 2012/30/EU concerning the acquisition by an undertaking of its own shares to be given in the notes to the financial statements

3 Presentation of the Balance Sheet and the Profit and Loss Account

Table 4 illustrates the choices made in the different jurisdictions regarding the layout of the balance sheet. In most cases, the countries analysed allow only a horizontal layout. The vertical layout is optional in the United Kingdom, France and the Netherlands. No jurisdiction requires a vertical layout.

The alternative presentation of the balance sheet, based on the distinction between current and noncurrent items (as opposed to the layouts reported by Annexes III and IV of the Directive, which do not require such a distinction[14]), is not allowed in most jurisdictions. However, it is mandatory in the United Kingdom (given the reliance of the UK GAAP on IFRS) and Spain (consistent with Spain's other efforts to reduce the differences between Spanish national rules and IFRS[15]). The alternative presentation of the balance sheet has also been optional in Denmark since 2015, with the explicit intent of adapting Danish national rules to prevailing international practices.[16] Given the relevance of the distinction between current and noncurrent items for financial statement analysis (Penman, 2006; White et al., 1994), and since this classification of assets and liabilities is required by the IFRS (IAS1.66), the alternative format would make for a more effective presentation of the company's financial position than the traditional layouts proposed by the Directive. The rarity of its adoption among the jurisdictions analysed contributes to the lack of comparability between the financial statements prepared according to IFRS and those based on local accounting standards.

Table 5 illustrates the choices made in the different jurisdictions regarding the profit and loss account layout. There is more variety among the countries selected for this study regarding the presentation of profit and loss accounts. In fact, five jurisdictions (Germany, the United Kingdom, Denmark, Sweden and the Netherlands) allow both layouts (nature of expenses and function of expenses); France, Italy and Spain only allow the nature of expenses layout. As already noted, classifying expenses by nature in the profit and loss account is considered typical of "weak equity" accounting systems, typical of contexts where most of the financing is provided by the banking system, and equity investors play a limited role in financing firms (Nobes, 1998).[17] Sometimes, these national preferences for specific financial

[14] Not even the vertical layout, in which the presentation of "net current assets" is a requirement, achieves a full distinction between current and noncurrent items, for item D.II (Debtors) of the Annex IV layout requires to report separately for each item the amounts owed more than one year after the balance sheet date.

[15] See Chap. 7 (Spain).

[16] See Chap. 8 (Denmark).

[17] Another effective classification of financial systems distinguishes between "outsider" systems and "insider" or "relationship-based" systems, depending on how capital is channelled to investment opportunities and how information asymmetries between contracting and financing parties are reduced See: Leuz (2010).

Table 4 Presentation of the balance sheet

Directive 34/2013/EU	Germany	United Kingdom	France	Italy	Spain	Denmark	Sweden	The Netherlands
One or both of the layouts set out in Annexes III and IV	One	Both (SI 2008/410)	Both	One	One	One	One	Both
Annex III: horizontal layout	Horizontal layout	Horizontal layout	Horizontal layout	Horizontal layout	Horizontal layout	Horizontal layout	Horizontal layout	Horizontal layout
Annex IV: vertical layout	Not provided	Vertical Layout	Vertical layout	Not provided	Not provided	Not provided	Not provided	Vertical layout
Alternative presentation (items on the basis of a distinction between current and noncurrent items)	Not provided	Mandatory distinction between current/ noncurrent items	Not provided	Not provided	Mandatory presentation (items on the basis of a distinction between current and noncurrent item	Optional	Not provided	Not provided

Table 5 Presentation of the profit and loss account

Directive 34/2013/EU	Germany	United Kingdom	France	Italy	Spain	Denmark	Sweden	The Netherlands
One or both of the layouts set out in Annexes V and VI	Both	Both	One	One	One	Both	Both	Both
Annex V: layout by nature of expense	Layout by nature of expense	Layout by nature of expense	Layout by nature of expense (both vertical and horizontal layout)	Layout by nature of expense	Layout by nature of expense	Layout by nature of expense	Layout by nature of expense	Layout by nature of expense
Annex VI: layout by function of expense	Layout by function of expense	Layout by function of expense	Not provided	Not provided	Not provided	Layout by function of expense	Layout by function of expense	Layout by function of expense
Alternative presentation (Statement of performance)	Not provided	Not provided	Mandatory in some cases, but not alternative to the layout by nature of expense.	Not provided	Not provided	Not provided	Not provided	Not provided

statement layouts persist, even among companies preparing their financial statements according to the IFRS (Doupnik & Perera, 2012; Stadler & Nobes, 2014). Given that the German accounting system is often identified as the most egregious example of a weak equity system (Nobes & Parker, 2020; Radebaugh & Gray, 2002), the choices made by the German law when adopting the Directive seem interesting and, in this sense, reduce the distance between German GAAP and IFRS (which also permit both layouts). It is not surprising that the UK rules allow both formats since it is also a feature of IFRS, on which UK GAAP is based. In the case of the Netherlands, the option of preparing a cost of goods sold profit and loss account is consistent with international accounting research, which classifies the Dutch accounting system as being closer to strong equity systems rather than to the weak equity systems of France, Belgium and Germany (Nobes, 1998; Radebaugh & Gray, 2002). The United Kingdom and the Netherlands are the only jurisdictions, among those analysed, that allow the adoption of all four financial statement layouts described by the Directive. In case of the Netherlands, this is consistent with the generally permissive Dutch attitude in implementing the accounting directive, which implies wide use of the options provided therein.[18]

On the other hand, the choices made by Spain, France and Italy seem consistent with these countries' accounting traditions and with the typical "weak equity" approach to financial reporting (classification of expenses by nature, little flexibility, etc.).

Finally, only France, among the jurisdictions examined, allows the production of a statement of performance; however, this statement must be presented in addition to, and not in place of, the traditional profit and loss account classified by nature of expense.[19] The scarce success of this particular provision of the accounting directive can probably be attributed to its elusiveness, as Art. 4, Section 1, of the Directive does not explain the specific content and objectives of this alternative presentation layout. However, given the introduction of fair value measurements in several jurisdictions, or their broader scope of application, it would probably have been helpful to widen the content of the profit and loss account to encompass comprehensive income. In fact, the introduction by national lawmakers of hedge accounting rules modelled after those contained in IFRS without, at the same time, introducing the concept of comprehensive income, on which most of those rules are based, risks widening the gap between local accounting standards in Europe and the IFRS instead of closing it.

[18] See Chap. 10 (The Netherlands).

[19] The statement of performance, known in France as *Tableau des soldes intermédiaires de gestion* is required in the "developed" French system, on top of the traditional profit and loss account. See Chap. 5 (France).

References

Doupnik, T. S., & Perera, M. H. B. (2012). *International accounting* (3rd ed.). McGraw-Hill.

IFRS Foundation. (2022). *IFRS application around the world. Jurisdictional profile: United Kingdom*. Retrieved December 13, 2022, from https://www.ifrs.org/content/dam/ifrs/publications/jurisdictions/pdf-profiles/united-kingdom-ifrs-profile.pdf

Leuz, C. (2010). Different approaches to corporate reporting regulation: How jurisdictions differ and why. *Accounting and Business Research, 40*(3), 229–256. https://doi.org/10.1080/00014788.2010.9663398

Nobes, C., & Parker, R. (2020). *Comparative international accounting* (14th ed.). Pearson Education.

Nobes, C. W. (1998). Towards a general model of the reasons for international differences in financial reporting. *Abacus, 34*(2), 162–187. https://doi.org/10.1111/1467-6281.00028

Penman, S. H. (2006). *Financial statement analysis and security valuation* (3rd ed.). McGraw-Hill.

Radebaugh, L. H., & Gray, S. J. (2002). *International accounting and multinational enterprises* (5th ed.). Wiley.

Stadler, C., & Nobes, C. W. (2014). The influence of country, industry, and topic factors on IFRS policy choice. *Abacus, 50*(4), 386–421. https://doi.org/10.1111/abac.12035

White, G. I., Sondhi, A. C., & Fried, D. (1994). *The analysis and use of financial statements*. John Wiley & Sons.

Write-Down for Impairment Losses

Silvano Corbella, Cristina Florio, and Giulio Greco

1 Introduction

With a view to promoting the harmonization of the financial statements prepared by those European companies which—by choice or by obligation—do not adopt IAS/IFRS but comply with national regulations, the Directive 2013/34/EU on "*the annual financial statements, consolidated financial statements and the related reports of certain types of undertakings*" (*i.e.* the EU-D-34/2013 or the EU Directive hereinafter) introduces specific provisions on value adjustments of fixed assets.

This is a critical evaluation procedure in the context of financial statement preparation. Indeed, the debate on value adjustments has been going on for long internationally, especially after the decision taken early in the 2000s by both the US Financial Accounting Standard Board (FASB) and the International Accounting Standard Board (IASB) to abandon the amortization model and adopt an impairment-only approach for goodwill and other identifiable intangible assets with indefinite useful life (Amel-Zadeh et al., 2023). The issue is especially relevant for goodwill, which is proven to represent the largest single asset acquired in an average business combination (EFRAG, 2017): throughout Europe, goodwill amounts to 50% of the purchase price and 41% of the shareholders' equity on average (Florio et al., 2018; Glaum et al., 2007). Moreover, goodwill accounting

S. Corbella · C. Florio (✉)
Università degli Studi di Verona, Verona, Italy
e-mail: silvano.corbella@univr.it; cristina.florio@univr.it

G. Greco
Università degli Studi di Pisa, Pisa, Italy
e-mail: giulio.greco@unipi.it

A. Incollingo, A. Lionzo (eds.), *The European Harmonization of National Accounting Rules*, SIDREA Series in Accounting and Business Administration,
https://doi.org/10.1007/978-3-031-42931-6_12

is complex and highly discretionary (Amel-Zadeh et al., 2023), thus subject to accounting opportunism: for instance, in Sweden, family-listed firms tend to allocate a larger portion of the purchase price to goodwill compared to nonfamily firms (Frii & Hamberg, 2021).

As for any other accounting policy, both the impairment model and the amortization model have pros and cons. The impairment test is meant to ensure that long-lived assets are not recognized at a value higher than their recoverable amount and to provide more useful and relevant information than the amortization model (Ramanna & Watts, 2012). However, within an impairment-only approach, the recognition of an impairment loss can have significant effects on income and the year-end shareholders' equity, while if no loss in value is recognized, all else being equal the company will appear more solid to investors (Jordan & Clark, 2004). The main cons are that the goodwill impairment test is complex, time-consuming and subject to discretion (IASB, 2019). Financial statement preparers criticize it as unduly costly (IASB, 2020; Amel-Zadeh et al., 2023) and as having led to overpayments (Frii & Hamberg, 2021). Conversely, the amortization model reduces the risk of a possible overvaluation of goodwill and increases the level of comparability between companies that grow organically (*i.e.* internally) and those that grow through acquisitions. It also allows highlighting the cases in which the activities of which goodwill is made up are consumed over time (*e.g.* the acquired workforce leaves the company). Nonetheless, the valuation of the useful life of goodwill is difficult—if not arbitrary (Amel-Zadeh et al., 2023; IASB, 2019). Moreover, the amortization model does not fully replace the impairment test, as it would still be necessary in case of impairment signals.

As part of its due process, in 2014 the IASB conducted a post-implementation review (PIR)[1] of the 2008 revised version of IFRS 3 Business Combinations, which among the others regulates goodwill recognition. Many participants in such PIR suggested the reintroduction of goodwill amortization combined with an impairment test in case there are signals of impairment of the asset. Therefore, in June 2015, the Board undertook a follow-on project relating to goodwill and impairment and decided on the point later in November 2022, when it tentatively decided to maintain the impairment-only approach (IASB, 2022, 2023). However, the debate on goodwill impairment is going to continue because in December 2022, the IASB added a new project to its standard-setting work plan, named *Business Combinations—Disclosures, Goodwill and Impairment*, in which it intends (*inter alia*) to simplify the application of the impairment test in IAS 36 Impairment of Assets and improve the effectiveness of the impairment test of cash-generating units containing goodwill.

[1] As stated on the IASB website, "*[T]he objective of a PIR is to assess whether the effects of applying the new requirements on users of financial statements, preparers, auditors and regulators are as intended when the IASB developed those new requirements. [. . .] A PIR includes consideration of how contentious matters that the IASB considered during development of the new requirements and how market developments since those new requirements were issued are being addressed in practice*".

The debate was heated and long-lasting even overseas, where in July 2019, the FASB issued an invitation to comment on *Identifiable Intangible Assets and Subsequent Accounting for Goodwill* (FASB, 2019), which underlined that the Board was considering whether changes to the subsequent accounting for goodwill were suitable for cost-benefit reasons. In December 2020, during the deliberation of the responses, the FASB tentatively decided to reintroduce amortization of goodwill on a straight-line basis over a 10-year default period or an estimated period (using an open list of factors to consider), limited to a 25-year cap and not modifiable. It also considered several options to simplify goodwill impairment testing. However, in June 2022, the FASB unanimously decided to end this four-year project because Board members were not convinced that the change pursued as regards the subsequent accounting of goodwill would have improved current rules, especially considering the marginal benefits perceived by investors.[2]

Within the framework outlined, it appears crucial to understand which regulatory choices have been made as regards value adjustments by the EU and its Member States. Therefore, this chapter analyses point by point the provisions dedicated to the value adjustments of fixed assets in the eight EU Member States examined in this book (*e.g.* Denmark, France, Germany, Italy, the Netherlands, Spain, Sweden and the UK). Whenever relevant, it underlines the room for discretion granted to the Member States and examines the implementation choices made by each Member State. National regulations on impairment loss recognition and accounting standards (if relevant) are reviewed, commented on, and confronted. Such a comprehensive analysis of how different jurisdictions have transposed the Directive into national law allows similarities and differences among Member States to emerge, thus contributing to extant knowledge on the current level of harmonization of the discipline on value adjustments.

The rest of the chapter is structured as follows: Section 2 analyses the regulatory and legal background in force in each Member State examined as regards value adjustments. Section 3 discusses the differences across various jurisdictions regarding value adjustments of financial assets, while Sect. 4 focuses on tangible and intangible fixed assets. Section 5 analyses the possibility of reversing a value reduction. Section 6 compares the disclosure on value adjustments across jurisdictions, while Sect. 7 discusses disclosure regulations for specific types of companies (*i.e.* SMEs).

[2]For a complete overview of the FASB project, please see the following webpage: https://www.fasb.org/page/PageContent?pageId=/projects/recentlycompleted/identifiable-intangible-assets-and-subsequent-accounting-for-goodwill.html.

2 Regulatory Sources at the National Level

In this section, the regulatory and para-regulatory sources that guide the accounting treatment of write-downs for impairment losses are highlighted concerning each country subject to analysis.

In Denmark, the EU Directive is transposed into the *Årsregnskabsloven*, *i.e.* the Danish Financial Statements Act or Annual Accounts Act (hereinafter, the Act). Section 42 of the Act provides for the impairment test for those fixed assets that are not regularly adjusted to fair value, while Section 43 deals with the depreciation of tangible fixed assets and intangible fixed assets with limited useful life. Both Section 42 and Section 43 apply to all companies that do not voluntarily or mandatorily apply IAS/IFRS and are required to submit an annual report to the Business Authority, *i.e.* all companies in accounting class B (micro- and small-sized companies), C (medium- and large-sized companies) and D (listed companies and state-owned public companies) in the Act. In Denmark, there are no official national accounting standards; yet, reference is made to IAS 36 Impairment of Assets as regards impairment losses measurement and recognition.

In France, the key regulatory source on value adjustments is the *Plan Comptable Général* (PCG), regulation ANC 2014-03, which is the cornerstone of the French accounting system and is applied to corporate accounts. The PCG is prepared by the Autorité des Normes Comptables (ANC). The first section (*i.e.* Book 1) deals with the general arrangements applicable to the various items in the financial statements, including financial and non-financial assets. The regulation relating to write-downs for impairment losses of non-financial assets is included in Title II (Assets), Chapter 1 (Non-financial assets), Section 4 (Subsequent measurements or measurements after the initial recognition). For financial assets, the reference is Title II (Assets), Chapter 2 (Financial assets).

The German legal basis for accounting is the *Handelsgesetzbuch* (HGB), *i.e.* the Commercial Code. Within this code, the Third Book (§§238-342) deals with accounting and reporting. In detail, §253 of the First Chapter (Provisions Applying to All Merchants) deals with the evaluation criteria to be applied to both financial and non-financial fixed assets. The HGB provisions are supplemented by accounting standards issued by a private standard setter, the German Accounting Standards Board (GASB), whose status is recognized—according to §342 of the HGB—by the German Ministry of Justice. As far as here is concerned, the GASB has published standards that cover the accounting for intangible assets and goodwill, including their impairment. Specifically, GAS 23 Accounting for Subsidiaries in Consolidated Financial Statements is focused on goodwill accounting, presents aspects that are relevant for assessing the question of whether any goodwill impairment is permanent and describes the procedure for determining the amount of the write-down in detail; in turn, GAS 24 Intangible Assets in Consolidated Financial Statements sets out detailed guidance on the requirements of German commercial law relating to the accounting for other intangible assets.

The primary reference for Italian accounting legislation is *Codice civile*, *i.e.* the Civil Code, which defines the criteria for evaluating financial and non-financial assets and mandates write-downs for permanent losses in the value of such assets in Article (Art.) 2426. The Civil Code provisions are then interpreted and integrated by the national accounting standards issued by the Italian Accounting Body (Organismo Italiano di Contabilità—OIC). As far as here is concerned, it is appropriate to mention OIC 9 Write-downs for Impairment Losses of Tangible and Intangible Fixed Assets, OIC 16 Tangible Fixed Assets, OIC 20 Debt Securities, OIC 21 Equity Investments and OIC 24 Intangible Fixed Assets (OIC, 2023).

In the Netherlands, the EU Directive is transposed into Book 2, Title 9 of the *Duch Law* (DL), *i.e.* the Dutch Civil Code, which provides the rules for preparing financial statements and applies to a wide range of legal entities that exercise commercial activities, both profit and non-profit. Within the DL, value adjustments are regulated by Art. 387 *Other decreases in the value of assets*. Moreover, the Dutch Accounting Standards Board (DASB) has included extensive requirements in a specific Dutch Accounting Standard (DAS). Indeed, DAS 121 Impairment of Assets offers guidelines on the value adjustment of assets according to Art. 387(4) of the DL and reversal of such reductions in value under Art. 387(5) of the Dutch Civil Code. Designed with a structure like IAS 36, DAS 121 describes possible indications of impairment from internal and external sources, offers detailed guidelines to measure the recoverable amount, the impairment loss, and the reversal of an impairment loss for individual assets and cash-generating units, and provides for disclosure requirements. In addition, DAS 210 Intangible Fixed Assets offers guidelines on the amortization of intangible assets.

The key Spanish regulation dealing with the write-downs for impairment losses is represented by the Spanish Generally Accepted Accounting Principles (GAAP), also known as *Plan General de Contabilidad* (PGC), *i.e.* General Accounting Plan. The current PGC was issued in 2021 (ICAC, 2021a), and there is a PGC simplified for SMEs (ICAC, 2021b). Regarding the provisions on impairment, it is included in the Part Two *Rules of recognition and measurement*, with specific rules regarding tangible, intangible and financial assets. The regulation for SMEs is included in the General Accounting Plan for SMEs (PGC PYMES) and is aligned with the PGC.

In Sweden, the EU Directive is transposed into the *Årsredovisningslagen* (ÅRL), *i.e.* the Annual Accounts Act, which regulates at a general level the reporting formats, the classification criteria, the principles of recognition and measurement, and disclosures. The provisions for value adjustment of assets are contained in Chapter 4. Moreover, the Swedish Accounting Standards Board has issued two sets of national accounting standards for non-listed legal entities depending on the size of the firm (K2 and K3). K3 (BFNAR 2012:1) contains the guidelines for the annual report and consolidated financial statements. Within K3, Chapter 27 Impairments is structured into general recommendations and comments. It describes possible indications of impairment from internal and external sources, offers detailed guidelines to measure the recoverable amount, the impairment loss, and the reversal of an impairment loss for individual assets and cash-generating units, and provides for disclosure requirements. In its turn, K2 (BFNAR 2016:8) offers the guidelines for the annual report of smaller companies. Within K2, Chapter 10 Intangible and Tangible Fixed Assets deals with intangible and tangible fixed assets and introduces some simplifications compared to the provisions for large-sized companies as regards depreciation and impairment of machinery, equipment and intangible assets. It also deals with the reversal of an impairment loss and introduces special rules for limited companies.

The United Kingdom legal framework for a company's annual report and accounts is attributable to the *Companies Act, The Large and Medium-sized Companies and Groups (Accounts and Reports) Regulations 2008* (SI[3] 2008/410), and *The Small Companies and Groups (Accounts and Directors' Report) Regulations 2008* (SI 2008/409). Moreover, there are accounting standards (UK GAAP) set by a private-sector body, the Audit, Reporting and Governance Authority. The relevant local UK GAAPs are FRS 100 Application of Financial Reporting Requirements, FRS 102 The Financial Reporting Standard applicable in the UK and Republic of Ireland and FRS 105 The Financial Reporting Standard applicable to the Micro-entities Regime. FRS 102 and FRS 105 dedicate a specific section (Section 27 and Section 22, respectively) to the impairment of assets and the recognition of impairment losses.

3 Permitting or Requiring Value Adjustments to Financial Fixed Assets

Art. 12 of the EU Directive contains *Special provisions relating to certain balance sheet items* and deals, among others, with the accounting for value adjustments to financial fixed assets. In detail, at point 6(a), the EU Directive provides for an explicit option, that *"Member States may permit or require value adjustments to be made in respect of financial fixed assets, so that they are valued at the lower figure to be attributed to them at the balance sheet date"*. Mentioning the *lower figure* that can be attributed to an asset at the year-end, this provision refers to the recognition of value reductions, or write-downs or impairment losses.

Although the great majority of Member States included in this analysis opted for requiring the recognition of value adjustments to undertakings in their country, some distinctive features can be underlined as regards: (a) the presence or absence of

[3] A Statutory Instrument (SI) is the principal form in which delegated legislation is made in Great Britain. SIs are governed by the Statutory Instruments Act 1946. A SI is used when an Act of Parliament passed after 1947 confers a power to make, confirm or approve delegated legislation on: (i) the Queen and states that it is to be exercisable by Order in Council; or (ii) a Minister of the Crown and states that it is to be exercisable by SI. On the website of the UK Parliament, it is stated that SIs *"are the most common form of secondary (or delegated) legislation. The power to make a statutory instrument is set out in an Act of Parliament and nearly always conferred on a Minister of the Crown. The Minister is then able to make law on the matters identified in the Act, and using the parliamentary procedure set out in the Act*".

specific provisions for financial fixed assets (compared to other fixed assets); (b) the permission or requirement to recognize value adjustments; and (c) the prediction about the permanence over time of the value reduction.

In Italy, a unique evaluation criterion is set for all fixed assets, notwithstanding their nature as tangible, intangible or financial assets. Indeed, Art. 2426, point 3, of the Civil Code requires that fixed assets whose year-end value results as permanently lower than the book value (computed as historical cost less accumulated depreciation, when applicable) must be written down (Codice Civile, 2023). The requirement of permanence over time is thus an integral part of the provision common for all fixed assets, including financial assets. The local GAAP OIC 20 and 21 require an impairment test for financial assets only if there are indicators of impairment. OIC 20 underlines that the loss is lasting whenever it is unlikely that the causes of the loss will disappear in the short term. Even for investees, a loss for the year may not be considered lasting if, for example, the investee has a convincing business plan and expects a return to profit in the short term. However, specific provisions are set for financial instruments that shall be measured with the equity method or at amortized cost (*e.g.* for equity investment held for sale, an impairment loss is recognized in case the carrying value is higher than the fair value).

The Spanish PGC classifies financial instruments into the following categories: (a) instruments measured at fair value through profit and loss; (b) instruments at the amortized cost; (c) instruments measured at fair value through equity; and (d) instruments measured at historical cost. The instruments in category (a) are always benchmarked with fair value at the end of each period. For the instruments in all other categories, the Spanish PGC requires a check at least every year on the presence of impairment indicators, among which the modification of the contractual cash flows of a financial asset due to the issuer's financial difficulties is mentioned (PGC, 2021, Part Two, Section 9 Financial Instruments). In such case, the recoverable amount of the financial asset shall be estimated (PGC 2021, Part Two, Sections 2, 5 and 9), but there is no explicit reference to the permanence of the value reduction over time (PGC, 2021, Part Two, Section 9 Financial Instruments).

In France, the measurement criteria for financial assets are included in a specific section of the *Plan Comptable General Version Consolidée* (PCG), namely in the Title 2—Assets. Chapter 2 of this Title is dedicated to the financial assets and requires write-downs, providing specific rules for each category. Like Spain, there is no explicit reference to the permanence of the value reduction over time (PGC, 2019, Title 2, Chapter 2 Financial Assets, Art. 221-1 and following).

The Danish Financial Statement Act (Årsregnskabsloven) states that if a company has financial fixed assets that are measured at cost and are recognized at a higher value than the fair value, then the company must provide information on the fair value of the assets, the recognized value and the reason why a write-down has not been recorded (§88b). Such financial fixed assets can be identified as investments in subsidiaries and associated companies, investments in joint ventures and joint operations, and unqualified shares. Considering this provision, Denmark has decided to permit value adjustments against financial fixed assets, without requiring them.

Similarly, no specific reference is found in the regulation as regards the permanence over time of the value reduction.

In Germany, a general statement is set out for all fixed assets. Indeed, the HGB, Third Book, First Chapter, states that fixed assets shall be reduced by depreciation and by impairment losses in the event of a prospective permanent reduction in value (§253 (1).1 and (3).5)). However, a provision is added for financial assets, whose impairment losses may also be recognized if the prospective reduction in value is not permanent (§253 (3).6).

In the UK, Part 2, Section B of Schedule 1 of SI 2008/410 and SI 2008/409 contains specific provisions for diminution in the value of fixed financial assets (or fixed asset investments). The general provision goes in the sense of permitting value adjustments of financial fixed assets. However, regulation is stricter in case the value reduction is expected to be permanent. Indeed, provisions for diminution in value must be made for any fixed asset (whether its useful economic life is limited or not) that has diminished in value if the reduction in its value is expected to be permanent and the amount to be included in respect of it must be reduced accordingly (§19.(2)).

Provisions like the UK ones have been introduced also in the Netherlands and Sweden. In the Netherlands, Art. 387, §3, of the Dutch Law, titled *Other decreases in value of assets*, introduces the evaluation criterion provided for all fixed assets and states that account shall be taken of any reduction in their value, if this is expected to be permanent. It then proceeds with a specific rule for financial fixed assets, stating that all events of any reduction in value occurring on the balance sheet date shall be accounted for. This last statement means that value adjustments of financial fixed assets, differently from value adjustments of other fixed assets, may also be considered when the value adjustment is not permanent. In Sweden, these rules are contained in the ÅRL, Chapter 4, §5.

Table 1 provides a summary of the provisions about value adjustments of financial fixed assets in the countries analysed.

4 Value Adjustments for Tangible and Intangible Fixed Assets

In line with IAS/IFRS, the EU Directive recognizes that fixed assets may have limited or indefinite useful lives. Indeed, Art. 12, point 6(b), of the EU Directive states that "*value adjustments shall be made in respect of fixed assets, whether their useful economic lives are limited or not, so that they are valued at the lower figure to be attributed to them at the balance sheet date if it is expected that the reduction in their value will be permanent*". The EU Directive does not list which assets may have an indefinite useful life; however, such a decision is left to the single Member States.

Table 1 Cross-country overview of value adjustments of financial fixed assets

Provisions	Germany	Italy	Spain	France	Denmark	Sweden	Netherlands	UK
Specific provisions	Yes	No	Yes	Yes	Yes	Yes	Yes	Yes
Permitted (perm.) or required (req.)	Req.	Req.	Req.	Req.	Perm.	Permanent req. Temporary perm.	Permanent req. Temporary perm.	Permanent req. Temporary perm.
Permanent	No	Yes	No reference	No reference	No reference	See above	See above	See above

Source: Authors' elaboration on country-specific regulation

Although the EU Directive provides for an evaluation criterion for all fixed assets to be applied by all Member States (without any option), it is worth considering whether the latter have adopted different policies as regards specific aspects, namely (a) the distinction between fixed assets with finite or indefinite useful life; (b) the existence of specific rules on depreciation of certain assets; (c) the timing of the assessment for value adjustments (*e.g.* impairment test execution); and (d) any details introduced about the permanence over time of value adjustments.

In Sweden, the Act of Law ÅRL, Chapter 4, §4, requires that fixed assets with a finite useful life are depreciated systematically over the period during which the company expects to use the asset. All fixed assets are deemed to have a finite useful life. As regards tangible assets, the only exception is land, which is supposed to have an unlimited useful life and thus is not depreciated (K3, Chapter 17 Tangible Fixed Assets). As regards intangible assets, the Swedish regulation admits that companies may face difficulties in assessing the useful life of those intangible assets that represent capitalized development costs. Therefore, if the useful life of such assets cannot be determined with a reasonable degree of certainty, the depreciation period shall be of five years. Similarly, the useful life of goodwill is assumed in five years maximum, unless another longer period can be determined with a reasonable degree of certainty (ÅRL, Chapter 4, §4(2)). As specified by K3 in Chapter 19 Business Combinations and Goodwill, this means that goodwill may only in rare cases be written off for longer than five years. Moreover, the Swedish regulation requires that if, on the balance sheet date, a tangible or intangible fixed asset has a lower value than the one determined as the historical cost net of depreciation, it must be written down to this lower value under the condition that the decline in value is assumed to be permanent (ÅRL Chapter 4, §5). In Chapter 27, K3 specifies that an entity shall assess at each balance sheet date whether there is any indication of impairment and provides a list of the external and internal information that shall necessarily be considered for such an assessment. Some examples are a significant decline in the market value of the asset due to reasons other than its age or normal use (external information) and a return on the asset that is or will be lower than previously assumed (internal information). Finally, as regards permanence over time of the value reduction, Chapter 27 underlines that the recoverable amount reflects an assessment of the cash flows expected to be generated by the asset throughout its remaining useful life and that this implies there is a long-term perspective in such an assessment.

In Germany, the HGB, Third Book, First Chapter, states that impairment losses must be recognized on fixed assets in the event of a prospective permanent reduction in value, irrespective of whether they have a limited useful life (§253 (3).5). Moreover, the HGB provides for the costs of acquisition or production of all fixed assets with a limited useful life being depreciated according to a regular schedule, *i.e.* over the financial years in which the asset can prospectively be used (§253 (3).1 and (3).2). Differently from IAS/IFRS, the German regulation explicitly identifies purchased goodwill as an asset of limited useful life (§246 (1).4). The accounting standard GAS 23 adds that the cost incurred for goodwill must be amortized over the financial years in which it is expected to be used. Other specific provisions are also introduced by the HGB for the depreciation of goodwill and self-produced intangible fixed assets, which shall be amortized over 10 years whenever, in exceptional cases, their prospective useful life cannot be estimated reliably (§253 (3).3 and (3).4). Moreover, GAS 24 states that intangible assets that can be used indefinitely are not amortized. However, in case in case maintenance measures are the only reason why intangible assets can be used indefinitely, such assets must be amortized.[4] As regards value adjustments of goodwill, GAS 23 specifies the carrying amount of goodwill must be reduced by write-downs in the event of expected permanent impairment, thus confirming the general rule.

The Italian Civil Code sets the evaluation criteria of fixed assets in several points of Art. 2426. It states that the cost of tangible and intangible fixed assets, whose useful life is limited, must be depreciated according to the residual possibility of usage. Companies are granted the option to modify the depreciation plan, however providing disclosure on the reasons for the change in the notes to the financial statement (point 2). OIC 16 specifies that depreciation does not apply to land and artworks, because their usefulness is potentially unlimited. In turn, OIC 24 specifies that no temporal limit is identified for the amortization of intangible assets other than goodwill; however, it is not possible to extend the amortization timeframe beyond the legal or contractual limit. Useful life may be shorter than such limit, in consistency with the period during which the company intends to use the asset. Concerning brands, amortization shall be accomplished in 20 years maximum. Point 6 of Art. 2426 is dedicated to goodwill, to confirm it shall be amortized over its useful life and require goodwill amortization in no more than 10 years in case its useful life cannot be estimated reliably. OIC 24 (§66) adds that the useful life of goodwill shall be estimated at its initial recognition and cannot be modified subsequently. Moreover, it allows goodwill amortization in more than 10 years, if companies have concrete expectations that its useful life is so long, based on objective facts and circumstances. In no case, goodwill amortization can be longer than 20 years, however. Finally, as regards value adjustments, a unique evaluation criterion is set for all fixed assets, notwithstanding their nature as tangible, intangible or financial assets. Indeed, according to Art. 2426, point 3 and OIC 9, the book value (computed as historical cost less accumulated depreciation, when applicable) must be written down when there is a long-lasting loss in value. A check on the presence of impairment indicators is due at the end of each accounting period, examples of which are provided by OIC 9. This accounting standard also provides detailed guidance on how to calculate the recoverable amount. The procedure is consistent with the IAS36 approach using discounted cash flows. In addition, the OIC 9 provides the option to adopt a simplified approach to impairment for companies below certain dimensional thresholds (*i.e.* small entities and micro-entities). The simplified approach is based on the concept of "depreciation capability", that is the ability of the prospective economic flow (*i.e.* EBITDA) to cover the depreciation expenses. The economic flow is not discounted.

---

[4]For an example list of these assets, see Section 248(2) of the HGB.

The Dutch Law does not introduce any distinction between assets with a finite or indefinite useful life; yet, it disciplines amortization and value adjustments in detail. First, Book 2, Title 9, Art. 386(1) introduces a general rule according to which depreciation shall be independent of the result of the financial year. Moreover, according to Art. 386(4), all fixed assets with a limited useful life are subject to annual depreciation consistent with their expected future useful life. A few constraints are introduced for a few asset categories, however. First, the capitalized costs related to the issue of shares shall be depreciated over five years maximum (Art. 386(3)). Second, it is admitted that in exceptional cases, the useful life of development costs and goodwill cannot be estimated reliably. When this happens, these costs are amortized over a period that cannot exceed 10 years. In such cases, the reasons for the amortization period for goodwill must be disclosed in the notes. DAS 210 (§401) complements the Dutch Law by maintaining that there is a rebuttable presumption that the maximum useful life on an intangible fixed asset is 20 years from the time the asset is available for use. Art. 387(3) generically states that in valuing fixed assets, any value reduction shall be accounted for, under the condition it is expected to be permanent. The Dutch Law does not indulge in any other specific provision, and especially, it does not introduce any guidelines for assessing value reductions, or any requirement for compulsory annual impairment testing. However, DAS 121 (§202) states that a legal entity shall assess at each reporting date whether there is any evidence that an asset may be impaired.

In the UK, SI 2008/410 and SI 2008/409 state that provisions for diminution in value must be made for any fixed asset (whether its useful economic life is limited or not) that has diminished in value if the reduction in its value is expected to be permanent and the amount to be included in respect of it must be reduced accordingly (§19.(2)). FRS 102 and FRS 105 do not explicitly mention permanence over time of the value reduction. They state that an intangible asset other than goodwill shall be carried at cost or fair value at the date of revaluation[5] less any subsequent accumulated amortization and subsequent accumulated impairment losses (FRS 102, §§18.18A and 18.18B and FRS 105, §13.8). As regards goodwill, the acquirer shall measure it at cost less accumulated amortization and impairment losses, following the principles stated by FRS 102 (§§18.19-18.24) and FRS 105 (§§13.9-13.14). All intangible assets (including goodwill) shall be considered to have a finite useful life; thus, their depreciable amount shall be allocated on a systematic basis over its useful life. The entity shall choose an amortization method that reflects the pattern in which it expects to consume the asset's future economic benefits. If the entity cannot determine that pattern reliably, it shall use the straight-line method (FRS 102, §§18.21-18.22 and FRS 105, §§13.11-13.12). The useful life of an intangible asset that arises from contractual or other legal rights shall not exceed the period of the contractual or other legal rights but may be shorter depending on the period over which the entity expects to use the asset (FRS

[5]FRS 105 (§§13.6 and 13.8) states that a micro-entity shall measure a separately acquired intangible asset only at cost.

102, §18.19; FRS 105, §13.9). If, in exceptional cases, an entity is unable to make a reliable estimate of the useful life of an intangible asset (including goodwill), the life shall not exceed 10 years (FRS 102, §18.20 and §19.23; FRS 105, §13.10 and §14.2). As regards value adjustments, in the UK an entity shall assess at each reporting date whether there is any indication that an asset may be impaired, providing some examples of indicators of impairment (FRS 102, §27.9; FRS 105, §22.7). If there is no indication of impairment, it is not necessary to estimate the recoverable amount. If any such indication exists, the entity shall estimate the recoverable amount of the asset by applying the provisions of FRS 102 (Section 27, §18.25 and §19.23) or FRS 105 (Section 22, §13.15 and §14.2). Local GAAP state also that if there is an indication that an asset may be impaired, this may indicate that the entity should review the remaining useful life, the depreciation (amortization) method or the residual value for the asset and adjust it following the section of this FRS applicable to the asset, even if no impairment loss is recognized for the asset (FRS 102, §27.10; FRS 105, §22.8).

In France, Art. 214-15 of the PCG requires that an entity assesses at each year-end whether there is any indication that an asset may have lost value. When there is an indication of impairment, an impairment test shall be performed by comparing the net book value of the asset to its present value. According to the same article, goodwill is tested for impairment at least once a year notwithstanding the existence of signals of a loss of value. This is because goodwill is assumed to have an unlimited period of use, as stated by Art. 214-3. However, this assumption does not apply in case the company expects that goodwill has a limited period of usage (Art. 214-3). In the latter case, goodwill is amortized over its useful life or, if this duration cannot be reliably determined, over 10 years. As regards value adjustments, the general rule is that if the present value of a fixed asset falls below its net book value, the latter is reduced to the present value by recognizing an impairment loss (Art. 214-17). France indulges in enlisting possible signals of impairment in its regulation: according to Art. 214-16, a company should at a minimum consider market value, significant changes, interest rate or return as external sources. It also should at minimum consider obsolescence or physical degradation, significant changes in usage patterns, and/or lower performance to consumers as external sources.

Regarding Spain, the cost model is applied to tangible and intangible fixed assets. As a rule, intangible assets are considered to have a definite useful life (PGC 2021, Part Two, Section 5 Intangible Assets). If the useful life cannot be estimated, the PGC establishes a maximum of 10 years. This rule applies to goodwill too. Intangibles shall be tested for impairment if there are indications of loss in their value. The Spanish PGC requires a check on the presence of impairment indicators at least every year for both tangible and intangible assets (PGC, 2021, Part Two, Section 2 Fixed Assets; Section 5 Intangible Assets). The Spanish PGC requires the estimation of the recoverable amount only when there is evidence of impairment for all types of assets, including financial assets (PGC 2021, Part Two, Sections 2, 5 and 9). It also provides some guidance on how to calculate the recoverable amount.

In Denmark, *Section 43* of the Act requires that the value of tangible fixed assets and intangible fixed assets with a limited useful life is reduced by systematic depreciation over their useful life. However, this rule does not apply to assets that are continuously adjusted to fair value under *Section 38*, *i.e.* investment property and living animals and plants which are biologically transformed for sale, processing, consumption or breeding of additional animals and plants measured according to the fair value model. This second provision limits the application of *Section 43* to fixed assets valued according to the cost model. The amount of the depreciation must take into account the expected residual value of the asset at the end of its useful life (Subsection 2). Moreover, in exceptional cases when a company is not able to reliably estimate the useful life of goodwill and development costs, this is assumed to be 10 years (Subsection 3). Before the EU Directive was adopted in Denmark, *Section 43* (Subsection 3) fixed a maximum of 20 years for the depreciation period for intangible assets. However, this provision was considered as consistent with Art. 12(11) of the new EU Accounting Directive, which maintains that intangible assets, in the same way as tangible assets, shall be depreciated over their useful life. Therefore, an amendment to the Danish Financial Statements Act was introduced in 2015 for the sake of consistency with the EU Directive. The explanatory note to the amendment explicitly states that if a company has intangible assets with a useful life of 50 years, these intangible assets shall be amortized over 50 years. However, if the intangible asset is amortized over a particularly long period, the justification for such a long useful life of the asset is more demanding. As regards value adjustments, *Section 42* provides that fixed assets are written down to the recoverable amount if the latter is lower than the carrying amount (Subsection 1). IAS 36 shall be used in Denmark as the basis for interpreting the provisions of the Act on the impairment of non-current assets.

Table 2 provides a summary of the provisions about value adjustments of tangible and intangible fixed assets in the countries analysed.

5 Reversal of a Value Reduction

As regards the reversal of an impairment loss, Art. 12, point 6(d), of the EU Directive explicitly maintains that the value adjustment (*i.e.* impairment loss) "*may not continue if the reasons for which the value adjustments were made have ceased to apply; this provision shall not apply to value adjustments made in respect of goodwill*". In this case, no room for discretion is granted to Member States, which have literally transposed these provisions in their respective regulations (*e.g.* the Italian OIC 9, the German GAS 23, the Swedish ÅRL 4:5). Most national regulations specify that the impairment can be reversed up to threshold set by the pre-impairment carrying value of the asset. Goodwill is an exception because in this case, the assumption is that an increase in its recoverable amount would likely

Table 2 Cross-country overview of the requirements on value adjustments for tangible and intangible fixed assets

Provisions	Germany	Italy	Spain	France	Denmark	Sweden	Netherlands	UK
Useful life	May be indefinite	Finite only, except for land and artworks	Finite only	Finite only, except for goodwill	Finite only	Finite only, except for land	Finite only	Finite only
Rules on depreciation of certain assets	Yes, for goodwill and self-produced intangible fixed	Yes, for goodwill and brands	Yes, for intangible assets	Yes, for goodwill	Yes, for goodwill and capitalized development costs	Yes, for goodwill and capitalized development costs	Yes, for goodwill, capitalized costs related to the issue of shares and capitalized development costs	Yes, for intangible asset
Timing of impairment indicator assessment		Annual	Annual	Annual	Annual	Annual	Annual	Annual
Timing of value adjustments	Upon impairment indicators	Upon impairment indicators	Upon impairment indicators	Annual for goodwill. Upon impairment indicators for other assets	Upon impairment indicators	Upon impairment indicators	Upon impairment indicators	Upon impairment indicators
Permanence over time of value adjustments	Not detailed	Not detailed	Not detailed	Not detailed	Not detailed	Detailed	Not detailed	Not mentioned

Source: Authors' elaboration on country-specific regulation

represent internally generated goodwill, which is a hardly identifiable resource. The provision is aligned with IAS 36.

In several jurisdictions, it is indicated that the assessment of a reversal in an asset's value reduction must be referred to the same reasons which led to the initial impairment (*e.g.* OIC9 in Italy or PCG in France). Namely, when the causes of the impairment no longer exert their impact, there shall be a reversal. The reversal cannot be attributed to other reasons, instead. For example, a tangible asset impaired because of physical obsolescence cannot be re-evaluated because of generically improved market perspectives. This is consistent with the exclusion of the revaluation model for fixed assets by such jurisdictions.

6 Disclosure Requirements on Value Adjustments

All the jurisdictions examined required disclosure of value adjustments, in most cases by providing for their separate recognition in the profit and loss statement. Some countries like Germany, the Netherlands and the UK allow disclosure in the footnotes as an alternative. Focusing on the specific disclosure on impairment of fixed tangible and intangible assets (*i.e.* additional to other information included in the footnotes regarding such assets), jurisdictions can be classified into two groups. Belonging to the first group, Italy and Spain strictly follow IAS 36 and mandate the most extensive disclosure requirements. More specifically, these two countries require information on:

- Basic assumptions and methodology used to determine the fair value less cost to sell or the value in use.
- Time horizon of cash flow projections.
- Discount rates used.
- Growth rate used to determine the terminal value.

Spain also requires a description of the triggering events and is the only jurisdiction requiring information on the cash-generating units. More specifically, Spain requires a description of the cash-generating unit that includes goodwill and other intangible assets or items of property, plant and equipment, and details on the method used to aggregate assets for identifying the cash-generating group, if this has changed compared to prior reporting periods. France is the closest jurisdiction requesting information on criteria used to determine fair value less cost to sell or value in use and on the triggering events.

The second group includes Sweden, the Netherlands, Denmark, Germany and the UK, which do not require disclosure that helps external reports' users to understand how the impairment has been calculated. The UK only requires information on events and circumstances leading to the impairment. Denmark's regulation has a provision which can cover issues related to value adjustments, as it is required that financial statements disclose any material uncertainties about the recognition and measurement of assets and liabilities in the footnotes and in the management report.

If there is a "material uncertainty", then an impairment is likely or needs to be recognized. Information on value adjustments of financial assets is usually required together with other information about the measurement of such assets. This emphasizes the patchwork approach of European countries on the topic of disclosure, which is summarized in Table 3.

7 Specific Provisions for Smaller Companies

Regulators and standard setters of some of the countries examined have formulated specific provisions according to the company size, to better meet the needs of smaller companies and those of the stakeholders who gravitate around them. Most of these provisions focus on the disclosures required in the notes to the financial statement.

France provides a very detailed regulation on disclosure: indeed, it requires a description of the movements that occurred during the year for each asset category. Table 4 shows the "basic system" of disclosure on write-downs provided for in Art. 841-3 of the PCG.

Compared to the framework presented in Table 4, a synthetic model is established for SMEs. In detail, Art. 831-1 provides that legal entities placed on an option or by operation of law under the simplified tax regime may submit an abbreviated annexe focused on information of significant importance on the assets and financial situation as well as on the result of the company. As regards fixed assets, Art. 831-2 requires disclosure of what follows: the valuation methods applied to the various items of the annual accounts, the methods for calculating depreciation and the movements in account items relating to fixed assets, amortization, provisions and depreciation. In separate financial statements, small businesses (as defined in Art. L. 123-16 of the Commercial Code) can amortize goodwill over 10 years. This simplification measure can be adopted at any time and will be applied to all goodwill subsequently recognized.

As regards Germany, the Second Chapter—Supplementary Provisions for Corporation (Stock Corporations, Partnerships Limited by Shares and Limited Liability Companies) and Certain Commercial Partnerships included in the Third Book of the HGB contains, *inter alia*, some specific provisions for small corporations and micro-corporations. More precisely, such companies (defined in §267 and §267a, respectively) are only required to prepare an abridged balance sheet (§266). Moreover,

Table 3 Cross-country overview of disclosure requirements

Disclosure requirements	Germany	Italy	Spain	France	Denmark	Sweden	Netherlands	UK
Impairment separate recognition in P&L	Yes (footnotes alternatively)	Yes	Yes	Yes	Footnotes	Yes (reversal also)	Yes (footnotes alternatively)	Yes (footnotes alternatively) (reversal also)
FVLCS /VIU (amount)	No	No	No	No	No	No	No	No
Base assumptions/methodology used to determine FVLCS or VIU	No	Yes	Yes	Yes	No	No	No	No
Time Horizon	No	Yes	Yes	No	No	No	No	No
Discount rate	No	Yes	Yes	No	No	No	No	No
Growth rate	No	Yes	Yes	No	No	No	No	No
Triggering events	No	No	Yes	Yes	No	No	No	Yes
Information by CGUs	No	No	Yes	No	No	No	No	No

Source: Authors' elaboration on country-specific regulation

Table 4 Example of "Table of Write-Downs" disclosure from the France PCG (2019, Art. 841-3)

	Situations and movements (b)			
	A	B	C	D
Rubrics (a)	Write-downs at the beginning of the year	Increases: allocations for the year	Decreases: value recoveries of the year	Write-downs at the end of the year (c)
Intangible fixed assets				
Tangible fixed assets				
Inventory				
Debt				
Financial fixed assets				
Total				

Source: PCG (2019, Art. 841-3)
[a]To be developed if necessary
[b]Entities subdivide columns as needed
[c]The amount of impairment at the end of the year is equal to the algebraic sum of the previous columns (A + B – C = D)

§288[6] states that small corporations do not need to provide the disclosures under §284 (3), §285 No. 18 and No. 26[7] (§288 (1)). Focusing on the core aspect, smaller companies are exempted from providing a separate breakdown in the notes on the development of the individual items of the fixed assets, *i.e.* of the additions, disposals, transfers, depreciations, impairment loss recognition and reversals recognized in a financial year (§284 (3)).

As for the legislation in force in Italy, it is noted that companies that do not exceed the size limits provided for in Art. 2435-*bis* of the Civil Code can draw up the financial statements in abbreviated form. In this regard, OIC 9 dedicates a few paragraphs to the information to be indicated in the notes to the financial statements. In detail, the standard provides for the following. First, it recalls Art. 2427, §1, of the Civil Code, which requires indicate in the notes the criteria applied in the valuation of the items represented in the financial statement, in the value adjustments and the

[6]See §288—Size-related relief.

[7]§285, *inter alia*, states that the following information shall be included in the notes: "18. for financial instruments pertaining to financial assets (§266 (2) A. III.) that are shown with a value above their fair value since an extraordinary depreciation was omitted pursuant to §253 (3) sentence 6, . . . the reasons for an omission of depreciation including factual evidence which indicates that the impairment will presumably not be of a permanent nature; . . . 26. on units in investment funds within the meaning of §1 (10) of the Investment Code or investment shares in investment stock corporations with variable capital within the meaning of §§108 to 123 of the Investment Code or comparable EU investment funds or comparable foreign investment funds of more than one tenth, broken down by investment objectives, the reasons for an omission of depreciation in accordance with §253 (3) sentence 6, including factual evidence suggesting that the impairment will presumably not be of a permanent nature; Number 18 is not to be applied insofar" (§285 No. 18, No. 26).

movements of fixed assets, specifying for each item: the cost; previous revaluations, depreciation and write-downs; acquisitions, shifts from one item to another, disposals that occurred during the year; the revaluations, depreciation and write-downs made during the year; and the total of revaluations regarding existing fixed assets at the end of the year (OIC 9, §40). Second, it recalls Art. 2423, §4, of the Civil Code, which states that it is not necessary to comply with the obligations regarding recognition, evaluation, presentation and disclosure when their observance has irrelevant effects on providing a true and fair view. In this case, entities illustrate the criteria with which they implemented this provision in the notes to the financial statements (OIC 9, §41). Third, regarding write-downs for permanent losses in value, the OIC 9, §42, underlines that the entities electing the adoption of the simplified method (*i.e.* small entities or micro-entities) must disclose the choice in the notes to the financial statements (see above Sect. 4).

In Spain, reduced disclosure is established for SMEs (PGC for SMEs). In detail, those drafting financial statements must analyse of the movement during the year of each of these balance sheet items and their corresponding accumulated depreciation and value adjustments due to accumulated value impairment, indicating the following: (a) opening balance; (b) entries, (c) exits and (d) final balance.

The Swedish Accounting Standard K2, Chapter 10, maintains that, for reasons of simplification, the useful life of machinery, equipment and intangible assets may be set at five years (§10.27). Machinery, equipment and intangible assets with a useful life of five years or less are written down if there is an apparent need to do so (§10.34). In case such assets have a useful life of more than five years, they should be written down if the usefulness of the asset to the entity has been significantly reduced as a result of an event (indication of impairment) that impairs the function or usefulness of the asset to the entity and the asset's usefulness to the entity cannot be expected to be recovered within two years after the indication of impairment occurred (§10.35). If the asset's usefulness to the entity is expected to be recovered within two years after the impairment indication occurred, the impairment is considered to be temporary and there is no need to recognize a loss. For example, an impairment may be triggered by a change in legislation that prevents the entity from using the asset in an economically viable way. If there are clear indications that legislation will change soon, so that the entity will regain an economically viable use of the asset, there would be no need to recognize an impairment. The Swedish regulation requires a sort of counterfactual proof. Permanence in time is proven in the absence of clues that the reasons for an impairment will fade shortly. A two-year time horizon appears to be a reasonable time frame for this assessment. Moreover, in the case of machinery, equipment and intangible assets, the asset should be written down either to the value the asset would have had if depreciation had been provided over a useful life of five years or to its fair value if that value is lower. An entity may write down an asset to a value higher than the value it would have had if it had been depreciated over a useful life of five years if it can demonstrate that the asset has a higher fair value (§10.36).[8]

As regards the UK, FRS 102 includes a specific section dedicated to small entities (*i.e.* Section 1A—Small Entities). This section sets out the information that shall be presented and disclosed in the financial statements of a small entity that chooses to apply the small entity regime (FRS 102, §1A.1). Section 1A "*requires small entities to apply the recognition and measurement requirements of FRS 102 but with a different disclosure regime, reflecting the fact that the EU Accounting Directive limits the number of specific disclosures that may be mandated for small entities*" (KPMG, 2015, p. 7). For example, as regards each item which is shown as a fixed asset in the small entity's statement of financial position, the cumulative amount of provisions for depreciation and impairment of assets included under that item at the beginning and the end of the reporting period shall be stated, as well as the amount of any other adjustments made in respect of any such provisions during the reporting period (FRS 102, §§1AC.13, 1AD.14). As regards impairment losses recognized by small entities in the UK, FRS 102 (§§1AC.20 and 1AD.20) states that provisions for impairment of fixed assets (including fixed asset investments) must be disclosed separately (or, for small entities in the Republic of Ireland, also in aggregate) in a note to the financial statements if not shown separately in the income statement. Finally, any provisions for impairment of fixed assets that are reversed because the reasons for which they were made have ceased to apply must be disclosed (either separately or in aggregate) in a note to the financial statements if not shown separately in the income statement (FRS 102, §§1AC.21 and 1AD.21).

In Denmark and in the Netherlands, no significant simplifications can be found to the advantage of smaller companies as regards the assessment of value adjustments and related disclosures.

8 Conclusions

The above analysis suggests that the level of convergence across countries varies concerning recognition, measurement, and disclosure of write-downs. As regards recognition, value adjustments are required in most jurisdictions. However, some jurisdictions permit them even if not permanent, like Sweden, the Netherlands and the UK. Voluntary write-downs of non-permanent value reductions may reduce cross-country comparability of financial statements. This can be an indication for future research as most research on cross-country comparison of accounting choices throughout the EU is still focused on different applications of IAS/IFRS (*e.g.* D'Arcy & Tarca, 2018; Fifield et al., 2011). Not only: permitting non-permanent value reduction allows managerial discretion, which prior research suggests is

[8] It shall be noted, however, that K2 (§10.4) provides a general advice to smaller companies not to recognize self-constructed intangible assets as assets, yet to prefer recognition as an expense.

mostly used to avoid write-downs (*e.g.* André et al., 2016; Ramanna & Watts, 2012; Riedl, 2004). The topic can be easily acknowledged as relevant if one thinks of the COVID-19 crisis, which sparked a heated debate about the transitory effect of lockdowns versus permanent changes in the market conditions, in the decision about going concern assessment and write-downs, with the latter being strictly related to going concerns issues (Geiger et al., 2021; Levy, 2020).

The analysis suggests a substantial degree of convergence on how to measure the value adjustments. Most jurisdictions appear to be aligned to the IAS 36, and some of them were aligned even before the Directive (*e.g.* the UK). Notably, only Italy allows a simplified approach to write-downs for small entities and micro-entities. This in turn highlights that future research is needed to understand how small entities cope with complex measurements, such as the projection of future cash flow, the selection of a proper discount rate and the calculation of the value of cash-generating units.

Furthermore, disclosure is the issue on which jurisdictions differ the most. Several jurisdictions like Sweden, the Netherlands and the UK do not require almost any disclosure on write-downs. The lack of standard requirements is a significant limitation to the comparability of financial statements across jurisdictions. More disclosure could also reassure financial reporting users about the reliability of write-downs in SMEs, in jurisdictions where there is no simplified approach for them. A policy implication of this analysis may be the recommendation to use the IAS 36 as a benchmark for disclosure in all jurisdictions.

Finally, and assuming a wider perspective, whether, under which conditions and to what purposes value adjustments in conformity with Directive 2013/34/EU are subject to managerial opportunism remains an empirical issue. Prior literature provides evidence of different behaviour according to a firm's ownership, as nonfamily firms use write-offs of tangible and intangible assets for earnings management purposes, while family firms recognize write-offs consistently with the firm's pre-write-off performance (Greco et al., 2015). Moreover, during economic crises goodwill impairments are found to be lower than expected in listed firms (Amel-Zadeh et al., 2023). The propensity towards value adjustments by private firms and the drivers of their accounting choices in this regard deserves specific attention, especially considering the relevance of such firms in the EU business arena.

References

Amel-Zadeh, A., Glaum, M., & Sellhorn, T. (2023). Empirical goodwill research: Insights, issues, and implications for standard setting and future research. *European Accounting Review, 32*(2), 415–446. https://doi.org/10.1080/09638180.2021.1983854

ANC 2014-03 (2019). Règlement de l'ANC n° 2014-03 du 5 juin 2014 relatif au Plan comptable général. available at: https://www.anc.gouv.fr/files/live/sites/anc/files/contributed/ANC/1_Normes_fran%c3%a7aises/Reglements/Recueils/PCG_Janvier2019/PCG_2019.pdf

André, P., Filip, A., & Paugam, L. (2016). Examining the patterns of goodwill impairments in Europe and the US. *Accounting in Europe, 13*(3), 329–352. https://doi.org/10.1080/17449480.2016.1260748

Codice Civile (2023). Italian Civil Code full text available in Italian at: https://www.gazzettaufficiale.it/sommario/codici/codiceCivile

d'Arcy, A., & Tarca, A. (2018). Reviewing IFRS goodwill accounting research: Implementation effects and cross-country differences. *The International Journal of Accounting, 53*(3), 203–226. https://doi.org/10.1016/j.intacc.2018.07.004

Danish Financial Statement Act (2019). Bekendtgørelse af årsregnskabsloven, LBK nr 838 af 08/08/2019. Full text available in Danish at: https://www.retsinformation.dk/eli/lta/2019/838

Dutch Accounting Standard Board (DASB). DAS 121 Impairment of Assets.

Dutch Accounting Standard Board (DASB). DAS 210 Intangible Fixed Assets.

Dutch Civil Code, Book 2 Legal Persons, Title 2.9 Annual accounts and annual report. Full text available at: http://www.dutchcivillaw.com/civilcodebook022.htm

European Financial Reporting Advisory Group. (2017, June). *What do we really know about goodwill and impairment?* (Discussion Paper).

Excerpt of German Commercial Code in the revised version published in the Federal Law Gazette Part III, section number 4100-1, last amended by Article 14 of the Act of December 22, 2020 (Federal Law Gazette I p. 3256).

Fifield, S., Finningham, G., Fox, A., Power, D., & Veneziani, M. (2011). A cross-country analysis of IFRS reconciliation statements. *Journal of Applied Accounting Research, 12*(1), 26–42. https://doi.org/10.1108/09675421111130595

Financial Accounting Standards Board (FASB). (2019, July). Identifiable intangible assets and subsequent accounting for goodwill (Discussion Paper).

Financial Reporting Council (FRC). FRS 100 (March 2018). Application of Financial Reporting Requirements.

Financial Reporting Council (FRC). FRS 102 (January 2022a). The Financial Reporting Standard applicable in the UK and Republic of Ireland.

Financial Reporting Council (FRC). FRS 105 (January 2022b). The Financial Reporting Standard applicable to the Micro-entities Regime.

Florio, C., Lionzo, A., & Corbella, S. (2018). Beyond firm-level determinants: The effect of M&A features on the extent of M&A disclosure. *Journal of International Accounting Research, 17*(3), 87–113. https://doi.org/10.2308/jiar-52226

Frii, P., & Hamberg, M. (2021). What motives shape the initial accounting for goodwill under IFRS 3 in a setting dominated by controlling owners? *Accounting in Europe, 18*(2), 218–248. https://doi.org/10.1080/17449480.2021.1912369

Geiger, M. A., Gold, A., & Wallage, P. (2021). *Auditor going concern reporting: A review of global research and future research opportunities*. Routledge.

German Accounting Standards Board (GASB). GAS 24. Summary (last revision 22.09.2017). Intangible assets in consolidated financial statements.

German Accounting Standards Board (GASB). GAS 23. Summary (last revision 09.03.2021). Accounting for subsidiaries in consolidated financial statements.

Glaum, M., Street, D. L., & Vogel, S. (2007). *Making Acquisitions Transparent: An Evaluation of M&A-Related IFRS Disclosures by European Companies in 2005*. Available at: https://www.pwc.dk/da/publikationer/assets/pwc-m-og-a-ifrs-survey-0307.pdf

Greco, G., Ferramosca, S., & Allegrini, M. (2015). The influence of family ownership on long-lived asset write-offs. *Family Business Review, 28*(4), 355–371. https://doi.org/10.1177/0894486515590017

Instituto de Contabilidad y Auditoria de Cuentas (ICAC). (2021a). *Plan general de contabilidad*, available at: https://www.boe.es/biblioteca_juridica/abrir_pdf.php?id=PUB-PB-2022-227

Instituto de Contabilidad y Auditoria de Cuentas (ICAC). (2021b). *Plan general de contabilitad de pequena y medianas empresas*, available at https://www.icac.gob.es/node/1703

International Accounting Standard Board (IASB). (2019, June). Goodwill and Impairment – Reintroduction of amortisation of goodwill (Staff Paper, Agenda ref 18B).
International Accounting Standard Board (IASB). (2020, March), Discussion Paper DP/2020/1, Business Combinations— Disclosures, Goodwill and Impairment.
International Accounting Standard Board (IASB). (2022, November). Goodwill and Impairment – Cover paper (Staff Paper, Agenda ref 18).
International Accounting Standard Board (IASB). (2023, January). Business Combinations – Disclosures, Goodwill and Impairment – Cover paper (Staff Paper, Agenda ref 18).
Jordan, C. E., & Clark, S. J. (2004). Big bath earnings management: The case of goodwill impairment under SFAS No. 142. *Journal of Applied Business Research, 20*(2), 63–70. https://doi.org/10.19030/jabr.v20i2.2206
KPMG. (2015). *Cutting through UK GAAP. KPMG's guide to the new financial reporing regime*, 2nd edition.
Levy, H. B. (2020). Financial reporting and auditing implications of the COVID-19 pandemic. *The CPA Journal, 90*(5), 26–33.
OIC. (2023). Italian Accounting Standards, available in Italian at: https://www.fondazioneoic.eu/?cat=14&lang=en
Ramanna, K., & Watts, R. L. (2012). Evidence on the use of unverifiable estimates in required goodwill impairment. *Review of Accounting Studies, 17*, 749–780. https://doi.org/10.1007/s11142-012-9188-5
Riedl, E. J. (2004). An examination of long-lived asset impairments. *The Accounting Review, 79*(3), 823–852. https://doi.org/10.2308/accr.2004.79.3.823
Swedish Annual Accounts Act (Årsredovisningslagen, ÅRL).
The Large and Medium-sized Companies and Groups (Accounts and Reports) Regulations 2008 (SI 2008/410).
The Small Companies and Groups (Accounts and Directors' Report) Regulations 2008 (SI 2008/409).
The Swedish Accounting Board's Guidelines. Annual report and consolidated accounts (K3) (last revision 12.11.2021) (Bokföringsnämndens VÄGLEDNING Årsredovisning och koncernredovisning (K3) Vägledning till BFNAR 2012:1 Uppdaterad 2021-11-12)
The Swedish Accounting Board's Guidelines. Annual report in small companies (K2) (last revision 12.11.2021) (Bokföringsnämndens VÄGLEDNING Årsredovisning i mindre företag (K2) Vägledning till BFNAR 2016:10 Uppdaterad 2021-11-12).

Accounting for Capital and Reserves, OCI and Profit Distribution

Marco Ghitti, Amedeo Pugliese, and Francesca Rossignoli

1 Introduction

One of the discerning features of the process leading to the passing of the Directive 2013/34/EU on 'the annual financial statements, consolidated financial statements and the related reports of certain types of undertakings' (i.e. the EU-D-34/2013 from now onwards) was the attempt to balance the need for a unified set of accounting rules and principles that would homogenise accounting practices of smaller and private firms in the EU, while allowing national legislators to exert enough flexibility to adapt the national general accounting principles to the specific features of the firms and the national economy (Andrè, 2017).

Such general trade-off subsumes most if not all the accounting issues analysed in this book and represents a key issue in relation to major changes in accounting rules and principles (Breuer, 2021). This is especially relevant regarding the accounting for equity, other comprehensive income and dividend distribution (i.e. Capital and Reserves onwards). Notwithstanding the homogeneity in terms of the items constituting part of the section Capital and Reserves, as detailed in the Annex IV,[1] noticeable differences still feature across jurisdictions in terms of what affects equity composition and which transactions (and accounting items) lead to increases or

[1] Annex IV details the structure of the Section L. Capital and reserves into the following: I Subscribed capital; II Share premium account; III Revaluation reserve; IV Reserves; V Profit or loss brought forward; VI Profit or loss for the financial year.

M. Ghitti · A. Pugliese (✉)
Università degli Studi di Padova, Padua, Italy
e-mail: marco.ghitti@unipd.it; amedeo.pugliese@unipd.it

F. Rossignoli
Università degli Studi di Verona, Verona, Italy
e-mail: francesca.rossignoli@univr.it

A. Incollingo, A. Lionzo (eds.), *The European Harmonization of National Accounting Rules*, SIDREA Series in Accounting and Business Administration,
https://doi.org/10.1007/978-3-031-42931-6_13

decreases in equity and consequently the extent of distributable income and reserves. As a general tenet, the definition of equity and distributable income is still largely affected by the 'prudence' principle that continues to be a key attribute of financial statements according to the EU-D-34/2013. In fact, both the recognition and measurement of assets and liabilities, and changes thereof are largely affected by the degree of prudence, thus bearing a direct effect on income and its volatility, equity, reserves and dividend distribution.

This chapter analyses how the accounting for Capital and Reserves and dividend distribution has been defined across different jurisdictions; in doing so, it offers three major contributions: first, it describes how the accounting for Capital and Reserves has been shaped by the adoption of the EU-D-34/2013 in the eight chosen countries (Denmark, France, Germany, Italy, the Netherlands, Spain, Sweden and the United Kingdom). For the sake of conciseness, our focus will be primarily on financial instruments, given the prominence of fair value measurement therein. As a matter of fact, changes in the way standard setters allow (or not) to make fair value(s) relevant to income or OCI largely affect capital, reserves and dividend distribution.

Second, given the relevance of Capital and Reserves as a 'contracting device' among the enterprise and its stakeholders, we point out the close connection between a series of real economic decisions (e.g. financing and investor protection) and accounting for Capital and Reserves (Bischof & Daske, 2016). Indeed, although the measurement of equity stems from accounting rules, such a measurement has implications along two main dimensions. In most countries, especially with code law traditions, equity serves as a 'third-party guarantee' when other corporate governance mechanisms perform poorly (Leuz et al., 2003; La Porta et al., 2008). For example, in countries like Italy or Spain, equity depletion (i.e. equity falling below a minimum threshold) triggers mandatory actions for board members and statutory auditors—such as calling on shareholders' meetings or filing for bankruptcy—as well as for shareholders (e.g. through a request of replenishing capital). In these countries, accounting rules tend to 'preserve' equity and limit dividend distribution, thus constraining the recognition of distributable income to stricter conditions. Next, most of the covenants in the private debt market rely on the book value of liabilities and equity (Beatty et al., 2008). That is, the degree of 'prudence' in measuring equity has direct implications on the breach of covenants and thus on the main financing terms (e.g. interest rates). In this light, we sought to analyse the underlying contextual conditions—at the country level—potentially explaining the different choices made by the national parliaments.

Third, we sought to pinpoint which accounting items and 'areas of considerations' (e.g. fixed assets, financial instruments and intangible assets), whose measurement and recognition criteria directly affect the measurement and representation of Capital and Reserves, drive the observable differences. For example, according to the EU-D-34/2013, Member States were offered the opportunity to opt for revaluation of fixed assets (Art. 7) and in the case they did, any revaluation should be booked in the balance sheet as part of the Capital and Reserves in which the higher value compared to the carrying amount should be part of the revaluation reserve that is not available for distribution unless it represents a gain fully realised (Alexander & Fasiello, 2021a).

Another major source of difference exists in terms of the fair value measurement: Member States are required to adopt it (Article 8 (1.a)) with the related changes in value to be included in the profit and loss account. The source of heterogeneity across Member States exists in terms of how to apply the prudence principle at the level of dividend distribution and the trade-off between a stricter adoption of the prudence principle and the accrual basis principle. For example, a key responsibility of the Member States relates to whether unrealised profits are accounted for in the profit and loss or included in a reserve, whereas losses in value are recognised at once in the profit and loss, with the prudence principle constraining and reducing the operation of the accrual basis principle.

The rest of the chapter is structured as follows: Sect. 2 discusses the nexus between the legal origin and background of a country/jurisdiction and the accounting for equity and reserves and dividend distribution. Section 3 analyses the differences across various jurisdictions in terms of specific accounting items playing a major role in affecting equity and dividend distribution. Section 4 concludes and offers avenues for potential future research.

2 Regulatory and Legal Background: Impact on Accounting for Capital and Reserves

The rules subsuming accounting for equity (i.e. Capital and Reserves) have two major economic implications typically disciplined by legal rules: limits to equity distributions and breaches of covenants. The heterogeneity across countries is highly significant in these matters.

Accounting-based information is key in transactions between different providers of capital, labour and good and the firm. Most financial contracts rely on accounting information. The positive accounting theory is based exactly on the idea that the use of accounting information enhances the efficiency of contracting by minimising contracting costs (Holthausen & Leftwich, 1983; Watts & Zimmerman, 1978).

The theory of incomplete contracts broadens this perspective on the role of accounting information in debt contracting (Christensen et al., 2016). The central tenet of this theory is that contracts are inherently incomplete, as the parties cannot negotiate all the possible future states of the world. When an unforeseen state occurs, incompleteness of contracts will inevitably trigger contract renegotiations, during which parties can behave opportunistically (e.g. borrowers may use asset substitution as a threat). Thus, incompleteness leads to post-contractual opportunism and hold-up problems that adversely affect the incentives of the parties to enter contracts. Incomplete contract theory suggests that ex-ante allocation of control rights alleviates hold-up problems in a contractual relationship. This happens because control rights determine the status quo in future renegotiations. Accounting information plays a determinant role within incomplete contract theory because the optimal allocation of control rights is contingent on a contractible signal (i.e. information) that reflects the underlying economics of the borrower (Aghion & Bolton, 1992; Hart

& Moore, 1998; Zender, 1991). As accounting information produces summary measures of firm performance, accounting signals are primary candidates for governing the state-contingent allocation of control rights.

The seminal papers in the law and finance field have shown that differences in legal protections for investors help explain why firms are financed and owned differently in different countries (La Porta et al., 1997, 1998). In the context of investor protection, rules are as important as the quality of their enforcement. Both the content of the law and its enforcement vary across countries and legal families (Djankov et al., 2008), explain the development of private credit markets (Djankov et al., 2007) and are linked to differences across bankruptcy codes (Davydenko & Franks, 2008). Countries with poor laws or enforcement have other substitute mechanisms of corporate governance. These adaptive mechanisms may in fact be incorporated into the law, or they may lie outside the law. One adaptation is to legally introduce mandatory standards of retention and distribution of profits and reserve to investors, which limit the opportunities for managerial expropriation (La Porta et al., 1998). For example, mandatory dividends may protect minority shareholders from incumbent managers. In some countries, companies are mandated by law to pay out a certain fraction of their earnings as dividends. Mandatory dividends have been documented only in French civil-law countries, consistent with the evidence that these countries do not have a strong legal protection for shareholders (La Porta et al., 1998). Another remedial mechanism is the existence of a legal reserve requirement to protect creditors. This requirement forces firms to maintain a certain level of minimum reserve as a percentage of share capital before distributing dividends. Such a mechanism is often coupled with the requirement of a minimum share capital to avoid automatic liquidation. This protects creditors, who have few other powers, by forcing an automatic liquidation before all the capital is wasted by the insiders. The evidence on the legal reserve requirement shows that it is almost never used in common-law countries but is often prescribed in all civil-law families (i.e. French and German), which tend to be less protective of unsecured creditors, and particularly in countries with German civil-law roots (e.g. Austria, Germany and Switzerland).

In this light, we could interpret the different implementations of the EU-D-34/2013 with regard to accounting for equity. All legal rules that discipline retention or distribution of Capital and Reserve rely on financial statements and thus depend on the equity measurement and representation. Therefore, accounting for equity and its implications for distributions should be stronger in southern European countries adopting the EU-D-34/2013, whose laws were influenced by the Napoleonic codes. As shown in Table 1, French civil-law countries (e.g. France, Greece, Italy and Spain) have systematically a creditor protection lower than English common-law countries.

Financial covenants are a second important tool of financial contracting that relies on accounting for equity. Financial contracts use covenants to regulate state-contingent control allocation when firms access external finance (Christensen et al., 2016). Typically, accounting information is a signal of debtor financial performance that triggers the application of covenants: that is, accounting proves

Table 1 Creditor rights index across time and regions

Legal origin	1978	1983	1988	1993	1998	2003
English	2.417	2.417	2.444	2.361	2.333	2.278
French	1.311	1.311	1.311	1.328	1.297	1.313
German	2.429	2.429	2.429	2.143	2.333	2.333
Nordic	2.250	2.250	2.500	2.000	1.750	1.750
Socialist	–	–	–	2.000	2.273	2.182
All	1.787	1.787	1.806	1.774	1.812	1.797
t-test English vs. French	4.664***	4.664***	4.719***	4.298***	4.364***	4.039***

Table 1 reports the creditor rights index (La Porta et al., 1998) by legal origins. Data are taken from Djankov et al. (2007). The creditor rights index scores the level of creditor protection based on four legal rights. It ranges from 0 to 4, where an higher index means a stronger protection for creditors

whether a covenant is fulfilled of breached. For example, the contract could impose explicit restrictions on borrowing whenever the leverage ratio exceeds certain thresholds, such as limits to distributions or the composition of the board of directors. The leverage ratio is an important covenant in financial markets (Nikolaev, 2010). Leverage computation is taken from financial statements; it thus depends on the measure of book value of equity.

Moreover, the link between covenants and accounting goes also in the direction of an increase in demand for accounting conservatism where there are covenants in financial contracts (Nikolaev, 2010). Therefore, country-level decisions about the adoption of the EU-D-34/2013 concerning accounting for equity can have a direct effect on the implementation and usage of covenants in the credit market.

For example, following Article 8 of the EU-D34/2013, Member States can require or authorise to evaluate derivates at fair value. If a state requires fair value accounting for derivatives while another state does not, the value of derivatives on the balance sheet will be different. In turn, this would lead to a different measurement of covenants, especially when derivatives are a liability like it is typically the case for interest rate swaps that are common for small and medium entities. Then, covenants are measured differently, and this affects financial contracts. Another example relates to the presence of micro-firms in a state. Micro-firms may avoid recognising derivatives on their balance sheet, while providing a minimum disclosure. If in each EU country, we have more micro-enterprises than in another country, covenant measurement and comparability may be affected.

3 An Analysis of the Key Accounting Items Affecting Equity Formation

Capital and Reserves incorporate values generated according to the recognition and measurement criteria stated for individual assets and liabilities. Consequently, values reported in the Capital and Reserves are likely to vary across the Member States in relation to the combination of the options allowed by the Accounting Directive EU-D-34/2013 matched with the options exerted by each Member State. Therefore, we focused on the effects on reserves of the accounting items whose treatments are more likely to be heterogeneous. This section shows the effects on reserves with reference to three specific accounting items: the revaluation of fixed asset, the change in fair value of financial instruments and the capitalisation of development costs (Table 2).

The first accounting item is the revaluation of fixed asset. The EU-D-34/2013 left the Member States the option to allow the revaluation of fixed assets (Article 7). In case the Member State exerts the option, the Directive requires that the exceeding value over the asset's carrying amount is recorded in a revaluation reserve included in the Capital and Reserves and 'no part of the revaluation reserve may be distributed, either directly or indirectly, unless it represents a gain actually realised' (Article 7 (2)). The Member States may lay their own rules governing the use of the revaluation reserve while respecting the provision that it must be tied up until it corresponds to a realised gain (Alexander & Fasiello, 2021b). Therefore, the cross-countries differences are observable referring to whether they have opted for the fix assets revaluation, and the potential use of the revaluation reserve while respecting the provision that no part of the reserve may be distributed, directly or indirectly, unless it corresponds to a realised gain.

In most of the countries, the local law sets strict conditions to be met for the entities to revaluate fix assets.

In France, the revaluation may be carried out occasionally either voluntarily or as required by the law, but it is admitted only for the entire class of assets, while it is not allowed in isolation (Le Manh, 2017). The revaluation gain is recorded in the revaluation Capital and Reserves (Code de commerce L. 123-18 and PCG art. 214-27). In Italy, the revaluation of assets is allowed only in case of specific laws permitting the revaluation for anomalous loss in the purchasing power. Accordingly, the Italian accounting standard setter (OIC) permits revaluations of assets only if these are authorised by special legislation (Provasi & Sottoriva, 2015). In the Netherlands, the current value of fixed assets should be measured as the current cost or lower recoverable amount (higher of value in use or realisable value). The measurement at current value is allowed for most investment properties, while agricultural products may be measured at fair value less costs of disposal (EY, 2020). In Sweden, the revaluations of fixed assets are allowed if: (i) there is a substantial value increase above the carrying amount; (ii) the value increase is not temporary; and (iii) there is a reliable measurement of the estimated fair value. The unrealised gain is booked as restricted equity (revaluation fund). The Danish Financial Statement Act (sections 58 and 53) did not set conditions for the revaluation, but it requires thorough explanations in the notes on revaluation amounts and the movements therein.

The change in the fair value of the fixed asset is mostly required to be recorded in the Capital and Reserve. An exception is the United Kingdom requiring the change in the fair value of investment properties to be recognised in the profit and loss instead of through reserves (PWC, 2013).

Table 2 Treatment of accounting items across countries

Accounting items/ countries	Asset revaluation	Financial instruments	Development costs
Denmark	Revaluation amounts that are tied up and thorough explanations in the notes on revaluation amounts and the movements therein are required.	The Danish Financial Statements Act introduced a requirement for a fair value reserve on currency conversion (Section 39) and on accounting hedging (Section 49. PCS. 3).	An amount corresponding to the recognised development costs must be tied up in a special reserve under equity (§ 83, para. 2, cf. Act no. 738 of 1 June 2015).
France	Occasional revaluation admitted under conditions. There is no possibility to revalue an asset class in isolation. The revaluation gain is recognised in equity (Code de commerce L 123-18 and PCG art. 214-27)	France did not exert the option of fair value measurement, allowing financial instruments to be recorded only with the cost model. Financial assets are generally recognised at acquisition cost, and liabilities at amortised cost based on the contractual repayment schedule. Therefore, there are no changes in fair value to be tied up in the reserve.	Development costs can be expensed or capitalised (preferred treatment). When capitalised, they are amortised over their useful life or over maximum of five years if the useful life cannot be reliably estimated (Art. 214-3)
Germany	Revaluation of fixed assets is not allowed.	The fair value measurement is required for short-term financial instruments but forbidden for long-term financial instruments	Research costs are required to be expensed as incurred, while costs arising during development are allowed to be capitalised. When internally generated, intangible assets are recognised, profits may only be distributed if the reserves available for distribution remaining after such a distribution are at least of the same amount as the recognised intangible assets.
Italy	Specific laws allow the revaluation of certain types of assets to consider their current value. OICs permit revaluations of assets if, and only if, these are authorised by special legislation. Fair value is permitted only if	The Civil Code and then OIC 19 established amortised cost as the general method of measurement of receivables and payables. Fair value measurement is mandatory only for derivative financial instruments.	The Italian Civil Code allows entities to capitalise start-up and expansion costs and with development costs that generate economic benefits over several years subject to approval of the Board of Statutory

(continued)

Table 2 (continued)

Accounting items/ countries	Asset revaluation	Financial instruments	Development costs
	lower than cost and to measure the recoverable amount of a fix asset.		Auditors. Start-up and expansion costs are amortised over a period not exceeding five years; development costs should be amortised over their useful life; and if reliable estimation is absent, they must be amortised over a period not exceeding five years. No distribution of profits takes place unless the amount of the reserves available for distribution and profits brought forward is at least equal to that of the costs not written off.
Netherlands	The current value of fixed assets should be measured as the current cost or lower recoverable amount. The measurement at current value is allowed for most investment properties.	There is no general fair value option, but fair value through profit or loss is allowed for all financial assets, except for loans granted and receivables. Other financial liabilities (except for trading portfolio and derivatives) are required to be measured at amortised cost. The decreases in value to below cost are required to be recognised in the statement of profit or loss: a negative revaluation reserve is not possible.	Development costs can be capitalised. In case their useful life cannot be reliably estimated, they shall be written off within a period not exceeding 10 years (DL, article 396:3)
Spain	Cost model is required, and revaluation is not allowed.	The financial assets evaluated at fair value with changes in reserve are a residual category for investments in debt securities or equity instruments that cannot be either classified as held-for-trading or considered an investment in associates.	Research expenditures: capitalisation permitted when the company can properly justify technical, commercial and financial success; amortisation over a maximum of 5 years. Development expenditures: capitalisation required when the

(continued)

Table 2 (continued)

Accounting items/ countries	Asset revaluation	Financial instruments	Development costs
			company can properly justify technical, commercial and financial success; amortisation in a maximum of 5 years.
Sweden	Swedish GAAP allows companies to make revaluations of fixed assets if certain criteria are met. The unrealised gain is booked as restricted equity.	Only in the consolidated financial statements in privately held groups, fair value accounting for financial instruments was introduced by offering preparers a policy choice between historical cost-based accounting and fair value-based accounting. Companies are not allowed to mix the two different choices.	Swedish GAAP does not allow for capitalisation of development costs for small limited liability legal entities, while large limited liability legal entities are allowed to make a policy choice between the 'expense model' and the 'capitalisation model'. Companies opting for the latter model had to apply the new EU requirement and create a development cost fund as part of restricted equity.
United Kingdom	Property, plant and equipment and intangible assets may be revalued. Changes in the fair value of investment properties will need to be recognised in the profit and loss instead of through reserves.	Initial measurement of financial instruments varies between transaction price (excluding transaction costs) for those held at fair value through profit or loss (FVTPL), present value of future payments for financing transactions and transaction price for those that are not held at FVTPL or financing transactions. Many equity investments will need to be fair-valued, with changes recognised through profit or loss.	Development costs and borrowing costs may be capitalised in certain circumstances.

Next, we turn our attention to the accounting for financial instruments. According to the Accounting Directive EU-D-34/2013, the adoption of the fair value measurement for financial instruments is optional for the Member States. If the Member States exert the option, the Directive requires that the change in fair value of hedging instruments under a system of hedge accounting (Article 8 (8.a)) the exchange difference on monetary items in investment in a foreign entity (Article 8 (8.b)) must be recorded in a tied reserve preventing the distribution of not realised gains (Alexander & Fasiello, 2021b). With reference to available sale financial assets, the Member States may permit or require that the change in fair value be recognised directly in reserve or, alternatively, in the income statement. The changes in the fair value of the other financial instruments must be included in the profit and loss account (Article 8 (8)) (Alexander & Fasiello, 2021b).

Denmark has implemented the option in Article 8 (6) of the Directive and permits the recognition, measurement and disclosure of financial instruments in conformity with international accounting standards adopted in accordance with Regulation (EC) No. 1606/2002 (Frank & Thinggaard, supra). The Danish Financial Statements Act introduced a requirement for a fair value reserve on currency conversion (Section 39) and on accounting hedging (Section 49. PCS. 3). The reserve must be dissolved or reduced to the extent that the change in the value is alternatively: (i) realised or eliminated from the activity, (ii) written down due to lower recoverable amount, (iii) associated with deferred tax that must be provided for, (iv) reversed due to a change in accounting estimates or (v) reduced due to depreciation. France did not exert the option of fair value measurement; therefore, there are no values to be tied up in the reserve. Germany exerted the option for fair value measurement of financial instruments with certain limitations. In Italy, the fair value measurement is mandatory only for derivative financial instruments, and values flowing into the reserves are limited to the variation in the fair value of some derivative financial instruments. Under Dutch laws and regulations, there is no general fair value option, but fair value through profit or loss is allowed for all financial assets, except for loans granted and receivables. Other financial liabilities (except for trading portfolio and derivatives) are required to be measured at amortised cost. The decreases in value to below cost are required to be recognised in the statement of profit or loss: a negative revaluation reserve is not possible. If bonds are measured at fair value and the changes in value are accounted for via the revaluation reserve, Dutch laws and regulations do not permit a negative revaluation reserve. If investments in equity instruments are measured at fair value and changes in value are taken through other comprehensive income, they are transferred to profit or loss when realised. A negative revaluation reserve is not permitted (EY, 2020). The current Spanish Plan General de Contabilidad is mostly aligned with IFRS 9 on Financial Instruments. The financial assets evaluated at fair value with changes in reserve are a residual category for investments in debt securities or equity instruments that cannot be either classified as held-for-trading or considered an investment in associates (Gisbert & Mora, supra). In Sweden, the historical cost has been dominating valuation approach; in fact, Swedish Financial Accounting Standards Committee never issued Swedish standard corresponding to the fair value standard IAS 39 (now IFRS 9). Only in the consolidated financial statements in privately held groups, fair value accounting for financial instruments was introduced by offering preparers a policy choice between historical cost-based accounting and fair value-based accounting. Companies are not allowed to mix the two different choices.

In the United Kingdom, the Financial Reporting Standard requires financial instruments to be initially measured at the transaction price, in the case of the instruments held at fair value through profit or loss (FVTPL), present value of future payments for financing transactions and transaction price for those that are not held at FVTPL. Many equity investments will need to be fair-valued, with changes recognised through profit or loss (PWC, 2013).

The third accounting item we discuss is the capitalisation of development costs. The Accounting Directive states that national law may authorise the inclusion of costs of development under 'Assets'. Until those costs have not been completely written off, Directive EU-D-34/2013 further introduced a requirement that no distribution of profits takes place unless the amount of the reserves available for distribution and profits brought forward is at least equal to that of the costs not written off. In Denmark, the Section 83, para. 2, of the Act No. 738 of 1 June 2015 requires that an amount corresponding to the recognised development costs must be tied up in a special reserve under equity.

According to the French General Accounting Plan, development costs can be expensed or capitalised, being the latter the preferred treatment. When capitalised, they are amortised over their useful life or over maximum of five years if the useful life cannot be reliably estimated (Art. 214-3) (Le Manh, 2017). German GAAP requires research cost to be expensed as incurred, while allowing capitalisation of costs arising during development. When internally generated intangible assets are recognised, profits may only be distributed if the reserves available for distribution remaining after such a distribution are at least of the same amount as the recognised intangible assets. The Italian Civil Code allows entities to capitalise start-up and expansion costs and with development costs that generate economic benefits over several years subject to approval of the Board of Statutory Auditors. Start-up and expansion costs must be amortised over a period not exceeding five years; development costs should be amortised over their useful life; and if this cannot be estimated reliably, they must be amortised over a period not exceeding five years (PWC, 2019). According to the Dutch Law, development costs can be capitalised. In case their useful life cannot be reliably estimated, they shall be written off within a period not exceeding ten years (DL, article 396:3). According to the Spanish PGC-2021, the capitalisation is, respectively, permitted for research expenditures and required for development expenditures, either way when the company can properly justify technical, commercial and financial success. Once capitalised, the amortisation is required over a maximum of five years (Gisbert & Mora, supra). Swedish GAAP does not allow for capitalisation of development costs for small limited liability legal entities, while large limited liability legal entities are allowed to make a policy choice between the 'expense model' and the 'capitalisation model'. Entities opting for the latter model had to apply the new EU requirement and create a development cost fund as part of restricted equity (Hellman, supra).

In the UK, development costs and borrowing costs may be capitalised in certain circumstances (PWC, 2013).

4 Conclusions

This chapter overviewed and discussed the differences and similarities emerged in relation to the accounting for Capital and Reserves across Member States, following the adoption of the EU-D-34/2013. In fact, while the IASB neglected to devote a specific standard to discipline the accounting for Capital and Reserves, hence favouring homogeneity, the process through which the EU allowed Member States to retain a certain degree of autonomy in terms of tailoring the adoption of the Directive on their own companies' needs brought to significant differences in terms of the accounting rules and economic meaning of the Capital and Reserve items.

Interestingly, we started off our analysis based on the ex-ante assumption that Capital and Reserve is not like any other balance sheet item: in fact, it is affected by other recognition and measurement criteria in relation to several other individual assets and liabilities. Consequently, values reported in the Capital and Reserves are likely to vary across the Member States in relation to the combination of the options allowed by the Accounting Directive matched with the options exerted by each Member State. Therefore, the reasons why cross-country differences exist are threefold. First, existing legal differences across jurisdictions, surfacing well before the adoption and transition to the Accounting Directive, map into the underlying role of equity as a 'third-party' protection for other stakeholders. Second, we argue that the 'size' and functioning of the Capital and Reserve accounts are mostly generated by the changes in the assets and liabilities at fair value; the fact that the Accounting Directive left Member States with the option to embrace either cost measurement instead of the fair value surfaced as a major trigger of differences. Third, we highlight that another major source of difference stems from—again the option left to Member States—to account for changes in the fair value either in the income statement or in the reserves, depending on the existing accounting discipline in the first place and on the State Members option in the second place.

We believe this overview opens up several avenues for future empirical research; below we offer two examples: the heterogeneity in terms of possibility to revalue fixed assets may subsume a significant difference in terms of loan amounts and pricing. In fact, if accounting rules allow (do not permit) to revalue upward fixed assets, loan officers should (should not) be able to better assess the firm's ability to recover from missed loan payments if assets are reported at a value closer to current valuations. On the other hand, an implicit form of unconditional conservatism may serve as an ex-ante screening tool and offer a lower bound in terms of cash flow in the case of missed payments (Ryan, 2006). Second, the existing differences both across countries and within countries—due, for example, to different accounting rules applying to firms' meeting size requirements or being waived application of the EU-D-34/2013—offer a nice setting to test whether governments react differently in terms of designing relief mechanisms in the aftermath of financial crisis.

References

Aghion, P., & Bolton, P. (1992). An incomplete contracts approach to financial contracting. *The Review of Economic Studies, 59*(3), 473–494.

Alexander, D., & Fasiello, R. (2021a). Prudence and Directive 34 – reality and rhetoric in accounting regulation. *Accounting in Europe, 18*(1), 26–42.

Alexander, D., & Fasiello, R. (2021b). Prudence and directive 34–reality and rhetoric in accounting regulation. *Accounting in Europe, 18*(1), 26–42.

Andrè, P. (2017). The role and current status of IFRS in the completion of national accounting rules evidence from European countries. *Accounting in Europe, 14*(1–2), 1–12.

Beatty, A., Ball, R., Bushman, R. M., & Vasvari, F. (2008). The debt-contracting value of accounting information and loan syndicate structure. *Journal of Accounting Research, 46*(2), 289–295.

Bischof, J., & Daske, H. (2016). Interpreting the European Union's IFRS endorsement criteria: the case of IFRS 9. *Accounting in Europe, 13*(2), 129–168.

Breuer, M. (2021). How does financial-reporting regulation affect industry-wide resource allocation? *Journal of Accounting Research, 59*, 59–110.

Christensen, H. B., Nikolaev, V. V., & Wittenberg-Moerman, R. (2016). Accounting information in financial contracting: the incomplete contract theory perspective. *Journal of Accounting Research, 54*(2), 397–435.

Davydenko, S. A., & Franks, J. R. (2008). Do Bankruptcy codes matter? A study of defaults in France, Germany, and the U.K. *The Journal of Finance, 63*(2), 565–608.

Djankov, S., Hart, O., McLiesh, C., & Shleifer, A. (2008). Debt enforcement around the world. *Journal of Political Economy, 116*(6), 1105–1149.

Djankov, S., McLiesh, C., & Shleifer, A. (2007). Private credit in 129 countries. *Journal of Financial Economics*.

EY (2020). IFRS: A comparison with Dutch Laws and regulations 2020.

Hart, O., & Moore, J. (1998). Default and renegotiation: a dynamic model of debt. *The Quarterly Journal of Economics, 113*(1), 1–41.

Holthausen, R. W., & Leftwich, R. W. (1983). The economic consequences ff accounting choice implications of costly contracting and monitoring. *Journal of Accounting and Economics, 5*, 77–117.

La Porta, R., Lopez de Silanes, F., Shleifer, A., & Vishny, R. W. (1997). Legal determinants of external finance. *The Journal of Finance, 52*(3), 1131–1150.

La Porta, R., Lopez de Silanes, F., Shleifer, A., & Vishny, R. W. (1998). Law and finance. *Journal of Political Economy, 106*(6), 1131–1155.

Le Manh, A. (2017). The role and current status of IFRS in the completion of national accounting rules–Evidence from France. *Accounting in Europe, 14*(1-2), 94–101.

Leuz, C., Nanda, D., & Wysocki, P. D. (2003). Earnings management and investor protection: an international comparison. *Journal of Financial Economics, 69*, 505–527.

Nikolaev, V. V. (2010). Debt covenants and accounting conservatism. *Journal of Accounting Research, 48*(1), 137–175.

Provasi, R., & Sottoriva, C. (2015). Preliminary considerations about the transposition of Directive 2013/34/EU into Italian accounting system. *Journal of Modern Accounting and Auditing, 11*(6), 302–312.

PWC (2013). New UK GAAP or IFRS? Your questions answered.

PWC (2019). Financial statements: looking to the future.

Ryan, S. (2006). Identifying conditional conservatism. *European Accounting Review, 15*, 511–525.

Watts, R. L., & Zimmerman, J. L. (1978). Towards a positive theory of the determination of accounting standards. *Accounting Review, 53*, 112–134.

Zender, J. F. (1991). Optimal financial instruments. *The Journal of Finance, 46*(5), 1645–1663.

Income Taxes in Financial Statements

Giuseppe Zizzo

1 The Relationship Between Taxable Income and Accounting Income

Briefly summarized, the relationship between taxable income and accounting income can be managed using one of the following models:

- At one extreme, there is the "single track" (or "full legal link") model, according to which accounting income acts also as taxable income.
- On the other, the "double track" (or "no legal link") model, according to which taxable income is calculated (analytically or synthetically) independently of accounting income.
- In the middle, the "derivation" (or "partial legal link") model, according to which accounting income constitutes a starting point for the measurement of taxable income. To calculate taxable income, tax legislation provides a set of rules that impose or allow to operate adjustments meant to increase or decrease accounting income.

2 The "Single Track" Model

Historically, the "single track" model reflects the need to relate the tax obligation to the actual ability to pay connected to business activities. While it is true that reference to accounting rules confers to taxable income a reliable economic basis, it is also true that income escapes a single definition, depending, to a large extent, not

G. Zizzo (✉)
Università Carlo Cattaneo LIUC, Castellanza, Italy
e-mail: gzizzo@liuc.it

A. Incollingo, A. Lionzo (eds.), *The European Harmonization of National Accounting Rules*, SIDREA Series in Accounting and Business Administration,
https://doi.org/10.1007/978-3-031-42931-6_14

only on the cultural context that defines it (different jurisdictions express different GAAP), but also on the scope of its calculation (determining the amounts distributable to shareholders, protecting creditors, informing investors). The existence of a plurality of accounting systems (domestic GAAP, IAS/IFRS), and therefore of economically reliable incomes, inevitably affects the range of solutions available in shaping taxable income. Indeed, it shows that the need to connect the taxable base to the ability to pay does not necessarily imply the choice of the "single track" model. This connection may be ensured not only by calculating taxable income referring to the same accounting system used in calculating accounting income, as in the "single track," but also by calculating taxable income autonomously, according to an accounting system different from the one used in calculating accounting income, according to the "double track."

In light of the above, today the main feature of the "single track" model is probably its efficiency, as it does not require companies to prepare two separate income reports, one based on accounting rules and one based on tax rules. It therefore significantly simplifies the fulfilment of the tax obligation, lowering the associated compliance costs. It also ensures transparency of the tax burden because it reduces the gap between the effective tax rate and the nominal one and promotes comparability.

On the other hand, this model, lacking flexibility, is unfit to fully comply with the requirements that characterize the drafting of the rules relating to the computation of taxable income. These requirements may indeed deserve a different approach and therefore push in the direction of the other two models. Moreover, it gives to accounting standard setters the power to define the tax base. Every change in accounting rules leads indeed to a change in the tax base, depriving governments of their control over public revenues.

As a consequence, no jurisdiction identifies taxable income in accounting income. Either it is used as a starting point or it is left altogether aside.

3 The Requirements That Characterize the Drafting of the Rules Relating to the Computation of Taxable Income

Among the requirements that characterize the drafting of the rules relating to the computation of taxable income, it shall be mentioned in the first place the need for legal certainty, which responds as much to the interest of taxpayers in the predetermination of the tax burden connected to their business activities, as to the interest of the Tax Administration in an easy and prompt collection of taxes.

The "single track" model implies that accounting rules act also as tax rules and, therefore, that the Tax Administration is entrusted with the power to assess the correct application of the former. This may lead to disputes with taxpayers, undermining legal certainty, especially when, to measure an item of income, accounting rules refer to one or more general principles or require appraisals or assessments of a technical or probabilistic nature.

The "double track" and the "derivation" models offer the opportunity to enact mechanisms suitable for removing the relevance of these processes in calculating taxable income. This removal may take the form (i) of rules prohibiting the inclusion in the taxable income of certain revenues or charges recognized in the income statement, and (ii) of rules, the observance of which is objectively and easily verifiable by the Tax Administration, which set barriers to the transfer of certain revenues or charges from the calculation of accounting income to the one of taxable income. When these tax rules apply, the compliance with accounting ones becomes irrelevant for the purposes of determining taxable income. Indeed, they imply (i) the acceptance of divergences between the items of income recognized by accounting rules and those recognized by tax ones and (ii) the understanding that the inclusion of the items in taxable income depends on the fact that their amount falls within the boundaries drawn by the latter and not on the compliance with the criteria set forward by the former.

Alongside the need for legal certainty, the "double track" and the "derivation" models allow to address, in building taxable income, other needs.

The need for stability of the tax base, and therefore of the tax revenue, may be jeopardized by taking into consideration, in calculating taxable income, value adjustments included in accounting income. These items are volatile, thus susceptible to both expanding and contracting and even transforming into one another (capital gains into capital losses and vice versa). In jurisdictions in which fair value accounting prevails, the trend is therefore to set autonomous rules for determining taxable income (André et al., 2021, p. 6).

There is a need to prevent tax evasion and avoidance. To this end, both models allow to enact measures: (i) which prohibit in whole or in part the deduction of certain expenses shown in the income statement; (ii) which prescribe the inclusion in the taxable income of certain revenues in whole or in part not shown in the income statement; (iii) which adopt the arms' length principle, in place of consideration, as a mean to recognize and evaluate certain items of income.

Another need that these two models may fulfill, contrary to the "single track" one, is the need for the prevention of economic double taxation on companies' profits in the form of an exclusion from taxable income of dividends received and gains realized through the sale of shareholdings.

Furthermore, when companies liable to tax apply different accounting systems, the adoption of the "single track" model fosters inequality. Indeed, the closer the link between taxable income and accounting income, the greater the influence of accounting rules on the measurement of taxable income and, therefore, the chance that differences in the amounts of the tax owed are due not to differences in the ability to pay but to differences in the set of accounting rules applied. While the "double track" model overcomes entirely this critical issue, the "derivation" may or may not, according to the breadth of the adjustments to the accounting income imposed or allowed.

All requirements described above relate to tax law and its drafting techniques. Taxable income is also affected by other factors, extraneous to tax law. The rules relating to the calculation of the taxable income may be used, and are actually often used, to accomplish a wide range of government policies, particularly to stimulate or discourage certain investments and/or productions and/or funding's forms. Although it is not always easy to bring a rule into one or the other set, the distinction is relevant, helping to define the scope of the different tax rules. Indeed, the rules that are attributable to the first category, having been introduced into the legal system for technical requirements, are by their nature intended to operate exclusively in the determination of the taxable income to be shown in the tax return. The other rules, on the other hand, serving other purposes, are not subject to the same limit.

4 The "Double Track" Model

The "double track" model is, of course, the one that best suits all the mentioned requirements.

On the other hand, it requires tax law to regulate in full the calculation of taxable income, covering all related issues. For this reason, the model looks particularly fit when companies liable to tax refer to more than one accounting system. It provides the same set of tax rules to all of them, and therefore, it ensures that the calculation of the taxable income is not affected by differences in the accounting systems. For this reason, it is the model that has been adopted in the UE Commission's 2016 proposals for a directive on a common corporate tax base (CCTB)[1] and on a common consolidated corporate tax base (CCCTB),[2] although during their elaboration there has been some debate on the opportunity of using the International Accounting Standards as a starting point for computing this tax base (Schöen, 2004).

When all companies liable to tax apply the same accounting system, this model is not as attractive as the "derivation" one, for it is considered more complex, implying the preparation of a second, and completely separate, report of income, and more subject to the possibility of being twisted to revenue needs by the government, weakening the connection between taxable base and ability to pay. Currently, it is applied in the Netherlands, where the tax base is determined according to the principles of goed koopmansgebruik (sound business practice), mainly developed by case law (Essers, 2016, p. 153), and in Denmark (Langhave, 2023). The UK is a jurisdiction that has been historically classified among the ones experiencing this model. In time, though, as accounting rules evolved, their role in the computation of taxable income has been strengthened by case law, anticipating the formal adoption of the "derivation" model that occurred in 1998 (Freedman, 2023).

[1] COM (2016) 683.

[2] COM (2016) 685.

5 The "Derivation" Model

The "derivation" model is the one mostly adopted. It is adopted in Germany (Eggert, 2016), France (Jaune, 2016), Italy (Grandinetti, 2016a), Spain (Baez Moreno, 2016), Sweden (Olsson, 2023), and, more recently, in the UK (James, 2016). It combines the advantages of the two other models, allowing to refer to the accounting rules when there is no need for a special tax rule and to have such a rule when there is a need for it.

To be precise, this model may take different forms. It may refer directly to accounting rules: Taxable income is determined according to accounting rules except for those items that are specifically dealt by tax rules. In the UK, for example, according to Art. 46 of the Corporation Tax Act of 2009, "The profits of a trade must be calculated in accordance with generally accepted accounting practice, subject to any adjustment required or authorized by law in calculating profits for corporation tax purposes." It may refer to the profit and loss statement: Taxable income is determined using as a starting point the result of the profit and loss statement, adjusting it with the increases and decreases that are required or authorized by tax rules. In Italy, according to Art. 83 of the Income Tax Code, "The total income is determined by applying to the profit or loss resulting from the income statement, relating to the financial year ended in the tax period, the increases or decreases resulting from the application of the criteria established in the subsequent provisions of this section." Similarly, in Spain, according to Art. 10.3 of the Corporate Income Tax Code, the taxable base "shall be determined by correcting, according to the special provisions of this law, the accounting profit or loss calculated in accordance of the Commercial Code, other laws relevant for that calculation and the regulations implementing the former." Finally, it may refer to the balance sheet: Taxable income is determined using as a starting point the difference between the value of the net assets at the beginning and at the end of the fiscal year, adjusting it with the increases and decreases that are required or authorized by tax rules. In France, according to Art. 38.2 of the French Tax Code, "The net profit is the difference between the value of the net assets at the beginning and at the end of the fiscal year." Similarly, in Germany, according to Art. 4 of the Income Tax Act, "Profit is the difference between the business assets at the end of the financial year and the business assets at the end of the previous financial year, increased by the value of the withdrawals and reduced by the value of the contributions."

While in the first case it is quite clear that accounting rules, when not derogated by tax rules, act also as tax rules, likewise the "single track" model, in the others, two options are conceivable. Based on the first, the result of the profit and loss statement or the difference in the value of the net assets is a figure relevant for tax purposes in itself, as a mere fact. The Tax Administration does not have the power to check if accounting rules have been correctly applied in determining them. It has only the power to check if the special tax rules that require or permit increases or decreases to their amount have been correctly applied. Based on the second option, the aforesaid result or difference is relevant insofar as they were determined by applying accounting rules correctly. Therefore, likewise in the "single track" model, the Tax Administration has the power to check if accounting rules have been correctly applied, except when they are derogated by special tax rules. Indeed, in this latter case the correct computation of taxable income depends on the correct application of these special tax rules not of the accounting ones. This option is expressly provided for by Spanish tax law, which requires compliance with "the Commercial Code, other laws relevant for that calculation and the regulations implementing the former" (Baez Moreno, 2016). Similarly, in Germany, Art. 5(1) s.1 of the Income Tax Act refers to the "commercial law principles of proper accounting" (Meyer, 2023). It is unquestionable that the second option appears more aligned with the basic assumption for referring to accounting rules in calculating taxable income, i.e., the assumption whereby accounting income provides a highly reliable indicator of the ability to pay arising from business activities. Since only compliance with accounting rules ensures accounting income of this quality, it would be incoherent to prevent the Tax Administration from verifying their correct application (Zizzo, 2014).

In this respect, it is important to underline two circumstances. The first is that the power to assess the correct application of accounting rules is conferred to the Tax Administration for the purpose of determining the correct taxable base and not of changing accounting income. The second is that, when it is exercised, the Tax Administration is not responsible for replacing the drafters of the financial statements in the recognition and measurement of its items, but for verifying whether the relevant accounting rules have been correctly applied. It follows that the greater the elasticity of these latter rules, i.e., the greater the room for choices they foresee, the wider the circle of solutions compatible with them is, and the narrower the space available to the Tax Administration for a correction should be, having to demonstrate, in order to affirm that their application has not taken place correctly, that the item shown on the income statement cannot be placed within the aforementioned circle.

In any case, the "derivation" model involves the enactment of a set of rules that require or allow the company to operate adjustments with a positive and a negative sign to accounting income. The adjustments to accounting income make it possible to adapt the accounting rules to the requirements, both of tax and non-tax nature, which characterize the drafting of the rules on taxable income.

The range and the intensity of these adjustments may vary significantly, across jurisdictions and time. The tax system may be characterized by few, and of low intensity, adjustments at a certain moment, and by many, and of strong intensity, adjustments at another moment. In the first case, it approaches the "single track" model, as most of the items building up taxable income are taken from accounting income. In the second, it approaches the "double track" one, as most of the items building up taxable income are determined autonomously from the ones that build up accounting income. Moreover, when some companies use IAS/IFRS in preparing financial statements while others use domestic GAAP, the number and intensity of adjustments may vary significantly across these two groups of companies. On the one hand, these differences may reflect the concern to avoid taxable income being affected by the differences existing between accounting systems, or the need to accommodate tax rules to take into account the specificities of these systems in light of the aforementioned requirements. On the other, it may just be the consequence of the different impact of tax rules on the items that make up accounting income under the two systems. In Italy, where some companies use (mandatorily or electively) IAS/IFRS in preparing financial statements while others use domestic GAAP, the scope of the relevant tax rules evolved in time. The concern to avoid different taxable incomes, which prevailed at first, gave quick way to the need to remodel tax rules, meant to operate in connection with domestic GAAP, to better deal with the specificities of IAS/IFRS (Zizzo, 2008).

Adjustments to accounting income act as countermeasures with respect to the weak points of the "single track" model, eliminating or containing them. They inevitably call for a judgment of reasonableness both in light of their objectives and of their adequacy and proportionality with respect to them.

In the first place, unreasonableness should be predicated when the measure does not reflect any interest worthy of protection, but only the interest to increase public revenues. It is true that the scope of tax law is to raise revenue to fund public expenditures, and the selection of the means to reach this objective is essentially in the hand of the legislature; however, once a certain economic base is chosen to levy a tax, it is unacceptable to invoke the objective to raise revenue to justify rules that drive the tax base away from the economic base chosen. Indeed, admitting such justification, tax rules, insofar as they are informed, as they generally are, to this objective, would always be reasonable.

Moreover, unreasonableness should be predicated also when, despite being connected to an interest worthy of protection, the measure proves to be inadequate to protect it, or, despite being connected to an interest worthy of protection, and adequate to protect it, manifests itself as non-proportional, going beyond what is necessary for this purpose.

The adjustments with a positive sign derive from (i) tax rules that require the inclusion in the taxable income of revenues in whole or in part not relevant for accounting income or (ii) tax rules that require, or allow for, the exclusion from the taxable income of expenses relevant for accounting income, because they are wholly or partially non-deductible, or because they are wholly or partially deductible in subsequent fiscal years.

The adjustments with a negative sign derive from (i) tax rules that require, or allow for, the exclusion in whole or in part from the taxable income of revenues relevant for accounting income, or (ii) tax rules that allow for the inclusion in the taxable income of expenses not relevant for accounting income, because they are not includable or because they were included in the accounting income relating to previous fiscal years.

Some adjustments have a temporary nature, being that they are the source of adjustments with opposite sign in one or more of the following fiscal years. For the items affected by these adjustments, accounting income and tax income deviate only for the time interval between the two opposite adjustments. It follows that, when the adjustment belongs to this category, either there is an anticipation of the moment in which the tax is due or a postponement of the same. More in detail, either (i) in the fiscal year of the adjustment the company will owe more tax than the one it should owe on the basis of the items shown in the income statement, but then, in one or more of the following years, due to adjustments of the opposite sign, it will owe less tax than the one it should owe on the basis of the items shown in the income statement, or (ii) in the fiscal year of the adjustment the company will owe less tax than the one it should owe on the basis of the items shown in the income statement, but then, in one or more of the following years, due to adjustments of the opposite sign, it will owe more tax than the one it should owe on the basis of the items shown in the income statement.

Other adjustments have a permanent nature, affecting only the taxable income of the fiscal year to which they refer. For the items affected by them, accounting income and tax income take positions that are irreconcilable. The higher or lower tax produced by these adjustments will not be offset subsequently.

Thanks to the adjustments described, when an accounting rule and a tax rule regulate the same situation, linking different legal consequences to it, there is no antinomy between them. Indeed, it is possible to comply with both, drawing up financial statements in compliance with the former, and tax returns in compliance with the latter. Accounting rules therefore provide the standard to judge the correctness of the financial statements, tax rules in turn provide the standard to evaluate the correctness of the tax returns.

The adjustments often affect the value of the company's net assets, opening a gap between their accounting value and the tax one.

On the one side, it may happen that there is an increase in the value of net assets, which is not recognized for tax purposes. This difference, due to an adjustment with a negative sign to accounting income, may have its source in an exemption, and therefore be permanent, or in a postponement, and therefore be temporary. In some cases, the postponement is allowed on condition that the company creates a special (tax-free) reserve and may last until the occurrence of certain events affecting the reserve. The range of these events varies considerably. Indeed, it may be limited to its distribution to shareholders. It may encompass any use of the reserve other than to cover losses. Lastly, it may be extended to any form of utilization of the reserve. Furthermore, alongside events affecting the reserve, such as those just mentioned, the postponement may be linked to events regarding the assets carrying the aforesaid increase. In this case, to avoid double taxation, it is necessary to establish a connection among these two series of events. This means that, if tax is collected because an event affecting the reserve has occurred, then a corresponding increase in the value recognized for tax purposes of the assets shall be admitted. Vice versa, if the tax is collected because an event affecting the assets has occurred, then the reserve shall be released from its constraints for a corresponding amount. Sometimes, moreover, the same law that regulates the creation of these reserves, or a subsequent one, provides for the opportunity of releasing these reserves from their constraints by paying a special tax, as a substitute for corporate income tax.

On the other side, it may happen that there is a decrease in the value of net assets, which is not recognized for tax purposes. This situation, due to an adjustment with a positive sign to accounting income, is common, deriving from depreciations, value adjustments, and/or provisions included in accounting income that are not recognized for tax purposes. As a consequence, the assets shown in the balance sheet will have an accounting value lower than the tax one and/or the liabilities shown in the balance sheet will have an accounting value higher than the tax one.

6 "Reverse Derivation"

The expression "reverse derivation" is here used to describe situations in which tax rules affect accounting income, with a reversal of the ordinary relationship between taxable income and accounting income, where the former is dependent on the latter (in Germany, this relation between tax and accounting rules is labeled "reverse authoritativeness," Eggert, 2016).

A legal "reverse derivation" may occur when tax rules are enacted with the purpose of stimulating or discouraging certain conducts in the preparation of financial statements. In such cases, "reverse derivation" is therefore the effect of tax rules, which, for certain items of income, expressly allow companies to detour from accounting rules in the preparation of financial statements as to obtain a tax benefit.

Aside from a legal "reverse derivation," there is a factual "reverse derivation." In the "derivation" model, a factual "reverse derivation" may occur as a side effect of tax provisions that either (i) allow the items shown in the income statement to concur to the taxable income only if their amount falls between a minimum and maximum, or over a minimum or under a maximum, or (ii) refer to accounting rules that confer options to companies. When these rules are coupled with other rules that prohibit to include in taxable income an expense in an amount higher than the one shown in the profit and loss statement or a revenue in an amount lower than the one shown in the profit and loss statement, they may be capable of exerting a strong influence on the preparation of this document. Indeed, if, on the basis of these rules, the aforesaid inclusion cannot be accomplished autonomously, because higher expenses or lower revenues can be computed in the taxable income only in so far that they are computed in accounting income, then companies will be pushed to "pollute" the income statement as to achieve a reduction in the tax due, aligning the amounts of the expenses or of the revenues included in the profit and loss statement to the ones recognizable under tax rules, regardless of accounting rules.

This restriction to the adjustment mechanism, known as "formal dependence" (Baez Moreno, 2023), characterizes, albeit in different degrees, the Italian (Grandinetti & Strampelli, 2023), the Spanish (Lopez et al., 2023), and the French tax systems (Dinh, 2023). It is also present, although in a weaker form, in the Swedish tax system (Olsson, 2023). The main reason given for it stems from the assumption according to which the State is, in substance, a partner of the company. A special partner, indeed, rewarded through income tax instead of dividend distributions. It follows that shareholders should not, as a rule, receive dividends on profits that were not taxed, otherwise they would get from the company's profit a benefit that the special partner, the State, was not able to get. To this end, taxable income should not, in principle, be lower than accounting income.

It follows that one critical issue of the "derivation" model is, when it is not shaped to avoid "pollution" of the profit and loss statement, its capacity to undermine the information function of this document, unless it is structured in such a way as to separate the amounts booked according to accounting rules from those booked according to tax rules, allowing therefore the readers to separate those items included only to obtain a tax benefit from the others and identify, despite the tax "pollution," the actual accounting income (i.e., the accounting income not affected by the tax inducted items).

The Italian experience is emblematic (Grandinetti, 2016b, p. 94), recording in the last decades many attempts to tackle this issue, at first, working on accounting rules, to enhance their capacity to inform readers about tax "pollution," subsequently, working on tax rules, as to limit their impact on financial statements. The most significant innovation to this end was the enactment of a rule allowing the deduction of depreciation of tangible and intangible assets, other value adjustments and provisions without their previous charge to the profit and loss statement, on condition that, in a specific statement of the income tax return, was indicated their total amount, the accounting and tax values of the assets and those of the provisions. Moreover, to avoid the distribution of untaxed profits as a result of these deductions, in the event of distribution, the amounts paid had to be included in the taxable income of the distributing company to the extent that the remaining reserves and profits carried forward did not cover the excess of the aforesaid deductions in respect of depreciations, value adjustments, and provisions charged to the profit and loss statement. In 2007, this rule was abolished, claiming, incongruously, that it was a mere tax relief. Since then, the deduction of these items has been again subject to the general rule that requires, for deduction against taxable income, the previous charge to the profit and loss statement; therefore, in substance, restoring the questionable situation pre-existing to the attempts described.

In Germany, as in Italy, options provided for by tax rules had to be previously exercised in financial statements, with the same tax "pollution" effects. Unlike in Italy, in Germany the rule that established this requirement was repealed in 2009, putting an end to these effects (Eggert, 2016, 119), even though the actual scope of this abolition is an issue still open to debate (Meyer, 2023).

7 Conclusion

As pointed out, both accounting rules and tax rules are interested in measuring the financial performance of companies. Their purposes do not entirely match, though, preventing the use of the same set of rules to determine accounting and taxable income ("single track").

Notwithstanding, the determination of taxable income is seldom totally independent from accounting rules. A direct or indirect link with these latter rules is in many cases clearly recognizable even under the "double track" model, as tax rules often duplicate accounting rules or refer to accounting rules. It follows that, although the "double track" model and the "derivation" model, which is the most common, imply different processes to calculate taxable income, the difference in their outcomes may be immaterial (Andrè et al., 2021, p. 6).

In certain jurisdictions, moreover, tax rules affect the determination of accounting income. This effect may reflect the purpose of stimulating or discouraging certain conducts in the preparation of financial statements (legal "reverse derivation"), but it may also stem from the prohibition to calculate in taxable income an expense in an amount higher than the one to be shown in the income statement or a revenue in an amount lower of the one to be shown in the income statement (factual "reverse derivation"). The unintended "pollution" of the profit and loss account that these restrictions may cause is, undoubtedly, a critical element of the "derivation" model. Notwithstanding, their withdrawal faces resistance. Among those tax systems that prescribe them, only Germany apparently gave it up, repealing the relevant provision.

References

Andrè, P., Schaubschlaeger, M., & Schultze, W. (2021). The Cash-Relevance of IFRS – European Legislation Regarding Dividends and Taxation in the Context of IFRS Reporting, electronic copy available at https://ssrn.com/abstract=3849492

Baez Moreno, A. (2016). Accounting and taxation: Spain. In M. Grandinetti (Ed.), *Corporate Tax Base in the Light of the IAS/IFRS and EU Directive 2013/34* (p. 183). Wolters Kluwer Eucotax.

Baez Moreno, A. (2023). General Report, 2023 Congress of the European Association of Tax Law Professors, Luxembourg, 8–10 June 2023, available on EATLP website.

Dinh, E. (2023). France National Report, 2023 Congress of the European Association of Tax Law Professors, Luxembourg, 8–10 June 2023, available on EATLP website.

Eggert, A. (2016). Accounting and taxation: Germany. In M. Grandinetti (Ed.), *Corporate Tax Base in the Light of the IAS/IFRS and EU Directive 2013/34* (p. 115). Wolters Kluwer Eucotax.

Essers, P. H. J. (2016). Accounting and taxation: Netherlands. In M. Grandinetti (Ed.), *Corporate tax base in the light of the IAS/IFRS and EU Directive 2013/34* (p. 151). Wolters Kluwer Eucotax.

Freedman, J. (2023). UK National Report, 2023 Congress of the European Association of Tax Law Professors, Luxembourg, 8–10 June 2023, available on EATLP website.

Grandinetti, M. (2016a). Accounting and taxation: Italy. In M. Grandinetti (Ed.), *Corporate tax base in the light of the IAS/IFRS and EU Directive 2013/34* (p. 125). Wolters Kluwer Eucotax.

Grandinetti, M. (2016b). *Il principio di derivazione nell'IRES*. Wolters Kluwer CEDAM.

Grandinetti, M., & Strampelli, G. (2023). Italy National Report, 2023 Congress of the European Association of Tax Law Professors, Luxembourg, 8–10 June 2023, available on EATLP website.

James, S. (2016). Accounting and taxation: UK. In M. Grandinetti (Ed.), *Corporate tax base in the light of the IAS/IFRS and EU Directive 2013/34* (p. 203). Wolters Kluwer Eucotax.

Jaune, R. (2016). Accounting and taxation: France. In M. Grandinetti (Ed.), *Corporate Tax Base in the Light of the IAS/IFRS and EU Directive 2013/34* (p. 101). Wolters Kluwer Eucotax.

Langhave, I. (2023). Denmark National Report, 2023 Congress of the European Association of Tax Law Professors, Luxembourg, 8–10 June 2023, available on EATLP website.

Lopez Lopez, H., Martinez Laguna, F. D., Sanz Gadea, E., Vega Borrego, F. A. (2023). Spain National Report, 2023 Congress of the European Association of Tax Law Professors, Luxembourg, 8–10 June 2023, available on EATLP website.

Meyer, A. (2023). Germany National Report, 2023 Congress of the European Association of Tax Law Professors, Luxembourg, 8-10 June 2023, available on EATLP website.

Olsson, S. (2023). Sweden National Report, 2023 Congress of the European Association of Tax Law Professors, Luxembourg, 8-10 June 2023, available on EATLP website.

Schöen, W. (2004). International accounting standards – A "Starting Point" for a Common European Tax Base. *European Taxation, 44*, p. 426.

Zizzo, G. (2008). L'Ires e i principi contabili internazionali: dalla neutralità sostanziale alla neutralità procedurale. *Rassegna tributaria*, p. 316

Zizzo, G. (2014). Il principio di derivazione a dieci anni dall'introduzione dell'Ires. *Rassegna tributaria*, p. 1303

Non-Financial Reporting in the European Union: Current Issues and Prospects

Roberto Maglio and Rosa Lombardi

1 Introduction

This chapter aims to illustrate the state of the art in the presentation of non-financial reporting by companies in the European Union in order to ensure sustainable behaviour and actions, be accountable to stakeholders and create long-term value. Non-financial reporting is also referred to as sustainability reporting, developed by companies increasingly dedicated to corporate social responsibility (CSR) and sustainability (Adams & Abhayawansa, 2021; Lokuwaduge & Heenetigala, 2017; Stacchezzini et al., 2016; Stolowy & Paugam, 2018).

In this scenario, the analysis of non-financial outcomes or sustainable performance of companies is jointly linked with environmental, social and governance (ESG) factors and the United Nations Sustainable Development Goals (SDGs) (www.un.org).

Our analysis contributes to the main theories of corporate reporting and disclosure (Marchi, 2019; Potito, 2021) and social and environmental accounting (research) or sustainability accounting—SEA or SEAR—(Bebbington et al., 2009; Bebbington & Unerman, 2020; Deegan, 2002; Gray et al., 1995; Gray & Bebbington, 2001; Guthrie & Parker, 1989; Larrinaga & Bebbington, 2001) to advance the literature examining non-financial reporting or sustainability reporting and sustainable disclosure. We further develop the analysis of mandatory and

R. Maglio (✉)
Department of Management, Economics, Institutions, University of Naples "Federico II", Napoli, Italy
e-mail: roberto.maglio@unina.it

R. Lombardi
Department of Law and Economics of Productive Activities, University of Rome "La Sapienza", Rome, Italy
e-mail: rosa.lombardi@uniroma1.it

A. Incollingo, A. Lionzo (eds.), *The European Harmonization of National Accounting Rules*, SIDREA Series in Accounting and Business Administration,
https://doi.org/10.1007/978-3-031-42931-6_15

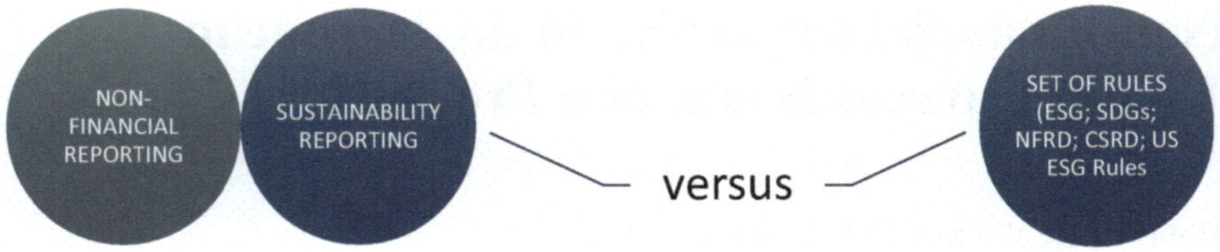

Fig. 1 Sustainability reporting and rules

voluntary reporting and disclosure (Perrault Crawford & Clark Williams, 2010) from a sustainability perspective and present the renewed accounting framework.

On the one hand, the revision of the European regulation on non-financial information—the Directive 2014/95/EU on disclosure of non-financial and diversity information (European Union Directive, 2014) and its guidelines, as well as the new Directive CSRD 2022/2464 (European Union Directive, 2022) —has acquired relevance for the structure of non-financial reporting and disclosure, affecting corporate accountability; on the other hand, standards, guidelines and frameworks (e.g. Global Reporting Initiative GRI, Climate Disclosure Standards Board CDSB, Sustainability Accounting Standards Board SASB, UN Global Compact) are used to implement sustainability reporting.

The chapter's findings provide academics and practitioners, as well as preparers and users of financial statements (e.g. companies and investors), with an update on the topic of non-financial and sustainability reporting and disclosure, including the recent Corporate Sustainability Reporting Directive 2022/2464 (CSRD) and EFRAG and IFRS standards, as well as key US regulations in this area, which add to the existing literature. In summary, this chapter addresses (i) changes in accounting rules related to non-financial information (reporting and disclosure) in the European Union, (ii) a summary of US regulations on sustainability reporting and disclosure and (iii) potential accounting impacts and improvements (sustainability reporting) as a path to harmonization in the European scenario (Fig. 1).

The chapter is organized as follows after this introductory section: Section 2 proposes corporate reporting and disclosure from the perspective of ESG and SDGs; Section 3 defines the European accounting rules for the structure of sustainability reporting and disclosure; Section 4 proposes the harmonization of non-financial reporting in the European Union; Section 5 proposes the main provisions of US ESG on sustainability issues; and Section 6 summarizes the impact and improvements in accounting (sustainability reporting) as a path to harmonization in the European scenario and future research.

2 Corporate Reporting and Disclosure in the ESG and SDGs Factors' Perspective

Corporate reporting and disclosure studies and SEA-SEAR (Bebbington et al., 2009; Deegan, 2002; Eugénio et al., 2010; Gray et al., 1995; Guthrie & Parker, 1989; Larrinaga & Bebbington, 2001; Lodhia & Sharma, 2019) help analyse non-financial versus sustainability reporting. The study of corporate reporting and disclosure has developed along several research paths, with a significant increase in the number of publications, especially since the 2000s (www.scopus.com). SEAR focuses on social and environmental issues from an accounting perspective, with reporting and disclosure and performance playing an important role. Lodhia and Sharma (2019, p. 309) argue in their study: "*Social and environmental accounting or sustainability accounting and reporting has become one of the major issues that organisations grapple with daily. Sustainability accounting is but one aspect of sustainability*".

Since this study focuses on reporting and disclosure from a sustainability perspective, the research starts from a primary lever of analysis: ESG and SDG factors. Interest in ESG factors coincides with increasing awareness of environmental, social and governance issues on a global scale by nations, governments, institutions, corporations and society (www.un.org). The adoption of an ESG perspective by an entity, including companies, goes hand in hand with the analysis of opportunities and risks arising from environmental, social and governance issues.

Following ONU's 2030 Agenda for Sustainable Development and the 2015 Paris Agreement, the 17 Sustainable Development Goals (SDGs) complement the ESG perspective by setting specific targets in this area. In Italy, for example, ISTAT reports on the achievements of the SDGs and presents data and trends in this context (ISTAT, 2021).

Several organizations have contributed to the ESG guidelines and metrics. For example, in the European scenario, Euronext set some targets in the area of climate change prevention, justifying its commitment to ESG (www.euronext.com). Nasdaq realized the "ESG Reporting Guide 2.0. A Support Resource for Companies" (Nasdaq, 2019) as a guide for ESG data reporting that promotes engagement between listed companies and investors. The World Federation of Exchange created the WFE ESG Guidance and Metrics (WFE, 2018) based on a set of environmental, social and governance metrics (e.g. E3 energy usage, S4 gender diversity and G2 board independence).

The SDGs are part of the United Nations' 2030 Agenda to Promote Action Plan for People, Planet and Prosperity (www.un.org). They consist of 17 Sustainable Development Goals (e.g. 1: no poverty; 11: sustainable cities and communities; 9: industry, innovation and infrastructure; and 14: life below water) and 169 targets.

3 Building Non-Financial Reporting and Sustainability Reporting Through the Changes in Accounting Rules in Europe

For several years, non-financial information represents a path to achieving sustainability developed along the ESG perspective and the European Green Deal (www.ec.europa.eu). It represents an open path towards sustainability issues to make the European Union *"...a modern, resource-efficient and competitive economy, ensuring:*

- *No net emissions of greenhouse gases by 2050.*
- *Economic growth decoupled from resource use.*
- *No person and no place left behind*" (https://ec.europa.eu/info/strategy/priorities-2019-2024/european-green-deal/delivering-european-green-deal_en).

The agenda in sustainability issues in the European scenario is based on several rules as reported below:

- Regulation (EU) 2019/2088. It is based on "sustainability-related disclosures in the financial services sector".
- Regulation (EU) 2020/852. It establishes a "framework to facilitate sustainable investment, and amending Regulation (EU) 2019/2088".
- Regulation (EU) 2019/2089. It is in the field of "EU Climate Transition Benchmarks, EU Paris-aligned Benchmarks and sustainability-related disclosures for benchmarks".
- Regulation (EU) 2021/1119. This is the European Climate Law setting direction and targets in the field of climate neutrality by 2050 (https://ec.europa.eu/clima/policies/eu-climate-action/law_en).
- Directive 2014/95/EU—Non-Financial Reporting Directive or NFRD—and the Corporate Sustainability Reporting Directive or Directive 2022/2464 (CSRD).
- Proposal for a Directive on corporate sustainability due diligence (https://ec.europa.eu/info/publications/proposal-directive-corporate-sustainable-due-diligence-and-annex_en). It is a proposal in the field of corporate due diligence fostering practices and responsibility in the field of sustainability (e.g. environment, human rights).
- Proposal for the European green bond standard (EU GBS) (https://ec.europa.eu/info/business-economy-euro/banking-and-finance/sustainable-finance/european-green-bond-standard_en). It represents a voluntary standard fostering the environmental propositions in the green bond market.
- Others in the field of ESG (e.g. EU Biodiversity Strategy for 2030; 2019/C 209/01 Guidelines in climate-related information and Task Force on Climate-Related Financial Disclosures (TFCD), 2017).

Among the previous regulatory path, Directive 2014/95/EU (NFRD) and Directive 2022/2464 (CSRD) (https://ec.europa.eu/info/business-economy-euro/company-reporting-and-auditing/company-reporting/corporate-sustainability-reporting_ en) is deputed to establish a framework for the sustainability reporting and disclosure by firstly regulating non-financial information.

Recently, annual financial reports developed by companies received great attention thanks to the focus on non-financial information (e.g. environmental and social issues) and sustainability issues (De Villiers & Sharma, 2020). The reporting and disclosure activities in the European scenario are invested by the adoption of Directive 2014/95/EU, to increase transparency, accountability, consistency and comparability of sustainability reporting (La Torre et al., 2018; La Torre et al., 2020; Lombardi, 2021; Monciardini & Conaldi, 2019). Hence, non-financial reporting becomes mandatory using the double materiality perspective (outside-in risks and inside-out risks), and it is currently realized by adopting existing guidelines and standards such as Global Reporting Initiative (GRI, International Integrated Reporting Committee (IIRC), OECD guidelines, Sustainability Accounting Standards Board (SASB), Climate Disclosure Standards Board (CDSB), Un Global Compact, and Task Force on Climate-Related Financial Disclosures (TCFD).

In the study by Dumay et al. (2019), the NFRD is defined as "*... the greatest revolution in corporate reporting for European listed companies since the introduction of International Financial Reporting Standards*" hoping to contribute to corporate accountability and trust in the market (European Union Directive, 2014; La Torre et al., 2018). The NFRD is widely connected to CSR and the stakeholder's engagement, contributing to the credibility of the mandatory annual report (Boyer-Allirol, 2013) as well as to environmental accountability, social responsibility and governance. For example, Cohen et al. (2015) state the non-financial information regulation serves to meet accountability requirements and respond to interest in CSR. The NFRD increases "*... transparency and improves uniformity and comparability*" (European Union Directive, 2014, art. 19) determining practices' changes in reporting and disclosure (Monciardini et al., 2017). Additionally, the shift from voluntary to mandatory non-financial disclosure on corporate accountability is a relevant issue that started to be investigated in the past (Cowan & Gadenne, 2005; Perrault Crawford & Clark Williams, 2010).

In the NFRD landscape, the non-financial report is a mandatory report for large public interest companies (or public interest entities or PIEs) having more than 500 employees. NFRD covers listed companies, banks, insurance companies and other companies intended as public interest entities. PIEs develop non-financial reports composed of the following topics:

- Environmental and social matters and treatment of employees.
- Human rights.
- Anti-corruption and bribery.
- Diversity on company boards (e.g. age, gender, educational issues).

The NFRD has been adopted in the EU member states following the transposition path in national laws, as discussed later.

The NFRD is accompanied by two guidelines, among which is a guideline for climate-related issues (2019/C 209/01) (https://ec.europa.eu/finance/docs/policy/190618-climate-related-information-reporting-guidelines_en.pdf).

In April 2021, the proposal of the Corporate Sustainability Reporting Directive (CSRD) (www.ec.europa.eu) intervened proposing an advance of the accounting regulation to be applied in the European scenario. The CSRD Directive has been approved for coming into force in January 2023 (CSRD 2022/2464) proposing the following main topics[1]:

- Increase the plethora of companies involved in sustainability reporting to be included in the management annual report, including listed companies, large companies and other companies (e.g. listed small and medium companies and other listed companies) foreseeing different steps of application about the company's category. The listed companies adopt the CSRD in 2024; the large companies (with over 250 employees and/or 20 million euros total assets and/or 40 million euros turnover) adopt the CSRD in 2025 and other companies since 2026 (extendible to 2028).
- Include detailed reporting requirements also following sustainability standards by the EU. It is realized assuming the topic of NFRD adding (i) long-term ESG objectives and policies, (ii) due diligence and (iii) intangibles disclosure.
- Double materiality.
- The audit assurance (limited or reasonable about fiscal years) of sustainability reports.
- Establish the digitally tagged information included in the sustainability report. The last one is proposed in the European Single Electronic Format or ESEF-HTML.

This scenario recalls the Sustainable Finance Disclosure and EU Taxonomy Regulations. Along with the CSRD 2022/2464, its application of the double materiality principle and the EU's goals included in the European Climate Law (Regulation EU 2021/1119), the European Financial Reporting Advisory Group (EFRAG) through the Project Task Force on European sustainability reporting standards (PTF-ESRS) prepared the reporting standards (www.efrag.org) that until now are exposure drafts "European Sustainability Reporting Standards" (ESRS). EFRAG PTF-ESRS has also some cooperation with the Global Reporting Initiative (GRI), WICI (www.wici-global.com) and Shift (www.shiftproject.org).

The ESRS' exposure drafts are grouped along the double materiality perspective into two general principles and the environmental, social and governance (ESG) principles as follows (EFRAG, 2022). Table 1 shows the list of ESRS drafts.

At the same time, the IFRS Foundation (www.ifrs.org) has published the "International Sustainability Standards Board" (ISSB) reporting standards to report to investors and capital markets on sustainability-related risks and opportunities of companies using a single materiality: the financial materiality perspective. The ISSB proposal is realized together with SASB, Climate Disclosure Standards Board (CDSB) and International Integrated Reporting Council (IIRC) under the Value Reporting Foundation (VRF).

[1] Its application is subordinated to the forthcoming national legislation in the European Union.

Table 1 European Sustainability Reporting Standards (ESRS) drafts

– General:
ESRS 1—general requirements.
ESRS 2—general disclosures.
– Environmental:
ESRS E1—climate change.
ESRS E2—pollution.
ESRS E3—water and marine resources.
ESRS E4—biodiversity and ecosystems.
ESRS E5—resource use and circular economy.
– Social:
ESRS S1—own workforce.
ESRS S2—workers in the value chain.
ESRS S3—affected communities.
ESRS S4—customers and end-users.
– Governance:
ESRS G1—business conduct.

4 The Harmonization of Non-Financial Reporting in the European Union: The Transposition of the NFRD by EU Member States

The transposition of the NFRD into national law was marked by controversial debates, probably due to the fact that the European system previously lacked coherence with regard to CSR. It is no coincidence that the EU has given national legislators some discretion in implementing the Directive (Aureli et al., 2019; Testarmata et al., 2020). Leaving many options to member states may mean that individual national interests are crucial to the success of harmonization (Evans & Nobes, 1998). While one country may simply opt for a normalization process and passively transpose the Directive mandate into its national legal system, another country might amend the mandate to adapt it to the specificities of its internal environment. Although some convergence has been achieved, the national status quo has been maintained in part by local circumstances, such as the existence of prior laws.

We examine how discretion has been used locally. The aim is to map the differences in the implementation of the NFRD in eight different European countries and to determine whether these differences jeopardize the original objectives of the NFRD. Some countries (e.g. France, the UK, Denmark, Sweden and the Netherlands) have already mandated disclosure of corporate social responsibility information for listed companies, while the leading European nation (Germany) did not have a comprehensive CSR reporting law before the NFRD.

Prior to the implementation of the NFRD, France, which is considered a model for CSR reporting, had already enacted a few pieces of legislation in this area. It was the first country to legislate mandatory reporting on sustainability issues in the 1970s with the introduction of the "bilan social", a document submitted by companies with more than 300 employees that includes information on 134 performance indicators related to employment issues. In France (where there is a solid welfare state), companies were expected to assume social responsibility for sustainable development. Thus, the state was used to promote or require CSR by enacting specific regulations.

In the United Kingdom, CSR initiatives emerged as voluntary actions by companies, and the government acted as a facilitator to provide incentives for CSR activities. Moreover, in line with English legal tradition, only principles were laid down, leaving management to fill in the gaps as they saw fit. Due to its distinct "liberal" market economy, as opposed to the coordinated market economies that prevail in continental Europe, the UK is considered as a case study in its own right. CSR disclosure is believed to be influenced by the UK's finance-oriented corporate culture. Since late 2013, listed companies in the UK have been required to publish an annual "strategic report", which serves as the primary authoritative source of data on environmental, social and governance (ESG) factors related to a company's operations.

Italy has less experience in CSR reporting than other European countries. A management report ("Relazione sulla gestione" ex article 2428 of the Civil Code) with an analysis of the situation, operating trends and performance is needed by limited liability firms in Italy. Since 2008, companies have been required to incorporate in the analysis relevant non-financial performance indicators, including information relating to environmental and employee matters, where this is necessary for a proper understanding of their situation, operating trends and performance. Companies are therefore not required to disclose this information if their financial statements and other financial indicators adequately describe their situation and performance. Companies not interested in the NFRD remain subject to the provisions of Article 2428 of the Civil Code.

In Spain, interest in CSR reporting began to awaken in this century. The publication of the Sustainable Business Act in 2011 was the country's first significant step in the field of sustainability (Sierra-Garcia et al., 2018). The Sustainable Business Act mandated that state-owned enterprises prepare annual corporate governance and sustainability reports according to generally accepted standards starting in 2012. The preparation of these reports had to take into account gender equality and the needs of persons with disabilities. In addition, this report had to be sent to the Spanish Council for Corporate Social Responsibility (Consejo Estatal de Responsabilidad Social Empresarial, or "CERSE") if the company had more than 1000 employees.

Before the implementation of the NFRD, there was no comprehensive CSR reporting legislation in Germany. After the financial crisis in 2007, CSR reporting gained more attention and in 2011 the German government adopted the Sustainability Code, which is not binding. The Sustainability Code is thus a reporting framework for NFRs that has been influenced by the OECD Guidelines for Multinational Enterprises, the UN Global Compact Principles and the GRI Guidelines. This code can be used by small and medium-sized enterprises and large companies (Jeffery, 2017).

In Denmark and Sweden, state-owned enterprises have been required to prepare annual sustainability reports according to the GRI Guidelines since 2009.

Most of the provisions of the NFRD have been implemented in a similarly way by EU member states. However, there are significant differences in implementation at the national level, as there have been significant adjustments to the implementation of the NFRD in some respects. These adjustments include which companies are subject to the non-financial reporting requirements, the definition of public interest entities (PIEs), the disclosure formats and the involvement of auditors.

The NFRD applies to large EU "public interest" entities (i.e. listed companies, credit institutions, insurance companies and other entities designated as such by member states due to their significant public importance) and to "public interest" entities that are parent companies of a large group. To be considered "large", companies (or groups on a consolidated basis) must have an average of more than 500 employees and (alternatively) a balance sheet total of more than € 20 million or a net turnover of more than € 40 million.

Member states differ in the way they:

1. Define an organization as a large undertaking.
2. Consider organizations as public interest entities.

In defining large undertakings, some member states (e.g. Denmark and Sweden) have decided to apply different (lower) size thresholds.

Most member states have broadened the concept of "public interest entities". It is difficult to consider the concept of public interest as clear and specific as there are numerous definitions: Denmark, France and Spain, for example, have extended the NFRD to unlisted companies that exceed certain size thresholds (CSR Europe and GRI, 2017).

Table 2 shows whether member states' requirements for the definition of large companies and public interest entities are the same as in the NFRD Directive or whether they have been adapted.

The Directive did not provide for a specific reporting format for non-financial disclosure, and specified the management report as the document reporting on non-financial disclosure. At the same time, a member state may exempt an undertaking from the obligation to prepare this non-financial statement if the undertaking prepares separate financial statements for the same financial year which contain the

Table 2 Transposition of the NFRD—company scope

Company scope	Ger.	Fra.	Ita.	Spa.	UK	Den.	Neth.	Swe.
Public interest entities with 500+ employees	≠	≠	≠	≠	=	≠	≠	≠
Listed companies with a balance sheet of at least €20 million or net turnover of €40 million and 500+ employees	=	=	=	=	≠	≠	=	≠

= Requirements are the same as in the Directive
≠ Requirements have been adapted
Authors' Elaboration

Table 3 Transposition of the NFRD—reporting format

Reporting format	Ger.	Fra.	Ita.	Spa.	UK	Den.	Neth.	Swe.
Part of the management report	×	×	×	×	×	×	×	×
As a separate report	×		×	×		×		×

Authors' elaboration

information required by the NFRD for the non-financial statement under the following conditions:

(a) If the entity publishes a separate report alongside the management report and makes reference to it in that report.
(b) If that separate report is published on the company's website within a reasonable time (not more than 6 months after the balance sheet date) and is referred to in the management report.

As shown in Table 3, the UK and France, for example, have required companies to include a statement of non-financial information in their management reports rather than allowing them to publish the statement separately. Still, Germany, Italy and Spain have allowed companies to prepare the NFR statement as a separate report.

Regarding the reporting framework, the NFRD takes a minimum harmonization approach to the reporting standards used for non-financial disclosures. It does not contain detailed rules on the content of non-financial reporting and does not prescribe mandatory EU standards. It also does not require companies to use a specific CSR framework as the basis for their reporting. Instead, companies are free to present such disclosures as they see fit (Wagner, 2018). The NFRD states that companies subject to these provisions can rely on national frameworks, EU-based frameworks or international frameworks to provide NFR.

In this scenario, member states have adopted the same requirements of the NFRD, namely the possibility for companies to choose between national, Union-based or international frameworks. As shown in Table 4, Italy has also given companies the option to use a mixed reporting methodology.

The non-financial statement should at least include information on the following categories: environmental, social and employee matters, respect for human rights, anti-corruption and bribery matters. NFRD (EU, 2014) mandates that companies disclose the following details for each of the aforementioned matters:

(a) A description of the company's business model.
(b) A description of the policies pursued by the company about those matters, including due diligence processes implemented.
(c) The outcome of those policies.
(d) The principal risks related to those matters linked to the company's operations including, where relevant and proportionate, its business relationships, products or services, which are likely to cause adverse impacts in those areas and how the undertaking manages those risks.
(e) Non-financial key performance indicators relevant to the particular business.

Table 4 Transposition of the NFR Directive—reporting framework

Reporting framework	Ger.	Fra.	Ita.	Spa.	UK	Den.	Neth.	Swe.
An international, national or EU-based reporting framework	×	×	×	×	×	×	×	×
A mixed reporting methodology constituted by one or more reporting standards			×					
Other specific frameworks (such as EMAS, UNGC, COP, PRI, UNGP, OCDE, ISO26000, the ILO Declaration or GRI)				×		×		

Authors' Elaboration

Table 5 Transposition of the NFR Directive—reporting topics and content

Reporting topics and content	Ger.	Fra.	Ita.	Spa.	UK	Den.	Neth.	Swe.
Information about the following non-financial topics: –Environmental matters –Social and employee matters –Respect for human rights –Anti-corruption and anti-bribery matters	x	x	x	x	x	x	x	x
A brief description of the company's business model	x	x	x	x	x	x	x	x
Company policies relating to non-financial matters	x	x	x	x	x	x	x	x
Company outcomes of policies relating to non-financial matters	x	x	x	x	x	x	x	x
Principle risks related to non-financial matters and business activities	x	x	x	x	x	x	x	x
Non-financial KPIs	x	x	x	x	x	x	x	x
Further specifications		x	x	x				x

Authors' Elaboration

According to Table 5, all member states comply with the NFRD in terms of both the non-financial topics (such as environmental concerns, social and employee concerns, respect for human rights and anti-corruption and anti-bribery issues) and the items (such as business model, company policies, outcomes, risks and non-financial KPIs) that should be disclosed in the NFR statement. Some member states have added further requirements for non-financial matters (Aureli et al., 2019).

Some countries require reporting on certain additional ESG aspects to each ESG factor. For example, Italian law requires reporting on the use of renewable and/or non-renewable energy when it comes to environmental issues. In France, other additional factors must be commented on (including some key performance indicators, such as frequency and severity of workplace accidents).

Table 6 Transposition of the NFR Directive—verification

Verification	Ger.	Fra.	Ita.	Spa.	UK	Den.	Neth.	Swe.
Auditor's involvement: Presence of statement	x	x	x	x	x	x	x	x
Auditor's involvement: Consistency check of disclosures as part of the review of the management report		x[a]	x		x	x	x	
Other						x[b]		

[a]In France, the auditor's involvement is required if the company has 500+ employees and has a turnover over €100 million or a balance sheet of over €100 million

[b]In Denmark, 10–20% of listed companies are subject to a regulatory review every year, which verifies the existence and content of the statement

Authors' Elaboration

Additional reporting requirements, such as assurance requirements and the imposition of fines in the event of non-compliance, have been outlined by the NFRD. NFRD mandates that NFR incorporated into a management report be subject to an audit by the company's auditors in terms of third-party assurances. While independent CSR reports are not obliged to be accompanied by third-party assurances, some member states may choose to do so (EU, 2014). Regardless of whether member states have mandated that the NFR disclosure be included in the management report, they must make sure that the auditor of the company verifies the existence and consistency of the NFR statement following Directive 2013/34/EU.

The approach to verification varies between states. Germany and Spain adopted the same requirements as in the NFRD (Table 6), whereas France, Italy and the UK included a consistency check as well. While Italy, for example, requires an internal and external audit of the information to be carried out concerning all reporting companies, in France the information provided is only required to be audited for companies above certain financial thresholds. Further, although in the UK the audit has to consider whether there are any false statements in the report, there is some lack of clarity over whether this is expressly required in the other surveyed states (Table 6).

Thus, NFRD and its implementation in national regulations seem directed towards corporate responsibility by increasing the consistency, transparency and comparability of NFR provided by companies. However, if the policy goals of the NFRD are to be met, more adjustments will probably be required. The fundamental flaw in the new rule is that the reporting methodology and format for NFR disclosure are not required by the NFR Directive or the member states, giving companies too much flexibility in these areas.

5 The US ESG Rules in Sustainability Reporting and Disclosure: A Summary

Following the first US rules in the field of environmental reporting and disclosure (e.g. Release No. 33-5170; guidance by SEC in 2010 about climate change disclosure), the mandatory reporting about sustainability issues is the greenhouse gas (GHG) reporting of heavy emitters (www.epa.gov/sites/default/files/2014-09/documents/ghgfactsheet.pdf). Other US companies' categories disclose ESG results voluntarily.

The recent US rule about sustainability has been proposed in 2022 adding a subpart to existing Regulation S-K (17 CFR 229.1500-1507): in March 2021, the Securities and Exchange Commission (SEC) proposed the rule "The Enhancement and Standardization of Climate-Related Disclosures for Investors" to enrich the climate disclosure by public companies in terms of climate-related risks and opportunities and metrics (www.sec.gov). The final rule became effective in December 2022 and is first applicable in 2023.

This proposal establishes the mandatory ESG data disclosure requirement in the USA (www.goldmansachs.com/insights/pages/gs-sustain-esg-regulations-us-sec-proposes-major-new-climate-disclosure.html) including climate-related opportunities and risks registration statements and annual reports (in a dedicated section or the Risk Factors, Description of Business, or Management's Discussion and Analysis section) by public companies: "*climate-related risks that are reasonably likely to have material impacts on its business or consolidated financial statements, and GHG emissions metrics that could help investors assess those risks*" (www.sec.gov/rules/proposed/2022/33-11042.pdf, p. 40). The proposal of mandatory ESG disclosure is not applied to non-listed companies.

The proposed rule is based on the following items:

(i) The adoption of the single materiality perspective.
(ii) The recalling TFCD standard.
(iii) The management's internal control and external audit (limited versus reasonable assurance about the fiscal years).
(iv) The electronic tag—narrative and quantitative—of climate-related disclosures in Inline eXtensible Business Reporting Language (Inline XBRL) format.

The US ESG proposal of disclosure is about the main following items (www.sec.gov/files/33-11042-fact-sheet.pdf) (Table 7):

Table 7 Enhancement and Standardization of Climate-Related Disclosures proposed by the SEC

– Climate-related risks/opportunities.
– Climate-related impact on strategy, business model and outlook.
– Governance.
– Risk management.
– Financial statement metrics.
– GHG emissions metrics.
– Attestation of Scope 1 and Scope 2 emissions.
– Targets and goals.

6 Sustainability Reporting' Implications, Conclusions and Future Research

Following the previous analysis, we mainly drafted (i) what are the changes in the accounting set of rules towards non-financial information (reporting and disclosure) in Europe and (ii) a summary of US rules in sustainability reporting and disclosure. Thus, we propose some potential impact and improvements in accounting (sustainability) reporting as a path towards harmonization in the European scenario.

Sustainability reporting is intended as an evolution of non-financial reporting developed by companies involved in corporate social responsibility (CSR) and sustainability paths (Adams & Abhayawansa, 2021; Lokuwaduge & Heenetigala, 2017; Stacchezzini et al., 2016; Stolowy & Paugam, 2018). Non-financial reporting stems from the NFRD on disclosure of non-financial and diversity information (European Union Directive, 2014). Sustainability reporting stems from the CSRD Directive (www.ec.europa.eu). Table 8 proposes the main similarities and differences in reporting and disclosure between NFRD and CSRD drafting their potential impacts and improvements in the field.

The chapter's results propose to scholars and practitioners and financial statement drafters and utilizers (e.g. companies and investors) the update in the sustainability reporting and disclosure and also contribute to corporate reporting and disclosure (Marchi, 2019; Potito, 2021) and SEA or SEAR (Bebbington & Unerman, 2020; Deegan, 2002; Gray et al., 1995; Gray & Bebbington, 2001; Guthrie & Parker, 1989) studies.

At the same time, Table 9 proposes the main similarities and differences in sustainability reporting and disclosure in the EU and USA, identifying some potential items impacting and improving the sustainability issues of corporate reporting and disclosure.

The path to sustainability reporting and disclosure is open, and continuous monitoring of progress seems important to keep track of key factors and levers in this area.

In this scenario, accounting regulations in Europe have been changed in recent years and new pillars have been proposed to advance non-financial reporting (before) and sustainability reporting (after). The current proposals included in the

Table 8 Main similarities and differences between NFRD and CSRD

KEY ISSUES	NFRD	CSRD
Regulation	Directive 2014/95/EU	Proposal COM/2021/189 final + Directive (EU) 2022/2464
Type of reporting/ disclosure	Non-financial reporting and disclosure	Sustainability reporting and disclosure
scope	Large public interest companies: – 500 employees – Total assets over 20 million euros – Total net sales revenues of over 40 million euros	Listed companies and non-listed companies are as follows: – Over 250 employees – Total assets over 20 million euros – Total turnover of over 40 million euros (other companies: listed small and medium companies and other listed companies)
Reporting standards	International guidelines and standards (e.g. GRI, IIRC, SASB, CDSB, TCFD, UN Global Compact)	Dedicated standards: European Sustainability Reporting Standards (ESRS) by EFRAG
Application	Since the fiscal year 2018	Since the fiscal year 2024
Main topics	Environmental and social matters and treatment of employees; human rights; anti-corruption and bribery; diversity on company boards	Environmental and social matters and treatment of employees; human rights; anti-corruption and bribery; diversity on company boards; long-term ESG objectives and policies; due diligence; and intangibles disclosure
Double materiality	Yes	Yes
Mandatory external assurance	Checking	Mandatory (limited versus reasonable about fiscal years)
Digitally "tag" information		– Digital tag – ESEF-HTML

Authors' Elaboration

broad EU sustainability strategy open up new insights that can be invested in the implementation of sustainability reporting by companies in the new context.

The comparison between the NFRD and CSRD applications at the company level is also useful to further define the "emerging reporting model" in this area. The additional comparison with the US ESG rule highlights similarities and differences that are useful for further developing some of the reporting and disclosure proposals. For example, the introduction of digital tags on the broad path of corporate

Table 9 Main similarities and differences between the EU and the USA in sustainability reporting and disclosure

Key issues	NFRD + CSRD	US ESG Regulation[a]
Regulation	Directive 2014/95/EU + Proposal COM/2021/189 final + Directive (EU) 2022/2464	Proposal of US ESG Regulation "The Enhancement and Standardization of Climate-Related Disclosures for Investors" (Release Nos. 33-11042; 34-94478; File No. S7-10-22). Effective Rule: December 2022
Type of reporting/ disclosure	Non-financial reporting and disclosure + Sustainability reporting and disclosure	Climate-related information
Scope	Until 2023: *Large public interest companies: - 500 employees* *– Total assets over 20 million euros* *– Total net sales revenues of over 40 million euros* After 2023: *Companies (listed and non-listed):* *– Over 250 employees* *– Total assets over 20 million euros* *– Total turnover (or net sales revenues) over 40 million euros*	Public companies
Reporting standards	NFRD: Voluntary standards (e.g. GRI, IIRC, SASB, CDSB) CSRD: European Reporting Standards (ESRS) by EFRAG	Guidelines: mainly TCFD
Application	NFRD: From the fiscal year 2018 to the fiscal year 2022 CSRD: since the fiscal year 2024	Since the fiscal year 2023
Main topics	NFRD: Environmental and social matters and treatment of employees; human rights; anti-corruption and bribery; and diversity on company boards CSRD: NFRD + long-term sustainability objective and policies; due diligence and intangibles	Climate-related risks/opportunities; climate-related impact on strategy, business model and outlook; governance; risk management; Financial statement metrics; GHG emission metrics; attestation of Scope 1 and Scope 2 emissions; targets and goals
Materiality	Double materiality	Single materiality
Mandatory external assurance	CSRD: Limited versus reasonable assurance about fiscal years	For Scope 1 and Scope 2 emissions Limited versus reasonable assurance about fiscal years
Digitally "tag" information	CSRD (digitally tagged information and ESEF-HTML)	Inline XBRL

Authors' Elaboration

[a]This is an estimation at the time of this writing

digitalization seems to promote the dissemination of information to stakeholders, with implications for corporate transparency and accountability.[2]

References

Adams, C. A., & Abhayawansa, S. (2021). Connecting the COVID-19 pandemic, environmental, social and governance (ESG) investing and calls for 'harmonisation' of sustainability reporting. *Critical Perspectives on Accounting*. https://doi.org/10.1016/j.cpa.2021.102309

Aureli, S., Magnaghi, E., & Salvatori, F. (2019). The role of existing regulation and discretion in harmonising non-financial disclosure. *Accounting in Europe, 16*, 290–312.

Bebbington, J., Higgins, C., & Frame, B. (2009). Initiating sustainable development reporting: Evidence from New Zealand. *Accounting, Auditing & Accountability Journal., 22*, 588–625.

Bebbington, J., & Unerman, J. (2020). Advancing research into accounting and the UN sustainable development goals. *Accounting, Auditing and Accountability Journal, 33*(7), 1657–1670.

Boyer-Allirol, B. (2013). Faut-il mieux réglementer le reporting extrafinancier? *Revue française de gestion, 8*, 73–95.

Cohen, J. R., Holder-Webb, L., & Zamora, V. L. (2015). Nonfinancial information preferences of professional investors. *Behavioral Research in Accounting, 27*(2), 127–153.

Cowan, S., & Gadenne, D. (2005). Australian corporate environmental reporting: A comparative analysis of disclosure practices across voluntary and mandatory disclosure systems. *Journal of Accounting & Organizational Change, 1*(2), 165–179.

CSR Europe, and Global Reporting Initiative (GRI). (2017). *Member State Implementation of Directive 2014/95/EU A Comprehensive Overview of How Member States are Implementing the EU Directive on Nonfinancial and Diversity Information*. Available online: https://accountancyeurope.eu/wp-content/uploads/NFR-Publication-3-May-revision.pdf

De Villiers, C., & Sharma, U. (2020). A critical reflection on the future of financial, intellectual capital, sustainability and integrated reporting. *Critical Perspective on Accounting, 70*, 101999.

Deegan, C. (2002). Introduction. The legitimising effect of social and environmental disclosures – a theoretical foundation. *Accounting, Auditing and Accountability, 15*(3), 282–311.

Dumay, J., La Torre, M., & Farneti, F. (2019). Developing trust through stewardship: Implications for intellectual capital, integrated reporting, and the EU Directive 2014/95/EU. *Journal of Intellectual Capital, 20*(1), 11–39.

EFRAG. (2022). EFRAG Public consultation on ESRS Exposure Drafts, Draft European Sustainability Reporting Standards. Appendix I – Navigating the ESRS: ESRS Exposure Drafts/ Disclosure Requirements, Application Guidance Index, April 2022, available at www.efrag.org

Eugénio, T., Costa Lourenco, I., & Morais, A. I. (2010). Recent developments in social and environmental accounting research. *Social Responsibility Journal, 6*(2), 286–305.

European Union Directive. (2014). 2014/95/EU of the European Parliament and of the Council of 22 October 2014 amending Directive 2013/34/EU as regards disclosure of non-financial and diversity information by certain large undertakings and groups, available at https://eur-lex.europa.eu/legal-content/EN/TXT/?uri=CELEX%3A32014L0095

European Union Directive. (2022). 2022/2464/EU of the European Parliament and of the Council of 14 December 2022 amending Regulation (EU) No 537/2014, Directive 2004/109/EC, Directive

[2]This study is the joint result of the work of the authors. The topic's investigation is directed to contributing to the aims and RQs of the research project "TOrnado or SUnshine? Mixing Accounting Regulation and Corporate Accountability in the Era of Non-Financial Information, Intangibles and Digitalization" of which Rosa Lombardi is a member and coordinator.

2006/43/EC and Directive 2013/34/EU, as regards corporate sustainability reporting, available at https://eur-lex.europa.eu/legal-content/EN/TXT/?uri=CELEX:32022L2464

Evans, L., & Nobes, C. (1998). Harmonization relating to auditor independence: the Eighth Directive, the UK and Germany. *European Accounting Review, 7*(3), 493–516.

Gray, R., & Bebbington, J. (2001). *Accounting for the environmental.* Sage Publications.

Gray, R., Kouhy, R., & Lavers, S. (1995). Corporate social and environmental reporting: a review of the literature and a longitudinal study of UK disclosure. *Accounting, Auditing & Accountability Journal, 8*(2), 47–77.

Guthrie, J., & Parker, L. (1989). Corporate social reporting: A rebuttal of legitimacy theory. *Accounting and Business Research, 19*(76), 343–352.

ISTAT. (2021). Rapporto SDGs 2021. Informazioni statistiche per l'agenda 2030 in Italia, available at: https://www.istat.it/storage/rapporti-tematici/sdgs/2021/Rapporto-SDGs-2021.pdf

Jeffery, C. (2017). Comparing the implementation of the EU non-financial reporting directive. *SSRN Electron J.* Available at http://www.purposeofcorporation.org/comparing-the-eu-non-financial-reporting-directive.pdf

La Torre, M., Sabelfeld, S., Blomkvist, M., & Dumay, J. (2020). Rebuilding trust: Sustainability and nonfinancial reporting and the European Union regulation. *Meditari Accountancy Research, 28*, 701–725.

La Torre, M., Sabelfeld, S., Blomkvist, M., Tarquinio, L., & Dumay, J. (2018). Harmonising non-financial reporting regulation in Europe: Practical forces and projections for future research. *Meditari Accountancy Research, 26*(4), 598–621.

Larrinaga, C., & Bebbington, J. (2001). Accounting change or institutional appropriation? A case study of the implementation of environmental accounting. *Critical Perspectives on Accounting, 12*(3), 269–292.

Lodhia, S., & Sharma, U. (2019). Sustainability accounting and reporting: Recent perspectives and an agenda for further research. *Pacific Accounting Review, 31*(3), 309–312.

Lokuwaduge, C. S. D. S., & Heenetigala, K. (2017). Integrating environmental, social and governance (ESG) disclosure for a sustainable development: An Australian study. *Business Strategy and the Environment, 26*(4), 438–450.

Lombardi, R. (2021). *The Going-Concern-Principle in Non-Financial Disclosure. Concepts and Future Challenges. SIDREA Series in Accounting and Business Administration.* Springer.

Marchi, L. (2019). *La creazione e la misurazione del valore: dalla prospettiva finanziaria alla prospettiva economico-sociale, Lectio Magistralis.* Università di Pisa, 19 ottobre 2019.

Monciardini, D., & Conaldi, G. (2019). The European regulation of corporate social responsibility: The role of beneficiaries' intermediaries. *Regulation & Governance.* https://doi.org/10.1111/rego.12248

Monciardini, D., Dumay, J., & Biondi, L. (2017). *Integrated reporting and EU law. Competing, converging or complementary regulatory Regulatory Frameworks?* University of Oslo Faculty of Law Research Paper No. 2017-23; University of Oslo Faculty of Law: Oslo, Norway, 2017; Available online: https://ssrn.com/abstract=2981674

Nasdaq. (2019). ESG Reporting Guide 2.0. A Support Resource for Companies, May 2019. Available at https://www.nasdaq.com/ESG-Guide

Perrault Crawford, E., & Clark Williams, C. (2010). Should corporate social reporting be voluntary or mandatory? Evidence from the banking sector in France and the United States. *Corporate Governance: The International Journal of Business in Society, 10*(4), 512–526.

Potito, L. (2021). L'origine dei principi contabili e il perduto senso dell'unitarietà del bilancio. Bilancio ed informativa economico-sociale, vol. 4. Giappichelli, Torino.

Sierra-Garcia, L., Garcia-Benau, M. A., & Bollas-Araya, H. M. (2018). Empirical analysis of non-financial reporting by Spanish companies. *Administrative Sciences, 8*(3), 29.

Stacchezzini, R., Melloni, G., & Lai, A. (2016). Sustainability management and reporting: The role of integrated reporting for communicating corporate sustainability management. *Journal of Cleaner Production, 136*, 102–110.

Stolowy, H., & Paugam, L. (2018). The expansion of non-financial reporting: An exploratory study. *Accounting and Business Research, 48*(5), 525–548.

Task Force on Climate-Related Financial Disclosures TFCD. (2017). *Recommendations of the Task Force on Climate-related Financial Disclosures*. Available at www.fsb-tcfd.org

Testarmata, S., Ciaburri, M., Fortuna, F., & Sergiacomi, S. (2020). Harmonization of non-financial reporting regulation in Europe: A study of the transposition of the Directive 2014/95/EU. In S. Brunelli & E. Di Carlo (Eds.), *Accountability, ethics and sustainability of organizations*. Springer.

Wagner, C. Z. (2018). Evolving norms of corporate social responsibility: Lessons from the European Union experience with non-financial reporting. *Tennessee Journal of Business Law, 19*, 619–708.

World Federation of Exchange (WFE), WFE ESG Guidance and Metrics, revised June 2018., Available at: https://www.world-exchanges.org/our-work/articles/wfe-esg-revised-metrics-june-2018

Private Firm Accounting in the EU: Still an Incomplete and Fragmented Picture

Alberto Incollingo and Andrea Lionzo

1 Private Firm Accounting Research: Issues and Perspectives

The country analysis section of this book has shown that the overwhelming majority of EU firms (around 98%–99%) are private and that they employ a large portion of EU workers (around 60%). Private firms are thus vital to the EU economy.

Researchers studying accounting have devoted increasing attention to private firms in the last decade (Bar-Yosef et al., 2019; Beuselinck et al., 2023). This is due not only to the desire to expand beyond the extensive literature on public firms but also to the need to understand the specific characteristics of these firms (e.g. in terms of ownership and managerial structures, firms' debts and relationships with lenders and supplier–customer relationships in the local and international supply chains in which they are embedded), the effects of such characteristics on accounting (Minnis & Shroff, 2017; Hope & Vyas, 2017) and the differences from public firms' reporting behaviours. The specific agency issues, business contexts and regulatory settings that characterise private firms make the study of these companies promising and richly interesting.

The EU setting deserves particular attention, as much country-level legislation requires private firms to publish at least their annual reports. Even if disclosure requirements are differentiated according to firm size between micro, small, medium and larger firms, in the EU, almost all limited liability firms are subject to specific

A. Incollingo (✉)
Università degli Studi della Campania Luigi Vanvitelli, Caserta, Italy
e-mail: alberto.incollingo@unicampania.it

A. Lionzo
Università Cattolica del Sacro Cuore, Milano, Italy
e-mail: andrea.lionzo@unicatt.it

A. Incollingo, A. Lionzo (eds.), *The European Harmonization of National Accounting Rules*, SIDREA Series in Accounting and Business Administration,
https://doi.org/10.1007/978-3-031-42931-6_16

mandatory requirements. This data availability makes the EU setting an attractive 'laboratory' (Beuselinck et al., 2023) in which to study private firms' reporting behaviours.

The framework presented in this textbook is thus significant, as it offers a view of the local financial reporting requirements (i.e. statement features and valuation approaches) of private firms across countries and time. Combining such information may allow the formation of promising research questions and consistent research contexts.

Directive 34,[1] which had to be transformed into national law by the EU Member States, has allowed broad national discretion in its adoption (André, 2017). As a result, there are still relevant differences in local accounting regulations across countries, as this textbook has shown.

For example, exemptions in filing income or cash flow statements and line item aggregation in balance sheets are not always homogeneous. In Italy and France, income statements are required for small firms, while in Germany, the Netherlands and the UK, income statements can be omitted by such firms. Income statement data (i.e. sales or costs) may thus be lacking for small firms in some jurisdictions. The exemption allowed in publishing cash flow statements does not make immediate data on operating, financing and investing cash flows available, so these data must instead be reconstructed from income statements and balance sheets.

Furthermore, in certain countries, unlimited liability firms are not required to publish their financial statements, except in cases where the company exceeds a certain size (as in Germany) or in relation to the types of shareholders (as in Spain). This contributes to the different availability of financial information for these entitites.

Another difference relates to the accounting standards applied, as country-specific rules either permit or prohibit the adoption of IFRS for private firms' consolidated and unconsolidated financial statements. For example, in most of the countries considered, IFRS can only be voluntarily adopted for consolidated financial statements, while in other countries (such as Denmark, Italy, the Netherlands and the United Kingdom) IFRS can be voluntarily adopted also for unconsolidated financial statements.[2]

---

[1] European Parliament (2013). Directive 2013/34/EU of the European Parliament and of the Council of 26 June 2013 on the Annual Financial Statements, Consolidated Financial Statements and Related Reports of Certain Types of Undertakings and Amending Directive 2006/43/EC of the European Parliament and of the Council and Repealing Council Directives 78/660/EEC and 83/349/EEC.

[2] Using a large sample of German firms, Bassemir (2018) documents that less than 10% of German firms voluntarily adopt IFRS for their consolidated statements. This paper documents that the adoption of IFRS is driven by growth opportunities, financing needs and external ratings; also, international orientation and auditors influence this decision.

As previously shown, notwithstanding Directive 34 and the move towards IFRS, the valuation approaches transposed in local rules still differ significantly from the IFRS, particularly in countries where historical cost accounting remains the central reference for financial statement valuations. This is particularly true in Italy, Germany and France. In such jurisdictions, taxation or credit protection still prevails over capital market pressures. In contrast, in Denmark and the UK, the local GAAP are very close to the provisions of the IFRS, having introduced for many assets the adoption of fair value or the revaluation model.

A fruitful research design should take into consideration the differences highlighted with the aim of composing meaningful and homogeneous samples. A research setting that includes private firms without considering the different local accounting rules they are required to follow may lead to unreliable results.

On the other hand, this heterogeneity in disclosure requirements and the variable availability of data could be harbingers of comparative research into the various incentives to increase the quality of financial disclosures. They may also be signs of the economic consequences of different accounting requirements. [3] The substantial freedom left to firms in how to aggregate specific line items or whether to publish income or cash flow statements may give rise to a promising context in which to analyse the different incentives to which firms respond (Burgstahler et al., 2006), also in managing size downward to avoid or reduce disclosure requirements (Bernard et al., 2018). In the same vein, different provisions for abridged financial statements may represent an opportunity, as it may be interesting to study which incentives prompt companies to provide this information on a voluntary basis. This kind of analysis may also foster a more precise understanding of the information needs of external parties—such as creditors, competitors, tax authorities, customers and suppliers—and of the ability of different local accounting rules to meet these different needs.

2 Levels of Harmonisation and Underlying Questions

The process of harmonising accounting in Europe began with EEC Directives 78/660 (known as the 4th Directive) and 83/349 (known as the 7th Directive), aimed, respectively, at standardising the rules governing the annual and consolidated accounts of companies.

A second important step in this process took place with the issuance of Regulation (EC) No. 1606/2002, through which the rules for preparing consolidated accounts for certain types of companies (all publicly listed EU companies, including

[3] This study contributes to answer the call of Beuselinck et al. (2023): ‘We are, however, not aware of any comprehensive survey allowing the in-depth comparison of current national GAAP systems. Such a granular overview would be particularly helpful in facilitating the analysis of alternative GAAP systems and their economic consequences’ (p. 45).

banks and insurance companies) were standardised on the basis of IFRS from 2005 onwards.[4] This regulation also allowed member countries the option (i) to permit or require publicly traded companies to also prepare their annual accounts in conformity with IFRS and (ii) to extend this permission or requirement to non-publicly traded companies (private firms) when preparing their consolidated or annual accounts.[5]

With the more recent Directive 2013/34/EU, which replaced the 4th and 7th Directives, the intention was to take a new step towards European accounting harmonisation, with the aim of further standardising accounting rules governing private firms and, at the same time, bringing them closer to IFRS.

The research carried out shows that there are at least three different levels of harmonisation in the EU today.

First, there are listed and financial companies for which the level of harmonisation is very strong, as these companies must adopt IFRS for their consolidated accounts.

On a second level, there are private firms that voluntarily adopt IFRS instead of local standards (*amplius*, Chapter 1). The adoption of IFRS is only optional, and the scenario within the eight countries is diversified: all countries have allowed the adoption of IFRS for consolidated accounts, but only four of these (Denmark, the Netherlands, the UK and Italy) have extended their use to annual accounts, while in the remaining four countries (Germany, France, Spain and Sweden) this is not allowed.

At a third level, which affects private firms more broadly, accounting harmonisation is weaker because Directive 34 retained the same high degree of flexibility that had already characterised the 4th and 7th Directives by granting member countries wide latitude in regulation. The analysis carried out in this book demonstrates that at this level the degree of harmonisation is quite weak.

The aim of this book is to examine how Directive 34 has been transposed into the legal systems of the major European countries in order to ascertain, almost 45 years after the enactment of the 4th and 7th Directives, the current degree of accounting harmonisation for private firms adopting local regulations. To this end, a vertical country analysis was carried out in conjunction with a cross-sectional survey of relevant accounting issues. At the end of this research, at least three questions emerged:

---

[4] Zeff (2007) points out that since 2005, when Regulation No. 1606/2002 came into effect, there has suddenly been a significant increase in overall comparability compared to what was previously the case, at least for companies adopting IFRS. However, Zeff had already indicated caution with respect to the fact that future progress in improving comparability would be difficult to achieve because cultures (corporate and financial culture, accounting culture, audit culture and regulatory culture) differed from country to country. It should be noted, however, that these differences have been relatively reduced over the past 15 years.

[5] According to regulations, using common accounting standards improves the transparency and comparability of company accounts, thus increasing market efficiency and reducing the cost of raising capital for companies.

(1) To what extent did the directives bring local accounting rules closer to IFRS, and what is the impact of this convergence on harmonisation?
(2) Is an accounting framework emerging for non-financial private firms?
(3) Would it be useful and appropriate to define a more uniform set of accounting rules for European private companies?

Before answering these questions, it is necessary to elaborate on the 'real' level of harmonisation achieved among local accounting regulations. This will double as a summary of the findings of previous chapters.

3 From the Directive to the 'Real' Degree of Accounting Harmonisation

As stated before, Directive 34 does not seem to have been structured with the aim of increasing the level of accounting harmonisation in the EU. Broad flexibility was allowed by this directive—for example, in defining abridged financial statements, identifying the simplification options for each size category, choosing between two options for each statement layout, requiring undertakings to include other statements in addition to the mandatory documents, allowing limits on the mandatory application of the materiality principle, exempting undertakings from the requirements of the substance-over-form principle, defining the extent to which the application of fair value is allowed and offsetting fair value changes in equity reserves or income statements.

The broad flexibility left by the directive resulted in different choices in different jurisdictions, as summarised below.

3.1 Financial Reporting Requirements for Different Size Categories

It is known that Directive 34 is based on the 'think small first' assumption to avoid disproportionate administrative burdens on smaller firms.[6] To this end, it identifies four size classes:[7] micro-, small- and medium-sized and large undertakings. Member states may (i) permit small undertakings to draw up abridged balance sheets, (ii) permit small- and medium-sized undertakings to draw up abridged profit and loss accounts, (iii) require the disclosure of different levels of information in the notes to financial statements, depending on the size classes of undertakings, and (iv) exempt small undertakings from the obligation to prepare management reports.

---

[6]Directive 34, 'Whereas', n. 10.

[7]Directive 34, Art. 3.

Not all countries have implemented the four size categories, with some limiting themselves to three (e.g. Italy and Sweden), while many have changed the quantitative thresholds (e.g. Germany, the UK, France, Denmark and the Netherlands). Moreover, as Chapter 11 shows, the requirements for financial statement formats and management reports for different size categories are not uniform across the countries analysed.

3.2 Presentation and Content of Financial Statements

As far as the statements included in annual reports are concerned, Directive 34 does not introduce any innovation, replicating what was already established by the 4th Directive: 'The annual financial statements shall constitute a composite whole and shall for all undertakings comprise, as a minimum, the balance sheet, the profit and loss account and the notes to the financial statements'.[8]

It is disappointing to observe that Directive 34 does not require statements of cash flow. Chapter 11 showed that all countries analysed, except France, reacted to the timidity of this provision by mandating cash flow statements in large undertakings, while Germany, the UK, Spain, Denmark and Sweden also require statements of changes in equity.

Regarding the presentation of balance sheets and income statements, Directive 34 allows member states to prescribe one or both of the layouts specified for both documents. For the balance sheet, five countries opted for a single format (Germany, Italy, Spain, Denmark and Sweden), while three countries allow the adoption of both (the UK, France and the Netherlands). For profit and loss accounts, the transposition of Directive 34 into individual jurisdictions led to widely differing behaviours among member states: five countries prescribe both layouts (Germany, the UK, Denmark, the Netherlands and Sweden), while three jurisdictions adopted only one format (France, Italy and Spain).

Regarding the alternative presentation of balance sheets ('Member States may permit or require undertakings, or certain classes of undertaking, to present items on the basis of a distinction between current and non-current items in a different layout from that set out in Annexes III and IV...'), our research demonstrates that the alternative format is mandatory for only two countries (the UK and Spain); for one, it is optional (Denmark), while for all other countries, it is not provided.

As far as the alternative presentation of profit and loss accounts ('...Member States may permit or require all undertakings, or any classes of undertaking, to present a statement of their performance instead of the presentation of profit and loss items in accordance with Annexes V and VI...'), we observed that the alternative presentation is mandatory only in France (in some cases, and not as an alternative to the ordinary scheme), while for all other jurisdictions analysed, it is not provided.

---

[8]Directive 34, Art. 4.

3.3 General Objective and Financial Reporting Statements

Directive 34 has not changed the true and fair view concept (TFV), which continues to represent the general objective of financial statements for private firms. As highlighted in Chapter 10, the TFV was introduced with the 4th and 7th Directives as a compromise rule between the German approach, which is traditionally characterised by a set of detailed rules to be observed without a general objective assigned to financial accounts, and the Anglo-Saxon approach, where a general objective assigned to annual accounts is accompanied by only a few detailed provisions. The need to reconcile these two opposing approaches has led to a hybrid system wherein the full application of the rules does not, in itself, guarantee the achievement of the TFV, even though it should, in theory, enable it.

Directive 34 therefore requires in undefined cases the provision of additional information beyond that required by the directive and the obligation to waive the same provisions of the directive in equally undefined exceptional cases.

The transposition of the TFV in the countries analysed did not lead to substantial changes with respect to the application of the 4th Directive. Most of the countries (Denmark, France, Italy, the Netherlands, Spain and Sweden) have implemented this directive in a substantially uniform way, while the UK and Germany have applied it in a different way. In the UK, the TFV has the role of a general objective to be respected without any explicit reference to the obligation to provide additional information or to waive certain provisions, as these options are considered implicit in the TFV concept. In contrast, in Germany, the TFV implies a reference to the generally accepted accounting standards, allowing only additional information, but it does not represent an overriding rule allowing the disapplication of specific provisions. Beyond these two opposite cases, the academic literature has repeatedly emphasised that the implementation of the TFV concept has been interpreted in different ways in different countries, both linguistically and philosophically (Alexander & Nobes, 2020). Another variation is found in Danish legislation, which allows for derogations only if the disapplication is compliant with IFRS.

The potentially major innovations of Directive 34 compared with the 4th and 7th Directives are related to the introduction of the 'substance-over-form' principle and the 'materiality' principle. Both represent a clear step towards IFRS.

Research has shown that the substance-over-form principle has not been explicitly included in all the legislation examined and that, in any case, its concrete application in national rules is not uniform.[9]

Directive 34 has weakly introduced the materiality principle, allowing its application only to presentation and disclosure, but member states have applied it in different ways: in some countries, such as France and the Netherlands, the

[9] Alexander et al. (2018) state that differences in understanding and use of concepts such as substance over form or true and fair view are rooted in the differences in the national patterns characterised by different cultural environments, legal systems and history. This questions the very existence of a Pan-European accounting community, or at best highlights its fragmentation.

application of the materiality principle is limited to presentation and disclosure, while in others, it is extended to recognition and measurement (e.g. in Italy and Spain). Our research also showed that the UK and Germany have not standardised the materiality principle, even though specific standards refer to it.

3.4 Measurement Basis

Directive 34 confirms historical cost as the general measurement basis for accounting estimates: 'Items recognised in the financial statements shall be measured in accordance with the principle of purchase price or production cost'.[10] According to this directive, historical cost ensures 'the reliability of information contained in financial statements'.[11]

Directive 34, however, allows for the adoption of two alternative measurement bases. Like the 4th Directive, Directive 34 allows member states to permit or require the measurement of fixed assets at revalued amounts[12]; in addition, following IFRS, it introduces the fair value model for some assets: 'Member States shall permit or require (. . .) the measurement of financial instruments, including derivative financial instruments, at fair value; and may permit or require (. . .) the measurement of specified categories of assets other than financial instruments at amounts determined by reference to fair value'.[13]

Among these measurement bases, the valuation criteria adopted in different countries largely derive from the objectives assigned to financial reporting and the consequent relationship with tax regulations.[14]

In this vein, the historical cost model represents the general valuation approach that informs the valuation criteria adopted in all EU countries examined. That said, this research shows that some countries allow a larger departure from the historical cost model, favouring the adoption of approaches that are less conservative and more oriented towards meeting the information needs of shareholders, whereas other countries are less inclined to allow the disapplication of historical cost because they favour a more conservative and creditor-based approach to measuring financial performance.[15]

[10] Directive 34, Art. 6, par. (i).

[11] Directive 34, 'Whereas', n. 18.

[12] Directive 34, Art. 7.

[13] Directive 34, Art. 8.

[14] Alexander and Nobes (2020).

[15] According to Alexander (2015), Directive 34, 'as finally issued allows, either by design or in despair, Member States to destroy comparability across Europe' (p. 20).

4 European Accounting Regulations and IFRS

In light of the differences in the transposition of recent legislative innovations into local accounting standards, it might be useful to return to the underlying questions posed at the beginning of the chapter.

Regarding the first question (*To what extent did Directive 34 bring local accounting rules closer to IFRS, and what is the impact of this convergence process on harmonisation*?), it can be pointed out that, while the Directive has not notably contributed to promoting harmonisation, it has nonetheless allowed some IFRS provisions to be introduced within local accounting regulations, although some countries have transposed them more extensively than others.

Since Regulation No. 1606/2002 forces listed companies to adopt IFRS for consolidated financial statements, EU countries have effectively been forced to address the problem of reducing the differences between the financial reporting of listed and non-listed companies. This research has shown that member states have taken steps in this direction, but the results are still mixed for two reasons: the previous accounting scenario and the intensity of the regulatory push towards IFRS.

According to our study, and despite some relevant differences, the greatest degree of compliance with IFRS has been achieved so far by Denmark, the Netherlands and the UK. These jurisdictions do not oppose the use of fair value, as it is considered an optional measurement basis for many financial and even non-financial assets, such as property, plant and equipment, investment property, intangible assets and equity instruments. In other jurisdictions, fair value is adopted only for financial instruments used for trading, shares without significant influence, derivatives, investment property and assets and liabilities that qualify as hedged items in a fair value hedge. In any case, the adoption of fair value measurements for non-financial assets is quite limited, mainly because positive adjustments to fair value are often required to be recognised in equity reserves, and recycling is allowed when assets are sold or required in the case of higher depreciation. In contrast, for investment properties, fair value changes are often recognised through profit and loss (with the exception of the Netherlands, where fair value changes in investment property are recognised through equity reserves); thus, for such items, the fair value model is more widespread.

Consistent with this accounting approach, in the UK and Denmark, inventory valuation cannot be carried out employing LIFO, while it is only permitted but not recommended in the Netherlands; this leads to inventories measured based on the average weighted cost of the period or on the most recent values using FIFO. Moreover, to offer a wider view of the assets used, in Denmark and the Netherlands, lease contracts can be recognised according to IFRS 16, but companies can also stop adopting only IAS 17. Accordingly, leased assets and leased liabilities related to both finance and operating leases can be recognised in financial statements. In contrast, in the UK, lease accounting is limited to the adoption of IAS 17. Goodwill is accounted for quite similarly in these countries: it is amortised over five years in the UK and the Netherlands unless a longer reasonable estimate can be made, while in Denmark, the amortisation period can be extended to the expected useful life or, if this is not foreseeable, a maximum of 10 years. It is also interesting to note that, in Denmark, the negative goodwill resulting from a business combination can be recognised as a gain on income statements, while this is not permitted in other countries. The Netherlands and the UK allow the impairment of fixed financial assets, even when the write-down is not permanent, whereas this is not permitted in Denmark. In addition, one must consider the presence of the IFRS options in the Dutch regulations, the extensive use of the overriding rule in the UK and the unique case of Denmark, where the derogation is allowed only if the non-application of the rules is compliant with IFRS. As for the statements, Denmark and the UK are the only countries (besides Spain) to allow (Denmark) or require (UK) alternative presentations of the balance sheet according to IAS 1, which separates items based on the 'current or non-current' criterion. Dutch SMEs can use the IFRS as standards, provided that there are no conflicts with the local legal requirements; similarly, the UK has adopted a modified set of IFRS for SME standards.

This brief summary highlights how, in these countries, broad discretion is left to firms. This can lead to large differences in application, even among firms adopting the same accounting rules. It can, therefore, be concluded that, the move towards IFRS is relatively more pronounced but still fragmented, and it must be defined on a firm-by-firm basis.

In contrast, Italy, Spain, France and Germany seem more rooted in the historical cost tradition, where contextual factors favour corporate financial reporting primarily oriented towards creditor protection (Leuz & Wüstemann, 2003). Even if this characterisation is still relevant, it does not fully describe the current valuation approaches allowed. The relevant legislative changes that have taken place over the last two decades, together with the transposition of Directive 34, have indeed placed these jurisdictions somewhere between the traditional conservative model of accounting and the Anglo-Saxon model. Among these countries, however, there are still relevant differences. For example, Italy allows the application of IFRS to the unconsolidated financial statements of non-listed companies, while Spain has, for many years, adapted its national GAAP to IFRS and extended the fair value model to activities other than derivatives while requiring the alternative presentation of the balance sheet. Both have extended the application of the materiality principle to recognition and measurement and have expressly provided for departure from specific accounting rules when their application is not material. Italy has also placed the materiality principle above the others, considering it instrumental to achieving TFV. In Italy, the fair value model is limited to derivatives, while in Spain, the fair value model is used with held-for-trading financial assets and liabilities, financial derivatives and hybrid financial assets, while the hedging rules are similar to IFRS 9. The possibility of exceeding historical cost in the valuation of single items is allowed in Italy only when permitted by law; however, long before this, the Directive's regulations had variously permitted the revaluation of fixed assets, thereby making possible tax-advantaged targeted revaluations. In Spain, asset revaluation has never been allowed, unless it is authorised by law, with the latest authorisation dating back to 1996. In addition, while, in Italy, LIFO is permitted and widely applied, and finance leases are not recognised, in Spain, LIFO is not permitted, and finance leases can find recognition, similarly to the provisions of IAS 17.

French accounting law is strongly attached to the principle of prudence, and even derivatives are valued using the cost model. Adjustments to fixed tangible and financial assets are occasionally possible, but they were allowed even before Directive 34. The definition of this occasional revaluation is unclear, leaving some room for discretion to companies. Finance leases cannot be recognised; LIFO is not permitted. Interestingly, unlike all other EU countries examined, in France, goodwill can be considered to have an indefinite useful life and is, therefore, subject to annual impairment testing. However, the indefinite useful life of goodwill can be refuted, and, in this case, the amortisation period is considered to be 10 years.

Otherwise, Germany remains the country where the push towards IFRS is weakest. The German accounting model is the most deeply anchored within the framework of the historical cost approach. The revaluation model is not foreseen for any fixed assets, and LIFO is allowed and widely used in measuring inventories. The fair value model is only allowed for assets exclusively held for coverage of pension liabilities and for trading securities of financial institutions. Exceptions to the historical cost also apply to short-term assets and liabilities (settlement within one year) in foreign currency, which are measured at the closing rate of the balance sheet date. Finance leases are included in financial statements, similarly to IAS 17.

Indeed, our research has shown that the TFV does not have the force of an overriding rule; materiality does not assume the rank of a general principle, and it only regulates certain cases. The use of fair value is permitted in extremely limited cases, and the revaluation model cannot be used.

In this second group of countries, the most recent accounting regulations did not intend to align local valuation approaches with IFRS. The use of fair value is only sketched out, and its extension is not even planned at the moment. Consequently, conservatism is likely to remain dominant in these countries.

Sweden can be placed in an intermediate position between these two groups of countries. Even if the Swedish scenario has traditionally been characterised by creditor protection and accounting prudence, since the 1980s Sweden has gradually opened up to the Anglo-Saxon approach, with a system of rules for non-listed companies based on IFRS for SMEs, albeit with substantial adaptations, mainly due to the link between accounting and taxation. In this vein, Sweden has allowed the adoption on a voluntary basis of the revaluation model as an alternative to historical cost for fixed assets, but its adoption is subject to multiple restrictions (i.e. a substantial value increase above the carrying amount, but not a temporary value increase, and reliable measurement of the estimated fair value). As a result, the adoption of the revaluation model is still limited. Furthermore, unrealised revaluation gain is not recognised in income statements but booked in equity reserves. These requirements steer the Swedish model towards a more conservative valuation approach.[16]

In conclusion, while Directive 34 has helped to bring European legislation closer to IFRS, it has done so in a heterogeneous and poorly organised way: heterogeneous in that Directive 34 leaves open even more areas of choice than the 4th Directive at both the state and firm levels; poorly organised in that the absence of a shared systematic framework has led to a transposition of the Directive into national legislations that is strongly influenced by the characteristics of each country's accounting environment.[17]

5 In Search of an Accounting Framework for Private Firms

Since there was no theoretical framework underlying Directive 34, such a framework cannot emerge from the transposition of this directive into local jurisdictions. The answer to the second question (*Is an accounting framework emerging for the financial statements of non-financial private companies*?) is thus clear.

Financial reporting has been conceived at the EU level as a hybrid model with 'various objectives' that cannot 'merely provide information for investors in capital markets but also give an account of past transactions and enhance corporate governance'; as a result, it has 'to strike an appropriate balance between the interests of the addressees of financial statements and the interest of undertakings in not being unduly burdened with reporting requirements'.[18] This choice of compromise has not been accompanied by a clear definition of the concepts of assets and liabilities or income and expenses; not even the concepts of capital maintenance are defined, and neither is the configuration of income that the financial statements should provide.

Nevertheless, it is possible to find some common elements in different jurisdictions. They can be seen as the 'lowest common denominators' among the local accounting rules of the countries examined. At a minimum, the following common elements can be highlighted:

(1) Unlike the *rule-based* accounting system in the United States, local EU regulations are generally more *principle-based*, allowing preparers greater professional judgement and reporting discretion. In the jurisdictions examined, accounting

[16]These conclusions are consistent with the classification suggested by André (2017) and summarised in Table 4 of Chapter 1.

[17]Other aspects unambiguously mark an incomplete approximation to IFRS, such as the absence in local regulations of any reference to the concepts of user primacy, decision-making utility, firms' cash-generating ability or information enabling users to assess '*the amount, timing and uncertainty of (the prospects for) future net cash inflows of the entity (...)*'. IASB *Conceptual Framework*, March 2018, par. 1.3.

[18]Directive 34, 'Whereas', n. 4.

rules provide guidance on recognition and measurement issues, but never as extensively as in the U.S. GAAP.[19]

(2) Generally speaking, the *historical cost model* represents the baseline measurement approach informing the valuation criteria for current and non-current items. The acquisition and production costs are measured and reduced (for accumulated amortisation and write-downs) in almost the same way in the countries examined.

(3) Local accounting regulations often provide that the historical cost model is accompanied by *another measurement approach*, which is useful in a more or less conservative approach to measuring financial performance. Examples include the use of fair value less cost to sell if lower than the cost of current assets, the equity method for investments in associates or joint ventures, the revaluation model for fixed assets, the value-in-use in impairment testing and the amortised cost for certain financial assets and liabilities.

(4) There is an emphasis on *early loss recognition* in local accounting regulations. Expected value reductions in current and non-current assets should be recognised in accordance with their specific characteristics.

In light of such elements, we wonder—this is the third underlying question—*whether it might be useful to identify a more uniform set of accounting rules for European private companies*. While the answer might be positive, given that most private companies operate in globalised financial and competitive scenarios, it should also be considered that private companies are not a monolith. As is well known, there are very large and internationalised firms, just as there are smaller and local ones; there are firms with broad ownership and a clear distinction between managers and owners, but there are other entities with very concentrated ownership.

Larger, internationalised private companies should be able to voluntarily adopt IFRS. This would enable these companies to adopt a widely shared accounting language and seize more opportunities in financial and business markets.

For more local private firms, there is a need to define an accounting model that can integrate financial reporting purposes with business size requirements.

To this end, it cannot be forgotten that financial statements in private firms perform a crucial 'statutory function' within corporate life. Think of the use of financial statement results for the purpose of protecting a company's capital integrity, or the use of net profits to shape shareholders' decisions regarding dividend distribution; again, think about the role of accounting income for income tax purposes; finally, consider the role of financial statement in estimates for M&A transactions (Bourveau et al. 2020). [20] In short, a good accounting model for private firms should take into consideration these needs, which local regulations have generally assigned to financial statements (Bonacchi et al., 2019). The translation

[19]Lisowsky and Minnis (2020).

[20]Bourveau et al. (2020) document that in M&A transactions the comparability between public and private firms accounting allows them to apply public firms' valuation multiples directly to private firms, increasing the value relevance of private firms' financial reporting.

of IFRS approaches into local accounting rules is impacting this statutory function. For example, it is changing the widespread conception of assets as divided into two broad categories: non-current assets, valued at cost, reduced by the depreciation process and write-downs in the case of lasting losses; and current assets, recorded at lower than their original value and the market value. Derivatives are measured at fair value independently of these two asset categories. Testing for impairment could lead to the deferral of a loss if the fixed asset is recovered through its use and not through disposal, because the recoverable amount is considered to be the higher of either value in use or fair value less costs to sell. In the case of amortised cost for financial liabilities, the negative components that explain the difference between the initial value and the value at maturity are deferred according to the accrual principle but in contrast with the prudence principle. Furthermore, the use of the revaluation model for fixed assets and the fair value measurement for certain assets other than financial instruments may have a significant impact on net income and net equity. These changes are altering the measurement of financial performance and, thus, its statutory role. Any accounting framework proposed for private firms should take these effects into consideration.

The path of harmonisation has thus far achieved disappointing results, as our survey has shown. This path began with a set of rules lacking a real conceptual framework (the 4th Directive), but after 45 years it has been made even more inconsistent by unsystematically inserting some of the IFRS provisions and expanding the level of flexibility even further, thereby reducing cross-country comparability.

Directive 34 did not overcome the limitations of the 4th Directive, namely (i) the absence of definitions for the concepts of assets, liabilities, capital maintenance and income to be accounted for; (ii) the excessive use of options across countries, regarding, for example, the use of LIFO, accounting for leasing, intangible assets and goodwill, and simplifications for smaller firms.

The consequence has been widening gaps between countries, gaps that are even greater today than in the past because of the timid and sometimes inconsistent grafting of IFRS into local accounting rules.

To overcome this situation, it would now be appropriate to develop a new accounting framework for private firms. Such a framework should be based on the following features:

- While remaining a principles-based framework, it should reduce the options available to bring the standards adopted in different countries closer together.
- The accounting framework should define the basic concepts of assets, liabilities, revenues, costs and capital maintenance, from which more uniform and comparable accounting choices among firms could result.
- The value-generation process should be based on the realisation principle, in which the introduction of fair value should be limited to a few clearly defined items.
- The role of information neutrality should be strengthened to ensure the balance of interests of all stakeholders.

– In simplified accounting regimes for different firm size categories, less leeway should be allowed in terms of documents to be prepared, accounting policies to be adopted, and disclosures to be provided in the notes.

A more decisive approach in this direction would allow a concrete step towards greater harmonisation of private companies' financial statements, improving comparability and ensuring the reliability of information. This could enable both firm internationalisation and a better capital allocation. In this vein, the acceleration in the EU of the sustainability reporting standardization (discussed in Chapters 1 and 15) is helping to bring local rules even closer together, promoting a disclosure culture more open to the adoption of a shared framework.

References

Alexander, D. (2015). Directive 2013/34/EU, Article 6. An analysis and some implications. A research note. *Financial Reporting, 1*, 5–22. https://doi.org/10.3280/FR2015-001001

Alexander, D., de Brébisson, H., Circa, C., Eberhartinger, E., Fasiello, R., Grottke, M., & Krasodomska, J. (2018). Philosophy of language and accounting. *Accounting, Auditing & Accountability Journal, 31*(7), 1957–1980. https://doi.org/10.1108/AAAJ-06-2017-2979

Alexander, D., & Nobes, C. (2020). *Financial accounting. An international introduction*. Pearson.

André, P. (2017). The role and current status of IFRS in the completion of national accounting rules – Evidence from European countries. *Accounting in Europe, 14*(1–2), 1–12. https://doi.org/10.1080/17449480.2017.1319965

Bar-Yosef, S., D'Augusta, C., & Prencipe, A. (2019). Accounting research on private firms: State of the art and future directions. *The International Journal of Accounting, 54*(02), 1950007. https://doi.org/10.1142/S1094406019500070

Bassemir, M. (2018). Why do private firms adopt IFRS? *Accounting and Business Research, 48*(3), 237–263. https://doi.org/10.1080/00014788.2017.1357459

Bernard, D., Burgstahler, D., & Kaya, D. (2018). Size management by European private firms to minimize proprietary costs of disclosure. *Journal of Accounting and Economics, 66*(1), 94–122. https://doi.org/10.1016/j.jacceco.2018.03.001

Beuselinck, C., Elfers, F., Gassen, J., & Pierk, J. (2023). Private firm accounting: The European reporting environment, data and research perspectives. *Accounting and Business Research, 53*(1), 38–82. https://doi.org/10.1080/00014788.2021.1982670

Bonacchi, M., Marra, A., & Zarowin, P. (2019). Organizational structure and earnings quality of private and public firms. *Review of Accounting Studies, 24*(3), 1066–1113. https://doi.org/10.1007/s11142-019-09495-y

Bourveau, T., Chen, J.V., Elfers, F., and Pierk, J., 2020. Public peers, accounting comparability, and value relevance of private firms' financial reporting. Review of Accounting Studies, published online, https://doi.org/10.1007/s11142-022-09707-y

Burgstahler, D. C., Hail, L., & Leuz, C. (2006). The importance of reporting incentives: Earnings management in European private and public firms. *The Accounting Review, 81*(5), 983–1016. https://doi.org/10.2308/accr.2006.81.5.983

Council of the European Union. (1978). Fourth Council Directive 78/660/EEC of 25 July 1978 Based on Article 54 (3) (g) of the Treaty on the Annual Accounts of Certain Types of Companies. http://data.europa.eu/eli/dir/1978/660/oj/eng

Council of the European Union. (1983). Seventh Council Directive 83/349/EEC of 13 June 1983 Based on the Article 54 (3) (g) of the Treaty on Consolidated Accounts. http://data.europa.eu/eli/dir/1983/349/oj/eng

European Parliament. (2013). Directive 2013/34/EU of the European Parliament and of the Council of 26 June 2013 on the Annual Financial Statements, Consolidated Financial Statements and Related Reports of Certain Types of Undertakings, Amending Directive 2006/43/EC of the European Parliament and of the Council and Repealing Council Directives 78/660/EEC and 83/349/EEC Text with EEA Relevance. http://data.europa.eu/eli/dir/2013/34/oj/eng

Hope, O. K., & Vyas, D. (2017). Private company finance and financial reporting. *Accounting and Business Research, 47*(5), 506–537. https://doi.org/10.1080/00014788.2017.1303963

IASB. (2018, March). *Conceptual Framework for Financial Reporting.*

Leuz, C., & Wüstemann, J. (2003). In J. P. Krahnen & R. H. Schmidt (Eds.), *The role of accounting in the German financial system.* Oxford University Press.

Lisowsky, P., & Minnis, M. (2020). The silent majority: Private U.S. firms and financial reporting choices. *Journal of Accounting Research, 58*(3), 547–588. https://doi.org/10.1111/1475-679X.12306

Minnis, M., & Shroff, N. (2017). Why regulate private firm disclosure and auditing? *Accounting and Business Research, 47*(5), 473–502. https://doi.org/10.1080/00014788.2017.1303962

Zeff, S. (2007). Some obstacles to global financial reporting comparability and convergence at a high level of quality. *The British Accounting Review, 39*, 290–302. https://doi.org/10.1016/j.bar.2007.08.001

The manufacturer's authorised representative in the EU is Springer Nature Customer Service Centre GmbH, Europaplatz 3, 69115 Heidelberg, Germany. If you have any concerns regarding our products, please contact ProductSafety@springernature.com

Printed and bound by CPI Group (UK) Ltd, Croydon, CR0 4YY
01/10/2026
02225896-0011